Criminalisation of Stalking

First published in 2001, *The Criminalisation of Stalking* fills a much-needed gap by drawing upon a range of methodologies to present a thorough and comprehensive examination of the way in which stalking became perceived as a pressing and prevalent social problem in need of legal intervention, as well as providing a critical evaluation of the efficacy and sufficiency of the legal responses.

Essentially this book has two main objectives- first, to provide a comprehensive account of the process by which stalking came to be regarded as a significant social problem which merited legal intervention and to evaluate that response. And secondly, to situate this within a wider theoretical context which addresses the role of the criminal law in dealing with social problems and the boundaries of criminalization. This illustrates how a detailed consideration of a particular issue can inform wider debate and provide a unique perspective on existing theoretical material. This socio-legal perspective facilitates the use of a range of methodologies to challenge the existing conceptualization of stalking and to present a wider range of potential solutions to this complex social problem. This is a must read for scholars and researchers of criminology.

Criminalisation of Stalking

Constructing the Problem and Evaluating the
Solution

Emily Finch

Routledge
Taylor & Francis Group

First published in 2001
by Cavendish Publishing Limited.

This edition first published in 2024 by Routledge
4 Park Square, Milton Park, Abingdon, Oxon, OX14 4RN

and by Routledge
605 Third Avenue, New York, NY 10017

Routledge is an imprint of the Taylor & Francis Group, an informa business

© Finch, E 2001

Publisher's Note
The publisher has gone to great lengths to ensure the quality of this reprint but points out that some imperfections in the original copies may be apparent.

Disclaimer
The publisher has made every effort to trace copyright holders and welcomes correspondence from those they have been unable to contact.

A Library of Congress record exists under ISBN: 1859416446

ISBN: 978-1-032-70457-9 (hbk)
ISBN: 978-1-003-55810-1 (ebk)
ISBN: 978-1-032-90446-7 (pbk)

Book DOI 10.4324/9781003558101

THE CRIMINALISATION OF STALKING:
CONSTRUCTING THE PROBLEM AND EVALUATING THE SOLUTION

Emily Finch
Lecturer in Law
University of Reading

Cavendish
Publishing
Limited

London • Sydney

First published in Great Britain 2001 by Cavendish Publishing Limited,
The Glass House, Wharton Street, London WC1X 9PX, United Kingdom
Telephone: +44 (0)20 7278 8000   Facsimile: +44 (0)20 7278 8080
Email: info@cavendishpublishing.com
Website: www.cavendishpublishing.com

British Library Cataloguing in Publication Data

Finch, Emily
The criminalisation of stalking: constructing the problem
and evaluating the solution
1 Stalking – Great Britain
I Title
345.4'1'025

ISBN 185941 644 6

Printed and bound in Great Britain

*To my father, Roy, who has been a constant source
of inspiration and encouragement.*

'Nowhere either with more quiet or more freedom
from trouble does a man retire than into his own soul.'

*Marcus Aurelius Antonious
Roman Emporor
121–180 AD*

ACKNOWLEDGMENTS

This book's main contentions were based upon the findings of the author's doctoral thesis 'The Criminalisation of Stalking: The Construction of the Problem and an Evaluation of the Solution'.

The author would like to thank the Department of Law at the University of Wales at Aberystwyth for the award of a studentship that facilitated this research and the invaluable advice and assistance provided by all members of the department.

Particular thanks are due to Gavin Dingwall and Elizabeth Macdonald without whom this project would not have been possible.

CONTENTS

TABLE OF CASES

TABLE OF LEGISLATION

CHAPTER 1

WHAT IS STALKING?

This chapter addresses the nature and extent of stalking. The interrelated issues of prevalence and definition are considered, with particular emphasis given to the question of why a definition of stalking is so difficult to formulate. This discussion focuses upon the legislative approach to the definition of stalking, both in England and Australia, in order to illustrate the problems involved in formulating a workable definition. Finally, this chapter considers whether this type of problem was a novel feature of the 1990s or whether it was in existence for many years before a commonly accepted terminology facilitated its rise to prominence as a prevalent social problem in need of a legislative response.

1.1 ISSUES OF PREVALENCE AND DEFINITION

The measure of the prevalence of any conduct is inextricably linked with the way in which it is defined. A definition provides a benchmark against which an incident can be measured in order to determine whether or not it can be classified as an example of the conduct being quantified. Therefore, a clear definition is an essential prerequisite to any exploration of prevalence. As such, it may seem axiomatic that a consideration of the prevalence of stalking should follow, rather than precede, a definition of stalking. However, the definition of stalking is not a straightforward matter and the absence of a commonly accepted definition has had a substantial impact on the measurement of the prevalence of stalking.[1]

English law contains no definition of stalking. Legislation enacted to combat stalking[2] and cases involving conduct that was labelled stalking[3] have not generated a generally applicable definition of the conduct. Therefore stalking, like shoplifting, mugging and vandalism, is a description of a particular manifestation of an offence rather than a legal category in its own right.[4] The Protection from Harassment Act 1997 based criminal liability upon the wider concept of harassment, which includes, but is not limited to,

---

1   Budd and Mattinson, 2000.
2   Protection from Harassment Act 1997.
3   *R v Burstow* [1997] 4 All ER 225; *R v Constanza* [1997] 2 Cr App R 492; *R v Morris* [1998] 1 Cr App R 386; *R v Haywood* [1998] 1 Cr App R(S) 358; *R v Notice* [2000] 1 Cr App R(S) 75.
4   Wells, 1997, pp 463–70.

stalking. Harassment itself is defined in wide terms by the Act as including causing alarm or distress.[5] The breadth of the scope of the statute was a deliberate attempt to extend protection against a variety of harassing activities:

> Those, then, are the Government's proposals to deal with stalking. As I have said, their effects will go beyond what might be termed classic stalking to provide protection for others who are persecuted by anti-social behaviour.[6]

In addition to stalking cases, there have been prosecutions under the Protection from Harassment Act involving disputes between neighbours,[7] 'peeping Toms',[8] school bullying,[9] the breakdown of relationships,[10] animal rights protestors[11] and harassment of public officials.[12] The diversity of the conduct encompassed within the term 'harassment' indicates that, whilst all stalking cases will amount to harassment, not all harassment cases involve stalking.

---

5 Protection from Harassment Act 1997, s 7(2).

6 Howard, M, *HC Deb* Vol 287 Col 786, 17 December 1996.

7 *R v Dunn* [2001] Crim LR 130; *R v Southwark Crown Court ex p Howard* (2000) unreported, 2 April (Divisional Court) – following the victim's refusal to engage in a relationship, Howard resorted to spreading rumours about the victim to discredit her. This included allegations that she was a prostitute, that she neglected her daughter and that she was a bad tenant. The recipients of these rumours included the Social Services, the Housing Association and the headmaster of the school attended by the victim's daughter.

8 *DPP v Williams* (1998) unreported, 24 July, Divisional Court – the first incident in this case involved the defendant, a homeless person, interfering with the bathroom window in the victim's home whilst the victim's flatmate was in the shower. The second incident occurred the following evening when the victim saw the defendant peering through her bedroom window.

9 *R v Barking Youth Court ex p B* (1999) unreported, 27 July, Divisional Court – in this case, a 15 year old schoolboy was prosecuted following three incidents in which he threw things at the victim, another pupil at his school, and shouted obscenities at the victim and the victim's mother.

10 *R v Liddle* [1999] 3 All ER 816.

11 *Huntingdon Life Sciences v Curtin* (1997) *The Times*, 11 December – Huntingdon Life Sciences is a research laboratory where experiments are conducted on animals and has been the subject of persistent protests by animal rights protestors for a prolonged period. An injunction was sought under the Protection from Harassment Act 1997 to end the protest, which had included the intimidation of employees, threats and attacks on directors' homes and a rooftop protest that continued for several weeks; *DPP v Moseley* (1999) *The Times*, 23 June – three animal rights protestors were prosecuted under the Protection from Harassment Act 1997, s 2 following a protracted period of protest at a mink farm. The farm was also home to the farmer and his young children. The conduct of the protestors included noisy all-night vigils, the waving of flaming torches and abuse shouted at the children as they travelled to and from school. This case is analysed in detail in Finch, 1999.

12 *Baron v Crown Prosecution Service* (2000) unreported, 13 June, Divisional Court – this involved two letters couched in abusive terms to a Benefits Agency employee in an attempt to coerce her into reinstating the defendant's benefit; *R v Rayson* (1998) unreported, 24 February, CA – the defendant targeted an educational welfare officer, who was dealing with the defendant's failure to ensure her child attended school, with letters and telephone calls. The victim was contacted both at home and at work. On one occasion, the volume of telephone calls was so intense that the Education Department was forced to close down its switchboard.

It can be seen that little guidance exists as to the nature of conduct that comes within the remit of stalking nor, for the purposes of the Protection from Harassment Act, does there need to be, as liability is based upon the reaction of the recipient.[13] The absence of a definition or guidelines enunciating the identifying characteristics of stalking does render this area rather uncertain, particularly in view of the range of variables that could be included:

> There are various definitions which could have been adopted forming a continuum from very narrow definitions to those which potentially encompass a wide range of incidents. Definitions can vary in terms of the type and frequency of the behaviours included, the length of time over which they occur and whether the intention of the stalker or the emotional, psychological and physical impact upon the victim are deemed relevant.[14]

The potential to include such a range of factors has led to the emergence of a disparate assortment of definitions of stalking in the US. All 50 States have enacted anti-stalking provisions or amended their existing legislation to encompass stalking, but this has resulted in 50 different definitions despite the formulation of a model anti-stalking code aimed at encouraging greater homogeneity of approach:

> Although there is a common purpose underlying all State anti-stalking statutes, there is little uniformity in how they define and address the problem.[15]

Such variance in definition has clear ramifications for any comparison between rates of prevalence as there is no guarantee that conduct that would amount to stalking in one State would satisfy the requirements of the anti-stalking provisions of any other State. As the Third Report to Congress on Stalking and Domestic Violence observes:

> Stalking prevalence varies with the level of fear included in the definition. A higher standard of fear produces lower prevalence rates, and a lower standard of fear produces higher prevalence rates.[16]

A narrow definition of stalking will encompass fewer situations, thus creating a lower prevalence rate than a broader, more inclusive definition. This factor was apparent in Sheridan, Davies and Boon's empirical study of stalking prevalence in England.[17] This study involved the analysis of 348 questionnaires completed by female members of UNISON. The questionnaire was designed to elicit the participant's experiences based upon a definition of stalking as 'a series of acts directed at one individual by another which, taken

---

13 'A person must not pursue a course of conduct (a) which amounts to harassment of another, and (b) which he knows or ought to know amounts to harassment of the other' – Protection from Harassment Act 1997, s 1(1).

14 Budd and Mattinson, 2000, p 2.

15 Bureau of Justice Assistance, 1996, p 11.

16 Department of Justice, 1998, p 8.

17 Sheridan, Davies and Boon, 2000.

as a whole, amount to unwanted persistent personal harassment'. On the basis of this definition, 23.6% of the participants had experienced stalking. The questionnaires were also analysed to determine how many would provide the basis for a prosecution under the Protection from Harassment Act, whereby the victimisation rate increased to 33%. This provides a clear illustration of the extent of variation of prevalence that can arise from the adoption of differing definitions of the conduct in question.[18]

The findings of the British Crime Survey do not support Sheridan et al's estimation of the prevalence of stalking.[19] This larger scale study[20] involved the analysis of self-completion questionnaires that had been deliberately designed to elicit a wide range of experiences that could be categorised as stalking. Based upon an extremely general definition, analysis of the questionnaires indicated that 2.9% of the population, or approximately 900,000 people, had experienced 'persistent and unwanted attention' during the previous year and that 11.8% of adults had experienced such conduct at some time in their lives. Acknowledging that the extent of stalking is inevitably affected by the way in which it is defined, Research Study 210 evaluated the experiences recounted by questionnaire respondents to determine the extent to which these were potentially prosecutable under the two criminal offences created by the Protection from Harassment Act. This confirms that the prevalence rates dropped as the definition of the conduct being measured narrowed, thus confirming that a wider definition is likely to result in the appearance of higher prevalence rates.

---

18 Although it should be noted that the definition originally formulated by Sheridan *et al* does not appear dramatically different from that used in of the Protection from Harassment Act 1997, s 1(1): 'A person must not pursue a course of conduct (a) which amounts to harassment of another, and (b) which he knows or ought to know amount to harassment of the other.'

19 Budd and Mattinson, 2000.

20 This was a nationally representative survey of 9,988 adults aged between 16 and 59.

Figure 1.1 **Estimated prevalence of stalking as determined by the definition adopted**

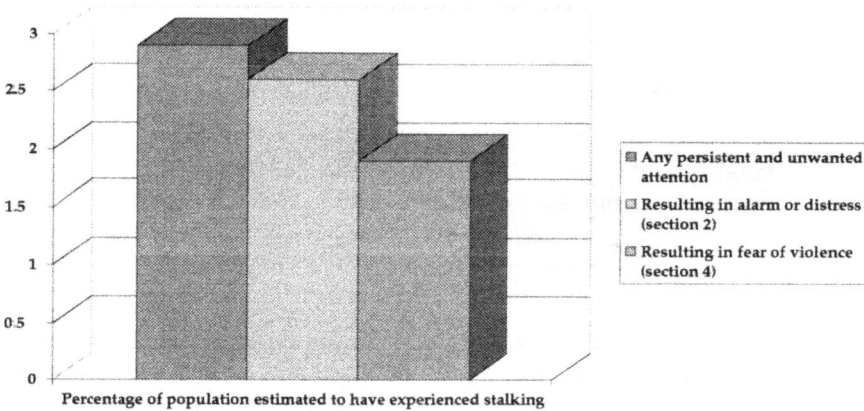

Percentage of population estimated to have experienced stalking

According to the British Crime Survey results, 2.6% of the population were the victims of stalking conduct that would come within the definition of harassment formulated by the Protection from Harassment Act. The research indicated that rates of prevalence of stalking victimisation differed dramatically between the sexes, with women being significantly more likely to encounter persistent and unwanted attention.[21]

Figure 1.2 **Prevalence of stalking by sex of the victim as affected by the definition adopted**

	WOMEN	MEN	ALL
Any persistent and unwanted attention	4.0	1.7	2.9
Resulting in alarm or distress (section 2)	3.7	1.3	2.6
Resulting in fear of violence (section 4)	2.7	0.9	1.9

21 There is some evidence to suggest that victimisation is more even than these figures would suggest; some studies suggest that there is no difference between male and female victimisation, merely a difference in the inclination to report incidents which could account for the apparent divergence: Hall, 'The victims of stalking', in Meloy, 1998, pp 119–20; Spitzberg, Nicastro and Cousins, 1998, pp 33–47.

Even when using the same definition based upon the provisions of the Protection from Harassment Act and focusing upon female victimisation, the rates of prevalence vary dramatically between Sheridan *et al*'s findings and those of the British Crime Survey. Certainly, there was no evidence to support Sheridan *et al*'s conclusion that:

> ... one in three British women will theoretically be able to prosecute a stalker at least once during their lifetime.[22]

Sheridan et al's findings have been criticised by von Heussen as lacking statistical validity and for making uncritical use of retrospective self-report measures, especially as previous research has indicated that there is:

> ... a profound discrepancy between women's responses in actual harassment situations and the evidence generated from analogue methodologies and from available samples of non-victims ... recruited specially for the task.[23]

Moreover, the Home Office evaluation of the findings of the British Crime Survey 1998 assert that, although Sheridan *et al*'s findings indicate the prevalence of stalking within a particular sub-group of women, they are unlikely to provide an accurate reflection of the rate of prevalence within the wider population.[24]

The emphasis of existing empirical research into stalking victimisation almost uniformly asserts that stalking is a crime committed by men against women. Certainly, the findings of the British Crime Survey seem to support that, as it appears that men were responsible for 90% of stalking cases involving female victims. Despite its frequent characterisation as a relational crime, men are also responsible for the majority of stalking cases involving male victims.

---

22 Sheridan, Davies and Boon, 2000.
23 von Heussen, 2000.
24 Budd and Mattinson, 2000.

Figure 1.3   Relationship between sex of stalker and victim (BCS)

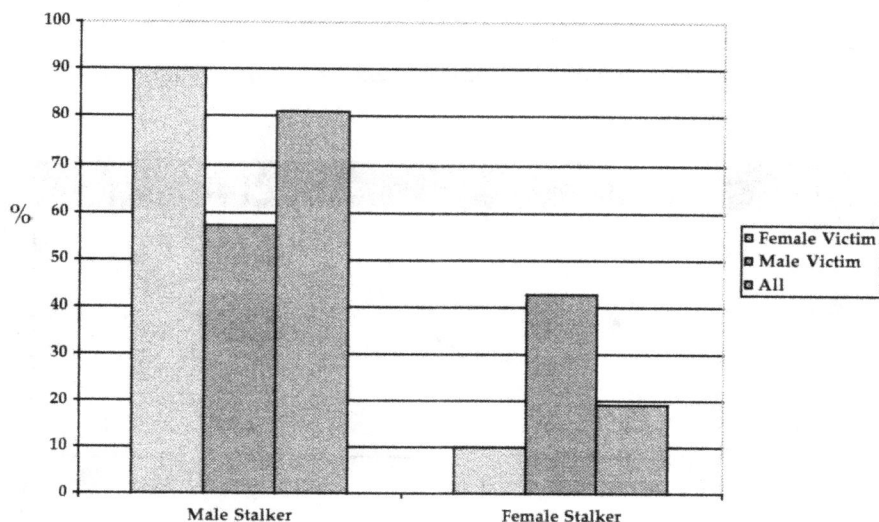

Despite the correspondence of these findings, caution should be exercised before accepting the characterisation of stalking as a 'woman's issue'. Research into stalking as a legal and social phenomenon is in its infancy. Although the current research findings do support the conclusion that this is a crime largely committed by men against women, there is also potential for this apparent fact to be based upon a greater disinclination to report victimisation by male victims. Certainly, this was the finding of two of the more recent empirical studies into stalking victimisation.[25] The influence of the social construction of stalking upon the 'reality' as represented by reported incidents is a crucial factor here, and one that will be explored in greater detail in Chapter 3.

This account of the attempts to establish the prevalence of stalking suggests that an accurate estimation is by no means a straightforward task. One of the central impediments to a measure of prevalence would appear to be an absence of a commonly accepted definition of stalking. Recourse to the general definition adopted by the Protection from Harassment Act does provide some common ground and this approach was used, with extremely different results, in both of the existing pieces of research which attempt to measure the prevalence of stalking in England. Reliance upon the statutory

25 Spitzberg, Nicastro and Cousins, 1998, pp 33–47; Hall, in Meloy, 1998. The issue of the relationship between victim and stalker is further considered at pp 51–58.

offences at least facilitates a form of measurement as the prosecution and conviction rates are published by the Home Office.

Figure 1.4   Number of prosecutions and convictions under the Protection from Harassment Act for the years 1998 and 1999 (Home Office)

	PROSECUTION	CONVICTION
1998		
Section 2	4304	1505
Section 4	2221	522
1999		
Section 2	5427	1632
Section 4	2709	488

Despite the precise information that is available if prevalence is to be based upon statutory definitions, there are substantial limitations to this approach. As mentioned previously, harassment is a wider notion than stalking, thus it is not possible to determine how many prosecutions and convictions relate to stalking and how many involve other forms of harassment covered by the statute.[26] Equally, it is accepted that official statistics do not provide an accurate measure of the prevalence of any type of crime.[27] The spectre of the 'dark figure' of unreported and unrecorded crime and the criticism of the official handling of crime figures[28] limit the efficacy of any attempt to estimate crime prevalence on the basis of official statistics. There is certainly evidence of under-reporting in relation to stalking cases. The Home Office evaluation of the British Crime Survey found that two-thirds of stalking cases were not reported, but that the police were aware of approximately 294,000 cases, a figure that suggests that the prosecution rate in stalking offences is incredibly low.[29] This links to the issue of police as 'gatekeepers' who determine whether a particular case will be permitted to enter the criminal justice system

---

26   No research has yet been conducted to examine the content of harassment prosecutions under the Protection from Harassment Act 1997.

27   Coleman and Moynihan, 1996; Koffman, 1996; Home Office, *Review of Crime Statistics: A Discussion Document*, 2000.

28   'There are three sorts of lie – statistics, crime statistics and police crime statistics ... [the Home Office has] reduced the art of public administration to that of finding beans and choosing which ones to count': Jenkins (2000) *The Times*, 1 December, as cited in Home Office, *Review of Crime Statistics: A Discussion Document*, 2000.

29   Budd and Mattinson, 2000, pp 50–52.

and hence figure in official crime statistics. A victim who receives a negative response from her first contact with the police is likely to be discouraged from making further complaints and will probably accept the officer's evaluation that the case does not merit police intervention.[30] There is evidence of an extreme discrepancy between prosecution rates in different regions, which suggests uneven enforcement on the part of different police authorities.[31] Concern over police involvement in stalking cases led the Home Office to sponsor research[32] to investigate approaches to stalking and harassment cases and to the publication of an *Investigator's Guide* to promote good practice across police authorities.[33]

The difficulties of establishing the prevalence of stalking are clearly associated primarily with issues of definition. The general definition of harassment used by the Protection from Harassment Act is not a sound basis for a measure of the prevalence of stalking. Official statistics do not provide a reliable measure of the occurrence of any particular crime as they note only reported and recorded crime. The high level of under-reporting of stalking and the indications of prevalence extrapolated from self-report surveys suggests that, in any case, the official figures represent only a small proportion of stalking cases. Thus, the absence of a commonly accepted definition of stalking is a substantial impediment to the determination of the rate of prevalence of the conduct. Even if a common definition of stalking were to be agreed, there is evidence to suggest that a number of factors inhibit the reporting of stalking cases, both to official and unofficial bodies.[34] This is also a significant obstacle to any accurate measurement of the prevalence of stalking.

Therefore, it is not possible to provide a conclusive measurement of the prevalence of stalking, although the British Crime Survey 1998 provides the most reliable basis for an estimation of the extent of stalking currently in existence.[35] It is probable that no accurate measurement of the prevalence of stalking is possible, but it is certainly true to say that it exceeds the estimate of 200 cases every year that was relied upon by the Conservative Government during the passage of the Protection from Harassment Act.[36]

---

30 Stephenson, 1997.

31 von Heussen, 2000.

32 Brown, 2000.

33 Conference on Stalking, Bramshill Police Training College, 22 March 2000.

34 Skogan's study of the British Crime Survey 1992 results addresses the issues that inhibit the reporting of crime: Skogan, 1994.

35 Although there are also limitations to the reliability of data obtained from such large scale victim surveys: Mayhew, P 'Researching the state of crime', in King and Wincup, 2000.

36 Maddox, D, *HC Deb* Vol 287 Col 803, 17 December 1996. References were also made to the estimates made by the Police Federation, believed to be more accurate, that there were approximately 3,000 stalking cases every year.

1.2 DEFINITIONAL DIFFICULTIES

The preceding section is based upon the assumption that a comprehensive definition is difficult, if not impossible, to establish. This section will examine the validity of this assumption and outline the reasons why a definition of stalking has proved to be so elusive. This examination will be based upon a consideration of the debates surrounding the definitional issues that arose during the enactment of the Protection from Harassment Act and an evaluation of the approach taken to the definition of stalking in Australia.

As has been discussed, formulating a definition of stalking is by no means a straightforward task. Indeed, one of the foremost difficulties that impeded the enactment of legislation to address stalking was the apparently insuperable impediment of devising a satisfactory definition. During an interview on *World at One* in May 1996, whilst being pressed to commit to a timetable for implementing legislation on stalking, then Home Secretary Michael Howard stated:

> Stalking is a particularly difficult thing to define, which is why we are taking so much care to make sure that we get it right. As soon as we are satisfied that we have a workable definition of the crime, we will legislate.[37]

However, six months later, when government proposals to legislate against stalking emerged, it became clear that the 'workable definition' had proved to be elusive, as the Protection from Harassment Bill contained no definition of stalking; indeed, the word is not mentioned anywhere in the legislation. Instead, there was a prohibition of the more general term 'harassment', which was deemed to need no definition, owing to the familiarity of the courts with the concept.[38] The rationale for this wide approach was that the behaviour engaged in by stalkers was so diverse that it was impossible to formulate a definition which encompassed all such activities.[39]

There is an immense variation in the conduct that occurs in stalking cases. There are categories of conduct such as following, unwanted communications and physical and verbal intimidation which commonly occur, but this conduct is not universal to all stalking cases. Equally, some stalking cases involve unusual, sometimes unique conduct, such as leaving dead animals on the victim's car windscreen,[40] sending the victim a used sanitary towel,[41] giving

---

37 *World at One*, 10 May 1996.
38 Howard, M, *HC Deb* Vol 287 Col 784, 17 December 1996. A general definition of harassment was provided in s 7(2) whereby harassment was said to include causing alarm or distress to another person.
39 Mclean, D, *HC Deb* Vol 287 Cols 823–27, 17 December 1996.
40 Case history 39 – the stalker drove around looking for animals that had been killed by cars on the road and left their corpses on the victim's car windscreen and on her front doorstep.
41 *R v Burstow* [1997] 4 All ER 225.

the victim over five hundred pairs of scissors[42] and shooting the President of the United States.[43] The conduct concerned may be perfectly lawful, involve the commission of criminal or tortious acts or be a combination of lawful and unlawful conduct.[44] It is usual for stalking cases to involve more than one type of harassing conduct; in fact, it is rare for a stalker to engage in only a single type of behaviour.[45]

Stalking conduct ranges from the outwardly innocuous to the seriously criminal, rendering it virtually impossible to find any common denominator to the conduct upon which to base a definition. This is an impediment to the formulation of a definition, as this would have to be sufficiently flexible to include a range of conduct whilst being sufficiently certain to ensure that the law was clear and accessible.

1.2.1 The legislative definition of stalking

The definition of stalking was a contentious issue during parliamentary debates in both Houses prior to the passage of the Protection from Harassment Act.[46] The delineation between the generality of the Conservative approach, which favoured the use of the more general term 'harassment' and the greater degree of specificity favoured by the Labour Party, who advocated the definition of stalking by reference to a list of prohibited activities, is notable throughout the debates. This divergence of approach to the definition of stalking was exacerbated by the conjunction of the imminent general election and the high level of media coverage devoted to the perceived inadequacies of existing legislation to counter stalking.[47] Both parties were keen to be seen to be taking a tough approach to law and order,[48] hence the

---

42 Case history 37 – the stalker was aware of the victim's extreme phobic reaction to scissors and gave her over 500 pairs during an eight month period.

43 John Hinckley had been stalking actress Jodie Foster for several years when his obsession led him to shoot the then President of the United States, Ronald Reagan, so that she would notice him and their names would be linked in history. Caplan, 1987.

44 See Chapter 4.

45 Harris, 2000, p 12. An example of a stalking case that involved only one type of behaviour is Case history 1, where the stalker's conduct was limited to standing outside the victim's house and watching it for hours whenever she was alone in the house.

46 HC Deb Vol 287 Cols 781–988, 17 and 18 December 1996; HL Deb Vol 578 Cols 917–43, 24 January 1997, 17 February 1997.

47 'Law in urgent need of reform' (1996) The Independent, 19 September; 'Ban on stalking is urged to protect victims' (1996) The Times, 9 September; 'Law call change after stalking acquittal', The Guardian (1996) 18 September; 'This man is stalking a girl aged TEN and the police cannot do anything' (1996) Daily Mirror, 2 July.

48 'In the run-up to the 1997 election both political parties view each other to come up with populist soundbites to prove who was toughest on crime': Wilson and Ashton, 1998, p 20.

competition to take credit for the introduction of legislation on this publicly visible issue.[49]

The Conservative Party had blocked attempts to introduce legislative measures to combat stalking on two previous occasions. The most recent of these was the introduction of the Stalking Bill by backbench Labour MP Janet Anderson under the Ten Minute Rule in March 1996.[50] The Stalking Bill defined stalking using the list approach and had been rejected by the then Conservative Government on the basis that it was flawed and unworkable.[51] The Conservative Government were then pressured to legislate against stalking and showed some reluctance to do so until directly pressured regarding this during the Queen's address to Parliament at the commencement of the new session.[52] In a hurried consultation, which was described as 'the first time the Cabinet's future legislation committee had met in public',[53] the Prime Minister, John Major, swiftly reversed the decision of the Home Secretary. He agreed to introduce stalking legislation as a government Bill if it received the all-party support that it had been promised.[54] The adverse reaction of the Home Secretary to this impromptu change of policy was apparent and the Shadow Home Secretary noted that:

> the Home Secretary's demeanour gave every indication that he had been subject to persistent and wanton harassment by his Right Hon friend the Prime Minister and wished for legal protection from it.[55]

It was in this political climate that the Protection from Harassment Bill was debated and a definition of stalking was discussed.[56] The Conservative Government were criticised both by members of other political parties and the

---

49 Bennett, A, *HC Deb* Vol 287 Col 809, 17 December 1996.

50 Anderson, J, *HC Deb* Vol 273 Col 370, 6 March 1996. The other attempt to introduce measures aimed at stalking had been proposed by Lady Olga Maitland during the passage of the Criminal Justice and Public Order Act 1994. The proposal would have inserted an additional section into the Public Order Act 1986: Standing Committee B Cols 1280–85, 8 March 1994.

51 In a letter to Janet Anderson, Michael Howard condemned her proposals as 'rushed, botched and unworkable' (letter from Michael Howard to Janet Anderson, 10 May 1996). His public justification for having rejected the Stalking Bill was that 'there was no time and there would not have been a full and proper consultation' (*World at One*, 10 May 1996). The official news release listed three areas of criticism against the Stalking Bill: (1) the definition of stalking was too wide; (2) legitimate activities would be curtailed; and (3) the combined use of criminal and civil measures was unprecedented and unworkable (Home Office News Release, May 1996).

52 'Howard leaves stalking laws at the back of the queue', *The Guardian*, 9 October 1996; '*Daily Mirror* victory over stalkers – Michael Howard will consider legislation against stalkers' (1996) Daily Mirror, 26 September; 'Stalkers face jail under new law' (1996) *The Independent*, 18 October.

53 'U-turn on stalking law' (1996) *Daily Telegraph*, 24 October.

54 *HC Deb* Cols 28–32, 23 October 1996.

55 Straw, J, *HC Deb* Vol 287 Col 793, 17 December 1996.

56 The relevance of the political context is discussed in Morgan, R, 'The politics of criminological research', in King and Wincup, 2000.

media for their lack of support for the Stalking Bill 1996,[57] thus a definition which bore any resemblance to that proposed by Janet Anderson was clearly out of the question.[58] However, there was a great deal of support amongst politicians from other political parties for the list approach to definition advocated by the Stalking Bill. This led to a protracted discussion of the merits of the definition of stalking posited by the thwarted Bill, which received more consideration during the passage of the Protection from Harassment Act than it ever did in its own parliamentary lifetime.

Clause 1 of the Stalking Bill defined stalking by reference to a list of prohibited activities:

> Stalking shall mean engaging in a course of conduct whereby a person –
>
> (a) follows, loiters near, watches or approaches another person;
>
> (b) telephones (which for the avoidance of doubt shall include telephoning a person but remaining silent during the call), contacts by other electronic means, or otherwise contacts another person;
>
> (c) loiters near, watches, approaches or enters a place where another person lives, works or repeatedly visits;
>
> (d) interferes with property which does not belong to him and is in the possession of another person;
>
> (e) leaves offensive, unwarranted or unsolicited material at a place where another person lives, works or repeatedly visits;
>
> (f) gives offensive, unwarranted or unsolicited material to another person; or,
>
> (g) does any other act in connection with another person so as to be reasonably likely to cause that other person to feel harassed, alarmed, distressed or to fear for his safety or for that of one or more third persons to whom he has a duty of protection or with whom he is associated.

This provides an extremely precise definition of the conduct element of stalking. Following another person is included, for example, as is watching another person, loitering near another's home or place of work, and making telephone calls. There is a clear list of conduct provided which potentially brings the perpetrator into conflict with the law. However, the difficulty arises when it is considered that in order to convert this *prima facie* lawful conduct into stalking, the conduct must be reasonably likely to cause one of the prohibited consequences also listed. How are the circumstances under which it is reasonably likely that following a person will cause them distress, or alarm, or to fear for their safety to be determined? What initially appears to set out a clear definition of the activities that will amount to stalking rapidly loses

---

57 'Home Office drops support for stalking Bill' (1996) *The Independent*, 7 May; 'Government rebuffs new stalking law' (1996) *Daily Mirror*, 7 May; 'Michael Howard's contempt for stalking victims' (1996) *Daily Mirror*, 11 May; 'Ministers block Labour Bill to outlaw stalking' (1996) *The Times*, 11 May; 'Stopping stalkers' (1996) *Daily Telegraph*, 11 May.

58 Confidential communication with Conservative Party official, June 1998.

clarity in the light of this qualification. Obviously, such a qualification is necessary, otherwise all telephone calls, for example, would automatically come within the definition of stalking, but the qualification detracts from the clarity of the activities listed and renders criminalisation contingent on an imprecise requirement. Certainly, it will be apparent that certain extreme and blatant examples will be encompassed within this definition, but not all stalking involves extreme conduct or overt criminal behaviour. The decision as to whether the listed conduct is reasonably likely to cause the prohibited result may not always be straightforward and may not be clear in advance to the person engaging in the conduct. As such, this list approach does not provide a clear definition of stalking, although it does identify some of the more common types of behaviour involved.

The Conservative Government attacked the list approach to the definition of stalking as being simultaneously too wide and too narrow. It was felt to be too narrow as the definition of stalking by reference to a list of prohibited activities meant that a stalker who engaged in an activity that was not listed could do so with impunity:

> I would be more relaxed about the list system if I thought that it could be complete. Unfortunately, we are dealing with people who have some very weird ideas ... they can get up to some pretty weird activities. It is impossible to define all the stalking activities that people could get up to.[59]

Evidence from stalking cases certainly supports this view. One stalker engaged in extremely diverse activities during his three year stalking campaign, which ceased only when he was imprisoned for inflicting psychological grievous bodily harm upon his victim.[60] She commented upon the proposal to define stalking by reference to a list of prohibited activities at the Suzy Lamplugh Trust conference on stalking where she stated:

> If you have a list of activities which you ban, my stalker will simply sit down and work out another activity with which to torment me.[61]

The accuracy of this statement was confirmed during an interview with this stalker, who stated that after he was imprisoned for burglary of his victim's house, he resolved not to use unlawful means in the course of stalking her as he was determined to avoid further arrest and imprisonment. He was indignant when referring to his conviction under s 20 of the Offences Against the Person Act 1861 which, he said, did not cover psychological harm until the courts decided to extend it to do so in order to convict him. This aggrieved the stalker, as he had gone to a great deal of effort to ensure that his continued pursuit of his victim involved only lawful means.[62]

---

59 Mclean, D, *HC Deb* Vol 287 Col 825, 17 December 1996.
60 *R v Burstow* [1997] 4 All ER 225.
61 Suzy Lamplugh Trust Conference on Stalking Laws, 18 October 1996.
62 Interview with Anthony Burstow, 29 March 1999.

This is not an isolated incident. There is evidence to suggest a tendency amongst persistent stalkers to develop activities that ensure that they are immune to legal intervention:

> There are many examples of stalkers, convicted of offences such as breaches of the peace, or making nuisance telephone calls, who learn to restrict their behaviour and keep just within the law.[63]

One stalker admitted that this was what he had done:

> You learn what not to do. I didn't know that sending her stuff through the post was illegal. I mean, I knew it was wrong but not that I could get nicked for it. I was gutted when I got arrested so I soon stopped doing that and, get this, when I thought of taking photos of her, I asked [the police] first if it were criminal and when they said 'no', I knew I was on a winner. It worked as well. Drove her round the bend. And the best thing was that she called the police about it and they did come and have a word with me and I was able to tell them straight out that they couldn't do nothing because I knew what I did wasn't illegal.[64]

A further example of the added attraction that remaining within the parameters of the law can hold for some stalkers is seen in the actions of the stalker who was the subject of a civil injunction prohibiting him from entering two adjacent towns. The stalker ascertained the boundaries of these towns and selected a position to park his car where he would be outside the geographical area prohibited by the injunction, but where he would still be visible to his victim as she drove into work. When approached by the police, who suspected that he was in breach of the injunction, the stalker was able to show the police a large scale map with the perimeters of the prohibited towns and his own position outside of this area marked upon it. This view is supported by the stalker's apparent satisfaction at having defeated the spirit of the injunction whilst remaining within its terms and his admission that he perceives his battle to be as much with the legal authorities as it is with his victim. He expressed his determination to continue with his conduct whilst remaining within the law so as to ensure that the police were powerless to intervene.[65]

The actions of the stalkers and their explanations for their conduct illustrate that some stalkers do go to great lengths to ensure that their conduct does not contravene the law and that they derive additional satisfaction from the knowledge that the police are powerless to intervene.[66] This desire for control and to render victims helpless has been identified as a dominant characteristic in stalking cases, thus indicating that flexibility to adapt to novel

---

63 Howarth, G, *HC Deb* Vol 287 Col 839, 17 December 1996.
64 Case history 38.
65 Case history 40.
66 See Chapter 2.

manifestations of harassing conduct should be an essential aspect of any definition of stalking.[67]

This potential objection to the exclusionary aspect of the list approach had been anticipated and the inclusion of a general 'catch-all' provision, whereby 'any act in connection with another person' that had one of the prohibited results was within the definition of stalking, was intended to counter this objection.[68] Despite the lack of clarity which arises from including within the definition of stalking any act which reasonably causes another person to be harassed, alarmed, distressed or to fear for the safety of themselves or another, this generality does address a specific characteristic of stalking. This is that the means employed during the course of stalking may be extremely diverse and include acts that may not be considered harmful if viewed in isolation. The inclusion of a provision that prohibits any act whatsoever provided it has one of the specified consequences equips the Bill with a certain degree of flexibility. This flexibility ensures that the Bill would have the power to address novel and unanticipated manifestations of stalking that would not otherwise be within its remit simply because they were so unusual. Under this provision, the stalker who had deliberately set up to take photographs of his victim to distress her would not be outside the scope of the law merely because he had thought up an original means of harassing his victim.

This general provision does not actually achieve what it sets out to do, as Conservative opponents of the Bill pointed out. Such a general provision would fall foul of the *ejusdem generis* rule of interpretation whereby words such as 'any other activity' would be construed with reference to the general characteristics of the other activities listed prior to the general provision:

> Adding a catch-all at the end does not achieve what it seems to achieve. Judges must interpret catch-alls at the end of lists in statutes according to certain rules that the courts have developed for the way in which they go about interpretation. The *ejusdem generis* rule assumes that if Parliament added a catch-all, Parliament intended it to be interpreted according to the other characteristics in the list. It is not a wide-ranging catch-all.[69]

Thus, the inclusion of such a general clause would result not in the wide 'catch-all' which would catch any harassing activity, but a narrower 'catch-some' which would cover only activities which the courts felt were similar in nature to those already listed within the Stalking Bill.[70] This would defeat the aim of the general provision and ensure that only a limited range of conduct was included within the remit of the Bill.

---

67   Babcock, RJ, 'Psychology of stalking', in Infield and Platford, 2000.
68   Anderson, J, *HC Deb* Vol 287 Col 818, 17 December 1996.
69   Mclean, D, *HC Deb* Vol 287 Col 825, 17 December 1996.
70   'Some conduct will be excluded directly but other conduct will have an ambiguous status': Mclean, D, *HC Deb* Vol 287 Col 828, 17 December 1996.

In addition to the criticism of the Bill as too narrow, the Conservative Government also condemned the Bill for being simultaneously too wide. This was based on the absence of a general defence of reasonableness that would be available to anyone who engaged in the prohibited conduct for a legitimate reason.[71] The key difficulty in formulating a legal definition of stalking is that it frequently involves conduct that is *prima facie* innocuous and the definition has to take account of this factor. Baroness Blatch summed up the difficulties inherent in this and notes the balance that has to be achieved:

> [Stalking] is a difficult area to legislate, since many of the individual actions in which stalkers engage are, in themselves, quite harmless – walking up and down a street, or standing on a street corner, for example. Much of the activity which can be described as stalking can, in another context, be something entirely innocent done as part of normal activity ... Any legislation in this area must be effective against stalkers and provide victims with adequate security and redress. But it must not inhibit people from going about their everyday business.[72]

This encapsulates the problem which has consistently impeded the formulation of a clear legal definition of stalking; how can a differentiation be made between the harassing conduct and the same conduct undertaken for perfectly legitimate reasons? Not all of the conduct that occurs during the course of stalking cases is manifestly objectionable. There is no outward distinction between a man waiting for a lift on a street corner and a man who is watching his victim's house in order to terrorise her. The conduct is the same; it is the unknown and frequently unprovable motivation of the perpetrator and the impact of the conduct on the recipient that transforms an apparently innocent act into a campaign of stalking. Merely because conduct is innocuous in the abstract does not mean that it cannot be extremely objectionable in the light of the context in which it occurs. There is nothing outwardly offensive in sending another person a picture of a new-born baby. However, should such conduct occur every year on the date upon which the recipient of the picture terminated her pregnancy, this context immediately changes the character of the act.[73] The context of the conduct renders that which is ostensibly pleasant into a hostile and distressing act.[74] Such

---

71 *HC Deb* Vol 287 Cols 798–01, 819, 17 December 1996.

72 Baroness Blatch, *HL Deb* Col 1824, 28 June 1996. After the Stalking Bill was blocked in the House of Commons, Lord Mcintosh reintroduced it in the House of Lords, hence the debate regarding the efficacy of the list approach to definition was taken up in the House of Lords.

73 Case history 12 – the victim has received a photograph or picture of a new-born baby on the same date for the past 14 years. She believes that the person responsible was a man with whom she had a casual relationship that ended when she found she was pregnant and decided to terminate the pregnancy.

74 'Often it is not the overt act itself which is harassing but the known, but unprovable, motives of the person concerned': Addison and Lawson-Cruttenden, 1998, p 35.

distinctions are difficult to encapsulate within a legal definition, particularly one that focuses upon conduct rather than motivation and consequences.[75]

To prohibit, for example, the making of all telephone calls which are reasonably likely to cause harassment, alarm or distress to the recipient must necessarily provide some defence for those who have legitimate reasons for doing so, such as those telephoning to impart bad news and those whose employment requires them to make unsolicited telephone calls. Telesales employees generally know that when they telephone private households in the evening, their calls are not usually welcomed, but it would not be reasonable to categorise such conduct as stalking, nor to use a statute aimed at the prohibition of stalking to render such behaviour unlawful. Equally, debt collectors[76] and insurance investigators[77] may follow and observe people, actions which doubtless cause the recipient of such conduct harassment, alarm or distress, but this is not the type of activity that the law was seeking to outlaw, thus it should not come within the remit of the Bill. The absence of a general defence of reasonableness would expose those engaged in legitimate activities that included any of the prohibited forms of conduct, such as political canvassers[78] and journalists, to potential criminal liability.[79] Whether any of the above activities should be subject to legal regulation is a separate question and one which the Stalking Bill did not seek to address, thus its provisions should not encroach upon what is, in the absence of specific legislation to the contrary, perfectly legitimate activity. A specific defence was provided in cl 4 of the Stalking Bill, which provided that:

> no person acting under statutory authority or other lawful authority insofar as he acts within that authority shall be guilty of an offence.

Whilst such a provision would ensure that certain categories of conduct that would otherwise incur liability would be exempted from the remit of the Bill, this would certainly not extend exemption to the activities of, for example, investigative journalists engaged in researching a story or persistent religious proselytisers.[80]

Clause 2(4) of the Stalking Bill did establish a more general defence that a person will not be guilty of stalking if he is able to establish that he did not know, nor had reasonable cause to believe, that his conduct would have the

---

75 Equally, it must be appreciated that not all stalking involved the deliberate causing of distress. As will be discussed further on in this chapter, some stalkers are oblivious to the impact of the conduct, whilst others hold a genuine belief that their attentions are welcomed. The need to encapsulate all these variables into a single definition of harassment makes the task of formulating a definition extremely challenging.

76 Lawrence, I (Sir), *HC Deb* Vol 287 Col 801, 17 December 1996.

77 George, B, *HC Deb* Vol 287 Col 798, 17 December 1996.

78 Lawrence, I (Sir), *HC Deb* Vol 287 Col 801, 17 December 1996.

79 *Ibid*, Cols 800–01, 17 December 1996.

80 Howard, M, *HC Deb* Vol 287 Col 819, 17 December 1996.

prohibited result.[81] As Lord Dixon-Smith pointed out, this would not prevent the imposition of liability on those involved in the listed activities for a legitimate reason if they realised that their conduct would be unwelcome to the recipient. Debt collectors and insurance investigators may be perfectly well aware that their activities would distress the recipient, but should still not incur liability under a statute aimed at combating stalking. Equally, private investigators and journalists seeking out salacious information would be likely to appreciate that their conduct is unwelcome to the target of their attentions, but should not be prevented from going about their lawful business.[82]

Thus, as Michael Howard asserted, the list approach to the definition of stalking was simultaneously too wide and too narrow. First, the activities listed were morally neutral in the sense that they could be undertaken for any number of reasons, but the Bill provided no means to differentiate between legitimate and nefarious purposes. In this sense, the proposed definition of stalking was too wide. Secondly, by establishing a list of conduct that would amount to stalking, any conduct not listed would be outside the remit of the legislation. The limitation of the efficacy of the catch-all provision imposed by the *ejusdem generis* approach to statutory interpretation ensured that only conduct directly analogous to that listed would be encompassed within the remit of the legislation. Therefore, a stalker who applied some ingenuity would be able to proceed with the pursuit of his victim whilst remaining beyond the reach of the criminal law. In this sense, the proposed definition was too narrow.

Whilst these criticisms appear logical, it should be noted that the Stalking Bill was drafted after careful consideration of anti-stalking legislation in operation in other common law jurisdictions,[83] where the list approach to definition is popular and appears effective.[84] Therefore, a consideration of this approach to stalking legislation will be informative both as a means of evaluating the efficacy of the list approach to definition and in determining why such a popular approach was deemed to be unworkable in England.

---

81 Stalking Bill 1996, cl 2(4): 'It shall be a defence to a charge under this section if the person charged proved that he did not know and had no reasonable cause to believe that his behaviour was likely to cause harassment, alarm, distress or fear for personal safety as mentioned in s 1 above, and the burden of proof shall lie upon the defendant.'

82 Lord Dixon-Smith, *HL Deb* Col 1821, 28 June 1996.

83 Anderson, J, *HC Deb* Vol 287 Col 824–25, 17 December 1996.

84 Eg, of the eight States in Australia, only New South Wales does not define stalking by reference to a list of prohibited conduct. Indeed, no definition of the conduct element of stalking is provided in the New South Wales legislation – Crimes Act 1900, s 562AB. The Canadian Criminal Code, s 264(1) contains a list of prohibited conduct and only five of the States in America do not specifically enumerate the type of conduct which is to be regarded as stalking: Bureau of Justice Assistance (1996) Regional Seminar Series on Implementing Anti-Stalking Codes.

1.2.2 The Australian approach to definition

All eight States in Australia have incorporated anti-stalking provisions into their legislation.[85] As was mentioned previously, seven of these States adopt the list approach to the definition of stalking. However, a consideration of these legislative definitions immediately reveals that although the seven States define stalking by reference to a list of prohibited activities, the conduct included on these lists is not identical. Can it be said, then, that each State has formulated a unique definition of stalking and that there is no consensus between these States as to the conduct that constitutes stalking?

1.2.2.1 The conduct element

There is a marked divergence between the States as to the conduct included within their definition of stalking. However, closer examination of these definitions reveals similar broad categories of conduct. It may be that the difference in terminology adopted accounts for the apparent diversity in conduct included in the definitions. For example, only four States include surveillance within their definition of stalking.[86] This does not necessarily mean that the conduct encompassed by the word 'surveillance' is not regarded as a manifestation of stalking in the remaining States, as analogous conduct may be labelled differently. The remaining three States all include the watching of a person or their place of residence or work or other place regularly visited within their list of prohibited conduct. As 'surveillance' is defined as 'watch or keep guard over a person ... often spying',[87] it is clear that the type of behaviour which would be regarded as surveillance is included within all the definitions of stalking using different terminology. Thus, despite the initial appearance of divergence caused by this different terminology, there is consensus regarding this aspect of the definition of stalking.

There is less agreement between the States regarding other types of conduct. Unwanted communications, whether by telephone or other means, and the sending of offensive material are not included in all the definitions of stalking despite the evidence of the prevalence of such conduct in stalking cases. However, this omission has to be considered in the light of the other legislative provisions that exist in these States. There is Commonwealth

---

85 Crimes Act 1900, s 34A (Australian Capital Territory); Crimes Act 1900, s 562AB (New South Wales); Criminal Code Act 1997, s 189 (Northern Territory); Criminal Code Act 1899, s 359A (Queensland); Criminal Law Consolidation Act 1935, s 19AA (South Australia); Criminal Code Act 1924, s 192 (Tasmania); Crimes Act 1958, s 21A (Victoria); Criminal Code Act 1913, ss 338D and 338E (Western Australia).

86 Australian Capital Territory, Northern Territory, Tasmania and Victoria.

87 Oxford English Dictionary.

legislation applicable to all States that deals with the use of the postal and telecommunications systems to menace, harass or cause offence to another.[88] In the light of such provisions, the decision to exclude conduct which is already prohibited is perfectly explicable. However, the inclusion of such conduct is also justifiable to extend the rather narrow scope of the communications prohibited by the Commonwealth legislation. Equally, as the list is used not merely to delineate prohibited conduct, but to provide a definition of stalking, it could be considered to be a weakness of this approach if a prevalent form of stalking conduct were to be excluded. If stalking is to be defined by reference to a list of characteristic activities, it is important that all prevalent manifestations of stalking are included, even if adequate provision is made to address such conduct in other legislation.

The surrounding legislative context is an important factor to take into account when engaging in comparative evaluation of similar legislative provisions in different jurisdictions. The context of the existing legislation is an important factor that influences the content of any subsequent legislation. Thus, any stalking legislation will necessarily be tailored to fill the gaps in the existing law, which may differ between jurisdictions, thus justifying discrepancies between content and level of penalty. An example of this can be seen when comparing the penalties available for basic stalking offences. Five Australian States distinguish between a basic offence of stalking and a more serious offence aggravated by such factors as use of a weapon and breach of a restraining order, injunction or bail conditions. The maximum penalty for the basic offence varies between two and three years' imprisonment; substantially more severe than the penalty of six months' imprisonment specified as the maximum under the basic offence created by the Protection from Harassment Act. This may be interpreted as an indication that stalking is viewed more seriously in Australia than it is in England. However, a consideration of the legislative context into which the Australian anti-stalking provisions were introduced reveals that most States already had an existing offence which would encompass minor incidents of stalking, thus there was a need for a more specific offence carrying a higher penalty to address more serious cases.[89] For example, in Southern Australia, s 7 of the Summary Offences Act 1953 prohibits 'offensive behaviour' and has been used successfully in minor stalking cases.[90] The absence of an analogous provision in English law meant

---

88 Crimes Act 1914, ss 85S and 85ZE (Commonwealth).

89 Summary Offences Act 1988, s 4 (New South Wales); Summary Offences Act 1953, s 7 (South Australia); Police Offences Act 1935, s 13 (Tasmania); Summary Offences Act 1966, s 17 (Victoria); Police Act 1892, s 54 (Western Australia).

90 *Stone v Ford* (1992) A Crim R 459. Conduct which would now be termed stalking also formed the basis for liability under this section prior to the emergence of stalking as a label to characterise certain conduct, as seen in *Grivelis v Horsnell* (1974) 8 SASR 43.

that a basic stalking offence had to encompass a lower level of conduct.[91] Indeed, it was at this lower end of the spectrum that English law was recognised to be particularly deficient as means of intervention were available in the more severe cases involving the commission of criminal offences or which caused the victim to suffer psychological harm.[92] If legislative provisions are enacted to target differing levels of severity of conduct, this should be taken into account when comparing the variance between approaches to the definition of the prohibited conduct.

1.2.2.2 The mental element

This variance in the legislative approach to definition is particularly apparent when comparing the approach to *mens rea* requirements between Australia and England in the formulation of a definition of stalking. The legislation of all eight Australian States specifies the intent with which the prohibited conduct must be undertaken. Although there is a degree of variance between the precise wording of the various provisions, generally they require either that the conduct should be undertaken for the purpose of causing fear or apprehension or for the purpose of causing serious harm, which includes psychological injury. Therefore, the motivation of the person engaging in the conduct is a determinative factor in establishing liability, thus is incorporated into the definition of stalking. This operates to limit the width of a definition of stalking based on a list of prohibited conduct. As previously discussed, the list approach was regarded as too wide to be adopted in England as it criminalised the actions of those engaged in perfectly legitimate activities. However, the requirement of a nefarious intent effectively limits the scope of the offence only to those who are deliberately intending their actions to have an adverse impact upon the recipient.[93] This limitation ensures that the legislation is applicable only to those to whom it was intended to apply and was also necessary to comply with the established principle of Australian common law that all serious offences require proof of intent.[94] The inclusion of a specific intent requirement is also seen as an essential element of any legal

---

91 Despite the potential availability of offences under the Public Order Act 1986, both the intent requirement of the offence and the disinclination of the legal authorities to apply this section to stalking limited its utility in this respect. Home Office, *Policing Low-Level Disorder: Police Use of Section 5 of the Public Order Act 1986*, 1994; Harris, 2000, *An Evaluation of the Use and Effectiveness of the Protection from Harassment Act 1997*. See Chapter 4.

92 'We need quick and effective remedies for the less serious cases': Howard, M, Home Secretary, Conservative Party Conference 1996. See Chapter 4.

93 When formulating the anti-stalking provisions in South Australia, for example, it was decided that 'the best way to limit the scope of the offence to the target group was to require proof of an intention to cause serious fear, harm or apprehension': Goode, 1995, p 28.

94 *He Kaw Teh v The Queen* (1985) 157 CLR 523.

definition of stalking in the US.[95] It is regarded as the most effective way to limit the breadth of the conduct requirement that acts as a measure of criminality to ensure that the defendant is actually culpable in relation to the conduct.[96]

The inclusion of an intent requirement to limit the width of the conduct element of the offence was not favoured in England where the greatest impediment to the use of potentially available existing offences was seen to be the requirement of intent to cause the prohibited harm.[97] By including a specific intent requirement within the definition of stalking, the remit of the offence is limited to those who appreciate that their conduct is unwelcome, but undertake it in any case with the purpose of causing distress. This is not the only motivating factor which leads to stalking; there may be a genuine misunderstanding regarding the reciprocity of feelings between the parties or the stalker may be delusional and have a genuine belief that the other party welcomes the attention. Nonetheless, the conduct may cause the same degree of alarm or distress to the recipient, despite the absence of any intention to do so, as the same conduct undertaken with a deliberately malevolent motivation, yet be excluded from the definition of stalking. For example, one stalker who has pursued his victim for four years claims that he wants to 'devote [his] life to making her happy'. Far from achieving this aim, his actions have caused his victim to move house 14 times and have damaged her health and her career:

> It's no exaggeration to say that he has stolen my life – all of it. He's taken everything away from me – my home, my family and friends, my job and my career prospects. I've changed job so many times that no one will employ me. I don't stay anywhere long enough to make friends and, besides, I don't really trust people any more. I take pills for depression and have counselling but it all seems so bleak that I can't see any purpose to my life at times. And the real joke, the real funny thing to all this, is that he is doing this because he thinks he is in love with me.[98]

Another stalker, whose conduct culminated in an arson attack on his victim's house, believed that she was the reincarnation of his lover who had burned at the stake for her adultery with him. He believed that they were bound together for all eternity by a 'karmic link' that meant that they were destined

---

95 The position in the US is somewhat restricted by the need to ensure that anti-stalking provisions are not invalidated by constitutional challenge on the grounds of vagueness or overbreadth. The inclusion of a specific intent requirement is regarded as the most effective means of ensuring that the legislation complies with constitutional standards of clarity and precision: Bjerregaard, 1996, pp 307–41.

96 Gilligan, 1992, pp 285–314.

97 'The greatest difficulty that the police find in using existing legislation against stalkers is the need to prove the intention of the stalker' Howard, M, HC Deb Vol 287 Col 783, 17 December 1996; Harris, 2000, *An Evaluation of the Use and Effectiveness of the Protection from Harassment Act 1997*, p 2.

98 Case history 26.

to be together.[99] It is unlikely that these stalkers would be found to have an intention to cause harm, as they both believe that their conduct is welcome to the recipient and that their feelings of love are reciprocated. Such situations do not solely arise in connection with delusional or mentally disordered stalkers, but may result from misunderstandings between the parties. In one such situation, a young man persistently asked a work colleague to go out with him. Not wanting to hurt his feelings with an outright refusal, she made excuses, expecting that he would understand that this was a rebuff. He, however, believed the expressions of regret that she was busy and her promise of 'some other time' to be genuine:

> If she didn't want to go out with me, she should have just said so but she never did. It was always 'not tonight, I'm busy' and 'maybe next week'. If she had ever said 'no thanks, you're not my type', I would have stopped asking her ... The first I knew that she didn't like me was when I got suspended from work and then arrested.[100]

Certainly there was no intention to cause harm or fear in the victim in these situations, but that was nevertheless the result of the conduct. Whilst it could be argued that deliberate stalking is morally worse than inadvertent stalking, whether due to mental disorder or misunderstanding, the impact on the victim may be equally harmful. It was in recognition of this factor that the Protection from Harassment Act included no intent requirement, focusing instead upon the impact of the conduct upon the victim in conjunction with whether the stalker knew or ought to have known that his conduct would have this effect.

Despite the extent of the reliance upon a specific intent requirement in the US and Australia, the limiting impact of such requirements are recognised:

> [Intent] requirements may mean that anti-stalking legislation will not reach people who, because they are delusional or otherwise, are not capable of forming the intent. The delusional offender may be acting out of 'love' for the victim, or out of a belief that he or she is, or is meant to be, bonded to the victim.[101]

Thus, it can be seen that an effective definition of stalking cannot refer exclusively to the conduct involved. However, reference to the intention behind the conduct may actually exclude situations which should be regarded as stalking and in which the victim needs and deserves the protection of the law.

The extent to which an intent requirement excludes instances of stalking is dependent upon the interpretation of 'intention' in this context. The

---

99 Case history 19.
100 Case history 18.
101 McAnaney, Curliss, and Abeyta-Price, 1993, pp 819–909.

Australian courts infer intention by reference to the absence of an alternative explanation for undertaking the conduct:

> A consideration of the conduct of the appellant is decisive in revealing intention ... The defendant offered no explanation for his conduct. He knew what he was doing. In the absence of explanation I think the facts here spoke for themselves. They bespoke an intention to be offensive, to threaten ... In my opinion, the irresistible inference is that the appellant intended to be offensive, to threaten.[102]

This inferential approach enables the Australian courts to extend the protection of stalking legislation beyond situations in which the stalker deliberately sought to cause an adverse reaction in his victim. If conduct is self-evidently harassing, it will be inferred that this was the intended effect unless the defendant can provide an alternative explanation.[103] Such an approach would not work in all jurisdictions, as it is dependent upon the approach taken to the inference of intention. Certainly it would have no place in the US as, owing to the need to avoid vagueness and overbreadth, precise definitions of all the elements of stalking must be provided.[104]

1.2.2.3 The impact on the victim

An alternative means of adding precision to a definition of stalking is to focus not on the purpose behind the conduct, but on the impact that it has on the recipient. This approach is used in some of the State legislation in the US as a further clarification of the nature of stalking that is used in conjunction with an intent requirement.[105] It is not enough that the stalker intends that the conduct will cause the victim fear of violence; the victim must actually fear violence. Thus, the intent requirement combines with a requirement that the victim actually experiences an adverse impact, thus further narrowing the scope of stalking. This focus on the impact of the victim was chosen as a means of limiting the offence of harassment. To incur liability under the Protection from Harassment Act 1997, the conduct must cause the victim to feel harassed, which is defined as including alarm and distress.[106] Thus, although there are no definitional restrictions imposed upon the conduct that can constitute harassment, it is limited by the requirement of an adverse reaction in the recipient of the conduct. This focus upon the impact of the

---

102 *Stone v Ford* (1992) Australian Criminal Reports 459, *per* Bollen J, pp 464–65.
103 Goode, 1995, pp 21–31.
104 Guy, 1993, pp 991–1027; Sohn, 1994, pp 203–41.
105 Bjerregaard, 1996, pp 285–314; Department of Justice, *Stalking and Domestic Violence: the Third Annual Report to Congress under the Violence Against Women Act*, 1998.
106 Protection from Harassment Act 1997, s 7(2).

conduct on the recipient was deliberately adopted to avoid the difficulties of formulating a definition of the conduct element of stalking:

> Let us not worry about what any one of 1,000 activities might be. Let us worry about the effect on the victim. If the effect is to cause harassment to the victim, we can trigger the offence.[107]

This approach avoids the difficulties inherent in formulating a definition of stalking. All conduct which has the proscribed result is included within the definition, thus providing a degree of flexibility that is absent in a more specific definition which delineates the precise nature of the prohibited conduct. Equally, the focus upon the impact of the victim limits the breadth of the conduct requirement without a need to establish the motivation behind the conduct.

The difficulty with this approach as the basis of a definition of stalking is that it bases liability upon that which inherently unknowable – the reaction of another person. Different people respond to similar situations in different ways. It is difficult, if not impossible, to predict with any degree of certainty how another individual will respond in any given situation. Extreme conduct will not pose a problem. It is inconceivable that anyone would have a positive reaction to being sent a used sanitary towel in the post, or having abusive comments painted in huge red letters on the road outside one's house. Such conduct would clearly provoke a negative response. Difficulty arises when more ambiguous conduct is involved, such as the sending of flowers. Such conduct, even if repeated on many occasions, would engender a range of responses in different people. Some may well feel harassed by constant unwanted attention, even of an innocuous nature, whilst others would be more readily able to dismiss the conduct as harmless. This renders the definition of conduct as stalking contingent on something that is neither ascertainable nor predictable, and is a substantial limitation of the use of this means of narrowing the definition of stalking.[108]

The scope of any definition of stalking is clearly problematic. It must be sufficiently wide to encompass the multifarious manifestations of stalking so as to provide comprehensive protection for victims. This will necessarily result in a wide definition. There are two ways in which it may be narrowed to ensure that no legitimate activities are subsumed within the definition. First, the inclusion of an intent requirement ensures that only those who deliberately set out to cause harm and distress by their conduct are labelled as stalkers. Differentiation between stalking and legitimate behaviour upon the basis of the motivation for the conduct is not straightforward. In the absence of an admission of guilt, a reliable basis upon which to make inferences of

---

107 Mclean, D, *HC Deb* Vol 287 Col 826, 17 December 1996.
108 Finch, 2000, pp 273–95.

intent must be established. Such a concept has proved troublesome in other areas of English criminal law.[109] The issue of intent is particularly difficult as an aspect of stalking, owing to the variable motivations which may arise. A delusional stalker who is convinced that the recipient of his conduct returns his feelings of affection cannot be deemed to have intended harm nor, presumably, would this fit within the approach taken by the Australian courts of inferring intent in the absence of any alternative explanation. Despite these difficulties, references to the intent behind the conduct are a common feature of stalking definitions in the US. The second way in which a more precise definition can be developed is by reference to the impact of the conduct upon the victim. The focus upon the reaction of the recipient narrows the scope of the conduct element of stalking without the necessity to consider the intent that motivates the conduct.

It is not easy to encapsulate the characteristics of stalking in a comprehensive yet concise definition. The need for both breadth and specificity is a particularly tortuous combination to encompass within a simple definition. Various combinations of the three key factors of conduct, motivation and impact have been utilised, but no definitional approach has proved to be unproblematic. These three key elements will be explored further in Chapter 2. However, before undertaking such an exploration, a final issue needs to be addressed in order to answer the question 'what is stalking?'.

1.3 NEW CRIME, OLD BEHAVIOUR

The preceding discussion has addressed the definitional difficulties associated with stalking. The question now arises as to whether this conduct has always been a feature, albeit it a hidden one, of interpersonal interaction, or whether it can truly be termed 'the crime of the nineties'; a development of the latter decades of the 20th century attributable to the changing nature of social and personal relationships.[110] There is plentiful evidence to suggest that, far from being a new type of behaviour, 'stalking' emerged as new terminology to describe behaviour that has been a recognised problem for a far longer period of time.[111]

---

109 The decision of the House of Lords in *R v Woollin* is generally heralded as eliminating the lack of clarity that has existed in the law of intention and murder for the last quarter of a century: Smith, 1998. Prior to this, there was some uncertainty as to the scope of intention that was exacerbated by seemingly inconsistent rulings by the courts: Simester and Chan, 1997. However, despite the clarity of the judgment in *Woollin*, not all academics are convinced that this is the final resolution to the problems posed to the criminal law by this complex concept: Norrie, 1999.

110 Emerson, Ferris and Gardner, 1998, pp 289–314; Meloy, 1999b, pp 85–99; Goode, 1995, pp 21–31.

111 'Violent behaviour toward self or others as the dénouement of unrequited love is as old as antiquity' – Meloy, 1992, p 19; 'Pursuit of one person by another is probably as old as human relationships' – von Heussen, 2000.

1.3.1 Fictional accounts of stalking

The recent emergence of the terminology impedes the location of reference to stalking in earlier fictional accounts. Nevertheless, by comparing the conduct that is characteristic of what we would now call stalking with literature and films that existed prior to the inception of the term, numerous examples of conduct that would now be termed stalking can be identified.

For example, *The Long Fatal Love Chase*, written in 1868, recounts the efforts of Rosamund to avoid the saturnine and sinister Tempest as he pursues her around Europe. Notable themes within the book, such as Tempest's pursuit of Rosamund despite clear evidence of the lack of reciprocity of his feelings, his obsessive determination to possess her, and his conviction of their shared destiny, are evident in contemporary stalking cases. One stalking victim described how she is forced to relocate on a regular basis to evade her stalker:

> I have to keep moving. It takes him on average four months to find me. This is the fourteenth place I've lived in just over three years. I always pick somewhere I've got no association with and that is really different to the last place I was to make it harder for him to work out. At first, I went where I knew people or places I'd always liked but he found me too quickly so I started making sure it was more random. I've learnt not to accumulate too much stuff or to get settled anywhere. And I keep a packed bag with me everywhere I go – work, the supermarket, friend's houses – so I can get away quickly if he finds me.[112]

Another victim explained that she changed her name and moved to a different town in order to escape an obsessive former partner, but that this means that she has no contact with her friends or family in case that provides a means for the stalker to track her down:

> It's like being new-born. I've got no past because I don't dare tell anyone where I'm from in case they know anyone there and it somehow gets back to him.[113]

---

112 Case history 26.
113 Case history 20.

Similarly, leading psychologist Dr Reid Meloy uses examples from Shakespeare to illustrate the longevity of stalking.[114] In particular, he refers to *Othello*, in which Desdemona is ultimately killed as a result of Othello's passionate obsession. Meloy links this to a common phenomenon in stalking whereby rejection by the object of desire leads to feelings of shame, humiliation and ultimately anger, leading the stalker to devalue the once adored object of his affections. Once destroyed, the object is restored to idealised perfection and can again be pursued; this love-hate-love pattern appears prevalent in relational stalking and is epitomised by Othello's words: 'I will kill thee and love thee after.'[115] Meloy likens this to OJ Simpson, who appeared distraught after the death of his wife. Three years after his trial for her murder, Simpson said: 'Let's say I committed this crime ... Even if I did do this, it would have been because I loved her very much.'[116]

Shakespeare's understanding of obsessive passion has been said to have been inspired by his conviction that a close friend was having an affair with his 'adored beloved'. Skoler argues that analysis of Shakespeare's last 14 sonnets, his so called 'dark lady' sonnets, reveals them to be: 'more like hate sonnets as his spurned affirmations of love become increasingly vicious, threatening, obscene, paranoid, irrational, desperate and devaluing of himself and her.'[117] Whether based upon Shakespeare's own experiences or his observations of others, much in these sonnets encapsulates the idea of obsessive love and rejection, leading to vilification, which appears frequently in relational stalking. As such, it is a sound illustration that this conduct was prevalent before it came to prominence as stalking.[118]

More recent representations of conduct that would now be termed stalking can be seen in major Hollywood films. A notable example is *Play Misty for Me*, made in 1971, which is a dramatic portrayal of stalking. Radio disc jockey Dave Garver receives regular requests from a female caller, Evelyn, to play the song 'Misty'. She contrives a meeting with him and

---

114 A quotation from *Othello* was used by one stalker, presumably in an attempt to communicate his feelings to his 15 year old victim. A letter written to her included the quotation:

> Yet she must die, else she'll betray more men.
> Put out the light, and then put out the light:
> If I quench thee, thy flaming minister,
> I can thy former light restore.

After this, the stalker commented: 'I guess Othello had a point.' Case history 24 (interview with victim's mother).

115 *Othello*, Act 5, Scene 2.

116 Interview in *Esquire*, February 1998, p 58, cited in Meloy, 1999, pp 85–99.

117 Skoler, G, 'The archetypes and psychodynamics of stalking', in Meloy, 1998.

118 Skoler also discusses Browning's *Porphyria's Lover* and *My Last Duchess*, both of which explore jealous fantasies of murdering an unfaithful lover so as to gain possession and keep her 'narcissistically alive'. Skoler also draws parallels with the murder of Nicole Brown Simpson, particularly in OJ Simpson's tendency to refer to his wife as if she were still alive and restored to him after attending her funeral: *ibid*.

seduces him, clearly expecting that this will be the beginning of a relationship. She appears convinced of their love for each other and immune to his attempts to orientate her to the reality of their situation. Evelyn's conduct becomes increasingly erratic and obsessive, including attempts to kill herself and him, as she degenerates further into violence and insanity. The gradual increase of the tension and the bloody conclusion of the film render it a memorable and graphic account of stalking at its most extreme, although predating the inception of the term by some 20 years.[119]

1.3.2 Case law

Examples can be found in reported cases where it is established not only that stalking is an old behaviour, but that it has long posed a challenge to the legal authorities. An early example can be seen in *Dennis v Lane* where, in 1704, Dr Lane was bound over to keep the peace following his disruptive attempts to force his attentions upon Miss Dennis. When she and her mother travelled to London in an attempt to avoid him, Dr Lane pursued them and assaulted those who impeded his access to Miss Dennis, forcing her mother to hire men to stand guard outside their lodgings.[120] In *R v Dunn*, the defendant sought a writ of habeas corpus following his imprisonment for refusing to enter into a recognisance to the keep the peace and be of good behaviour.[121] The conduct complained of included the sending of letters couched in 'strange language' to Miss Coutts, persistently following her and accosting her whilst she was out walking, causing her to fear for her safety, and his violence and abuse towards those who sought to keep him away from her. When he appeared before magistrates, the defendant referred to Miss Coutts as 'the damnedest whore' who deserved to be 'tarred, feathered and burnt' and he continued to pester her after his court appearance.

In both these cases, the victims had sought a surety of the peace by giving a Justice of the Peace an assurance upon oath (articles of the peace) that she was 'actually under such fear; and has just cause to be so, by reason of the other's having threatened to beat him, or lain in wait for that purpose'.[122] If the defendant did not assault the plaintiff or threaten bodily harm, the articles of the peace had to contain a statement by the plaintiff that she feared for her bodily safety. This was absent in *R v Dunn*, hence the court could offer no protection to Miss Coutts. Upon hearing the details of the case during the application for habeas corpus, Lord Denman commented that:

---

119 Similarly, the more recent *Fatal Attraction* charts the descent into violence of a woman who develops an obsession with a married man following a casual sexual encounter.

120 *Dennis v Lane* 87 ER 887; QB 1704.

121 *R v Dunn* (1840) QB 12 AD & EL 568.

122 Hawkins, *Pleas of the Crown*, 6th edn, 1878, p 254.

the law of England may be justly reproached with its inadequacy to repress the mischief, and obviate the danger, which the prisoner's proceedings render too probable; and we may naturally feel surprise if none of the numerous Police Acts have made sufficient provisions for this purpose.[123]

These cases would certainly be considered examples of stalking according to current terminology. The courts had extremely limited powers to address such conduct at the time, but clearly recognised the need to do so. Despite Lord Denman's words, legislation targeted at the type of conduct that occurred in *R v Dunn* did not appear on the statute books for a further 157 years.[124]

1.3.3 Research studies

There were two predominant strands of academic research that addressed stalking behaviour. First, there were studies which addressed the behaviour itself, albeit under different labels. For example, an American study conducted by Herold et al found that 24% of college students had been harassed and that the most common manifestations of harassment were unwanted telephone calls and following.[125] In a more detailed study, again based in the US, Jason *et al* studied post-relationship harassment and found that that 56% of women in their sample had been pestered for at least one month after terminating a relationship.[126] This study categorised the harassing conduct into unwanted telephone calls (92%), visits to the woman's home or place of work (48%), threats and assaults (30%), following and watching (26%), and unwanted gifts, flowers or notes (6%). The findings of this research in terms of the impact of the harassment upon the victims and of the coping strategies employed are comparable to more recent research into stalking.[127] Herold's study classified the conduct as a form of sexual offence[128] and Jason used the general term 'harassment' although it was, at the time, rare to apply this term outside of a workplace context. Stalking was also referred to as obsession, a form of sexual harassment and psychological rape.[129] Despite the variance in terminology, the conduct described under these labels would clearly amount to stalking as it is now understood.

---

123 *R v Dunn* (1804) QB 12 AD & EL, *per* Lord Denman, pp 602–03.

124 Protection from Harassment Act 1997.

125 Herold, Mantle, and Zemitis, 1979, pp 65–72.

126 Jason, Reichler, Easton, Neal and Wilson, 1984, pp 259–69.

127 Zona, Palarea and Lane, 'Psychiatric diagnosis and the offender-victim typology of stalking', in Meloy, 1998, pp 70–84.

128 Similarly, harassing conduct such as following and obscene calls are categorised as 'sexually stressful events', in DiVasto, Kaufman, Rosner, Jackson, Christy, Pearson and Burgett, 1984, pp 59–67.

129 Lowney, K and Best, J, 'Stalking strangers and lovers: changing media typifications of a new crime problem', in Best, 1995.

The second area of research concerns mental disorders that cause the sufferer to engage in stalking behaviour. This area of research features prominently in early psychiatric literature examining erotomania, which is now recognised as the cause of some stalking cases, notably those involving delusional stalkers.[130] The first use of the term 'erotomania' occurred in 1604,[131] but throughout the 17th and 18th century this term was used as a synonym for nymphomania and satyriasis. It was not until 1837 that the prominent French psychiatrist Jean Etienne Esquirol distinguished erotomania and nymphomania:

> In the latter, the evil originates in the organs of reproduction, the irritation of which reacts upon the brain. In erotomania, the sentiment which characterises it is in the head.[132]

Despite this clear distinction, debate over the nature of erotomania continued throughout the 19th century until it was finally recognised as a genuine psychiatric illness in 1892.[133] It was not until 1921 that a detailed exposition of erotomania developed which clearly identifies it as giving rise to conduct which would constitute stalking today. De Clérambault identified the characteristics of erotomania which are clearly recognisable as those which may give rise to stalking. The patient, usually a woman, holds a delusional belief that the victim, usually a man who is older and of greater social status than the patient and is frequently a public figure, is passionately in love with her. Any paradoxical conduct such as denial of this love or attempts to repulse or harm the patient are interpreted as confirmation of his love and attributed either to a test of the strength of her feelings for him or as an attempt to deceive others as to the nature of the relationship.

One of de Clérambault's patients provided a prototypical example of erotomania:

> A 53-year-old Frenchwoman suffered from the delusional belief that King George V was in love with her and was sending English sailors and tourists to France with messages of love for her. She travelled to England and followed the King as he moved between his various residences and waited patiently outside Buckingham Palace until she saw a curtain moving which she interpreted as the King signalling to her. She was convinced that their love was known throughout London and that people wished them well. Despite this, she was also convinced that the King was deliberately disrupting her travel plans and had arranged for her luggage to be misplaced. This paradoxical behaviour did not deter the woman who persisted in her belief that there was a relationship between herself and the King as she stated 'The King might hate

---

130 Harmon, Rosner and Owens, 1995, pp 188–96; Meloy and Gothard, 1995, pp 258–63; Zona, Sharma and Lane, 1993, pp 894–903.

131 Ferrand, *Erotomania or a Treatise Discussing the Essence, Causes, Symptoms, Prognosticks and Cure of Love or Erotique Melancholy*, 1640, cited in Enoch and Trethowan, 1991.

132 Esquirol, 1965.

133 Tuke, 1892: 'the erotomanic was the toy of his own imagination'.

me but he can never forget. I could never be indifferent to him, nor he to me'.[134]

This example provides a clear illustration of erotomanic stalking traits that can be seen in modern cases. One stalker echoed the words of the Frenchwoman when he said:

You'll be thinking of me. You may not be thinking good thoughts, but you'll be thinking of me.[135]

Equally, American chat show host David Letterman was stalked for several years by an obsessed fan, Margaret Ray, who showed clear indications of erotomanic delusions. She believed she was married to David Letterman and was once arrested after living in his house and driving his car whilst he was away. Nothing short of periods of imprisonment stopped her pursuit of him and she could not be convinced that he was not in love with her.[136] She eventually committed suicide.[137] Celebrity stalkers are significantly more likely to suffer from erotomania than stalkers who target a person known to them.[138] For celebrities, the distinction between a devoted fan and a stalker may not be easy to establish and, to a certain extent, classification is dependent upon the celebrity's reaction. For example, during the height of The Beatles' popularity during the 1960s, Margo Stephens stood outside Paul McCartney's London home for three years. He came to know her well during this time and frequently asked her to exercise his sheepdog and enlisted her help to unlock his security gates. Given the publicity surrounding attacks by stalkers on celebrity victims,[139] it is unlikely that a similar reaction to such prolonged attention would occur at the present time.[140] Celebrities are increasingly seeking advice from specialist agencies, such as the Threat Management Unit established to deal with stalking cases, and specialist security firms, such as leading stalking security consultant Gavin de Becker, on how to deal with persistent and obsessive fans.[141]

---

134 De Clérambault, 1921, p 259.

135 www.fiu.edu/~victimad/stalkvoi.html.

136 Ironically, despite being the partial inspiration for Connecticut's stalking legislation, Margaret Ray could not be prosecuted under it as she did not satisfy the 'credible threat' requirement. Her periods of imprisonment arose from charges associated with her persistent trespass on David Letterman's property and her theft of his car. Orion, 1997, p 240.

137 Paper given by Kerry Wells and Wayne Maxey, Stalking Task Force, San Diego Police Force at the Stalking Seminar held at Bramshill Police Training Centre, 22 March 2000.

138 Zona, Sharma and Lane, 1993, pp 894–903.

139 'Stalker planned to rape Spielberg' (1997) Daily Telegraph, 19 December; 'Madonna bodyguard shot fearless stalker' (1996) The Times, 5 January; 'Björk fan films his death after acid attack' (1996) Daily Telegraph, 19 September.

140 'Every star's nightmare: the fan who is fuelled by Madness' (1992) The Times, 24 May.

141 'When fans turn into fanatics: nervous celebs call for help from security expert Gavin de Becker' (1990) People, 12 February; Perez, 1993, pp 263–80.

1.4 CONCLUSION

Thus, although the preceding discussion clearly establishes that behaviour that would now be termed stalking is not a recent development but has existed for at least 300 years, it is also apparent that attitudes towards stalking have changed dramatically in more recent years. The reason for this change in attitude towards stalking is not clear. The courts were concerned about the lack of legal remedy for stalking victims as early as 1840, yet legislative intervention did not occur in any jurisdiction until the 1990s. An explanation for the emergence of stalking as a serious social problem at this time will be sought in Chapter 3. However, before engaging in sociological analysis of the genesis of stalking, it is important to gain a greater understanding of the characteristics of stalking and the nature of the association between stalker and victim. These issues form the basis of the next chapter.

CHAPTER 2

THE CHARACTERISTICS OF STALKING

This chapter elaborates on the discussion in the preceding chapter regarding the nature of stalking. The focus is upon three central issues – the characteristics of the conduct, the motivation of the stalker and the impact of stalking upon the victim. As the immense variability of the conduct involved precludes the formulation of a concise and comprehensive definition, it is particularly important to identify the defining characteristics of stalking. The first section of this chapter focuses upon the identification and exploration of such characteristics. This is followed by an account of the nature of the association between the parties concerned that seeks to dispel some common misconceptions regarding the relationship between stalker and victim. This discussion provides a context in which to consider the motivation of the stalker, which arguably provides a more accurate and useful means of classifying stalking cases than reference to the relationship between the parties. Moreover, an understanding of the motivational forces that lead to stalking is essential to any critical evaluation of the efficacy of various means of legal intervention. This chapter closes by considering the impact of stalking upon the victims, illustrating the potential severity of the nature of the harm, another essential factor to take into account when assessing the appropriateness of the legal response to stalking.

2.1 THE CONDUCT ELEMENT OF STALKING

One of the most notable features of stalking is the immense range of conduct that it encompasses. Many of the early studies were concerned with identifying the types of conduct that will commonly occur in stalking cases. These were relatively small scale studies that were usually focused upon a particular subject, such as domestic violence[1] or psychotic and mentally disordered stalkers.[2] Although there was a degree of consensus regarding the broad categories of conduct, the classification of conduct varied between studies, as did the prevalence with which particular types of stalking behaviour were found to occur. This can be attributed to a number of factors, such as the range of methodologies employed, the differing definitions of stalking that were used as a basis for the study and the focus of the research. Small scale, non-representative studies cannot be used as a basis from which

---

1   Coleman, 1997, pp 420–32; Zona, Sharma and Lane, 1993, pp 894–903.
2   Kienlen *et al*, 1997, pp 317–34; Harmon, Rosner and Owens, 1995, pp 188–96.

to extrapolate general findings regarding the wider incidence of the various types of stalking conduct, but they do reveal that certain types of conduct, such as following, unwanted communication and contact and threats to persons and property occurred uniformly regardless of the nature of the study. As such, these can be considered to be examples of common stalking behaviour.

The diversity of stalking behaviour precludes the creation of an exhaustive list of specific conduct. Some acts are so unusual that any such list would run to hundreds, possibly thousands of items. One way in which to address this is to create general categories of conduct. For example, examples of extremely unusual conduct that has occurred in stalking cases include giving the victim over 500 pairs of scissors,[3] leaving a box of cauliflower on a doorstep[4] and depositing a Bible and a severed chicken head in the doorway of the victim's home.[5] Such conduct is likely to be so rare that it would form a series of unique categories of conduct that are likely only to have arisen on a single occasion. However, the alternative is to ignore the particularities of the conduct and subsume all of the acts within the more general category of 'leaving unwanted items or gifts'.

This approach was adopted by the most comprehensive examination of the stalking in England, which was carried out as part of the British Crime Survey 1998. Fourteen general categories of common stalking conduct were established and the accounts provided by the participants were analysed to determine the extent to which their experiences disclosed conduct within these categories.

This approach identifies some of the more common stalking behaviours and gives some indication of the range of conduct that may arise during the course of stalking. However, each of the categories can itself encompass a continuum of conduct. For example, physical violence includes a range of conduct of varying degrees of severity from an isolated incident of minor violence to a protracted period of severe violence; it may result in little or no physical harm to the victim, or to the infliction of serious injury or even death. The behaviour that falls into any of these categories may be manifested in multifarious ways.

---

3   Case history 37.
4   'Cauliflower love tokens led to court' (1997) *The Times*, 17 December.
5   *R v Cox* [1998] Crim LR 810.

Figure 2.1   Types of stalking conduct experienced by participants in the British Crime Survey 1998

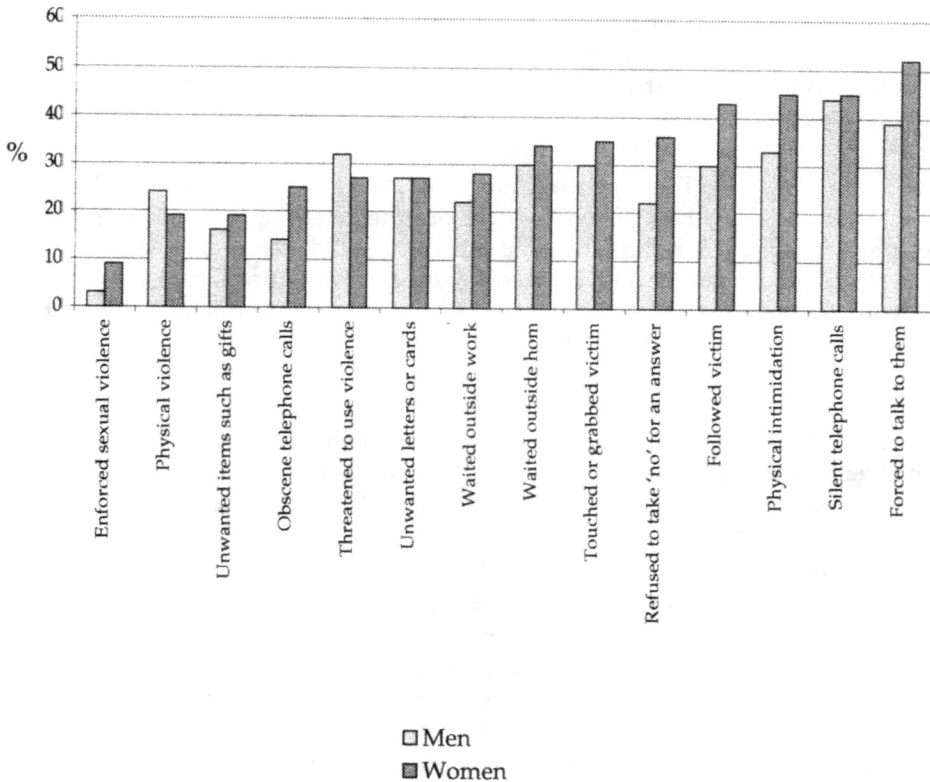

□ Men
■ Women

A comparison of the experiences of two victims whose stalkers refused to take 'no' for an answer provides a further illustration of this point. The first victim became distressed when a work colleague persistently asked her out.[6] He was always pleasant and polite, but she had no wish to go out with him. In order to avoid hurting his feelings with an outright refusal, the victim pretended that she was busy at the times that he suggested. This continued for a period of time and the requests became more frequent. The stalker began to leave gifts for the victim on her desk and started to call at her home. It was at this stage that she reported his conduct to her employer and the police became

---

6   Case history 18.

involved. Despite the obvious distress that this caused the victim, the conduct itself was ostensibly pleasant. This can be contrasted with the experiences of the second victim, who feels compelled to engage in intercourse with her ex-partner on a regular basis as she fears the consequences of refusal.[7] Her ex-partner refused to accept that their relationship was over and engaged in increasingly controlling and violent behaviour until the victim feared that she would be raped unless she complied with his demands. There is an immense difference between the experiences of these two victims and yet each case of stalking could be categorised as within 'refusal to take "no" for an answer'.

These cases also illustrate that the experiences of victims may fall into more than one category. The first case outlined here also involved silent telephone calls and leaving unwanted gifts, whilst the second involved actual and threatened violence and forcible sexual contact. Indeed, it is relatively unusual for a stalking case to involve only one type of conduct.[8] The British Crime Survey found that only 16% of cases involved conduct that fell into a single category and only two victims interviewed during the course of this research experienced only one form of conduct.[9]

In addition to involving multiple forms of behaviour, stalking usually involves repeated incidents of the same types of behaviour. The British Crime Survey found that silent telephone calls were the most likely to occur on multiple occasions with nine out of 10 victims receiving three or more calls and 43% of victims reporting in excess of 10 incidents.

The findings of the British Crime Survey indicate that the more indirect forms of stalking are likely to occur most repeatedly with telephone calls and unwanted written communications occurring most frequently. The more serious forms of conduct appeared less likely to occur on multiple occasions, although the repeat incidence was still relatively high.[10] Seven per cent of participants indicated that they had experienced persistent and unwanted conduct that did not fall into any of the 14 categories identified. It is impossible to speculate what forms of conduct were experienced by these participants, but notable omissions from the list include damage to property, threats to third parties, and interception of mail.[11] Again, this illustrates the difficulties inherent in an evaluation of stalking based upon listed activities.

---

7   Case history 34.
8   Harris, 2000, p 12.
9   Case history 1 involved only the watching of the victim's house; Case history 13 involved only silent telephone calls, although these were directed at multiple victims.
10 Eg, in cases involving forcible sexual contact, 14% of victims had experienced three or more incidents of this nature: Budd and Mattinson, 2000, p 38.
11 Budd and Mattinson, 2000, p 40. These types of conduct were amongst those identified as examplars of stalking by Sheridan, Davies and Boon, 2001.

Figure 2.2   **Percentage of victims that experienced each type of conduct more than 10 times (BCS)**

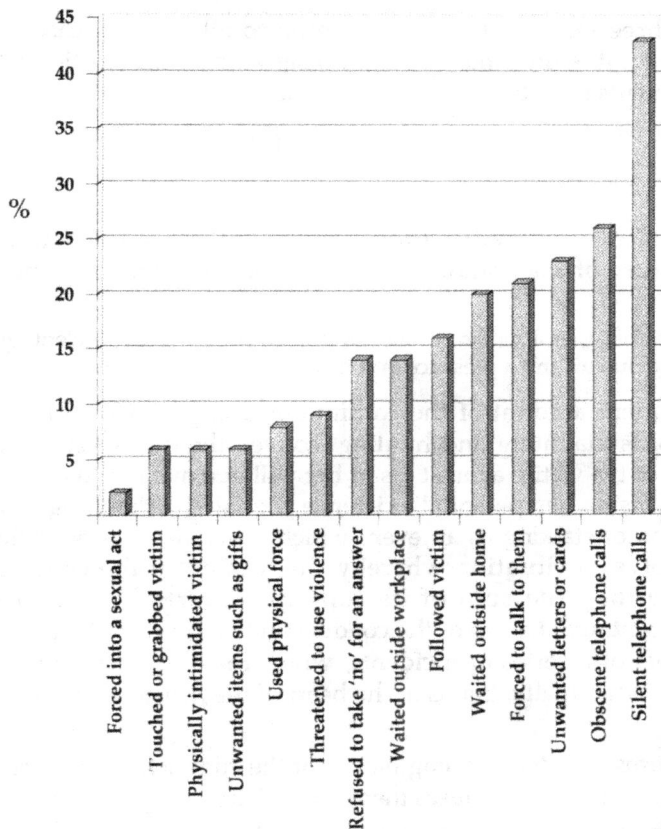

This further exploration of the nature of stalking illustrates the futility of attempting to encapsulate the totality of the conduct that may arise. Stalkers may use any combination of numerous forms of conduct during the course of the pursuit of their victims. Some general categories of behaviour occur with greater frequency, but there is an immense potential for variability within these general categories. Therefore, it is true to say that stalking conduct involves an incalculable number of combinations of an immense range of conduct.

It may appear as if different stalking cases have little commonality as regards the conduct involved. Whilst this is certainly the case as regards the particular manifestation of the conduct, three general characteristics of stalking are apparent. These characteristics were encapsulated by Earl Russell when referring to the experiences of a stalking victim:

I asked her whether she could define why what the person was doing to her was wrong and I received three answers. First, 'It was driving me round the bend', she said. There one has a classic definition of harassment. Secondly, 'It went on and on', she said. There is the course of conduct ... Thirdly, said my pupil, 'I didn't want it'.[12]

This identifies three features that are common to all stalking cases. The conduct is repeated, it is unwanted, and it causes an adverse reaction in the victim. These elements form the essence of stalking.

2.1.1 Repeated conduct

Stalking is characterised by the intransigence of the stalker and the interminable nature of the conduct. Baroness Park's characterisation of stalking as the:

haunting and hunting of a victim ... conducted simply through unrelenting and unremitting pursuit and a presence in someone's life at every turn.[13]

provides an eloquent account of the continuous and pervasive nature of stalking. The words 'haunting and hunting' convey the idea of stalking as obdurate pursuit of the victim against his or her will in a manner that invades every vestige of his or her personal existence. Equally compelling is Jack Straw's description of stalking as an event which ruins the lives of ordinary people and involves a situation whereby the totality of the conduct is infinitely worse than the sum of its composite parts.[14] This neatly encapsulates the continual nature of the conduct and emphasises that it is the cumulative impact of a series of incidents, which may be totally harmless when considered individually, that is at the heart of the nature of the harm in stalking cases.

For many victims, it is the ongoing nature of the conduct, rather than the nature of the conduct itself, that causes them most distress:

This is one of the defining characteristics of stalking: irrespective of the nature of the component acts, stalking can be distressing and threatening to a victim because of its sheer oppressive persistence.[15]

Some victims reported paradoxical feelings of relief when the stalking recommenced after a period of inactivity, especially if there had been previous periods of dormancy, which were attributed to the uncertainty 'of not knowing if, or when, it was all going to start again'.[16]

Thus, the apparent cessation of stalking provided little respite for many victims who, accustomed to the continual nature of the conduct, were merely awaiting the re-emergence of the stalker:

---

12   Earl Russell, *HL Deb*, Vol 577, 24 January 1997.
13   Baroness Park of Monmouth, *HL Deb*, Vol 477, 24 January 1997.
14   Straw, J, *HC Deb*, Vol 287, Col 788, 17 December 1996.
15   Brown, 2000, p iii.
16   Case history 17.

It was actually worse when it stopped. In fact, there was no point in it stopping because even when he wasn't following me I was constantly looking for him so he had just as soon kept going all the time. Sometimes it was a few days, often a couple of weeks, and once it was even about four or five months. All that did was make it worse, so very much worse, every time it started again.[17]

Many stalking victims agree that once the stalking is established and they realise that it is an ongoing problem, they remain in a state of tension waiting for the next incident. Any initial break in the conduct leads the victim to hope that the stalking is over, hence the disappointment and despair when it recommences:

Sometimes it's better when he has found me because then at least I know that every knock on the door is him rather than being afraid that it might be. He's just as destructive when he's not here because I live in constant fear that he'll turn up. For all the good it does me, getting away from him for a bit, he [might] just as soon be constantly outside the door.[18]

I spent every evening looking at the phone waiting for it to ring. The longer it went without calls the worse it was, because I got more and more optimistic that it was over and the agony would be so much more intense when it started again. When the phone was ringing, I knew what to expect. Once it stopped, the waiting was excruciating.[19]

Whilst the majority of victims experience repeated conduct, it is difficult to quantify the amount of incidents comprising individual stalking cases. The victim may not attribute all of the incidents to the stalker, particularly at the beginning when the realisation of the continued nature of the conduct has not been appreciated. Equally, once the stalking is established, a victim may become sensitive to unusual occurrences and attribute these to the stalker when, in reality, they have some other source. Incidents may be open to variable quantification: for example, if a victim receives 20 silent telephone calls within one hour, they may either view this as a single incident or 20 separate incidents. Not all victims will keep a record of each incident and may recollect only the more serious or unusual incidents. When asked to describe the extent of their victimisation, it is more usual for victims to refer to the period of time that the stalking spanned rather than to a particular number of incidents:

It's difficult to say how much of it there was. At first, things were just a bit strange and irritating so I didn't realise that there was a stalker responsible for them. Once I realised, I got a bit paranoid and started blaming him for everything. Like when one of my brake lights was smashed and I was sitting shaking in the kitchen thinking 'oh no, now he's started smashing up my car' when my neighbour knocked on the door and told me that she had done it parking and offered to pay for it. But there were other things that I didn't think

---

17 Case history 32.
18 Case history 26.
19 Case history 17.

of blaming on him like when I received all those holiday brochures – I just thought that they were junk mail. So it's difficult to say. It went on for about seven months and it was pretty unrelenting – there was no clear period when I thought it was over. I suppose there must have been couple of hundred incidents but it's incredibly difficult to work it out.[20]

The British Crime Survey addressed the length of victimisation, rather than the number of incidents, and found that the most common period of victimisation, experienced by one quarter of the victims, was between one and three months. However, approximately one in five victims were targeted for more than a year with the victimisation of 7% of respondents continuing in excess of three years. Obviously, there is scope for an immense variation in the amount of repeated conduct that occurs within different period of time.

Figure 2.3 – Duration of stalking victimisation (BCS)

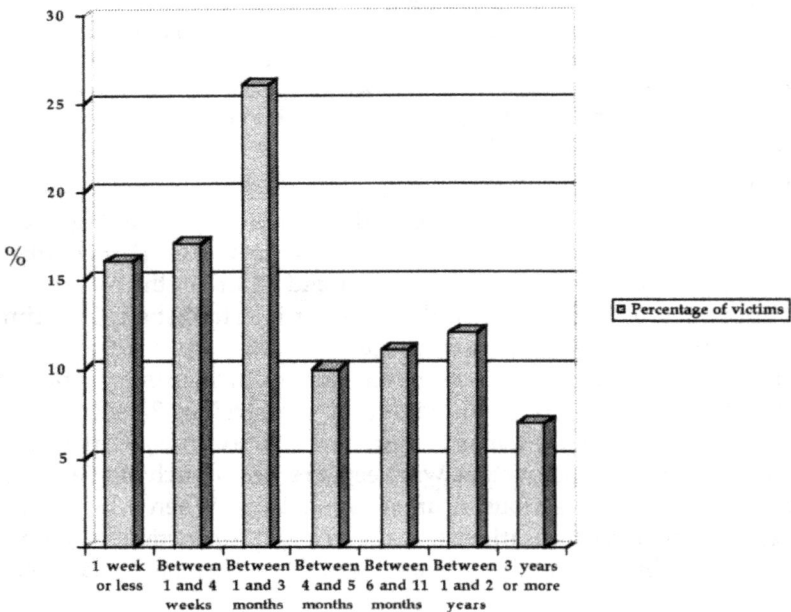

The repeated nature of conduct is a factor that contributes to the complexity of formulating a precise definition of stalking. The continuing nature of stalking is addressed within legislation by the qualification that the conduct is repetitive,[21] occurs on at least two occasions[22] or is part of a 'course of

20 Case history 25.
21 Canadian Criminal Code, s 264.
22 Crimes Act 1900, s 34A (Australian Capital Territory); Criminal Code Act 1997, s 189 (Northern Territory); Criminal Law Consolidation Act 1935, s 19AA (South Australia); the model Anti-Stalking Code proposed by the National Institute of Justice in the US includes a requirement that the conduct occur on two or more occasions.

conduct'.[23] Section 7(3) of the Protection from Harassment Act 1997 defines 'course of conduct' to mean conduct that occurs on at least two occasions. There has been some interpretation of the requirements of a course of conduct in recent cases. The tendency to regard any two incidents involving the same parties, regardless of the timing or the nature of the conduct, was viewed with disfavour by Schiemann LJ in *Lau v DPP*:

> the incidents which need to be proven in relation to harassment need not exceed two incidents but ... the fewer the occasions and the wider they are spread, the less likely it would be that a finding of harassment can reasonably be made.[24]

Schiemann LJ went on to reject the mathematical approach of 'incident plus incident equals a course of conduct' in favour of a requirement that there be some nexus between the incidents. This approach was approved by the Court of Appeal in *R v Hills*:

> Nevertheless the broad position had to be that if one was left with only two incidents it was necessary to see whether what happened on those two occasions could be described as a course of conduct. It was not possible to answer that question, adopting an essentially mathematical approach by saying that there were two incidents and that showed that there was a course of conduct.[25]

A different approach to the definition of 'course of conduct' is evident from an examination of Australian case law. Although the continuing nature of stalking is acknowledged, there has also been some development in the view taken of a single prolonged incident:

> In order for the conduct which is engaged in to be a 'course of conduct', the relevant conduct must be conduct which is protracted or conduct which is engaged in on more than one occasion.[26]

Consideration of such pronouncements during the consultation exercise conducted by the Queensland Government led to the amendment of the statutory definition of stalking to encompass protracted single incidents. Section 359A(2) defines 'course of conduct' to include (a) conduct that is protracted or (b) conduct that is engaged in on more than one occasion, whether the conduct is the same or different on each occasion.

The need to formulate legislation so as to encompass conduct on more than one occasion can be seen to be problematic in other areas of criminal law. For example, the requirement of 'persistence' in relation to various soliciting

---

23 Protection from Harassment Act 1997, s 2; Criminal Code Act 1899, s 358A (Queensland); Crimes Act 1958, s 21A (Victoria).

24 *Lau v DPP* [2000] 1 FLR 799, *per* Schiemann LJ, p 801.

25 *R v Hills* (2000) *The Times*, 20 December, *per* Otton LJ.

26 'The *actus reus* of the offence contemplates continuing conduct involving harassment or offensive behaviour towards a particular person': *Police v Leon Peter Flynn* (1997) unreported, 9 May, Supreme Court of South Australia, *per* Duggan LJ.

offences has posed difficulties for the courts in deciding what degree of repetition this implies, to whom the conduct must be directed and the timing of the various incidents.[27] In *Dale v Smith*, it was held that although 'persistence' implied a degree of repetition, this need not imply that the conduct must be repeatedly directed towards the same person.[28] Rather, that persistence included:

> either more than one invitation to one person or a series of invitations to different people.[29]

Further difficulties arose when it was held that a single ongoing incident could amount to the requisite persistence. In *R v Burge*, the Court of Session held that the display of a card in a window could amount to persistent soliciting even if it were only displayed for half an hour.[30] However, the decision was quashed as it was held that the work 'solicit' required the physical presence of the offender.[31] The finding that such a display satisfied the persistence requirement was not addressed but, as Rook and Ward note, the acceptance of this decision would reduce the persistence requirement to almost nothing.[32] It may be that the difficulties surrounding the interpretation of 'persistence' was a material factor in the decision to avoid the inclusion of the word in the Protection from Harassment Act 1997 when defining the nature of the prohibited conduct.

Regardless of the specific wording of the legislation, it is clear that most statutes take the progressive nature of stalking into account. The requirement of two incidents ensures that there is an element of repetition whilst providing a means of early intervention before the conduct escalated into a more harmful and dangerous situation. However, intervention should not be too early, as reliance upon only two incidents is considered a precarious foundation, because if one incident were to be disproved, the remaining incident would be an insufficient basis for the imposition of liability.[33]

Some recent psychological literature has examined the ongoing nature of stalking conduct and concluded that there is consistent evidence of escalation rather than mere continuance.[34] Therefore, if not addressed, the stalking will not just continue, it will become more serious. This worrying aspect of stalking is one that requires greater research in order to ascertain its accuracy and its implications.

---

27 Sexual Offences Act 1985, ss 1(2) and 2(1); Sexual Offences Act 1956, s 32.
28 *Dale v Smith* [1967] 1 WLR 700.
29 *Ibid, per* Lord Parker, p 704.
30 *R v Burge* [1961] Crim LR 412.
31 *R v Burge* [1962] 1 All ER 666.
32 Rook and Ward, 1999.
33 'If there are, say, three incidents alleged, if you can eliminate two of them the prosecution are left with an insufficient basis upon which to proceed. If they have waited a bit longer and allege 20 incidents, the defence job is nigh on impossible': interview with defence solicitor, 21 July 1998.
34 Meloy, in Pinard and Pagini, 1999; Meloy, 1999, pp 85–99.

2.1.2 Unwanted conduct

A second defining characteristic of stalking is that it involves conduct that is not welcomed by the recipient. Reference has been made to the range of conduct that may occur and it has been noted that much of the conduct is, of itself, lawful:

> Stalkers typically engage in behaviours that are threatening to the victim, but which may not, absent an anti-stalking statute, rise to the level of criminal violation.[35]

In situations where the conduct is not inherently criminal, the unwanted nature of the conduct delineates stalking from legitimate activities. An analogy can be drawn with rape.[36] The conduct element of rape is non-consensual sexual intercourse – the essence of the wrong is not the conduct itself, but in the fact that it imposes on another that which should only be engaged in voluntarily. The same reasoning can be applied to a significant amount of stalking conduct. Conduct which is *prima facie* lawful, such as sending flowers or giving another person gifts, becomes regarded as unlawful when it is imposed on another who has no desire to receive such attention. Thus, the wrong in stalking cases may not relate to the lawfulness or otherwise of the actual conduct, but in the persistent subjection of the victim to unwanted attention.

This will not always be the case, as many stalking cases involve conduct that, taken in isolation, would amount to the commission of a criminal offence. In such cases, each incident may be considered in isolation, thus addressing the criminality of the individual acts, or it may be viewed more holistically as a constituent element of stalking. Prior to the enactment of the Protection from Harassment Act 1997, approaching each incident as a discrete criminal offence was the only means by which the case could be brought within the criminal justice system.[37] This fragmentation of stalking cases which focuses upon the inherently criminal acts sends an unequivocal message that it is acceptable to cause manifest distress to another provided lawful means are used to do this. Clearly, this is unacceptable, and it was one of the primary motivating factors that led to pressure to formulate legislation that dealt with the totality of the conduct. Since the enactment of the Protection from Harassment Act 1997, an element of fragmentation remains if the stalking involves the commission of a discrete criminal offence of a particularly serious nature,[38] probably due to the low maximum penalty

---

35 Strikis, 1993, p 2772.

36 'A man commits rape if (a) he has sexual intercourse with a person (whether vaginal or anal) who at the time of intercourse does not consent to it': Sexual Offences Act 1956, s 1(2).

37 See Chapter 4.

38 *AG's Reference (No 22 of 1999)* [2000] 1 Cr App R(S) 253 (false imprisonment, indecent assault); *R v Hills* (2000) *The Times*, 20 December (rape, indecent assault).

available for the offence of harassment.[39] This is unavoidable if the stalking culminates in a serious offence such as rape or murder, but the overlap can be more problematic when stalking involves a combination of overtly lawful and minor criminal offences, as was recognised by the Supreme Court of South Australia:

> The individual acts need not amount to the commission of an offence in themselves, although the section recognises that a charge of stalking may arise out of the same circumstances as another offence.[40]

In cases involving a combination of lawful and unlawful behaviour, a decision has to be made whether to view the totality of the conduct as stalking or to separate the case into a series of composite criminal offences. There may be difficulties that prevent pursuit of both courses of action simultaneously if any of the criminal acts are relied upon as the basis of the harassment charge due to the possibility of double jeopardy.[41]

From the perspective of the victim, being targeted by unwanted lawful conduct may have the added disadvantage of not appearing serious due to the outwardly innocuous nature of the conduct. This lack of understanding may exacerbate the isolation of the stalking victim.[42] For example, one stalking victim, a teenage girl, was targeted by an unknown stalker who gained access to her house to leave gifts and carry out household chores such as changing the bed linen and cleaning the house. Her mother was unable to get the police to view her situation as serious even though it led her daughter to suffer such severe depression and anxiety that she began to inflict harm upon herself:

> [The police] thought it was funny that I was complaining that he had been in my house and left food and flowers. There was two of them who were particularly obnoxious who just laughed and said that they wished someone would tidy their houses and do the shopping. It's the ultimate intrusion when somebody invades your house like that but one of them said that I ought to go out more often because I'd save a fortune on groceries ... They were so condescending that it was unbelievable.[43]

Another victim recounted the isolation that she experienced due to the inability of those in whom she confided to take her situation seriously:

> It was pointless trying confide in anyone because everyone thought it was a joke. People kept saying things like 'I don't know what your problem is – I'd

---

39 'A person guilty of an offence under this section is liable on summary conviction to imprisonment for a term not exceeding six months, or a fine not exceeding level 5 on the standard scale, or both': Protection from Harassment Act 1997, s 2(2).

40 *Police v Leon Peter Flynn* (1997) unreported, 9 May, Supreme Court of South Australia, *per* Duggan LJ.

41 *R v Cunningham* (1999) unreported, 23 November, CA.

42 See pp 72–73.

43 Case history 24.

love it if someone kept giving me chocolates and flowers'. But it wasn't funny. It was oppressive and really quite sinister to keep receiving these things when I'd made it clear I didn't want them and that he should stop – he was obviously just going to carry on regardless whatever I said or did.[44]

The words of this victim emphasise the powerlessness of the victim that is a common feature in stalking cases. Psychological studies of the actions and motivations of stalkers tend to agree that stalkers, either deliberately or unconsciously, seek control over their victims.[45] This is achieved, to a large degree, by imposing unwanted conduct upon the victim, as is illustrated in these words of a stalking victim:

> My life wasn't my own. It was his. He decided whether I had a good day or not. There is something really disempowering about having to plan every possible permutation of his behaviour that might occur before you leave the house in the morning. If he asked me for lunch, I had to have a believable excuse ready that wouldn't aggravate him. If I said I had plans with someone else, he might get angry because I'd made time for them and not for him. If I was playing squash, he would get cross because I cared more about a game than spending time with him. It was an absolute minefield. People just don't understand that you can't just say 'no'. It takes careful thought or you could easily make matters worse. But he never did anything to me, as such, just asked me out and gave me presents. But he was so manipulative in a way that is impossible to describe. I had to do what he wanted. How can you tell someone who has just spent £200 on a present for you that you won't go for a drink with them?[46]

This illustrates the sense of impotence experienced by victims in the face of the single-minded determination of the stalker to achieve his or her objective. This victim felt powerless to resist her stalker's determination to impose his company upon her and is illustrative of the indifference of the stalker to the wishes of the victim.

Thus, it can be seen that the repeated and unwanted nature of the conduct provides a clearer characterisation of stalking than reference to specific forms of conduct. The final issue that provides a potential means of isolating stalking from non-stalking conduct relates to the reaction of the recipient of the conduct.

2.1.3 The reaction of the recipient

This final characteristic of stalking is particularly relevant to conduct which is overtly innocuous. The very nature of criminal acts dictates that they are

---

44 Case history 18.

45 Babcock, RJ, in Infield and Platford, 2000; Meloy, in Pinard and Pagini, 1999; Meloy, 1999, pp 85–99.

46 Case history 26.

presumed to have a deleterious impact – whether physical, psychological, or both – on the victim. However, not all behaviour that occurs during stalking amounts to a discrete criminal offence. When considering the unwanted nature of stalking conduct, reference to the words of stalking victims emphasised the incredulity with which others may react to the victim's distress at being given gifts and flowers, for example.[47] It is not easy for a person who has not experienced the relentless intrusion of stalking to appreciate the impact of persistent unwanted attention, whatever its nature.

This is not to say that all victims respond to stalking in the same way. There are a range of possible reactions to stalking ranging from amusement, indifference and tolerance to the more unfavourable reactions such as anger, distress and anxiety. The nature of the reaction to victimisation is dependent upon factors such as the duration of the stalking, the extremity and frequency of the conduct and the character of the victim.[48] As such, generalisations made regarding the reaction of victims are likely to be incomplete and inaccurate. It is clear that each victim may experience a combination of different reactions during the course of the stalking:

> At first, it was quite funny. We used to laugh about my 'devoted admirer'. But after a while, it became really irritating. I couldn't go anywhere without him turning up. The longer it went on, the more worried I got because I knew it wasn't normal to behave like that. It got to the stage where I was really frightened of him – afraid of what he would do. Right now, I'm angry. Angry with him because he's controlled my life for the past year; angry with me for letting him get away with it; and angry with the police for persistently refusing to do something about him.[49]

This progression of emotion was quite usual amongst the stalking victims interviewed during the course of this research. As the conduct continues, or escalates, the level of concern experienced by the victim tends to increase. The fluctuation between fear and anger is also common and, as the above quotation illustrates, anger is not solely reserved for the stalker. Some victims may resort to violence against their stalker. For example, one female victim attacked her stalker in the street with a kitchen knife in what was described as a 'prolonged, violent and determined' attack. Despite psychiatric evidence that the woman was suffering from 'acute stress reaction' caused by the prolonged period of harassment, the Court of Appeal upheld the sentence of two years' imprisonment.[50]

---

47 See pp 46–47.
48 See pp 71–81.
49 Case history 35.
50 There are few examples of violence retaliation by stalking victims and this is not an area that has been addressed by any of the existing research into stalking victims. As such, it is impossible to estimate the frequency of such occurrences.

The Protection from Harassment Act 1997 recognises the importance of the impact of the conduct upon the victim and includes this as an element that is required in order to establish liability under the Act. Section 1(1)(a) prohibits the pursuit of a course of conduct 'which amounts to harassment of another'. This enables the Act to encompass otherwise lawful behaviour that causes harassment due to the context in which it occurs or the nature of the relationship between the parties. Rendering criminality contingent upon the reaction of the recipient of the conduct widens the reach of the law. For example, the police told one victim that they were powerless to intervene to prevent an unknown man watching her house because he was not contravening the law. The victim was disturbed by this man's conduct especially as it only ever occurred when she was alone in the house.[51] Although not intrinsically unlawful, this conduct would come within the remit of the Protection from Harassment Act as it caused the victim to feel harassed. This ensures that a stalker who employs only lawful means during his pursuit of the victim will no longer be immune from legal intervention. However, the less favourable aspect to this emphasis on the reaction of the victim is that it bases criminal liability on that which is inherently unknowable – how another person will react to a particular situation.[52] It is in this respect that stalking could be said to be a context-dependent crime as the response of the victim becomes the determinative factor that delineates lawful and unlawful conduct. This is particularly apparent in relation to stalking that involves only *prima facie* lawful conduct, such as giving gifts or sending flowers, as such actions are as likely to provoke a favourable reaction as they are an unfavourable response. As Jaconelli notes, the critical element in determining whether a context-dependent crime has occurred concerns the susceptibility of the person to whom the conduct or speech is directed.[53] The law is concerned with whether the harm that it seeks to avert has materialised; in the case of harassment, whether the victim has been caused alarm or distress by the defendant's conduct. The absence of such a response by the victim places the conduct outside the remit of the law even if it were undertaken with the express intention of causing such an adverse reaction. This adds a further element of uncertainty to the criminalisation of stalking, as there is no stock response that can be guaranteed to follow a particular type of conduct. Of course, the more unpleasant the conduct, the more likely it is that an adverse reaction will result, but the range of responses to ostensibly harmless conduct is more varied and less amenable to accurate prediction.

The range of responses can be illustrated by reference to a case in which three women experienced similar behaviour from the same person, but reacted in different ways. The man, whom they described variously as 'a

---

51 Case history 1.
52 Finch, 2000, pp 273–95.
53 Jaconelli, 1995, pp 771–82.

manipulative nuisance',[54] 'overpowering and needy'[55] and 'harmless in a weird sort of way',[56] persistently sought their company, being termed 'the office weirdo who liked to have one special friend, always a woman, and no one else'. All three women experienced discomfort at the extent to which this man sought to become closer to them and spend increasing amounts of time with them. His initial contact was limited to 'chance' meetings, but soon escalated to calling at their homes uninvited, following them and demanding more and more exclusive attention. The first of the women to be targeted acted promptly when he admitted to following her home from work to ascertain her address:

> He admitted that he had followed me home from work and I was furious. He said that he only wanted to be my friend and I told him straight that that's not how I expect my friends to behave ... I told him that I considered him to be my friend and I was happy to spend time with him but he wasn't to invade my personal space any more ... I told him firmly how it was going to be and after that we were all right.

The second subject of his attention developed a different means of dealing with the unwanted attention. She was less direct; using excuses and changes in her behaviour to limit the amount of contact between them. She changed her working hours and her car to make it harder for him to keep track of her and even considered moving house. She felt that it was essential to maintain a semblance of normality with regard to their interaction, as, if they were forced to confront what was really happening, the situation might decline:

> We both pretended that everything was normal but I did everything I could to avoid him and he did everything he could to catch me. But it was important to keep things pleasant on the surface. If I tried to make him stay away and it didn't work, we would both be confronted with how powerless I was and that he was in control. At least by what I was doing, I kept some sort of control and he had to keep pretending to be nice to me. If he didn't have to pretend, I think he would have got far more unpleasant and aggressive. Sometimes when I had been avoiding him, I could see him only just hanging on to his temper. Once it was out in the open, he wouldn't have had to do that and it would have been so much worse.

This second victim was only relieved of the stalker's attention when he became interested in the third victim. Although the third victim finds the constant presence of the stalker somewhat overpowering and would welcome the opportunity to spend more time alone, she does not object to his friendship in general. As a newcomer to the area who describes herself as slow to make new friends, she was glad of his company. She says that he is not a stalker, but a lonely person who is eager for friendship and who has

---

54 Victim 2, Case history 33.
55 Victim 3, Case history 33.
56 Victim 1, Case history 33.

been treated abysmally by other women. According to the definition adopted by the Protection from Harassment Act 1997, only the second woman was a victim of harassment despite being targeted with the same conduct by the same person as the other two women. The first victim set the parameters of acceptable conduct and left no scope for negotiation, which curtailed the stalker's attention towards her. She claims that his actions annoyed her briefly, but that she did not feel harassed, alarmed or distressed, therefore this situation would not fall within the parameters of the Protection from Harassment Act. Likewise, the third victim is not alarmed or distressed. The contrast is evident when considering the reaction of the second victim, who was extremely distraught by her inability to limit the frequency of the conduct between her and the stalker. She used evasion and excuses in an attempt to avoid his company and claims that he appreciated this and contributed to the maintenance of the façade of social convention that regulated their dealings with each other. This reaction to the conduct she is experiencing would bring her situation firmly within the reach of the Protection from Harassment Act.

These three differing reactions to the same conduct illustrate that each individual will respond in a way that is in keeping with their own character and interpretation of the situation. Whether a situation can be correctly termed 'stalking' if the recipient does not have an adverse reaction to the experience is open to debate, but as such matters are unlikely to come before the courts for want of a complainant, it is a point of little practical purpose.[57] However, as the distinguishing feature between lawful conduct and stalking is frequently the perception of the conduct by the recipient, it seems logical to regard the requirement of an adverse reaction as an essential element of stalking. This being so, the deliberate stalker who targets a particularly strong minded or phlegmatic victim would, as a matter of chance rather than design, not be considered to be a stalker, nor would he engender liability under the Protection from Harassment Act. This element of contingency based on factors outside the perpetrator's control adds an additional uncertainty to the definition of stalking and the attribution of criminal liability to an already tortuous difficulty of defining and outlawing stalking.

2.2 STALKERS AND VICTIMS

The focus thus far has been upon the nature and prevalence of the conduct element of stalking. Having explored this aspect of stalking in detail, the next area of investigation concerns the stalkers and victims themselves. This will focus predominantly upon the motivation of the stalker and the impact of stalking upon the victim. This discussion will be preceded by a consideration

---

57 Chapter 6.

of the research studies that have investigated the typology of stalking and the nature of the relationship between stalker and victim.

Many early studies of stalking sought to develop a system of classification of stalking cases. Some of these were based solely upon the nature of the relationship between the parties such as Roberts and Dziegielewski who divided cases into three categories: domestic violence, erotomania, and nuisance cases.[58] Other classifications were based upon the psychiatric diagnosis of the stalker. For example, Zona, Sharma and Lane examined 102 cases dealt with by the Threat Management Unit and classified them as either erotomanic, love obsessional or simple obsessional.[59] Other studies concentrated upon the motivation of the stalker. For example, a study of 145 stalkers referred to a psychiatric clinic for treatment classified the stalkers as rejected, intimacy seeking, incompetent, resentful or predatory, noting that these categories were not necessarily mutually exclusive.[60] Some studies sought a more complex typology by combining factors, such as Wright et al, who first categorised the cases in a law enforcement experiential paradigm according to whether they were domestic or non-domestic. These were then analysed to determine whether or not the stalkers were delusional, finding that non-domestic stalkers were significantly more likely to be delusional than domestic stalkers.[61] A more detailed combination of variables was used by Harmon et al, who sought to classify 379 stalkers referred to a forensic psychiatry clinic according to two variables:

> one relating to the nature of the attachment between the defendant and the object of their attention, and another relating to the nature, if any, of the prior relationship between them.[62]

However, the findings of these studies do not form the basis for extrapolation of general principles applicable to the wider population of stalkers. They were all based upon a non-random sample of convenience, and thus do not provide a representative view of all stalkers and victims. Little emphasis, in particular, should be given to the finding that stalkers have a high propensity to mental illness, as many of these studies were focusing upon stalkers who had been referred for psychiatric assessment or who had been detained following a stalking conviction.

Meloy examined the findings of 10 clinical research studies to ascertain whether these formed the basis for the formulation of a typology of stalking.

---

58 Roberts and Dziegielewski, 1996, pp 359–68.

59 Zona, Sharma and Lane, 1993, pp 894–903.

60 Mullen, Pathe, Purcell and Stuart, 1999, pp 1244–49.

61 Wright et al, 1996, pp 487–502.

62 Harmon, Rosner and Owens, 1995, pp 188–96. The nature of attachment variable was divided into two categories: affectionate/amorous and persecutory/angry. The relationship variable had six categories: personal, professional, employment, media, acquaintances, and no prior relationship.

His analysis of the cumulative findings of these research studies enabled him to identify the common characteristics of stalkers and victims. In relation to the characteristics of the stalker, examination of the 10 studies revealed that the prototypical stalker is an older, well educated man[63] who is likely to be unmarried, either unemployed or underemployed and suffering from a psychiatric or psychological disorder. There was little consensus regarding victims and the only characteristics that could be attributed to the prototypical victim were that she was a woman who was likely to have had a prior relationship with the stalker.

Meloy concluded, after consideration of these 10 clinical research studies, that the different classification systems cause confusion and could be simplified by the adoption of a tripartite categorisation that could be applied to all cases. His proposal was that there should be three categories based upon the relationship between the stalker and victim. These categories – acquaintance, sexual partners, and strangers – could be applied to all existing studies and would eliminate any potential for overlap between the categories.[64]

Although the accumulation of data as a means of classifying stalking cases may be of value in clinical studies where it can be used to assist in the case management of stalking cases, the information is of less relevance in a legal context. It is surely of little consolation to a stalking victim to find that her situation is not at all typical and she was actually at an extremely low risk of victimisation. Moreover, the creation of a prototypical stalker and victim may be an impediment to the investigation and prosecution of stalking cases. Perceptions of stalking as a crime committed by a man against a woman in the context of a dysfunctional relationship may influence legal intervention in stalking cases. This could be due to the 'domestic' taint, which may still discourage police intervention.[65] Several victims have reported that the police were disinclined to intervene once it was revealed that the stalker was an ex-partner.[66] This has, somewhat surprisingly, been confirmed by interviews with the police conducted during the course of this research:

> There are some things that the law shouldn't try and interfere with and this is one of them. They need to get on with it themselves and sort themselves out.

---

63 In comparison to a random sample of other mentally disordered offenders: Meloy, 1996, pp 147–62.

64 *Ibid*, pp 147–62.

65 'Part of the reason for law enforcement's unresponsiveness is that, historically, domestic discord was considered a private matter. It was not considered a crime against society but against a family member and, as a result, police officers did not feel comfortable intervening. At most, police officers perceived their role as that of counsellor or mediator; most officers did not view domestic violence as a legitimate violent crime. In addition, for some officers, there remains awkwardness in removing a man from his own home.' Jordan, 1995, pp 363–83.

66 Edwards, 2000; Lockton and Ward, 1997.

It's hard enough working through a big relationship bust-up without one person dragging the police into it every five minutes. It makes things worse and, to be honest, we've got better things to do.[67]

The converse may also be applicable and the police may be disinclined to intervene in cases falling outside of the paradigm stalking case. Certainly, that is the fear of many victims; they have an insufficient knowledge of what 'proper' stalking is like so they are reluctant to involve the police lest they be perceived as over-reacting or wasting police time:

It took me ages to get up the courage to try and involve the police. I had heard about stalking cases but it didn't seem like what he was doing was that bad. But it seemed bad to me and I wanted him to be made to stop so I did tell the police and I had been right all along. They didn't think it was serious enough to do anything about.[68]

Although socio-demographic information may be of little practical use within the criminal justice system, such studies may increase the wealth of knowledge about stalking. The British Crime Survey gathered such information as an aspect of its evaluation of the nature and prevalence of stalking. It found that women were significantly more likely to be stalked than men and that the risk of victimisation was higher amongst young, single women, particularly students, who were at the lower end of the accommodation and income scale.[69] Less information was gathered on stalkers although it appeared that they were predominantly male. The favoured means of classification of stalking cases was by reference to the nature of the relationship between the parties. The British Crime Survey found a fair degree of differentiation between the relationship dependent upon whether the victim was male or female. The significance of this was not discussed.

---

67 Interview with a police officer involved in Case history 35.

68 Case history 1. The perceptions of victims regarding police attitudes and responsiveness to their complaints about stalking is discussed in Chapter 7.

69 Budd and Mattinson, 2000.

Figure 2.4   The relationship between stalker and victim according to the sex of the victim (BCS)

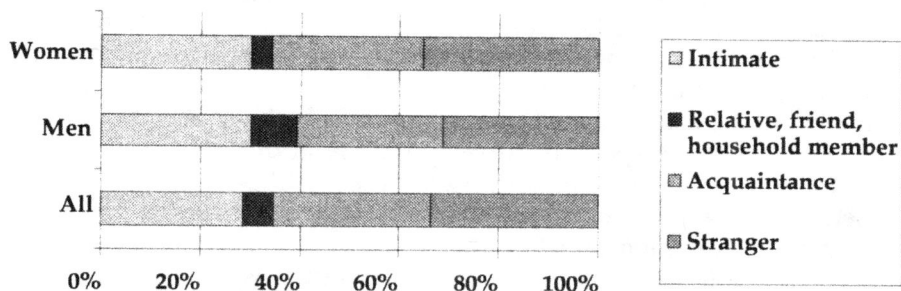

This delineation between relational and non-relational stalking is a feature of almost every study of stalking typology and yet nowhere is it questioned whether this distinction is desirable. For what purpose is such a distinction to be made? The bifurcation of 'domestic' and stranger stalking may create a situation whereby both are perceived to be different species of the same conduct. This does not, of itself, create problems. However, if this is just another example of conduct that is viewed less seriously when committed by a current or former partner, such as 'marital' and 'date' rape and 'domestic' violence, then it is a distinction that should not be made. There is, however, evidence to suggest that the dichotomous treatment of domestic and non-domestic victims is decreasing. The abolition of the marital exemption for rape,[70] the Home Office requirement that police respond effectively to domestic violence,[71] and the recent acknowledgment that so called 'date rape' should not be viewed less seriously than any other form of rape suggest an increasing recognition that the right to inviolability and personal autonomy should not be excluded from those in intimate relationships.[72]

Clearly, the tendency to associate stalking with dysfunctional relationships suggests that there may be some association between stalking and domestic violence. It is, therefore, relevant to consider whether there is a justifiable distinction between stalking in a relational and non-relational context.

Certainly, all the research studies conducted to date have found that a significant amount of stalking cases arise in a relational context, but the extent to which this is so varies enormously between different research studies. Few

---

70   *R v R* [1992] 1 AC 599.

71   Home Office Circular 60/1990, quoted in the Home Affairs Committee Third Report, *Domestic Violence*, HC 245, para 14.

72   'The review did consider whether there should be a lesser degree of offence to deal with acquaintance rape (sometimes called "date rape") but was unanimous in rejecting this proposal. The evidence placed before the review was that rape by an acquaintance could not only be as traumatic as stranger rape, but that the betrayal of trust involved could cause further long term physical damage to the victim.' Home Office [*Setting the Boundaries: Reforming the Law on Sexual Offences*, 2000, London: HMSO], para 0.10.

of these studies have explored the nature of the relationships in which stalking occurs in order to determine whether they were abusive. This is an important factor as there is no evidence to suggest that all relational stalking takes place against a background of domestic violence. Kurt's study of the interrelation between domestic violence and stalking led him to conclude that stalking was a significant feature in some domestic violence cases, but no estimation of the extent of the overlap was made.[73] Approaching the issue from the opposite perspective, Burgess et al found that 30% of their non-random sample of domestic violence victims had been stalked by their abuser.[74] Salame attributes the overlap to the need to assert control over another that is common to both domestic abuse and stalking cases.[75] She asserts that the termination of a violent relationship is likely to cause the abuser to stalk the victim as a means of re-asserting control over him or her. Coleman agrees that the stage at which a person leaves a violent relationship is usually the point at which violence increases and harassment is most likely.[76] However, Coleman also suggests that domestic relationships that lead to stalking have usually already been characterised by excessive control and violence:

> Results suggest that males who are verbally or physically abusive during relationships are more likely to pursue their partners in a harassing or violent manner after the relationships have dissolved.[77]

These studies suggest a degree of overlap between stalking and domestic violence, although the extent of the overlap is unclear and is an area that would benefit from further research. Moreover, Walker and Meloy suggest that domestic abusers and stalkers share characteristics that lead domestic violence to constitute a form of stalking:

> Domestic violence has been conceptualised as an abuser's attempt to use physical, sexual or psychological force to take away a woman's power and control over her life. One of the most successful ways of doing this is by isolating women from their friends and family and other means of support.[78]

Walker and Meloy explain that when the means by which this isolation is achieved, such as the monitoring of the woman's behaviour, surveillance and overpossessiveness, reach an oppressive and restrictive degree, this would amount to stalking within the domestic relationship.

Furthermore, although the subject of only a small amount of research, there is evidence to suggest that relational and non-relational stalkers have

---

73 Kurt, 1995, pp 219–30.
74 Burgess et al, 1997, pp 389–403.
75 Salame, 1993, pp 67–111.
76 Coleman, 1997, pp 420–32.
77 Ibid, p 430.
78 Walker, LE and Meloy, JR, in Meloy, 1998.

distinct characteristics and differ in their use of violence. Studies conducted to date suggest that the relational stalker is significantly less likely to be delusional than the non-domestic stalker,[79] but has a greater propensity to resort to physical violence.[80] These findings were confirmed by the recent study of 50 convicted stalkers, of which 40% were former sexual partners of the victim. This research found significant differences in the mental state and level of violent conduct between relational and non-relational stalkers and concluded:

> Our results indicate that the greatest danger of serious violence from stalkers in the UK is not from strangers or from people with psychotic illness, but from non-psychotic ex-partners.[81]

A distinction between relational and non-relational stalking would not be justifiable if the nature of the relationship between the parties were the sole determining factor. However, if it can be established that the nature and severity of the conduct involved differed significantly between such cases, this would have clear ramifications for the management and intervention strategies that would be appropriate, hence justifying the bifurcation of relational and non-relational stalking.

Figure 2.5 **Prevalence of psychotic illness and violence according to the relationship between the parties (Farnham)**

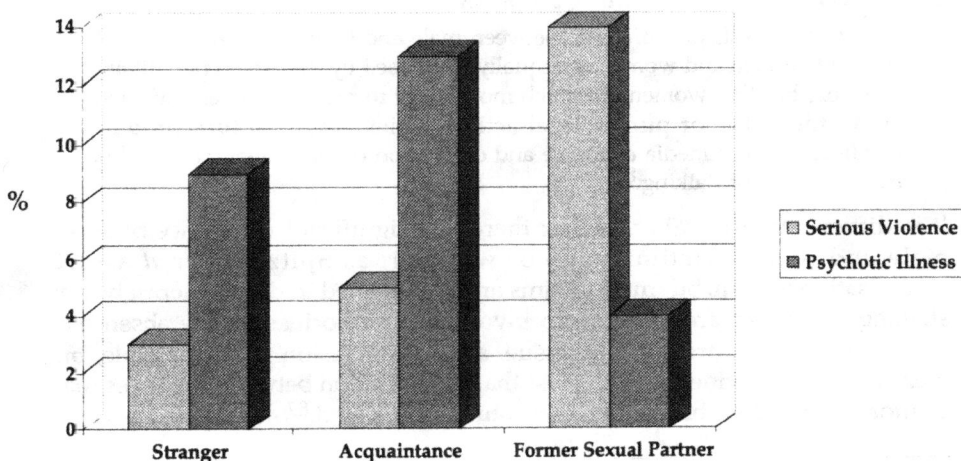

---

79 Wright *et al*, 1996, pp 487–502.
80 Schwartz-Watts and Morgan, 1998, pp 241–45.
81 Adapted from the findings of Farnham, James and Cantrell, 2000.

A second major point that emerges from a consideration of the many typologies of stalking that abound is the extent to which stalking is viewed as a crime against women. Certainly, the studies reveal a disparity of victimisation between men and women, but this is not questioned. There appears to be a common acceptance that, although men can be victims, such cases are an aberration and a departure from the norm. The two studies that have questioned this issue have concluded that there is a serious under-reporting of male victimisation.[82] This can be partially attributed to the popular conception of stalking as a crime against women; male victims either do not perceive themselves as stalking victims or are deterred from reporting their experiences for fear of a negative response.[83] Two male stalking victims interviewed during the course of this research who approached the police felt that their complaints were not taken seriously because they were men:

> I felt as if I was the one in the wrong. The police basically said that I was causing the situation by refusing to speak to the woman. I felt as if they were more inclined to arrest me than her ... I didn't fit the 'stalking victim' mould and that's all there was to it.[84]

> This policeman said: 'Let's see if I've got this right. This lovely girl is pestering you to sleep with her and you want us to arrest her.' That's when I knew that I had absolutely no chance of them taking any notice of me.[85]

This leads to a situation whereby official figures reflect and thus confirm the popular conception of stalking as a crime committed against women, therefore creating a self-fulfilling prophecy:

> This study reveals no difference between male and female victimisation ... It may be that men and women are equally victimised by unwanted pursuit and intrusion, but that women are much more likely to perceive threats sufficient to call the police or pursue legal action, which would in turn produce significantly more media exposure and cultivation of the stereotype that they are the victims of stalking.[86]

It is difficult to ascertain whether there is a significant difference between male and female victimisation or whether, as Spitzberg *et al* assert, victimisation is even, but male victims are less inclined to define themselves as stalking victims or are reluctant to involve the authorities. In the absence of further research addressing this issue, a firm conclusion is not possible, but there is certainly evidence to suggest that victimisation between the sexes may be more evenly distributed than early studies indicated.[87]

---

82 Spitzberg, Nicastro and Cousins, 1998, pp 33–47; Hall, DM, 'The victims of stalking', in Meloy, 1998.
83 Hall, in Meloy, 1998.
84 Case history 5.
85 Case history 14.
86 Spitzberg, Nicastro and Cousins, 1998, pp 33–47.
87 von Heussen, 2000.

2.3 THE MOTIVATION OF THE STALKER

Stalking is, in many respects, an unusual type of behaviour. The continuation of conduct often spans months, even years, and many stalkers appear unaffected by any means of intervention that attempts to end their behaviour:

> One of the things which is often hard to understand about stalking is its persistence in defiance of apparent benefit, common sense or legal threat. Some stalkers persist in their activity no matter what and remain undeterred by courts, legal action and even imprisonment.[88]

It is essential to seek an understanding of the motivation that drives what appears to be essentially unrewarding behaviour. Knowledge of the factors that prompt such behaviour should provide some insight into what measures might operate to end the conduct, thus facilitating an estimation of how effective various means of legal intervention are likely to be.

Many studies that have sought to determine what drives the stalker have focused upon the clinical causes of such behaviour.[89] Samples of stalkers already convicted of stalking offences, incarcerated under mental health provisions or required by law to seek treatment, have revealed a high incidence of mental disorder amongst stalkers. However, given the sources from which the samples were drawn, such a finding is hardly a surprise. Meloy conducted an analysis of existing research on this issue and summarised the findings:

> Most stalkers have both Axis I and Axis II diagnoses. The most common Axis I diagnoses, in descending order of frequency, are drug abuse or dependence (eg, alcohol or stimulants), a mood disorder or schizophrenia ... Axis II diagnoses are most likely to be Cluster B (ie narcissistic, histrionic, antisocial or borderline) with paranoid (Cluster A) and compulsive (Cluster C) features not uncommon.[90]

The psychiatric analysis of stalking motivation has been criticised as an oversimplification of a complex issue. The samples are condemned as unrepresentative and overselective of the pathological and the extreme.[91] Moreover, such an approach conceptualises stalking as the result of mental imbalance and ignores the complex social processes involved. This approach has been accused of ignoring the divergence between stalker and victim perceptions of the conduct, thus privileging the victim's version and dismissing the stalker's perception as pathology.[92]

---

88 Babcock, RJ, 'The psychology of stalking', in Infield and Platford, 2000, p 6.
89 Harmon, Rosner and Owens, 1995, pp 188–96; Leong, 1994, pp 378–85; Zona, Sharma and Lane, 1993, pp 894–903; Mullen and Pathe, 1994, pp 469–77; Meloy, 1999, pp 85–99.
90 Meloy, 1999, p 87.
91 Emerson, Ferris and Gardner, 1998, pp 289–314.
92 *Ibid.*

Evidence of this prioritisation of the victim's perceptions can be seen in studies that seek to determine the motivation for stalking by asking the victim why they feel that they were stalked.[93] Analysis of perceived motivations for stalking identify two predominant driving forces that account for the vast majority of stalking behaviour; entering or leaving a relationship and revenge, with most attention being given to the first category.[94]

2.3.1 Relational stalking

Research conducted by Meloy and Gothard found that stalkers are rarely involved in functional relationships and are frequently socially isolated.[95] This finding is common to many such studies of stalkers. Meloy and Gothard assert that this difficulty in establishing relationships may account for the high incidence of stalking cases that have a relational motivation.

It must be understood that stalking can be categorised as driven by relational motivation even when the parties are strangers to each other, provided the stalker is prompted to act by the desire to form a relationship with the victim. Emerson, Ferris and Gardner share this view:

> Many forms of what comes to be identified as stalking grow out of glitches and discontinuities in two very common and normal relationship processes – coming together and forming new relationships on the one hand, and dissolving and getting out of existing relationships on the other. In this way, the processes and experiences of being stalked are intricately linked to normal, everyday practices for establishing, advancing and ending relationships.[96]

Thus relational stalking can either arise from non-reciprocal desire to establish a relationship with an acquaintance or a stranger, or from attempts to maintain an existing relationship when one party wishes to terminate it:

> Relational stalking thus includes both people who were initially complete strangers, as well as those who have had a long-standing intimate relationship that one party has sought to end.[97]

It may appear rather contradictory to classify stalking by a stranger as relational stalking, but the emphasis here is upon the motivation of the stalker, not the actual status of the parties. These two categories of relational stalking are quite distinct from each other in terms of the behaviour involved, particularly in terms of the timing and likelihood of violence. When the stalking arises due to the unilateral desire of a stranger or acquaintance to

---

93 There appears to be a universal reluctance to seek an answer from the stalker, an omission that is remedied by this research.

94 Emerson, Ferris and Gardner, 1998, pp 289–314.

95 Meloy and Gothard, 1995, pp 258–63.

96 Emerson, Ferris and Gardner, 1998, p 290.

97 *Ibid*, p 295.

establish a relationship, initial contact is usually ostensibly pleasant and would be considered part of the normal preliminary behaviour to the initiation of a new relationship if the desire were mutual. This generally involves neutral activities such as waiting for the victim, sending gifts and flowers, communications between stalker and victim, all of which would be perfectly innocuous if welcomed by the victim. However, unrequited love does not continue indefinitely and there comes a 'turning point' whereby the stalker's affection and admiration for the victim curdles into vituperation, threats and possibly violence. This is usually caused by the final recognition or acknowledgment of the victim's rejection, which the stalker had previously been ignoring or been unaware of. When admiration turns to hatred, the nature of the conduct alters to become more hostile and intrinsically unpleasant, as opposed to merely unwelcome but innocuous conduct. It is at this stage that this may overlap with the second motivation for stalking: the need for revenge.[98]

This transformation of the nature of the stalking, both in terms of conduct and motivation, is graphically illustrated by reference to the conduct of Anthony Burstow, whose persistent harassment of his victim led to his conviction for inflicting psychological grievous bodily harm.[99] According to Burstow, his victim had initially welcomed his friendship and he had hoped that a relationship would develop between them. However, an incident occurred, the nature of which was not revealed, which caused his victim to react in an adverse manner and attempt to sever contact between them. Burstow attributed his initial attempts to contact his victim to his desire to 'sort out the misunderstanding' between them. When she resisted his attempts to communicate with her by telephone, he began to call at her home. The more she avoided Burstow, the greater his determination to contact her. Throughout this period, Burstow maintained that his only intention had been to restore their relationship to its previous amicable status. However, after one abortive attempt to see the victim at her home, Burstow telephoned her from a public telephone. Unfortunately, the telephone was not working and although Burstow could hear his victim, it was apparent that she could not hear him:

> It was when I was standing there in the telephone box listening to her voice getting more and more hysterical that I suddenly stopped wanting to talk to her and started wanting to hurt her. Every positive thing that I had felt for her turned to hate in an instant. I could hear the panic in her voice and realised how badly she had been affected by me constantly trying to contact her so I decided to keep doing it but this time with the intention of hurting her.[100]

This identification of the point at which feelings of admiration and affection are curdled by constant rejection to feelings of hatred and malice are common

---

98 See pp 67–71.

99 *R v Burstow* [1997] 4 All ER 225.

100 Interview with Anthony Burstow, 29 March 1999.

when stalking arises from a unilateral desire to instigate a relationship. When the stalking is related to the desire to maintain an existing relationship that the other party wishes to terminate, the adverse emotions and motivations are generally present from the outset:

> In such cases, the eventual stalker seeks almost simultaneously to reinstate the prior relationship and punish the ex for having shattered it.[101]

It is these cases that are most likely to take place against a background of domestic abuse. As Coleman notes, partners who are verbally or physically abusive during relationships are more likely to pursue their partners in a violent or harassing manner after the relationship is over.[102] Equally, the need for control over the autonomy of another has been noted as a feature of both abusive relationships and stalking.[103] Certainly, there seems to be an element of ownership that characterises situations in which a former partner refuses to allow the other to end the relationship:

> It was sort of like the principle of the thing – he wanted us to be finished and I didn't. So I sort of thought 'why should he get it all his way' and started following him and phoning and all that. It was just to make him know that he couldn't just cast me aside because he'd changed his mind.[104]

> I told him that he had to understand that he couldn't just turn up any more because I had finished with him. He said: 'you might think you've finished with me but I haven't finished with you. It takes two people to end a relationship.' That was when I realised how determined he was and that I'd have to move away if I wanted to escape from him.[105]

Despite the clear distinction between the two categories of relationally motivated stalking, they do share a common feature, as both involve the imposition of a relationship upon a person who has no desire for such a relationship.

Attempts by a stranger or acquaintance to initiate a relationship are not likely to be interpreted as stalking from the outset. The similarities and overlap between activities involved in this type of relational stalking and normal pre-dating behaviour and the societal rules of dating behaviour create scope for a variety of interpretations to be placed on the same events. If the conduct is welcomed, a relationship develops and no question of stalking will arise. Equally, if the advances are unwelcome and this is communicated to the suitor, who then discontinues his attempts to initiate a relationship, again there will be no question of stalking. Difficulties arise if the suitor is unwilling

---

101 Emerson, Ferris and Brooks Gardner, 1998, p 290.
102 Coleman, 1997, pp 420–31.
103 See pp 53–54.
104 Case history 14.
105 Case history 4.

or unable to interpret the victim's words or actions as a rejection or is unwilling or unable to abandon his pursuit following the rejection:

> In the instances that came to be seen as stalking, however, those receiving proposals reported that they rejected them, but that rejection failed to end pursuit, and that implicit or explicit proposals continued.[106]

Continued pursuit in the face of clear rejection will lead the victim to interpret the conduct as stalking, although the stage at which this occurs will depend upon such factors as the personality of the victim and the nature of frequency of the behaviour. There are numerous reasons why rejection may be misinterpreted or ignored. The erotomanic stalker has a genuine belief that his love is reciprocated and the nature of the delusional disorder is such that he is capable of interpreting the most unequivocal rejection as encouragement.[107] The borderline erotomanic, or love obsessional, lacks the belief in the reciprocity of his emotions but has a strong conviction that the victim will soon return his love:

> I know he thinks he doesn't want to go out with me but if he would just relax for a bit and stop pushing me away, he would see how much I love him and how we are meant to be together.[108]

Both the erotomanic and the borderline erotomanic may blame third parties for the victim's failure to respond to their advances. One victim interviewed during the course of this research was targeted by a man who believed she was the reincarnation of his lover from a previous existence and that they were bound by a 'karmic' link to be together in all existences. He attributed her reluctance to be reunited with him to the presence of her husband and two year old son, so he tried to kill them by setting fire to their house when the victim was not present.[109] Hostility directed towards a third party in such circumstances has been termed 'triangulation' and can have fatal consequences.[110]

Not all incidences of stalking arising from unilateral desire to initiate a relationship can be attributed to mental disorder. Some stalkers may suffer from personality disorders that inhibit their interpretation of, and reaction to, normal social intercourse, or lead them to develop such severe obsessions that they are incapable of detaching from the situation. Babcock identifies a tendency to obsessive behaviour and a need for control as two factors that can be a dangerous combination and are frequently exhibited in stalkers.[111] These tendencies are illustrated by the words of one stalker:

---

106 Emerson, Ferris and Brooks Gardner, 1998, p 290.
107 Orion, 1997.
108 Case history 14.
109 Case history 19.
110 Meloy, 1999, pp 421–24.
111 Babcock, RJ, 'The psychology of stalking', in Infield and Platford, 2000, pp 4–5.

> At first, I used to telephone to see if he was in. I was just curious because he'd said there wasn't anyone else so I wondered if it was true. If he had been out a lot, I'd have known he was with someone else. Even if he was in, I'd phone five minutes later, in case he'd gone out. I couldn't stop thinking about it – it took over my life. Then it got to the stage where I just had to hear his voice and even though I knew that he knew it was me, I kept doing things to make sure that he didn't forget about me. I can't understand it now but, at the time, it was better that he was hating me than just not thinking about me at all.[112]

An inability to tolerate apparent indifference may also be an aggravating factor.[113] The words of the stalker quoted above indicate that negative feelings towards her were preferable to no feelings at all. Richard Farley, whose obsession with a work colleague eventually led him to shoot seven of his workmates, expressed a similar sentiment:

> You'll be thinking of me. You may not be thinking good thoughts, but you'll be thinking of me.[114]

Although the predominant desire of the stalker may be to establish or rekindle a relationship, the potential for overlap with revenge stalking is clear here as the stalker fluctuates between love and hate. Even though the stalker knows that his actions are alienating the victim, thus lessening the chance of reconciliation, the burning desire for revenge will not permit him to desist:

> I couldn't bear that she couldn't care less about me any more. I could've coped better if she'd hated me, but she just didn't care. I could cry and beg her to come back to me but she was unmoved by everything I did. My heart had been ripped out of my body by her leaving me but she didn't care. So I thought 'right, bitch, let's see you ignore this'. But even when I was doing it and it made me feel better because I knew it would hurt her, it was tearing me apart because I loved her so much.[115]

An additional difficulty that arises in relational stalking, both when seeking to initiate a new relationship and in the ending of an existing relationship, is the divergent interpretations of the same events by the stalker and victim that can be caused by the prevailing societal standards of dating behaviour:

> In many instances the proposer is not explicitly and forcefully told that his or her proposal would never be accepted under any imaginable conditions; most relational rejections are delivered in ways that offer the proposer at least some opportunity to save face.[116]

The harshness of an outright rejection is not an option for many people, who prefer to mitigate the rejection by offering an excuse or using avoiding tactics.

---

112 Case history 14.
113 Auchincloss and Weiss, 1992, pp 1013–38.
114 Florida Victim Advocacy Centre website – www.fiu.edu/~victimad/stalkvoi.html.
115 Case history 30.
116 Emerson, Ferris and Gardner, 1998, p 290.

To refuse the offer of a date on the basis of a prior engagement, for example, is kinder than telling another person that you have no desire to spend time in their company. However, a conditional refusal leaves scope for renegotiations, as one stalking victim found out when she used washing her hair as an excuse to refuse invitations from a work colleague. She felt that using such a trite excuse sent a clear message of rejection to her colleague. He did not interpret it as such, and continued to ask her out, with increasing regularity, for seven months until the situation escalated out of control, culminating in his arrest and prosecution under s 2 of the Protection from Harassment Act 1997.[117]

It may appear that excuses are insufficiently equivocal and create ambiguity that justifies a certain degree of persistence. However, the determined stalker will ignore, deny or rationalise even the clearest of rejections. Deputy District Attorney Kerry Wells uses an example from the comedy film *Dumb and Dumber* to illustrate this point. One character is enamoured with a woman who has no feelings for him. They have a discussion about the likelihood of her ever agreeing to go out with him, and she tells him that there is a one in 10 million chance. He is ecstatic and jumps up shouting: 'I've got a chance, I've got a chance.'[118]

Although this is a fictitious example, taken from a comedy film, it does illustrate the ability of stalkers to interpret the most unlikely words or actions as an indication of the victim's interest in them. One victim took pity on a man who had been stalking her for several months as he stood on her doorstep bleeding profusely from a self-inflicted wound:

> What was I supposed to do? Slam the door in his face and let him bleed to death? I wanted to really, after all that he had put me through, but I didn't have it in me to treat anyone like that. So I took him in, cleaned him up and put a bandage on his hand. The next day he left a note for me saying that he had almost given up hope of us ending up together until he saw the tender way that I had taken care of him.[119]

Other examples have included a woman who knew her victim was in love with her because she had her arrested,[120] a single smile to a stranger at a bus stop that led to a protracted and vicious campaign of violence when the relationship that the smile 'promised' did not materialise,[121] and an unremarkable customer transaction that led the sales assistant to accuse the customer of 'leading him on'.[122]

---

117 Case history 18.
118 Paper given by Wells, K and Maxey, W, Stalking Task Force, San Diego, at the stalking conference held at Bramshill Police Training Centre, 22 March 2000.
119 Case history 4.
120 Orion, 1997.
121 Case history 6.
122 Case history 31.

Difficulties may arise in less extreme cases, partially as a result of ambiguous messages and partially because of the popular conception that a refusal to an initial invitation is all part and parcel of the 'dating game'. This problem is encapsulated by the words of a young man who was convicted of harassment:

> I didn't think twice about asking her out a couple of times even though she said 'no'. My brother's girlfriend told me to, in any case. She said that all women say 'no' a couple of times so that they don't look too keen and to test if the bloke is really interested. She never mentioned that I could end up getting arrested.[123]

It is clear that the early stages of relational interaction create a range of potential situations in which normal dating behaviour and stalking may overlap. The difficulty comes in separating the situations that arise from a genuine misunderstanding and those that stem from a deliberate and persistent refusal to take the wishes of the victim into account. This is possibly the most difficult type of stalking to distinguish from normal behaviour. The second type of relational stalking, which relates to the desire of one party to continue a relationship that the other wishes to end, generally involves more overtly harassing conduct.

When stalking occurs in the context of a prior relationship, this is usually done with the purposes of continuing or re-establishing a relationship that one party wishes to terminate. This divergence in synchronicity of feelings regarding the relationship creates immense potential for stalking, as one party remains committed to the relationship whilst the other is discontented and seeks to extricate herself from it. The destruction of a shared social world generally has an extreme negative impact upon the party who wishes to salvage the relationship.[124] Again, social constraints upon behaviour may cause this party to seek to soften the blow, for example, by implying that the separation will not be permanent or that the parties will remain in contact. Such promises may merely operate to foster hope in the partner who wishes to maintain the relationship and can actually led to bitterness as the promises are not honoured.[125] Obviously, not all situations such as this culminate in stalking, but of those that do, several stalkers attribute their hostility to the unclear messages they received from the victim. Clearly, it is impossible to speculate upon whether these stalkers would have behaved differently if the relationship were ended in a clear and unequivocal manner. It may be that those who are likely to use avoiding tactics and offer excuses are more vulnerable to exploitation by those with controlling and obsessive personalities. As Clark and LaBeff noted, even the firmest rejections are ignored, with:

---

123 Case history 6.
124 Vaughan, 1986.
125 Clark and LaBeff, 1988, pp 245–67.

the receiver of the news [making] extraordinary efforts, occasionally violent, to either hold on to the relationship, or make the life of the deliverer miserable.[126]

It is in such circumstances that stalking is likely to occur.

2.3.2 Revenge stalking

As has been discussed, there is clear potential for overlap between relational stalking, which is motivated by a desire to establish or rekindle a relationship, and revenge stalking, whereby the stalker deliberately engages in conduct designed to cause distress to the victim. Many relational stalkers switch between categories of stalking as they alternate between affection and hatred for their victim. Meloy explains the fluctuation between positive and negative feelings towards the victim as a cyclic concept. The stalker develops what Meloy terms 'a narcissist linking fantasy' towards another person which is based either upon reality (when the partner is known to the stalker) or delusional (where the victim is a celebrity or a stranger to the stalker). This leads the stalker to commence romantic pursuit. This may either receive a positive response, in which case a relationship may develop, or be met with rejection. Meloy asserts that, owing to the socially isolated and characteristically narcissistic nature of the stalker, he is unable to react to rejection in a normal way and his feelings mutate to hatred and the urge to harm the victim:

> Rejection stimulates shame and humiliation, the sensitive ventral underbelly of pride, which is quickly defended against with rage ... The perception is one of abandonment or disillusionment, and defence constellate around these emotions, such as the devaluation of the rejecting object to maintain rage and diminish envy. The latter emotion, prominent in narcissistic psychopathology, is the wish to possess the goodness of another. If she is sufficiently devalued, the stalker begins to see the victim as unworthy of having. These emotions fuel the pursuit of the object to hurt, injure, control, damage or destroy him or her.[127]

Thus the rejection leads the stalker, who will generally suffer from low self-esteem, to experience self-doubt and feelings of inadequacy. These are blamed upon the victim, who must then be made to suffer in order for the stalker to feel better.[128] This can be illustrated by an extract from a letter written to a stalking victim:

---

126 *Ibid*, p 262.

127 Meloy, 1999, pp 88–89.

128 'People who stalk feel better about themselves as a result of the process. This may be simply a feeling of relief from inner tension or from a sense of inadequacy, but it may also be an experience of feeling positively better.' Babcock, RJ, 'The psychology of stalking', in Infield and Platford, 2000, p 3.

Time to remove the kid gloves. I asked you to see me and you refused, that is your right. It's my option to make your life miserable, if that's what you really want. You asked me what I could do. Kill you? The answer was and still is no. If I killed you, you won't be able to regret what you did.[129]

However, as Meloy notes, aggressive and destructive pursuit restores the value of the victim to the stalker and re-establishes the narcissistic linking fantasy, hence the cycle begins again with the urge to possess the victim. This is the most paradoxical aspect of stalking, as the diminished value of the victim is restored only once the stalker has inflicted an adequate amount of hurt upon the victim. The victim is adored once more and the romantic pursuit recommences. For the victim, there may be little distinction between these phases:

> Sometime he loved me and made my life a misery because of it. Sometimes he hated me and made my life a misery because of it. But the bottom line was that he made my life a misery.[130]

Not all revenge stalking has a relational aspect. In the absence of any initial feelings of affection or admiration, this type of stalking is marked by hostility from the outset. Contrary to the position regarding relational stalking, there is little research exploring the psychology and pathology of the pure revenge stalker and its importance tends to be under-emphasised in the literature. Therefore, greater reliance will be placed upon the experiences of victims and stalkers as a means of providing examples of this type of stalking.

The revenge stalker is primarily motivated by the perception that he has been maltreated and acts out of a sense of grievance towards the victim. The maltreatment may be real or imagined and need not be attributable directly to the victim.[131] One stalker felt maltreated by the other students on her course as they failed to make sufficient effort to befriend her and include her in their social arrangements. The target of her grievance was a student who was extremely popular and outgoing, thus epitomising all that the stalker wished to be, which led her to feel an overwhelming need to destroy the victim's confidence:

> I tried so hard to be like her, all bubbly and chatty, but still nobody wanted to be my friend. She had friends everywhere and got included in everything and I hated her for that. I resented her so much that I couldn't think about anything else. When I started to phone her and I heard how frightened it made her, I felt so much better, for a while anyway. Then she got even more attention because she was being stalked so I had to keep doing it.[132]

---

129 Florida Victim Advocacy Center website –
   www.fiu.edu/~victimad/stalkvoi.html.
130 Case history 4.
131 Emerson, Ferris and Gardner, 1998, p 290.
132 Case history 17.

There is a clear parallel here with aspects of relational stalking. There are similar feelings of inadequacy that lead to strong feelings of envy and a consequent need to attack the victim's peace of mind. There is an element of rejection, but this need not be rejection from the person who is targeted by the stalker. This appears to be linked to a need to blame another person for the things that go wrong in the stalker's life. For example, one stalker was responsible for a prolonged campaign of stalking that was initially provoked by the victim's adulterous liaison with the stalker's husband. However, the stalking continued for many years after the affair was ended. The stalker explained that every time her husband was unfaithful, she blamed it upon the victim and started to harass her again:

> If she hadn't taken him away, he would never have started to mess around with other woman. It was all her fault. And she went off and married this rich bloke and lives in a huge house and doesn't have to work. When things go wrong, the first thing I think of is 'I bet [the victim] doesn't have to put up with this' and before I knew what I was doing, I'd start going after her again. I hate her so much that it frightens me. She has got everything and I've got nothing but it didn't stop her taking [my husband] away from me. She didn't have to do that and I have to make her pay. When I start to hate her, I can feel the pressure building up inside me and I have to do something to her or it's like I'll explode. As soon as I've got to her, whether it's phone calls, or pizzas, or her car, it's like the pressure just melts away.[133]

This tendency to target one particular person as a focus for a range of grievances that are not necessarily associated with the victim can made the identification of the stalker a particularly difficult matter. This anonymity appeared to increase the satisfaction of the revenge stalkers interviewed during the course of this research. For example, one stalker targeted more than 20 female members of the health club at which she was a receptionist. She was overweight and developed a grievance against those who lost weight successfully. She believed that these women were contemptuous of her failure to lose weight and that they flaunted their success in front of her to make her feel inadequate.[134] She described her campaign of silent telephone calls as her 'weapon' against the victims who 'deserved all they got and more' and she appeared to revel in their powerlessness:

> They didn't have a clue, any of them. It was great. They got more and more frightened but they didn't have the first idea who was responsible. They used to talk about 'him' and ask 'why is he doing this to us', it was brilliant. I wish I had one of those voice changers like in films so I could sound like a man and

---

133 Case history 15. The reference to pizza relates to one of the means of harassment used by this stalker who used to order a range of goods and services in the victim's name and cause them to be delivered to her home. Damage to the victim's car was also a common occurrence.

134 Case history 13. This illustrates the extreme egocentricity that is common in stalkers, as few of the victims could describe the receptionist: far from trying to distress her, they could barely recollect what she looked like.

then I could really have frightened them. I'd have said that I was watching their houses to see when they were alone and that I was going to come round and rape them so that they'd wish they were fat again so no one would want to rape them.[135]

Not all revenge stalking involves this indirect element. Some are more straightforward cases where the stalking can be linked to a particular act or set of circumstances that instils a sense of grievance in the stalker against the person they perceive to be directly responsible. For example, one stalker sought revenge against his former partner who had terminated a pregnancy against his wishes[136] whilst another targeted the sales assistant whose vigilance led to her arrest for credit card fraud.[137] Similarly, a student stalked a lecturer after he awarded her essay a poor mark[138] and a patient stalked her general practitioner after he gave her what she considered to be inadequate treatment. These cases all involve a direct grudge held by the stalker based upon some wrong that the victim is perceived to have committed.

It is probable that there are issues relating to the mental health and psychological condition of revenge stalkers, but this has not yet been addressed by professionals within these disciplines, where the focus has been exclusive on the motivation of relational stalkers. The four examples cited are not uncommon instances of behaviour, yet it is by no means common for stalking to result from their occurrence. This suggests that the reason that stalking occurred in these situations is peculiar to the stalker rather than the circumstances. The psychological, psychiatric and sociological research that exists on the motivational aspects of relational stalking has provided invaluable insights into the driving force behind stalking. Sufficient information is available to suggest that there are parallels to be made between relational and revenge stalking, but the dearth of research into the motivation that drives revenge stalking precludes any definite conclusions being reached on this issue.

What is clear from this examination of the motivation of stalkers is that not all harassment is deliberate, but may result from a failure to appreciate the impact of their conduct upon the victims, whether this is due to mental illness, psychological conditions or mere insensitivity. The tripartite categorisation of stalkers as mad, bad and sad, in many ways encapsulates the essential nature of the various motivations for stalking and is useful for legal purposes when determining the most appropriate means of intervention. The 'mad' stalker, suffering from a mental disorder that convinces him that his actions are not unwelcome, requires a different response than the 'bad' stalker, who fully appreciates the impact of his conduct and deliberately sets out to cause

---

135 Case history 13.
136 Case history 12.
137 Case history 23.
138 Case history 5.

distress to the victim. These can be contrasted with the 'sad' stalker who may be inept in dealing with social interaction and may genuinely not appreciate that his conduct is unwelcome. Such a stalker may be more easily deterred than the 'mad' or 'bad' stalker and may need only a clear indication that his behaviour is unacceptable and unwelcome. It is also important to intervene at an early stage lest the conduct and commitment to the course of action escalate into deliberate 'bad' stalking when the fact of rejection finally becomes apparent. This issue will be explored in greater depth in the final chapter, where the efficacy of various means of legal intervention will be addressed.

2.4 THE IMPACT OF STALKING ON THE VICTIMS

The motivation of the stalker is an important delineating factor in terms of establishing a typology of stalking and assessing the potential efficacy of different means of intervention. However, for the victim of stalking, the motivation of the stalker may well be of little relevance. As one victim stated:

> Sometimes he loved me and made my life a misery because of it. Sometimes he hated me and made my life a misery because of it. But the bottom line was that he made my life a misery.[139]

This illustrates the point that, for the victim, the conduct does not change in nature according to whether the stalker has benign or malicious motives. However, victims who knew the identity of their stalkers and were able to understand why they were being targeted appeared less fearful then those stalked by unknown persons or for a reason that they were unable to comprehend.[140] To this extent, the motivation of the stalker may have some impact upon the severity of the harm experienced by the victim. For example, one victim described her sense of relief when she discovered the identity of her stalker:

> The worst thing was not knowing who it was and imagining all sorts of people. Once we found out who it was, it was easier to deal with, mainly because we knew who to look out for. Before that, we had to be suspicious of everyone – every single person I saw in the supermarket, or wherever, could have been the stalker, that's why I pretty much stopped going out. Knowing who to look out for made it easier and more restful, if you see what I mean, than having to suspect everyone.[141]

---

139 Case history 4.

140 'The victim's confusion about the meanings and motives underlying their harassment augmented their fear, particularly when subjected to bizarre forms of harassment.' Pathe and Mullen, 1997, p 15.

141 Case history 24.

An additional feature that exacerbated the problems for this victim was the fact that the police were unwilling to intervene because she could not tell them who was responsible. She felt an increased degree of powerless because of this and ultimately paid a private investigator to find the stalker's identity. He was able to do so within two days.[142]

Another victim was stalked for almost three years before the identity of the stalker, who was a stranger to her, was revealed. She explained that not knowing who was responsible was one of the worst aspects of her ordeal:

> If I'd known who it was, I could've tried to work out why it was happening. You can't even guess at 'why' until you know 'who'. Then I did find out and it was this total stranger who had developed some sort of fantasy life that we were getting married, or something, so it was no use at all. In fact, finding out that it was someone who was mentally disturbed made it more frightening, but at least by then he'd been arrested.[143]

The experiences of these two victims reveal several themes that were prevalent amongst other victims.[144] First, the need to know the identity of the stalker is linked to a need for certainty. In the absence of such knowledge, almost everyone is potentially the stalker, thus increasing the anxiety of the victim. Knowledge of the identity of the stalker operates to return a vestige of control to the victim by ensuring that he or she knows exactly who to look out for. This appears to give the victims greater confidence to resume their normal activities. Secondly, an inability to name the person responsible appeared to decrease the likelihood of police intervention as several victims were told that the police could not act until there was a named suspect to approach. Only in cases of extreme harm did the police intervene in order to identify the stalker. Finally, once the identity of the stalker is ascertained, the victim has a basis upon which to determine why the stalking occurred. It does not necessarily follow that this will be possible once the stalker is identified, but the absence of identification prohibits any attempt at an assessment of the reason for victimisation.

The need to understand why they were targeted is almost universal amongst stalking victims. This can be linked to the need to attribute blame and to ensure that measures are taken to avoid future victimisation. If the victim can ascertain that the stalker had a mental disorder, her selection as a victim becomes almost random, thus absolving her of any responsibility. There is a strong tendency towards self-blame amongst stalking victims, even

---

142 At this stage, the stalking had been going on for over a year, but the police had continually asserted that they were not able to take action until they were told who was responsible. The influence on police attitudes on the social perceptions of stalking is discussed further in Chapter 3.

143 Case history 25.

144 These were extrapolated from the transcripts of the interviews using Ethnograph, a qualitative data analysis computer package. Ten per cent of the transcripts were analysed manually to ensure that the findings were reliable.

on the basis of the most trivial incident. One victim holds herself responsible for a nine month stalking campaign by a mentally disordered stalker who drove her from her home and her job. The basis for this was that she smiled at him whilst they were waiting at the same bus stop, which caused him to believe a relationship would develop between then. When this was not forthcoming, he attacked the victim and embarked upon a campaign of harassment that ended only when she gave up her job, sold her house and relocated to another part of the country.[145] It is common for victims to berate themselves for allowing the stalking to start and for being unable to bring it to an end.[146]

This element of self-blame and attribution of responsibility, whether full or partial, is one way in which stalking has a profound impact upon victims. However, this is only a single aspect of the impact that stalking can have upon those who are targeted. It is also important to note that the adverse affects are not limited to the direct victim, but impact upon family members and friends of the victim.

The impact of victimisation has not been greatly investigated, but the research that has been carried out suggests that stalking has a severe and long lasting impact on the lives of the victims. Pathe and Mullen's research found that all the victims experienced some deleterious impact upon their psychological, interpersonal or occupational functioning, with 37% fulfilling the criteria for a diagnosis of post-traumatic stress disorder.[147] The British Crime Survey addressed the impact of victimisation in terms of the emotional impact, the affect on the victim's lifestyle and the level to which victimisation affected the victim's fear of future victimisation. In terms of emotional impact, it was found that 91% of all victims were annoyed or irritated by the experience and 74% were distressed or upset.

---

145 Case history 6.
146 Pathe and Mullen, 1997, pp 12–17.
147 *Ibid.*

Figure 2.6   Emotional impact of stalking, by sex of the victim (BCS)

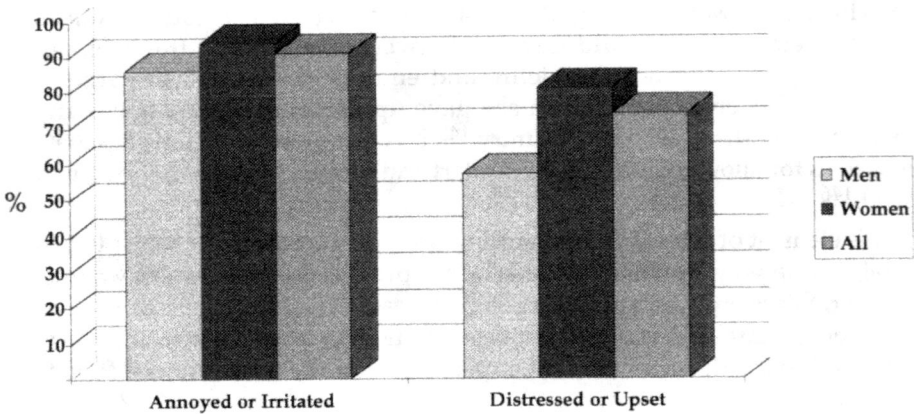

This indicates, therefore, that the majority of those targeted are likely to experience an adverse reaction.[148] It should be noted that the definition of stalking adopted by the British Crime Survey focused solely on the conduct involved – persistent and unwanted attention.[149] For the purposes of the Protection from Harassment Act 1997, such conduct would not incur liability unless it caused the recipient to feel harassed,[150] which is defined as including alarm or distress.[151]

Various factors may influence the nature of the victim's reaction, such as the duration, frequency and severity of the conduct concerned. The British Crime Survey considered the degree to which the victim was affected in relation to the nature of the stalking behaviour and found that the more serious behaviours of sexual assault and the use or threat of violence provoked a greater degree of annoyance and distress than conduct such as following and unpleasant telephone calls.

---

148 See pp 46–48.

149 Budd and Mattinson, 2000, p 6.

150 'A person must not pursue a course of conduct (a) which amounts to harassment of another': Protection from Harassment Act 1997, s 1(1).

151 'References to harassing a person include alarming the person or causing the person distress': Protection from Harassment Act 1997, s 7(2).

Figure 2.7 – Reaction of victims to different stalking behaviour (BCS)

	Silent Telephone Calls	Followed	Obscene Telephone Calls	Violence or Threat of Violence	Sexual Assault
Annoyed or Irritated	%	%	%	%	%
Yes – very	62	56	76	78	85
Yes – fairly	25	31	18	18	14
Yes – a little	12	11	5	3	2
Not at all	1	2	1	1	-
Distressed or Upset	%	%	%	%	%
Yes – very	42	36	57	57	79
Yes –fairly	24	31	27	23	12
Yes – a little	18	23	10	15	6
Not at all	16	11	6	5	3

Earlier in this chapter, the range of possible reactions to stalking was noted, as was the extent to which the emotional response of the victim may fluctuate during the course of the stalking. The findings of the British Crime Survey, as summarised in the above table, confirm that immense variability is possible between individuals subjected to conduct of a similar nature. However, as no account appears to have been taken of the duration and severity of the conduct, such findings are indicative only, as there is a wide range of conduct that is encompassed within any single category.[152]

It is important to look beyond the immediate emotional reaction of the victim to consider the wider impact that stalking has had upon the victim's life. Many victims have made major lifestyle changes as a result of being stalked:

> Lifestyle changes were a universal response to being stalked, with decline in social, occupational and/or academic functioning and sundry other disruptions. Over half of the victims had curtailed, changed or ceased work altogether ... A number of victims felt compelled to shift residence, in some cases overseas, sacrificing ties with an increasingly precarious social network.[153]

---

152 See pp 35–37.
153 Pathe and Mullen, 1997, p 15.

Such dramatic alterations illustrate the devastating affect that stalking can have. Suicide and attempted suicide amongst victims is not uncommon and one quarter of the victims interviewed by Pathe and Mullen had contemplated suicide.[154] Some victims resort to self-harm as a vent for their feelings of powerlessness, frustration and inadequacy.[155] Other severe consequences of stalking include the relocation of the victim to a new area in order to escape from the stalker, which often includes the severing of contact with friends and family. One victim has moved 14 times in the past three years in an attempt to be free of her stalker. She in unable to visit her parents, as the stalker keeps their house under surveillance in an attempt to track her down. Not only has this disrupted her relationship with her family and damaged her career, it has compounded her sense of isolation and vulnerability.[156]

A feeling of isolation is common amongst stalking victims. This may be attributable to physical factors such as forced relocation and/or mental and psychological isolation due to an absence of understanding and supportive friends and family. Many stalking victims were unable to communicate their experiences adequately to others or were met with a lack of comprehension. Comments such as 'why don't you just tell him to get lost', 'just be firm with him' and 'take no notice, he'll soon get fed up with it' are common and illustrate a complete misapprehension both as to the tenacity of stalkers and the traumatic impact of victimisation. Faced with the misunderstanding and trivialisation of their situation, many victims doubt their own interpretation of events or become increasingly less inclined to seek support from others for fear of further lack of understanding. Another factor that leads to a disinclination to confide in others relates to the attribution of responsibility for the stalking. Victims report comments such as 'you must have done something or why is he so keen on you' and 'people don't behave like this without encouragement' from friends and family, and even the police suggest that the victim is in some way to blame for their own victimisation. Such misunderstandings exacerbate the isolation of the victim, thus intensifying the trauma of the stalking experience, and can have a detrimental affect on the victim's relationship with those close to him or her. One victim reported that the most hurtful aspect of her victimisation was the fact that her family did not believe her until they had seen the stalker themselves some seven months after the stalking commenced.[157]

---

154 One interview conducted during the course of this research was with the sister of a stalking victim who had committed suicide exactly one year after her rape by a stranger who had been stalking her for five months – Case history 7. Four other research participants had attempted suicide as a result of their victimisation.

155 Eg, one 16 year old victim took to making deep cuts in her forearms and catching the blood in a bowl – Case history 24. Self-harm was a feature of six further cases encountered during the course of this research.

156 Case history 26.

157 Case history 1.

The victim's relationships with friends and family often appear to suffer as a result of stalking. Absence of understanding and support during the course of stalking is one aspect of this but, as noted previously, it is not only the direct victim who is affected by stalking. A great deal of stalking conduct will reach a wider audience than the intended recipient. Some stalking conduct cannot be directed exclusively at a particular person, hence abusive telephone calls, for example, may impact upon all household members. Equally, the stalker may deliberately target those close to the victim with a view either to distressing the victim or to driving away those who are viewed as impeding access to the victim. This is particularly common in a relational context. For example, one victim's boyfriend ended their relationship after his car was damaged on 16 occasions, once so severely that the car was beyond repair and had to be replaced. The victim's ex-husband was responsible for this, acting upon the belief that once his rival was driven away, his marriage would be restored.[158] The targeting of a person who is perceived as standing between the stalker and the victim is known as triangulation and can have fatal consequences.[159] Relationships may also suffer through claims and accusations made by the stalker. Relational stalkers frequently seek to damage the victim's existing relationships by making claims of infidelity that, in some cases, cause irreparable damage to this relationship.[160]

It is not just the personal and social life of the victim that suffers as a consequence of stalking. Stalkers appear to have no compunction about targeting victims at their place of employment, which can have an extremely adverse impact upon the victim's working atmosphere. Not all employers adopt a sympathetic attitude towards the victim whose stalker bombards the switchboard with requests to speak to the victim[161] or who causes a scene in front of customers when refused access to the victim.[162] Some victims have been reprimanded or threatened with dismissal if they fail to restrain the stalker's conduct and have been forced to give up their employment as a result.[163] Other victims leave their employment in order to escape from the stalker. This may involve a transfer between branches or a change of employer within the same industry, but the persistence of some stalkers to track down

---

158 Case history 30.

159 Meloy, 1999, pp 421–24; *R v Hough* (1997) unreported, 28 February, CA. The defendant, unable to accept that his marriage was over, stalked his estranged wife. She obtained an injunction which the defendant believed was done at the behest of her new boyfriend, so he broke into their home and stabbed the boyfriend, who died from his injuries. See also 'Stalker tried to kill ex-wife's new boyfriend' (1997) *Daily Telegraph*, 16 April.

160 Case histories 5, 19 and 28.

161 Case history 20.

162 Case history 2.

163 A large scale survey of stalking victims in the US found that 26% of victims had taken time off and 7% left work altogether as a consequence of stalking: Tjaden and Thoennes, 1998.

their victims sometimes requires the victim to change career completely. One victim, who was a qualified sports instructor, ultimately sought a new career when she realised that her stalker was tracking her down by visiting and revisiting sports centres in an increasingly wide area in order to locate her.[164] Such persistent changes in employment can have a deleterious effect on the victim's career. One victim outlined the gradual descent of her career:

> They were supportive at first and suggested a transfer. He found me within three days. My employer agreed to six further relocations, always on the pretext of widening my experience, before they ran out of patience. After three different jobs in five months, I was forced to take an unskilled job and now I just do temporary work. There's no point in me getting a permanent job because I'll only have to leave when he finds me anyway. It was a waste of time me getting a degree because he's destroyed my career prospects like he destroyed everything else.[165]

This victim is considering taking a second degree using a different name; a measure that she hopes will enable her to escape her stalker. Other victims have found that a complete change of identity was necessary to prevent the stalker locating them but, despite this, still live in fear of the stalker's appearance in their new life.[166]

Research into stalking in the US suggests that victims of stalking are significantly more likely to be in fear of becoming victims of other crimes than non-victims. This finding was mirrored by the results of the British Crime Survey where it was found that women who had been a victim of stalking were significantly more likely to fear for their personal safety, both in a generalised sense and in terms of victimisation from specific crimes.

---

164 Case history 25.
165 Case history 26.
166 Case histories 12 and 20.

Figure 2.8   Fearfulness of female stalking victims and non-victims (BCS)

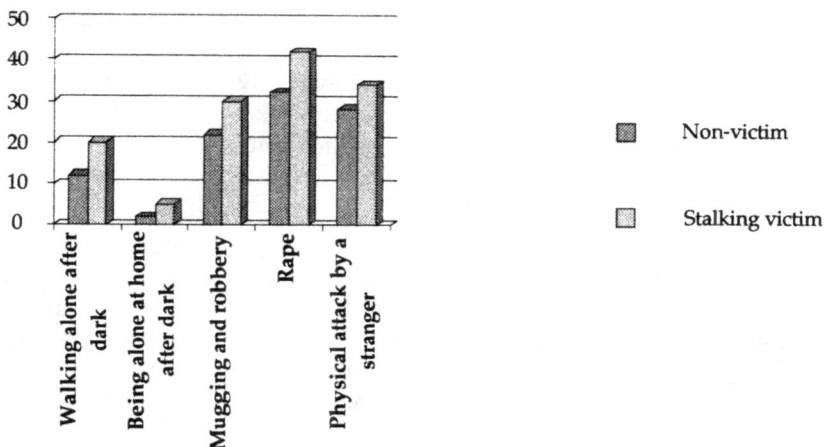

In addition to this accentuation of fearfulness, many victims report a heightened sense of wariness regarding other people. The need to rationalise the experience is common and is associated with the tendency to self-blame. Many victims attribute their victimisation to their tendency to trust others too readily and blame themselves for failing to be sufficiently cautious. Following their victimisation, many stalking victims find themselves unwilling or unable to trust others. This tendency to view strangers with suspicion leads to difficulties in making friends and forming new relationships. This can exacerbate the sense of isolation experienced by the victim, especially if they have relocated to a new area to avoid the stalker:

> I can't react normally to other people any more. People here have tried to be friendly but I have to push them away. On one level, I know this is stupid because these are perfectly normal people trying to make friends, but on another level I find myself thinking 'what do they really want' and 'why did she just ask me if I was doing something nice this weekend. Is it to find out where I'll be so she can watch me?' I wish I could stop but I can't. I don't think I'll ever be the same again.[167]

> I'm not sure I'll ever go out with anyone again. It's like everyone is a potential stalker. I'd rather spend the rest of my life on my own than risk it happening to me again.[168]

---

167 Case history 20.
168 Case history 4.

This statement encapsulates the enormity of the impact that stalking can have upon the lives of the victim. This victim moved away from her family and friends at the age of 19 to avoid her stalker. She has moved 23 times in the past five years and changed her name twice, but the stalker still manages to track her down. Her doctor has prescribed sleeping tablets and anti-depressants and has referred her for counselling as she suffers from agoraphobia. The victim is not able to work and has no friends; her only social contact is with her sister who travels to see her once a fortnight, taking the most circuitous route to ensure that she is not followed. She inflicts injuries on herself and has attempted suicide twice.

The devastation caused by stalking is immense. In many cases, no vestige of the victim's life remains unaffected – relationships, career, physical and mental health and feelings of self-worth may all be damaged by the experience. Victims develop a heightened sense of fearfulness and apprehension and appear unable to trust others or to develop ordinary social relationships. The effects of stalking can continue for many years after the actual stalking ceases. The far reaching impact of stalking is summed up by the words of one stalking victim:

He is everywhere. There is no part of my life that he hasn't destroyed.[169]

2.5 CONCLUSION

This chapter has identified the three central characteristics of stalking – repeated conduct that is unwanted and which provokes an adverse reaction in the recipient. To focus upon these characteristics obviates the necessity to seek a definition based upon the precise nature of the conduct itself. Moreover, a definition based upon these composite characteristics ensures that there is a sufficient degree of flexibility to encompass novel manifestations of stalking and to thwart those stalkers who deliberately engage in ostensibly lawful conduct in order to harass their victims. Further elucidation of the nature of stalking was provided by a consideration of the various means of classifying stalking that have been proposed by academic literature from various disciplines. This section of the chapter has challenged the typology of stalking based upon the pathology of the stalker and the relationship between the parties in favour of a motivationally based tripartite categorisation into the bad, the mad and the sad; a typology that is of particular use in a legal context. Furthermore, this section has sought to dispel some of the common misconceptions regarding stalking; that it is solely a relational problem, that it is a 'woman's issue' and that all stalking can be attributed to the mental health problems of the stalker. The bifurcation of the behaviour into relational and

---

169 Case history 26.

revenge stalking is not based upon the actual relational nexus between the parties but upon the motivation of the stalker in engaging in this conduct. Using this system of classification, stalking by a stranger can be classified as relational if the conduct is engaged in for the purpose of initiating a relationship between the parties. Finally, this chapter has addressed the impact of stalking on the victim. Stalking is frequently portrayed as a mere irritation that has a transient and insignificant effect upon the victim. This conceptualisation is far removed from the reality of victimisation, which can have far reaching and permanent effects upon the victim. It is essential to recognise the severity of the harm caused by stalking both in order to accord it the precedence that it merits amongst other types of criminal conduct and in order to evaluate the efficacy of legal responses to stalking.

During the course of this exploration of the characteristics of stalking, it has become clear that common misconceptions exist regarding this conduct and its consequences. Public perceptions appear to differ dramatically from the reality of stalking as experienced by the victims. This leads to a lack of understanding of the severity and impact of stalking that exacerbates the trauma and isolation of victimisation. Therefore, it is essential to address the nature of public perceptions of stalking and consider the extent to which such perceptions differ from the reality of stalking as experienced by the victims. This links to an issue discussed in the previous chapter regarding the ancestry of stalking. It was established that stalking is not a new type of behaviour but a new label given to a long standing form of harassing conduct which, possibly owing to a lack of universally accepted terminology, did not emerge as a serious social problem until the latter part of the 20th century. These issues will be addressed in the next chapter, which explores the social construction of stalking and seeks to account for its emergence as a social problem demanding a legislative response.

CHAPTER 3

THE SOCIAL CONSTRUCTION OF STALKING

Chapters 1 and 2 addressed the characteristics of stalking and considered the experiences and narratives of both stalkers and victims. It was established that stalking is not a new type of behaviour, but a long standing problem that was not publicly recognised, predominantly due to a lack of commonly understood terminology to describe the conduct. As such, the emergence of stalking as a social problem deemed to necessitate a legislative solution requires some explanation. This chapter examines the processes by which an issue becomes recognised as a social problem and questions whether the emergent construction accurately reflects the reality of the problem. The perceptions and misconceptions of stalking will be outlined as a prelude to a consideration of the problems that may arise if the social construction and actuality of stalking do not correspond, with particular emphasis on the implications of this for the efficacy of legal intervention.

3.1 SOCIAL CONTEXT OF CRIMINAL LAW

It is unhelpful to start from the assertion that stalking, or harassment, is a crime. To state that any particular conduct is a crime provides a limited and one-dimensional view of a multi-faceted concept. It explains nothing about how the conduct came to be perceived as appropriate for criminalisation and ignores the social context in which this perception was established. The social context of the criminalisation of stalking requires exploration in order to understand why stalking was deemed to merit legal intervention at a particular point in time. More than this, it is not just the decision to legislate that requires illumination, but the decision to legislate in a particular way – how was stalking perceived that it was decided that the legal response that was forthcoming was the most suitable way to address the conduct?

Criminal law is traditionally perceived as establishing prohibitive norms that proscribe certain conduct[1] or as creating disciplinary norms that delineate the parameters of acceptable behaviour.[2] Legal definitions of crime emphasise the norm violating nature of conduct, thus creating a situation whereby crime can be defined only by reference to criminal law.[3] Definitions that move

---

1   Quinney, 1970.
2   Foucault, 1977.
3   Tappan, 1947, p 100: 'only those are criminals who have been adjudicated as such by the courts. Crime is an intentional act in violation of the criminal law.'

beyond norm violation tend to focus upon the role of the State in initiating proceedings[4] or the particularities of criminal procedure in order to distinguish crime from conduct that contravenes the civil law.[5] Legalistic definitions of crime are frequently isolated from the social, political and economic contexts in which crime occurs and in which conceptions of criminality are formed.[6] Hence, to state that harassment is a criminal offence is merely to state that conduct which contravenes the provisions of the relevant statute is regarded as unacceptable and will result in the offender being brought before the criminal courts where his guilt will be determined by established criminal procedure and, where appropriate, punishment will be imposed. Thus, it can be seen that legalistic definitions address the 'what' of crime rather than the 'why and the how',[7] thereby overlooking what Lacey refers to as the contingent nature of the boundaries of criminality.[8]

A legalistic approach to crime merely identifies that which is regarded as criminal in a particular society at a given time. However, the categories of criminal conduct are not static or permanent in any society, but are a 'historically and socially specific concept'.[9] As Lacey notes,[10] the boundaries of criminality are constantly shifting as that which was prohibited becomes lawful, such as the decriminalisation of homosexuality,[11] and hitherto lawful conduct becomes prohibited, for example, the criminalisation of non-consensual intercourse within marriage.[12] The reasons for changing the status of conduct from permissible to prohibited require exploration.[13] It may be that

---

4   Marshall, WL and Clark, WL, 'The legal definition of crime and criminals', in Wolfgang and Johnston.

5   Hartjen, 1978, p 4.

6   Muncie and McLaughlin, 1996, p 9.

7   Loveland, I, 'Preface', in Loveland, 1995, pp ix–xvi.

8   Lacey, N, 'Contingency and criminalisation', in Loveland, 1995, pp 1–27. Here, Lacey asserts that the boundaries of criminality might have been, and might be, other than what they are. This being so, any genuinely critical approach to crime and criminal law should attempt to confront and understand how the boundaries of criminality are constructed and managed – how they shift, who or what determines shifts or resistance to change.

9   Muncie and McLaughlin, 1996, p 10; Wilkins, 1964, p 46: 'There are no absolute standards. At some time or another, some form of society or another has defined almost all forms of behaviour that we now call "criminal" as desirable for the functioning of that form of society.'

10 Op cit, Lacey, fn 8, pp 1–27.

11 Sexual Offences Act 1967, s 1(1): 'a homosexual act in private shall not be an offence provided the parties consent thereto and have attained the age of 21 years.' Further amendments were made by the Criminal Justice and Public Order Act 1994, s 143 and the Sexual Offences (Amendment) Act 2000.

12 The Criminal Justice and Public Order Act 1994 redefines rape by substituting a new s 1 to the Sexual Offences Act 1956 in which the word 'unlawful', which was considered 'mere surplusage' by the House of Lords in *R v R* [1991] 4 All ER 481, is omitted, hence non-consensual marital intercourse constitutes rape.

13 The process of decriminalisation also merits consideration, but the focus of this chapter is on criminalisation of hitherto lawful conduct with particular reference to stalking and harassment.

conduct is new; technological development may create novel situations that are deemed to necessitate regulation by the criminal law.[14] However, if the conduct itself is not new, as was the case with harassment and stalking,[15] an alternative explanation for its criminalisation must be sought, as it is the reaction to the conduct that has changed whilst the conduct itself remains constant:[16]

> Crime ... is not an objective 'thing' out there, but a product of socially created definitions: deviance is not inherent in an item of behaviour, it is a quality bestowed upon it by human evaluation.[17]

Thus, the prevailing social evaluation of conduct is determinative of its status as permissible or prohibited for the purposes of criminal law. As Heidensohn asserts, if criminal law is based upon conduct norms within society, it is axiomatic that it must change to reflect social changes.[18] This societal dimension of criminal conduct is not reflected by legalistic definitions, thus a greater understanding of the rationale from criminalisation of any particular conduct is to be gained by considering the social context in which the conduct takes place.

Further support for the need to look beyond legalistic definitions of crime in order to glean an understanding of the process by which conduct becomes deemed to merit criminalisation can be found when considering the range of criminal conduct. The criminal law covers an immense and diverse range of conduct with little in common other than that it is prohibited by the criminal law. Infractions of the criminal law do not form a meaningful or homogenous category of conduct. Therefore, no guidance can be derived as to why stalking was criminalised from considering existing categories of criminal law as there is nothing intrinsic to these behaviours that makes them criminal. In the absence of a general principle that justifies criminalisation, the reason why certain conduct is criminalised must come from something external to the conduct itself as this cannot be accounted for by reference to a purely legalistic notion of crime.

---

14 Croall, 1998, p 9. Technological change affects the opportunities for crime, the forms of crime that are prevalent and patterns of crime. Eg, the development of cars and computers have created new forms of crime which require new laws to keep pace with them. Heidensohn, 1989, p 13: 'Yet criminality does take novel forms from time to time, reflecting technological development: no one could hijack an aeroplane until powered flight was possible.'

15 See pp 27–34.

16 Heidensohn, 1989, p 13. 'Sometimes crimes are not so much new in themselves, rather they involve conceptual shifts as police or other agencies change their policies and practices, and this affects public perceptions in turn.'

17 Young, 1999, p 39 (original emphasis).

18 Heidensohn, 1989, p 4.

Legalistic definitions of crime as contravention of the criminal law are circular,[19] provide little insight into the variability of the conduct which is regarded as criminal and fail to encapsulate the complexity of the process by which certain conduct becomes deemed to be unacceptable within society.[20] As Packer asserts:

> crime is a sociopolitical artefact, not a natural phenomenon. We can have as much or as little crime as we please, depending upon what we choose to count as criminal.[21]

In order to achieve a clear understanding of the nature of crime and the reasons for criminalisation, the social setting in which the conduct occurs should be considered.[22] The operation of the criminal law is inextricably bound up with the society within which it exits. As Sartre contended, any notion of truth that is abstract and removed from the struggle of everyday life is a form of ignorance.[23] Crime is a social phenomenon, thus the process by which conduct becomes regarded as a social problem that merits criminalisation requires exploration. In order to understand the 'how and why' of the criminalisation of stalking, the factors which led to a commonality of understanding of such conduct as a social problem need to be understood, hence the need to explore the social construction of stalking.

3.2 THE CONSTRUCTION OF SOCIAL PROBLEMS

The study of social problems was traditionally undertaken from an objectivist perspective which concentrated on the quantification and investigation of an objectively established phenomenon[24] that was accepted to exist and constitute a problem on the basis that it harmed or endangered human life or societal well being.[25] There was no necessity for public concern or awareness of this phenomenon, provided that it caused harm in some clear cut and non-ideological fashion. The decision as to which conditions satisfied the

---

19 Michael and Adler, 1933, p 5: 'if crime is merely an instance of conduct which is proscribed by the criminal code, it follows that the criminal law is the formal cause of crime.'

20 Lacey and Wells, 1998; Muncie and McLaughlin, 1996.

21 Packer, 1968, p 364.

22 Lacey and Wells, 1998; Muncie and McLaughlin, 1996; Heidensohn, 1989.

23 Sartre, 1992.

24 Thompson, 1998, p 12: 'The objectivist accepts that a particular phenomenon exists ... and the role of the social scientist is to quantify that problem, to investigate its causes and suggest solutions.'

25 Bassis, Gelles and Levine, 1982, p 2: 'A social problem is a social condition that has been found to be harmful to individual and/or societal well-being'; Farley, 1987, p 2: 'A social problem, then, can be defined as a condition that: (1) is widely regarded as undesirable or as a source of difficulties; (2) is caused by the actions or inactions of people or of society; (3) affects or is thought to affect a large number of people.'

requirements for the existence of a social problem was a matter for the 'expert, armed with empirical evidence and scientific insight, and not the untrained general public',[26] thus conditions that sociologists considered to be social problems became established as social problems.[27] Other than their recognition as social problems, these conditions had little, if anything, in common with each other.[28] The absence of a unifying theoretical explanation of social problems was one of the two main criticisms of the objectivist approach.[29]

The other criticism concerned the way in which the objective approach ignores the subjective nature of social problems. It is not true to say that every condition that meets the harm criteria is considered a social problem and historic consideration of the evolution of certain social problems reveal that there was a time when such conditions were simply not regarded as problematic. For example, it was not until the rise of the feminist movement that a whole range of issues such as domestic violence, pay inequality and sex discrimination became accepted as social problems.[30] However, there is little doubt that these conditions were endemic prior to their recognition as social problems, thus it was not the conditions that had changed, but the subjective appraisal of them as problematic. It was this aspect of social problems that objectivism was unable to explain,[31] thus this perspective would be unable to account for the emergence of stalking as a social problem during the 1990s when it is clear that this conduct was not a new phenomenon.[32]

These limitations led to the objectivist approach being condemned as 'imprecise and ambiguous' by Spector and Kitsuse, who reformulated the sociology of social problems by their development of the social constructionist perspective.[33] This approach rejects the conception of social problems as objective conditions and focuses instead upon the processes by which

---

26 Goode and Ben-Yehuda, 1994, p 87. Manis, 1976, p 25: 'Social problems are those social conditions identified by scientific inquiry and values as detrimental to human well-being.'

27 Rubington and Weinberg, 1995.

28 Best, J, 'Typifications and social problems construction', in Best, 1995, p 5: 'Objectivist definitions of social problems lead to a hodge-podge list of topics with little in common. These problems do not have the same sort of causes, and they do not have the same sort of effects. Sociologists studying crime need to ask very different questions from those studying sexism. Saying that both are social problems does not offer a useful direction for research.'

29 Kitsuse and Spector, 1973, p 419: 'Prior approaches harbour crucial ambiguities as to the distinctive nature of the phenomenon of social problems and the kind of theory one would have to develop to account for it'; Spector and Kitsuse, 1977: 'There is no adequate definition of social problems within sociology and there is not and never has been a sociology of social problems.'

30 Op cit, Best, fn 28, p 4.

31 Jenkins, 1992.

32 See pp 27–34.

33 Kitsuse and Spector, 1973, pp 407–19; Spector and Kitsuse, 1973, pp 145–59; Spector and Kitsuse, 1977.

members of society define conditions as problematic. Spector and Kitsuse define social problems as:

> the activities of individuals or groups making assertions or grievances and claims with respect to some putative condition.[34]

This definition emphasises the role of activities which Spector and Kitsuse term 'claims making', whereby conditions, for example crime, racism and pollution, are not themselves social problems, but are merely the subject matter of claims.[35] The significance of objective conditions is the assertions made about them and not the validity of those assertions as judged from some independent standpoint. The objective existence of a harmful condition does not, of itself, amount to a social problem unless and until it is characterised as such by society. Goode and Ben-Yehuda illustrate this reference to attitudes towards disease in society – if people do not conceptualise a particular disease as problematic then, according to constructionists, it does not amount to a social problem, even if it has a significantly higher mortality rate than diseases that are considered to be social problems.[36] To constructionists, the validity of the assertion that a condition is problematic is irrelevant.[37] It does not matter whether or not the condition exists; it only matters that claims are made about it as the verification of assertions made about conditions is not a fundamental aspect of the analysis of social problems.[38] The fact that the conduct had been around for a long time without being viewed as problematic is irrelevant to the constructionist perspective, as the focus should be on the way in which this conduct became characterised as a social problem. Thus, social problems do not have an objective existence, but are constructed by social interaction; they are 'called into being by the definitional process'.[39] Indeed, a condition that does not objectively exist can qualify as a social problem. For example, it is irrelevant that women in Renaissance Europe did not really cavort with Satan; what matters is the process by which this situation was created as a

---

34 Spector and Kitsuse, 1977, p 75.

35 *Ibid*, p 73.

36 Goode and Ben-Yehuda, 1994.

37 Although the two predominant schools of constructionist thought are mainly distinguishable by their stance on the importance of the objective seriousness of a condition.

38 Spector and Kitsuse, 1977, p 76. Thus the only valid subject matter for sociological inquiry is how a condition became construed as a social problem. The actual validity of the claim is a matter for other disciplines. To hold otherwise would demand an immense spectrum of expertise from the sociologist given the range of conditions regarded to be social problems. As Fuller notes, the investigation of the objective validity of all conditions considered to be social problems would require the sociologist to 'hold himself out as an authority on everything from technological unemployment to dementia praecox ... He need not be an expert on social problems, but an expert on the sociology of social problems.' Fuller, 1938, p 424.

39 Goode and Ben-Yehuda, 1994, p 88.

social reality by the claims made about it.[40] The use of 'claims' should not be taken as a denial or affirmation of the moral validity or material facticity of the condition. A claim is a socially structured reality and it is this which is the subject matter under investigation regardless of its empirical validity. Social problems are constructed by members of society who, by the claims making process, attempt to call attention to a condition which they find objectionable or repugnant by asserting that such a condition ought not exist and that 'something ought to be done' to ameliorate or eradicate that condition.[41]

The divergence in objectivist and constructionist perspectives is clearly illustrated by their respective approaches to 'new' social problems, such as stalking. The objectivist accepts the creation of genuinely new problems, which are attributable either to the advent of novel forms of aberrant behaviour or to a dramatic increase in the seriousness or prevalence of an existing form of behaviour. By contrast, the constructionist believes that problems are rarely completely novel and that problematic behaviours are endemic in society, but are not problematised until they are named and defined in a particular way. Constructionists attribute the emergence of 'new' social problems to changes in social perceptions, attitudes and levels of tolerance to an existing condition or behaviour and seek to determine what social, political or bureaucratic forces influence these altered attitudes.

As has been established, stalking is not a novel kind of behaviour that originated in the 1990s. The objectivist perspective can only account for the emergence of stalking as a social problem if the conduct became significantly more prevalent or developed new levels of dangerousness at this time. Owing to the absence of a commonly understood and accepted terminology, it is impossible to ascertain whether stalking has escalated in dangerousness or prevalence. Babcock surmises that stalking must have increased in recent years, as under-reporting and under-recognition cannot account for its present incidence.[42] He offers no evidence to support this and, owing to the impossibility of measuring the prevalence of stalking prior to the inception of a commonly understood label, this can only be considered to be mere speculation. The way in which stalking emerged as a social problem is indicative of changes in public attitudes towards conduct of this nature. Wells attributes this to the association between stalking and two major contemporary concerns – the determination and regulation of the boundaries

---

40 Goode and Ben-Yehuda, 1994, p 95. Jenkins' chapter on ritual child abuse explains how the claims made about ritual child abuse successfully constructed this as a serious social problem which occupied the media, social services and the police for almost three years despite the claims being unfounded and almost wholly discredited: Jenkins, 1992.

41 Spector and Kitsuse, 1977, p 86. Value judgments lead people to experience conditions as offensive and to view them as social problems, therefore social problems are heavily freighted with morality and values. Claims are a normative phenomenon, as are statements about conditions that ought not to exist and which imply that something must therefore be done to improve the situation.

42 Babcock, RJ, 'The psychology of stalking', in Infield and Platford, 2000.

of acceptable sexual and relational conduct and the acceptance of psychological injury to the forefront of significant personal harms.[43] Moreover, there is evidence to suggest that stalking was 'repackaged' on several occasions before its acceptance as a social problem, thus indicating that a constructionist analysis will be the most appropriate and informative means of approaching this issue.

This perspective has developed since its inception and there now exist two predominant movements within constructionism which differ in the extent to which the objective validity of the condition is taken into account. The strict constructionist is not concerned with the accuracy of the claims made about the problem, but focuses exclusively upon the way in which people 'define, lodge and press claims; how they publicise their concerns, redefine the issue in question in the face of political obstacles, indifference or opposition; how they enter into alliance with other claims makers'[44] and believes that these factors must be accepted without regard to their objective validity.[45] This view is rejected as overly solipsistic by contextual constructionists on the basis that assertions made by claims makers are made as a response to something which objectively exists in the social world in which they live,[46] hence are potentially amenable to empirical verification.[47] The contextual constructionist, whilst concentrating on the subjective reality, does not discount the influence of the objective reality of the condition, but merely believes that the objective dimension alone cannot account for the emergence of a condition as a social problem. The plausibility and factual basis of the claims is a factor which contextual constructionists take into account when exploring the process by which social problems are constructed, brought into the arena of public debate and used to shape policy.[48] As this chapter follows from an exploration of the actuality of stalking from the perspectives of those with direct experience of the phenomenon, this will be used as the basis for a contextual constructionist approach that will evaluate the way in which stalking came to be perceived as a pressing social problem during the 1990s.

---

43 Wells, 1997, p 463.

44 Kitsuse, JI and Schneider, JW, 'Preface', in Best, 1995, pp i–iv.

45 Goode and Ben-Yehuda, 1994, p 95: the strict constructionist recognises no objective dimension but perceives all dimensions as subjective with there being no possibility of stepping outside the definitional process. All assertions about conditions, whether they are official crime statistics or leaflets proclaiming that UFO abductions are a serious problem, are equally valid in the process of constructing a social problem.

46 Sarbin, TR and Kitsuse, JI, 'A prologue to constructing the social', in Sarbin and Kitsuse, 1994.

47 Goode and Ben-Yehuda, 1994, pp 98–99: to strict constructionists, there is no objective reality, hence there is no way of empirically verifying or refuting any claim. Contextual constructionists emphasise the necessity of potential to verify the objective dimension although they acknowledge that existence is frequently easier to determine than extent.

48 Jenkins, 1992, pp 2–3.

3.3 THE IMPORTANCE OF THE SOCIAL CONSTRUCTION OF STALKING

If the conduct itself is not new, its emergence as a significant social problem in need of legislative response can only be justified by a change in social attitudes. Social constructionism facilitates an examination of the process by which social attitudes emerge and are formed. However, before considering the social construction of stalking, it is relevant to address the question of why the way in which people perceive and characterise such conduct is important.

Berger and Luckmann assert that everyday life is a reality that is interpreted by an individual in a way that is subjectively meaningful to him in a coherent world, but that this reality originates and is maintained in an individual's thoughts and actions.[49] It is shared understandings amongst society that facilitate the construction of the reality of any object or phenomenon. Thus, social facts are self-referential; that is, they exist because they are universally accepted as existing.[50] Searle uses money as an example to illustrate this point. Money is, after all, so many pieces of paper and metal. However, its common acceptance as currency gives it value. Should these objects cease to be accepted by society as money, they would no longer be money. This is because the notion of money is an institutional fact based upon shared understanding and common acceptance.[51] Language plays an essential role in this process of shared understandings, as different words come to symbolise immense and complex concepts and objects in a way that is publicly understandable.[52] Thus, without a common terminology to link together people's experiences, there was no potential for a shared understanding of stalking to develop, hence it was difficult, if not impossible, for victims to articulate what was happening to them. Victims whose experiences pre-date the inception of the term 'stalking' struggled to define and communicate what had happened to them. One victim encapsulates this difficulty:

> There was nothing to describe it then, of course. No one ever used the word 'stalking'; we called it 'pestering', but that didn't really sum up the whole of

---

49   Berger and Luckmann, 1967.

50   Searle, 1995.

51   *Ibid*, pp 31–35. Searle distinguishes between institutional facts, such as money, crime, marriage, tables and cars, which are dependent upon human agreement, and brute facts, such as mountains, water and other naturally occurring phenomena, which require no human institutions for their existence. Institutional facts are so called because they rely on human institutions for their existence. For a piece of paper to be a £5 note, there has to exist a human institution of money. The paper may objectively exist, but it only becomes a social reality as money if generally accepted to exist as money. For example, the half penny piece is no longer money, as it was withdrawn from circulation, which led to it not being regarded as money despite its physical existence being unaltered.

52   *Ibid*, pp 60–61.

what he was doing. I felt helpless and sort of hunted, like he followed me everywhere and I couldn't get away from him. But it was so hard to explain to people. I would say, 'there is this man following me and watching me' and you could see people trying to work out what I meant. When I tell people now, 'oh yes, I was stalked' they know exactly what I mean, so it's much easier to get people to understand. It was this thing about people not understanding that was half the problem because no one seemed to understand what I was going through and why I was so upset.[53]

This illustrates the point made by Berger and Luckmann when they explain the way in which the construction of social reality is limited by 'common participation in the available social stock of knowledge'.[54] Without an established terminology, people generate their own labels to describe their experiences. As different people will establish different labels, this makes it difficult to reconcile their experiences and to appreciate that they are referring to similar conduct. The previous quotation uses the word 'pestering' to describe very similar conduct to that experienced by another victim, who uses different terminology to describe her experience:

> We all used to refer to him as 'the prowler'. No one called him a stalker but it was back in 1982 so I don't think that anyone in our village would have heard of stalking.[55]

This victim and her family were amongst approximately a dozen households who were targeted over an 18 month period by a person who lurked in their gardens at night, banged on their doors and windows and made repeated silent telephone calls. This type of multiple victim scenario is relatively unusual.[56] Interestingly, the victim's use of the word 'prowler' to describe this conduct would be considered correct by Dr Richard Babcock who distinguishes between 'stalkers [who] stick to the same victims for long periods of time' and 'prowlers [who] tend to be more territorially orientated in their habits and therefore switch victims frequently as they move in and out of their territory.'[57] The victim, however, despite her use of the word 'prowler' at the time, now considers herself to have been the victim of stalking. This illustrates both the contingent reality of definitions that are constructed from

---

53 Case history 1 – this victim was followed and watched for approximately nine months by a stranger whom she had encountered during the course of her employment as a counsellor at a free advice centre.

54 Berger and Luckmann, 1967, p 56.

55 Case history 11 – this woman, along with her family and several other households within a small village, was targeted by a man who would watch their houses, bang on doors and windows and make silent calls.

56 Only one other instance was discovered during the course of this research: Case history 36, in which various families in a Derbyshire village were targeted by a man, dubbed 'the Phantom Photocopier' by the police and local press, who distributed malicious cartoons depicting scenes, real and invented, from people's lives. There is no reference in any of the existing literature on stalking which covers group stalking.

57 Babcock, RJ, 'The psychology of stalking', in Infield and Platford, 2000.

social experience and the need to make sense of one's experiences by relating them to an established category of conduct, even if this only occurs retrospectively. Therefore, at the time, this victim had never heard of stalking, so used the best word she could find in an attempt to encapsulate her experience. Her subsequent knowledge of the type of behaviour that is encompassed within the parameters of stalking has led her to conclude that the word would have been applicable to her situation. This conclusion is based upon her knowledge and experiences of stalking cases gleaned from a variety of sources. To label the conduct as stalking makes it meaningful for the victim and to those to whom she recounts her experiences. Berger and Luckmann acknowledge that language is used to typify new experiences and subsume them under broad categories within which they have meaning not just to the individual concerned, but to society in general.[58]

Therefore, until there is a publicly recognised and generally accepted label that can be used to draw these cases together, there is no reason for a connection to be made between them. This lack of recognition perpetuates the invisibility of the situation as it is impossible to measure the prevalence of an event that has no accepted name that can be used to identify all incidences of the conduct. This, then, illustrates the importance of the social construction of stalking. A wide range of disparate conduct was given a common identity that enabled those who had encountered such conduct to identify and name their experience. More than this, those without direct experience of the conduct gained awareness of it as, once named and defined, communication is possible.

Until such common terminology made a shared understanding of stalking possible, victims sought alternative methods of defining their experiences. One victim makes reference to the film *Fatal Attraction*[59] to communicate his experience to others in a way that was meaningful to them:

> This was a long time ago. I don't think I knew that she was a stalker then. I didn't know what one was, I don't think, although my mate reckoned she was going to turn out to be a bunny boiler, you know, like in *Fatal Attraction*, so that's what we all called her, even my mum in the end, the bunny boiler. But now I hear about stuff that happens to other people and think 'that's what happened to me, she was a stalker' even though I did know perfectly well who she was at the time.[60]

---

58 Berger and Luckmann, 1967, p 53.

59 *Fatal Attraction*, 1987, revolved around the actions of Alex Forrest, played by Glenn Close, who refused to accept that her weekend affair with happily married Dan Gallagher, played by Michael Douglas, was over. As the film develops, she appears increasingly unhinged and, amongst other things, kills his daughter's pet rabbit and leaves it boiling in a pot in the family kitchen.

60 Case history 14 – this victim was repeatedly telephoned and followed by his former partner who refused to accept the ending of their relationship. Her conduct included breaking into his home in order to ascertain his new telephone number and hitch-hiking about 12 miles every day so that she could see him during his morning coffee break.

These three accounts demonstrate the difficulties inherent in trying to contextualise previously unfamiliar experiences. However, although 'stalking' was not a term in common parlance, these victims adapted to the new terminology and considered it appropriate to describe their experiences although it was not in use at the time. At the time, it is extremely unlikely that these accounts of 'pestering', 'prowling' and 'bunny boiling' would have been linked with each other. However, the victims can now compare their own experiences with what they now understand to be stalking and are able to conclude that they were all stalking victims. This accords with Berger and Luckmann's belief that language provides a means by which the reality of experience can be objectified and understood.[61]

The social construction of stalking facilitates a common understanding which ameliorates the difficulties of communication of experience caused by the absence of an identifiable and meaningful terminology. As one victim states, merely to say 'I have been stalked' communicates the experience in a way which is immediately understandable to others.[62] However, a social construction of stalking does more than identify and name the conduct in question. It also characterises not only the conduct, but also the stalker and the victim. This characterisation of issue is an essential aspect of social constructionism. It is not merely a matter of drawing public attention to an issue, but also of presenting the problem in a particular way which shapes the way in which that issue is perceived or constructs the social reality of the issue. This is known within social constructionism as typification.[63]

The means by which people come to know of and understand stalking inevitably influences their perceived reality of stalking. If this perceived reality has sufficiently wide acceptance, it becomes a social reality which may or may not accord with the objective reality of stalking, depending upon how the issue has been presented during the claims making process.[64] Thus, the social construction of stalking is concerned with how stalking is perceived. This is important, as it effects each individual's understanding of the nature of stalking and influences whether or not they recognise stalking when confronted with it. For example, the male stalking victim quoted above categorises his experience as stalking, but adds the qualification that he feels this is so even though he knew who was responsible.[65] Equally, a woman who was followed and watched for more than three years by the man who

---

61 Berger and Luckmann, 1967, p 53.

62 Although there is a general understanding of the type of conduct involved in stalking, each individual's specific understanding may differ according to a variety of factors.

63 Best, 'Typification and social problems construction', in Best, 1995, p 8: 'Naming is just one way claims makers typify social problems. *Typification occurs when claims makers characterise a problem's nature.*' (Original emphasis.)

64 *Ibid.*

65 Case history 14.

lived in the flat opposite her stated 'it was like being stalked, but by somebody you know'.[66] These victims could relate their experiences to their understanding of stalking, but clearly perceived that an essential characteristic of stalking was that it was perpetrated by a stranger, or at least by a person whose identity was unknown. Although figures concerning the prevalence and nature of stalking vary enormously,[67] it is clear that a significant proportion of stalkers know their victims.[68] Therefore, this view does not accord with the objective reality of stalking, but nonetheless the perception of stalkers as unknown strangers is relatively common. Typification occurs when claims makers characterise a problem's nature.[69]

Therefore, the social construction of stalking can affect whether people consider themselves to be victims of stalking. A social problem such as stalking can have various typifications, and these may alter over time.[70] Other characterisations of stalking have been apparent in victim accounts:

> I didn't really think of myself as being stalked. I'm just ordinary and I knew he wasn't dangerous. Stalking to me, then at least, meant celebrities being stalked by sinister nutters with guns. He was just an ordinary bloke who had gone a bit strange.[71]

Several characteristics of the victim's perception of the prototypical stalking case are presented here. The victim sees herself as too ordinary to be stalked as she sees stalking as a celebrity problem. She is clear about her image of a stalker, as her description implies that he will be mentally ill, dangerous and likely to possess a weapon. Her 'stalker' did not fit that image, hence she did not, at the time, consider herself to be the victim of stalking. These events

---

66 Case history 35 – a young woman was followed for over three years by the man who lived in the flat opposite to hers. He would frequently call at her home and find excuses to stay and chat, and began to waylay her and telephone her at her work and her parents' and friends' homes when she tried to avoid him.

67 See Chapter 1.

68 Fremouw, Westrup and Pennypacker, 1997, pp 666–69: four empirical studies of campus stalking in the US revealed that between 16% and 18% of stalking cases involved strangers. Wallis, 1996, pp 25–29: Assistant Chief Constable Maria Wallis carried out research on behalf of the Association of Chief Police Officers into the nature and prevalence of stalking. Her survey of the 43 police forces of England and Wales and the British Transport Police revealed that 32% of the stalkers were unknown to the victims. The divergence in this figure is repeated throughout the available research on the prevalence of stalking. The difficulties associated with measuring the prevalence of stalking are discussed in Chapter 1.

69 Sheridan, Gillett and Davies, 1999 notice a significant demographic difference in perceptions of what constitutes stalking and predict difficulty in establishing the true incidence of stalking due to the problems inherent in reconciling victim definitions of stalking with the 'official' definition in the minds of the authorities.

70 Lowney, KS and Best, J, 'Stalking strangers and lovers: changing media typifications of a new crime problem', in Best, 1995.

71 Case history 31 – the victim was targeted by a much younger man who worked in her local garden centre. At first, she considered that he had a crush on her, but his attentions became increasingly oppressive and demanding until she became afraid to leave her home.

occurred in 1992 at a time when media attention was very much focused upon the issue of celebrity stalking in which, by its nature, the stalker is usually a stranger.[72] Her sentiments are echoed by another victim who refers explicitly to the influence of media accounts of stalking:

> I failed to connect these news items with my own ordeal for the obvious reason that they seemed always to concern famous, glamorous people, who risked such attention as part of the price of being in the public eye. I wasn't famous, I wasn't beautiful, I wasn't in the public eye. I have learned, though, that the harassment I experienced is far from an isolated experience.[73]

Celebrity stalking is now recognised to account for only a small percentage of total stalking cases. Nevertheless, such cases attract media attention, thus may reasonably be perceived as more prevalent than cases involving 'ordinary' victims.

It is not just victims who fail to characterise conduct as stalking because it fails to coincide with their conceptions of what a typical stalking case involves. One man who harassed his estranged wife for approximately two years with conduct which included spreading garbage and dog excrement over her garden, making silent calls during the night and breaking into her house and causing such substantial damage that it was uninhabitable for over six weeks, was indignant that she had called him a stalker:

> She's well out of order, accusing me of stalking her. I mean, I'm not a stalker, am I? Its not like I'm some weird psycho following her around with a knife in my pocket. I'm not mad and I'm certainly not dangerous – I'd never hurt her, or anyone else for that matter. I'm just an ordinary bloke who'd had enough.[74]

Although this man admits to being responsible for all the conduct of which he is accused by his wife, he denies being a stalker, as he does not believe that he possesses the appropriate 'stalker characteristics'. He is not mentally ill, nor is he dangerous and he does not possess a weapon. The absence of these characteristics was used by the victim quoted previously to explain why she did not consider her experience to be stalking. Equally, both of these people, in addition to considering the possession of these characteristics as definitive, considered that their 'ordinariness' precluded them from being either stalker

---

72 Dietz, Matthews, van Duyne, Martell, Parry, Stewart, Warren and Crowder, 1991, pp 185–209: paper given by Wells, K and Moxey, W, Stalking Task Force, San Diego, California, at the Stalking Conference at the Bramshill Police Training Centre, 22 March 2000.

73 Cited in Wilcox, 1982, pp 232–33, 291–96.

74 Case history 30 – interview with man accused of his stalking by his estranged wife. She was not aware for some time who was responsible for what was happening to her, but had interpreted her experiences as stalking almost from the outset. She had referred to 'the stalker' and saw no reason to change her characterisation when she realised who was responsible. Thus, she was not deterred from categorising her experience as stalking even though she knew who it was (unlike the other victim). However, she did regard her experience as unusual. 'I mean, how many people's stalkers turn out to be their husbands?'

or victim. Ordinariness, both in the stalker and the victim, is given as a negation of the experience of being stalked. By implication, there must be something extraordinary about 'real' stalkers and victims or something about them that justifies what has happened. This emphasis by victims on their ordinariness suggests that they are not to blame for what happened as they were too ordinary to be stalked, hence maybe the stalker mistook them for someone less ordinary. However, this also implies that some stalking victims might well be blameworthy by the mere fact of their lack of ordinariness.

The negation of an experience as stalking need not be solely based upon the conduct involved, but may also make reference to the motivation of the stalker:

> I wouldn't call him a stalker. He doesn't hide in bushes or follow you around – well, he does follow you a bit, but he doesn't mean any harm by it.[75]

Here the traditional conception of the word 'stalking' as 'stealthy pursuit' or 'to progress in a ominous and stealthy manner' is being employed by the victim.[76] This 'hiding and following' conception is common in victim definitions of stalking. However, even when this victim acknowledges that there was an element of 'real' stalking occurring, she is still reluctant to characterise this as stalking, as she does not consider it was done with intent to harm. This illustrates the popular misconception that the stalker must be malevolent. The conception of the stalker as dangerous and in possession of a weapon implicitly acknowledges that an intention to harm is regarded as an essential prerequisite to the construction of conduct as stalking.

Therefore, the role of the social construction of stalking is twofold. The labelling of certain conduct as stalking creates a shared understanding of the phenomenon that enables victims to communicate their experiences in a way that is meaningful to their audience. However, the social construction of stalking does more than identify the relevant conduct; it also outlines the parameters of the conduct encompassed by the terminology and characterises the stalker and the victim as well as the stalking conduct itself. Although the social construction of stalking facilitated a common perception of the conduct which enabled victims to understand and communicate their experiences, it is clear that some of the shared misunderstandings have affected victims' ability to comprehend their experiences as stalking. The implications of this will be explored after the process by which the social construction of stalking emerged has been examined.

---

75 Case history 33 – this victim was the first of three victims of a 'serial' stalker. Interestingly, they all perceive their experiences differently, with the second victim being unequivocally certain that she was being stalked.

76 *Webster's Encyclopaedic Dictionary of the English Language,* 1990. The *New Oxford Dictionary* expanded its definition of 'stalk' to include 'harass or persecute with obsessive attention' in 1998.

3.4 THE INFLUENCE OF AMERICAN EXPERIENCES

The construction of a social problem occurs as the public assimilate information from a variety of sources about the nature, scope and extent of a certain condition which is presented by claims makers as problematic. This information is used to create a conception that represents a shared social understanding of the problem. Although there are numerous sources of such information, the acceptance of the condition as a social problem in other countries will clearly be influential, especially if it resulted in a legislative response. The existence of a shared language and a comparable legal system ensure that Britain is particularly responsive to legal developments in other English speaking, common law jurisdictions such as Australia, the US and Canada. The similarities between the legal systems ensure that analogous decisions can be used in a meaningful manner by the British legal system[77] and the common language renders judicial decisions, legislation and academic research readily accessible for consideration.[78] Certainly, once the government of the day decided to consider legislation to address the problem of stalking, it was the approaches taken in the US, Australia and Canada that were considered.[79]

Stalking was first recognised as a serious social problem in America where the first anti-stalking legislation was enacted in California in 1990.[80] By the end of 1993, all the States, except Maine,[81] had enacted anti-stalking legislation.[82] The publicity given to stalking in the US was influential in raising awareness of the problem and shaping the legislative response in Canada and Australia.[83] Similarly, the publicity given to stalking in Britain predominantly framed it as an American concept and a great deal of media coverage was given to American stalking cases, particularly those involving celebrities.[84]

---

77 Decisions of the courts in Commonwealth countries – especially Australia, Canada and New Zealand – and the US can be cited in the English courts as persuasive authority. This is particularly appropriate where there is a shortage or total lack of English authority on the point – Ingman, 2000, pp 324–25.

78 Jenkins, 1992, p 219.

79 Home Office, *Stalking – The Solutions*, 1996, para 4.3.

80 California Penal Code § 646.9 (West 1990 and Supp 1994).

81 Maine was slow to enact anti-stalking legislation and, in 1993, was the only American State without a specific statute to address stalking, although some protection was available under the terrorising statute and the specifically amended protective order statute – Maine Revised Statutes Annotated, tit 17-A § 210 (West 1983 and Supp 1993). Specific legislation was finally enacted in 1995 – Maine 17-A § 210 (West 1997).

82 National Criminal Justice Association, *Monograph on Implementing Antistalking Codes*, 1996, p 11.

83 Goode, 1995, pp 21–31 (Australia); Cairns-Way, 1994, pp 379–400 (Canada).

84 'US clamps down on the psychos who stalk who stalk the stars' (1992) *The Times*, 5 July; 'In the shadow of the stalker' (1996) *The Times*, 2 February; 'Inside the mind of the stalker' (1996) *Sunday Times*, 29 September; 'Stalked by a terrible obsession' (1996) *The Guardian*, 31 January.

Therefore, the importance of the American construction of stalking was clearly influential on the way in which stalking was perceived in these other jurisdictions. The role of American characterisations in shaping perceptions of social problems is well documented within sociological theory[85] and the use of American terminology to facilitate the evolution of British social problems has been termed the 'export-import trade in social labels'.[86] As the US was the first country to recognise, name and define stalking, the impact of this American characterisation on the construction of stalking in Britain is important.

Jenkins identifies two distinctions between Britain and America which can be used to account for the emergence of so many social problems in America. First, the decentralised nature of American policing provides great scope for entrepreneurial policing.[87] For example, some police forces in America were so concerned about the threat of satanic activity that they took to disseminating information and raising the profile of the problem. Although many of the claims were never substantiated, there is little doubt that the activities of the police made a significant contribution to the construction of satanism as a social problem.[88] Equally, some campaigns for stalking legislation were supported by the police, who were frustrated at the lack of effective provisions to enable them to tackle stalking.[89] Such activism would not be acceptable within the more centralised British police system which promotes homogeneity of policy and practice, leaving no scope for the championship of specific issues by individual officers. As such, this means of raising the profile of contentious issues perceived to be in need of legal protection is not available in England.[90] Secondly, the political processes are distinctly different, with Britain having fewer electoral offices and a more homogenous and centralised party political structure. This contrasts with the American system with its many elected offices within the police, judiciary and local and central politics, which encourages 'official entrepreneurship' whereby the championship of problematic conditions can provide a direct route to electoral office.[91] Equally, the system under which concerned individuals are able to testify before Congress and campaign for changes in the law places a certain degree of power in the hands of those who are directly effected to bring conditions affecting them to the attention of the authorities.[92]

---

85 Best, 1990; Richardson, Best and Bromley, 1991; Richardson and Bacon, 1991.

86 Hall, Critcher, Jefferson, Clarke and Roberts, 1978, p 27.

87 Jenkins, 1992.

88 Hicks, 1991.

89 For example, Captain Dan Draovich of the Minot Police Department supported a campaign for stalking legislation and testified before the House Judicial Committee that the police were 'unable to do their jobs due to lack of appropriate legislation'. Cited in Kolb, 1994, pp 159–86, fn 16.

90 Jenkins, 1992.

91 *Ibid.*

92 Kolb, 1994, pp 159–86.

Thus, the American system provides more scope and more incentive for police, prosecutors, those seeking public office and directly affected individuals to raise the profile of conditions which they perceive as problematic.

The way in which social problems, once established in the US, become recognised in Britain is dependent upon two factors. First, the social problems must be communicated to Britain and, secondly, these problems must be accepted as relevant by a significant sector of British society.[93] The lines of migration of American social problems include high channels, such as professional and official contacts and publications,[94] and low channels, such as the mass media and popular culture[95] whose influences permeate the 'public arenas in which social problems are framed and grow'.[96] Even if the problem is originally dismissed as outlandish, exaggerated or bizarre, the information has still been disseminated and may provide a foundation for claims about similar problems to be made in Britain or even create an expectation that similar events will inevitably occur. The knowledge may lay dormant until some connection is made between the American problem and similar events that subsequently occur in Britain. Whatever the perception of the American situation, once the information has been communicated, it provides a basis and a shape for future claims in Britain.

Although many social problems appear to originate in the US and to travel to Britain by these lines of migration, this does not necessarily ensure that the problems are accepted in the form communicated. There is no evidence of straightforward assimilation, thus it is not suggested that mere awareness of the existence of an American social problem guarantees its automatic adoption in Britain. Social problems will only be 'naturalised' if they are perceived as being relevant to existing or emergent concerns in Britain.[97] The parallel social and cultural development of Britain and the US frequently leads to a situation where similar problems do develop, but this is not automatic. If the problem is relevant to the concerns of an existing interest group, the adoption of the problem in a relatively unaltered form should be straightforward.[98] However, if the condition is not perceived as problematic within the existing social and cultural climate, the issue will remain a 'foreign news item' and not become established in Britain as a social problem at that time. Even if the problem is accepted, local considerations may alter the way in which the problem is perceived and the fundamentally different structure

---

93 Jenkins, 1992.
94 Eg, research papers, addresses to Congress, official studies and academic publications.
95 Such as films, television series, newspapers, news broadcasts and chat-shows.
96 Best, 1990, p 16.
97 Jenkins, 1992, p 225.
98 *Ibid.*

of legislative, policing and prosecution practices in Britain may lead to a different response to the problem than that formulated in the US.[99]

The American influence is frequently found in the rhetoric and emphases of British social problems, but is rarely solely responsible for initiating concern over any particular issue. The parallel social and cultural development of the two countries ensures that similar issues will arise as problematic; it is merely that the ethos of policing and political life in the US is more conducive to the identification and championship of new social problems. Although the American perspective is influential rather than determinative, the way in which a problem is defined and tackled will be a relevant factor in the construction perceptions of the problem in Britain. It is therefore relevant to consider the emergence of stalking as a social problem in the US and the extent to which this influenced the social construction of stalking in Britain.

3.5 THE CONSTRUCTION OF STALKING IN AMERICA

Studies of social problem construction usually focus upon successful claims which attract media coverage, influence public opinion and provoke an official response. However, successful claims may not represent the first attempt at bringing any particular problem into the public arena, but may instead be the culmination of a protracted series of unsuccessful claims. Claims makers compete within a social problem marketplace and will often struggle to develop a rhetoric that will attract sufficient public attention to ensure that their claim is recognised rather than any of the other claims which are simultaneously trying to attract public attention.[100] The failure of a claim does not mean that the condition is eliminated, merely that the existing problem must be repackaged in such a way that attracts the necessary attention. The revision and alteration of typifications of the problem that is involved in this repackaging are often overlooked as the successful claim, which reflects a particular construction of the problem, becomes authoritative and confers 'ownership' of the problem upon a particular group of claims makers.[101] However, earlier unsuccessful claims are often an important stage in the evolution of the construction of the problem that provide insight into the reasons why a claim was rejected and what alterations were necessary to present the problem in a way which would gain public acceptance as a social problem.[102] This process of unsuccessful claims can be seen in relation to the construction of stalking as a serious crime problem in the US.

---

99 *Ibid*, p 227.
100 Hilgartnner and Bosk, 1998.
101 Gusfield, 1981.
102 Lowney, KS and Best, J, 'Stalking strangers and lovers: changing media typifications of a new crime problem', in Best, 1995.

The influence of earlier unsuccessful claims on the construction of stalking as a serious crime problem in the US was considered by Lowney and Best, who identify three distinctive stages: first, unrelated unsuccessful claims using diverse terminology, secondly, stalking as a celebrity problem, and finally, the association between stalking and domestic violence which widened the range of potential victims.[103] During the first stage, Lowney and Best identify seven articles which covered conduct that would now be regarded as stalking. These articles use a range of terminology to describe the conduct, such as sexual harassment, obsessive fantasy and psychological rape[104] and refer to those engaging in such behaviour as lovesick, compulsive and possessive.[105] Although the conduct described in these articles is remarkably similar, the divergence of terminology explains why these apparently different conditions were not linked together, which would have strengthened the individual claims. This illustrates how crucial a universally understood terminology is to the emergence of social problems.

Despite a lack of consensus regarding terminology, the articles describe similar findings regarding the nature of the conduct and those who are likely to engage in it. The most prevalent conduct is described as following, making telephone calls, sending letters and unwanted gifts. All emphasise the non-violent nature of the conduct, although acknowledging that violence can occur in some extreme cases. Only one of the articles, written after the success of the film *Fatal Attraction*, considered the possibility of male victims of female harassers, hence the agreed construction within the articles is of conduct that it is perpetrated by men and directed at women.[106] The continuing nature of the conduct was highlighted and it was given a relational emphasis, as the cases considered were all attributed either to actual relational difficulties or an unreciprocated desire to enter into a relationship.

One respect in which these characterisations of the problem differ from the construction of stalking which finally emerged is the tendency to attribute some blame to the victims.[107] This was so of the perpetrators,[108] the victims[109] and the experts.[110] The understanding that victims were in some

103 *Ibid.*
104 Mithers, 1982, p 36; Wilcox, 1982, pp 232–33, 291–96.
105 Wilcox, 1982, pp 232–33, 291–296; Heil, 1986, pp 128–30, 136–38.
106 Kunen, 1987, pp 89–98.
107 The issue of victim-blame in the current construction of stalking is explored above.
108 'I'll say I have a problem, the woman I love doesn't love me. It's the worst thing that can happen to anyone; I have no idea how to deal with it,' in Wilcox, 1982, pp 232–33, 293.
109 'He said I'd provoked him into anger last night and I had the guilty uneasy feeling that maybe that was partially true,' in Anonymous, 1980, pp 32–34, 39, 40.
110 'They can often get away with it because their ex-girlfriends unwittingly allow them to ... [a victim pursued for over 10 years] admits that even when [her former partner] was harassing her with phone calls and driving by her house in the middle of the night, she gave him a scarf she had knitted for him,' in Heil, 1986, pp 128–30, 138.

way responsible for their plight may have created an unsympathetic reaction towards those who complained of such conduct as the victims found the authorities reluctant to intervene and unreceptive to the impact of the experience. Complaints were invariably classified as 'boyfriend trouble', regardless of any actual relationship between the parties, and one judge, when granting an injunction prohibiting a man from continuing to harass his former partner, was persuaded to grant an injunction against the woman prohibiting her from cohabiting or spending the night with anyone other than her former partner on the grounds that it would be unfaithful to their relationship.[111] The other difficulty in convincing the authorities that the situation merited legal intervention was due to the non-violent nature of the conduct, as there was a lack of sympathy towards the idea of emotional harm at the time.[112]

The construction of the problem as relational tended to normalise the conduct even in circumstances where it was clear that no relationship had existed between the parties. John Hinckley's conduct towards actress Jodie Foster, which culminated in him shooting then President Ronald Reagan, was characterised as psychological rape and attributed to his desire to form a relationship with her.[113] As forensic psychologist Laud Humphreys noted, 'to some extent, all love behaviour is obsessive behaviour' and this characterisation of the conduct as based upon unreciprocated love is common to all the articles.[114]

Therefore, early characterisations of behaviour that would now be termed stalking were of non-violent conduct directed primarily by men towards women, who could be regarded as partially responsible for the situation, and which occurred predominantly, although not exclusively, in a relational context. This characterisation of the conduct failed to attract public support and failed to become regarded as a social problem because:

> [W]hilst occasional press coverage viewed the behaviour as problematic, the issue had not yet been packaged and presented to command public attention.[115]

The repackaging of the problem in a way that did attract public attention and prompt an official response occurred with the emergence of celebrity stalking which shared the essential elements of the previous claims, but which was typified in a different way.

---

111 Wilcox, 1982, pp 232–33, 293.

112 'A jury will want to know why *emotional* harassment is damaging when the victim is never touched. I see only six prosecutable cases of emotional harassment a year': Susan Kaplan, Deputy District Attorney for Los Angeles, quoted in Wilcox, 1982, pp 232–33, 295.

113 'I would abandon this idea of getting Reagan if only I could get your heart': letter from John Hinckley quoted in Wilcox, 1982, p 233.

114 Lowney, KS and Best, J, 'Stalking strangers and lovers: changing media typifications of a new crime problem', in Best, 1995.

115 *Ibid*, p 39.

The incident which is accepted as the impetus for the first anti-stalking law was the murder of 21 year old actress Rebecca Schaeffer by obsessed fan Robert Bardo.[116] After almost two years of sending letters and gifts to Rebecca Schaeffer through her New York agent, Bardo employed a private detective to obtain her address. He then travelled across America to her home, armed with a gun, having left a note to his sister, explaining where he was going, which finished: 'If I can't have her, no one shall.' Bardo rang the doorbell of Rebecca Schaeffer's home and shot her in the chest when she answered the door. He was sentenced to life imprisonment with no possibility of parole for first degree murder aggravated by the special circumstances of lying in wait.[117]

This case received world wide attention and, although it was not the first serious attack on a celebrity by an obsessed fan,[118] the focus this time was on the conduct which preceded the violence as much as on the violence itself. The stabbing of actress Theresa Saldana, for example, had been typified as an example of violent crime with little attention being paid to the obsessive pursuit that preceded the stabbing.[119] Rebecca Schaeffer's murder, however, became the typifying example of what the media termed 'star stalking'.[120]

Victims of star stalking were typified as celebrities and public figures of either sex and, despite the association with erotomania,[121] a psychiatric disorder which predominantly affects women, there appeared to be no suggestion that women were more likely to become star stalkers than men.[122]

---

116 Carmody, 1994, pp 68–71; Diacova, 1995, pp 389–421; Holmes, 1993, pp 317–27.

117 Salame, 1993, pp 67–111.

118 Eg, in 1982, Arthur Jackson repeatedly stabbed actress Theresa Saldana causing her serious injuries. Jackson was so obsessed with the actress that he moved from Scotland to America to track her down and be near her. In 1981, John Hinckley's obsession with actress Jodie Foster led him to shoot then President Ronald Reagan so that she would take notice of him and that their names would be linked in history. Reagan survived the shooting, although one of his bodyguards did not, and Hinckley was found not guilty of second degree murder by reason of insanity. In 1980, John Lennon died after being shot by Mark Chapman, a fan who had asked for his autograph only hours before the shooting. Chapman was refused parole in 2000, having served 20 years for second degree murder. Interestingly, horror writer Stephen King has been stalked for several years by Stephen Lightfoot, who claims to have evidence that Stephen King shot John Lennon – 'US clamps down on the psychos who stalk the stars' (1992) The Times, 5 July.

119 The differences in typification of these two similar cases illustrates the importance of contingency in social problems construction. Lowney and Best examine the external and internal contingencies which determined the way in which these cases were constructed – Lowney, KS and Best, J, 'Stalking strangers and lovers: changing media typifications of a new crime problem', in Best, 1995, pp 52–53.

120 Ibid.

121 American Psychiatric Association (1987) DSM-III-R, p 199: 'The central theme of an erotic delusion is that one is loved by another ... The person about whom this conviction is held is usually of higher status, such as a famous person or a superior at work, and may even be a complete stranger. Efforts to contact the object of the delusion, through telephone calls, letters, gifts, visits and even surveillance and stalking are common'.

122 Cosgrove, 1990, pp 31–32; Segal, 1989, pp 1261–66.

The connection between star stalking and erotomania was the first characterisation of the conduct as a mental health problem as earlier claims had attributed the conduct to ineptitude, loneliness and lack of social skills.[123] Thus, star stalkers were portrayed as suffering from mental disturbance which caused them to develop an obsession with a celebrity victim. The extent of the obsession was inexplicable and unreasonable, hence star stalking emerged as an irrational and essentially random act which, as with all random crime, absolves the victim from blame,[124] unlike earlier claims which presented the victim as partially responsible for the situation. Another major distinction between star stalking and earlier claims was the redefinition of the conduct as violent. The conduct, whether overtly or implicitly threatening, bizarre or merely inappropriate, was characterised as potentially dangerous.[125] Equally, where earlier claims had portrayed the conduct as ongoing, star stalking was presented as escalating – the situation was likely to deteriorate rather than merely to continue.[126]

Thus, star stalking became constructed as an unpredictable and potentially lethal form of random violence and attracted significantly more media coverage than previous claims.[127] This construction was accepted by the public and officials and led to the enactment of the first anti-stalking legislation[128] and the creation of the Threat Management Unit, which was established within the Los Angeles Police Department specifically to deal with stalking cases.[129]

Therefore, although the behaviour concerned does not appear to be materially different, it was presented very differently and gained acceptance as a serious social problem. The identification of a link between a single troublesome event and a pattern of problematic behaviour is an important element of the construction of social problems as the high profile event is used

---

123 Cosgrove, 1990, pp 31–32; Wilcox, 1982, pp 232–33, 291–96; 'A fatal obsession with the stars' (1989) *Time*, 31 July, pp 43–44.

124 Lowney, KS and Best, J, 'Stalking strangers and lovers: changing media typifications of a new crime problem', in Best, 1995.

125 Dietz, Matthews, van Duyne, Martell, Parry, Stewart, Warren and Crowther, 1991, pp 185–209.

126 Lowney, KS and Best, J, 'Stalking strangers and lovers: changing media typifications of a new crime problem', in Best, 1995.

127 *Ibid.*

128 Californian Penal Code § 646.9 (West 1990 and Supp 1994). Any person who wilfully, maliciously and repeatedly follows or harasses another person and who makes a credible threat with the intent to place that person in reasonable fear of death or great bodily injury is guilty of the crime of stalking. This original definition was amended in 1992 to include threats to family members, in 1993 to widen the definition of credible threat to include implied threats, in 1994 to improve the treatment of stalking victims, in particular regarding arrangements for the release of convicted stalkers, and in 1995 to remove the specific intent requirement mandating only an objective standard of fear on the part of the victim: Jordan, 1995, pp 363–83.

129 Lane, 1992, pp 23–29.

to publicise the extent of the problem. This involves 'defining a particular incident as an instance of some larger problem'.[130] This key juxtaposition occurred in California when the murder of actress Rebecca Schaeffer was linked retrospectively with the stabbing of actress Theresa Saldana in 1982, thus establishing stalking as a long standing problem, and with the murder of four women in Orange County, California, all of whom had obtained restraining orders to protect them from harassment by their former partners prior to the murder.[131] This association with ordinary victims widened the ambit of the problem beyond celebrities and led to its further reconstruction as a domestic violence problem. This augmentation of the relatively narrow focus of star stalking to encompass similar behaviour in a domestic or relational context is an example of domain expansion, whereby once a dramatic example of problematic conduct has been used to draw attention to a particular issue, its domain is expanded to include other similar conduct which also requires recognition.[132]

Stalking became the common denominator which linked star stalking and domestic abuse. The problem continued to be well publicised and other States introduced stalking legislation, usually in response to a serious and high profile local incident.[133] The problem became repackaged as a woman's issue and was seen as a precursor to serious violence, typically occurring in a relational context. The conduct was characterised as involving a deliberate intent to cause harm to the victim:

> The verb 'stalk' is defined as: (1) 'to move threateningly or menacingly'; (2) 'to pursue by tracking'; and (3) to go stealthily towards an animal 'for the purpose of killing or capturing it'. These definitions say much about the crime of stalking, suggesting that a stalker is a hunter, is dangerous, and thus should be avoided if at all possible.[134]

In addition to being constructed as violent and intentionally harmful, stalking was also portrayed as a common problem. An unattributed claim that 'up to 200,000 people exhibit a stalker's traits'[135] gained credence with repetition although, as is frequently the case with statistical estimates of social problem

---

130 Lowney and Best, 'Stalking strangers and lovers: changing media typifications of a new crime problem', in Best, 1995, p 48.

131 Morville, 1993, pp 921–35; Corwin, 1993.

132 'Regardless of the specific issue at hand, domain expansion ultimately involves rendering more and more conduct and/or social conditions "at issue".' Jenness, V, 'Hate crimes in the United States: the transformation of injured persons into victims and the extension of victim status to multiple constituencies', in Best, 1995, pp 232–33; Best, 1990.

133 'Behind almost every State stalking Bill has been at least one local tragedy': Morville, 1993, pp 921–35.

134 Perez, 1993, p 265.

135 The earliest incidence of this claim appears in Tharp, 1992, pp 28–30.

magnitude,[136] 'this number soon took on a life of its own; it was often repeated, but never examined or explained'.[137]

Thus, stalking became established as a serious and prevalent social problem in the US and, by the end of 1993, all States except Maine[138] had enacted stalking legislation.[139] Estimates of victimisation varied enormously,[140] but the consensus opinion was that stalking was increasing and was becoming a 'national epidemic'.[141] The association between domestic violence and stalking strengthened as the same characteristics were attributed to both forms of behaviour and stalking became perceived to be a manifestation of domestic violence. This association was sedulously fostered by domestic violence campaigners who were anxious to use this 'visible issue with connotations of extreme violence' to improve the legal protection available for victims of domestic violence.[142] This claim to 'ownership' of stalking appeared successful. For example, Illinois enacted stalking legislation following the murder of four women by their former partners after substantial pressure to legislate from the Illinois Coalition Against Domestic Violence.[143] Newspaper coverage of the decision to legislate emphasised the domestic violence context of stalking:

> Hundreds of women are threatened and harassed and intimidated by ex-boyfriends or ex-husbands ... [The stalking legislation] has the potential to be a helpful weapon against domestic violence.[144]

This typification of stalking as a form of domestic violence prevails as the predominant characterisation of the conduct in the US.[145] Certainly, this was

---

136 Best, 1990.

137 Lowney and Best, 'Stalking strangers and lovers: changing media typifications of a new crime problem', in Best, 1995, p 42.

138 Although no specific legislative measures were introduced to deal with stalking, protection was available under the terrorising provisions and the specifically amended protective order provisions. However, specific stalking legislation was finally enacted in 1995: Maine Revised Statutes Annotated, 17-A § 210 (West 1997).

139 National Criminal Justice Association, *Monograph on Implementing Antistalking Codes*, 1996, p 11.

140 Eg, it was estimated that one person in 40 would be stalked in their lifetime in Safran, 1992, pp 183, 263–66, one person in 30 in Tharp, 1992, pp 28–30, and one person in 20 in CNN *Prime News*, 'Michigan legal system takes stalking very seriously', 1 January 1993, cited in Lowney, KS and Best, J, 'Stalking strangers and lovers: changing media typifications of a new crime problem', in Best, 1995, p 42.

141 Gilligan, 1992, pp 285–342.

142 Lowney, KS and Best, J, 'Stalking strangers and lovers: changing media typifications of a new crime problem' in Best, 1995, p 43.

143 O'Reilly, 1993, pp 821–64.

144 'Police need help to stop stalkers' (1992) *Chicago Tribune*, 18 November, cited in Lowney, KS and Best, J, 'Stalking strangers and lovers: changing media typifications of a new crime problem', in Best, 1995, p 44.

145 Burgess *et al*, 1997, pp 389–403; Coleman, 1997, pp 420–32.

the construction of stalking that was adopted when the problem was 'exported' to Canada.[146]

The table below compares the characteristics identified by the typifying examples employed by the media in the US during the three stage evolutionary process of stalking: unsuccessful claims (1980–1988), star stalking (1989–1991) and domestic violence (1992–June 1994).

Figure 3.1   Characteristics of typifying examples of stalking used by the media in the US

	1980–1988 (%)	1989–1991 (%)	1992–June 1994 (%)
Victim is female	86	83	94
Victim is a celebrity	18	48	16
Stalker is male	82	78	90
Stalker and victim have been engaged or married	14	5	18
Stalker and victim are strangers	24	68	19
Stalking leads to homicide	5	10	30
	(n = 22)	(n = 23)	(n = 170)

Thus, the construction of stalking as a social problem was a progressive process which involved distinct periods of evolution. The final portrayal of stalking as a violent crime committed against women by their former partners was built upon earlier claims about star stalking, which in turn has precursors in still earlier claims about harassment, obsession and psychological rape. These three distinct stages in the construction of stalking all describe essentially the same phenomenon, but differ in their characterisation of the sex of both stalker and victim, the nature of the relationship between them, the degree to which the victim shares responsibility for the situation, the psychology and motivation of the stalker and the potential for the situation to end in violence. The issue was packaged in different ways during its quest for attention and it was by this the process that stalking ultimately emerged as a prominent social problem in America. Thus there was a ready-made notion of stalking that could be used as a basis for claims making in order to raise the profile of stalking in England.

---

146 'Stalking is one vicious manifestation of a broader spectrum of violence against women – one part of the multi-faceted whole, integrally linked to the systematic social, economic and political inequalities experienced daily by Canadian women': Cairns-Way, 1994, pp 379–400.

3.6 THE SOCIAL CONSTRUCTION OF STALKING IN ENGLAND

As has been discussed, it is unusual for social problems to be adopted unquestioningly and without modification in another country, thus the construction of stalking developed in America was not merely exported wholesale to England. A problem will not be 'naturalised' merely by awareness of its existence elsewhere; it must also be perceived as relevant to the emergent or existing concerns in the 'host' country. However, the availability of a terminology and examples of the conduct concerned provided a sound basis for the emergence of stalking in England. Moreover, it did link with two existing concerns – the boundaries of acceptable sexual behaviour and the need to acknowledge the seriousness of psychological injury. The pre-packaged problem and the receptive environment combined to provide fertile soil in which the seeds of stalking as a social problem could flourish.

References to stalking first appear, albeit infrequently, in the news media in 1992. A search of the database at the National Newspaper Archive at Colindale revealed eight relevant references to stalking in this year. These were of two types. The first category would inevitably convey the notion of stalking as leading inexorably to rape and murder as four stories reported sexual attacks and homicide that was preceded by a period of stalking. Despite the references to the 'stalker' who committed these offences, they do not appear to be correctly categorised as stalking cases. More accurately, these were cases where the primary objective of the perpetrator was the commission of the final crime, rape or murder, and the stalking was carried out in order to achieve this objective. This is in contrast to 'real' stalking cases in which the stalking itself is the main focus, although the situation may deteriorate to such an extent that more serious offences, even murder, are committed. Despite the focus upon stalking as a precursor to rape and murder, little attention is dedicated to these stories that merit only a cursory account of the facts. The second category of newspaper articles that make reference to stalking during this time are features concerning celebrity stalking in America. Articles in *The Times* and *The Guardian* do make reference to the fact that stalking is not restricted to celebrities and that 'perfectly ordinary women get stalked by nutters too',[147] but this is very much incidental to the main focus of the articles which detail celebrity cases. These editorials make frequent reference to the likelihood that stalkers of both celebrities and 'ordinary' people suffer from mental health problems. For example, *The Guardian* refers to stalkers as:

> Deviant creatures, loners, losers, compensating for their own inadequacies by writing endless letters to Shakin' Stevens.[148]

---

147 'Looking for trouble: fan letter to the adoring masses' (1992) *The Guardian*, 28 May.
148 *Ibid.*

Moreover, these feature articles all draw attention to the more extreme and dramatic consequences of stalking. All three make reference to Mark Chapman and John Hinckley, hence emphasising extreme cases involving murderous intent and potentially fatal outcomes. In addition to this, the articles feature unusual and outrageous acts by stalkers that emphasis the mental health issue. For example, *The Times* relates the story of Susan Dyer who lived under the floorboards of her former lover's house for months prior to discovery. The article continues with an account of the case of William Perry, who was obsessed with actress Olivia Newton-John and believed that she was sending him messages through her eyes. In his attempt to get to her, he murdered five people including his own parents. When he was arrested, he was watching seven televisions simultaneously, all of which were showing only static and upon which he had painted huge pairs of eyes.[149]

Thus stalkers are portrayed as dangerous and mentally ill with a tendency towards the commission of violent crime. There is little relational reference here; the message is that even when the victims are not celebrities, the mentally disordered stalker develops a dangerous obsession with a total stranger who is predominantly, but not exclusively, a woman. Although more references to stalking occur in 1993, the themes portrayed are the same. The stalker is a dangerous, mentally ill man who fixates on a celebrity or complete stranger, often with drastic consequences. The majority of the 22 articles appearing in 1993 mention the stabbing of tennis player Monica Seles by a stalker during a tennis match. The focus is still firmly on extreme examples of conduct:

> Reason has long deserted the fan who sent Cher a fingernail with the message 'next time it'll be part of my body'. He then sent her an ear.[150]

The focus of the 44 newspaper items that addressed stalking in 1994 was somewhat altered. Although the problem of celebrity stalking remains a constant theme, there is greater emphasis on the stalking of 'ordinary' victims, both by estranged partners and strangers. References to stalking as 'normal relationships gone wrong' are not uncommon and there is a preconception that all stalkers are seeking sexual relationships with the victim.

It is in 1994 that the first questions are raised as to whether the English legal system ought to intervene in stalking cases. Great emphasis is placed upon the inability of the law to protect victims until the conduct escalates to include serious violence, which is still portrayed as an almost inevitable consequence of stalking. Although stalking is beginning to be characterised as a legal problem,[151] there is greater emphasis upon the behaviour as a

---

149 'US clamps down on the psychos who stalk the stars' (1992) *The Times*, 5 July.
150 'Men who must pursue women' (1993) *The Guardian*, 26 June.
151 'Can laws stop the obsessed?' (1993) *The Times*, 22 February.

challenge for the medical profession.[152] Thus, the extent of stalking is recognised as greater attention is paid to non-celebrity victims, and the beginnings of the construction of stalking as a legal problem can be seen. This is particularly so following the conviction of Christopher Gelder for inflicting psychological grievous bodily harm as a result of a campaign of persecutory telephone calls, although the conviction was later quashed because of a misdirection by the trial judge.[153] These themes continue, with no appreciable variation, in the newspaper coverage of stalking in 1995.

In 1996, the attention paid to stalking by the news media increases dramatically, with 356 articles focusing upon the subject, particularly the issue of the extent and efficacy of existing legal protection. There is no longer any doubt that stalking is a legal problem. Instead, the debate concerns whether there is sufficient protection under the current law or whether new legislative measures are required.[154] The conviction and imprisonment of Anthony Burstow for inflicting grievous bodily harm received extremely high profile media coverage.[155] The Stalking Bill proposed by backbench Labour MP Janet Anderson was generally well received, although some reservations were expressed that its breadth would include those engaged in lawful conduct.[156] Predominantly, the question was presented as 'what should the scope of the new law be?' rather than 'should there be a new law?' The then Conservative Government's rejection of the Stalking Bill attracted a great deal of negative attention that did not really abate until the emergence of the Protection from Harassment Bill in December.[157]

Thus, it was not until 1996 that stalking became firmly established in England as a serious social problem that necessitated a legislative response. Although the construction of stalking was already complete when it was

---

152 'A dangerous obsession' (1994) *The Observer*, 9 January; 'In the mind of the stalker' (1994) *The Times*, 31 October; 'Stalked by a terrible obsession' (1994) *The Observer*, 27 November.

153 'Judge's error frees clerk jailed for anonymous calls' (1994) *The Times*, 16 December.

154 'The law and the stalker', *The Independent*, 30 January 1996; 'Police lack powers over dangerous obsession' (1996) *Daily Telegraph*, 30 January.

155 'Stalker jailed for terrifying sex obsession' (1996) *The Independent*, 5 March; 'Stalker jailed for causing grievous bodily harm' (1996) *The Times*, 5 March; 'Stalker jailed for mental GBH' (1996) *The Guardian*, 5 March; 'Nightmare ends with smile as stalker jailed for three years' (1996) *Daily Telegraph*, 5 March.

156 'Why not all stalkers are criminals' (1996) *The Independent*, 31 January; 'In the shadow of the stalker' (1996) *The Times*, 2 February.

157 'Ministers block Labour Bill to outlaw stalking' (1996) *The Times*, 11 May; 'Michael Howard's contempt for stalking victims' (1996) *Daily Mirror*, 11 May; 'Call for tighter law as victim tells of stalking campaign' (1996) *The Times*, 3 September; 'Law change all after stalking case acquittal' (1996) *The Guardian*, 18 September; 'Law in urgent need of reform' (1996) *The Independent*, 19 September; 'Judge says stalking should be a criminal offence' (1996) *The Independent*, 29 September; 'Stopping stalkers: how would the law change?' (1996) *Daily Telegraph*, 19 October; 'Its bad to stalk ... but the law needs careful drafting' (1996) *The Times*, 19 October; 'Major buckles as Labour calls Tories' bluff' (1996) *The Guardian*, 24 October; 'Stalking legislation clear the Commons' (1996) *Daily Telegraph*, 19 December.

'exported' from the US, this was not immediately adopted in England, despite the relatively high profile that the American response to stalking received in the news media. Some degree of similarity can be seen between the construction of stalking in England and America, with an initial focus on celebrity stalking before the focus widened to include 'ordinary' victims. The English news media portrayal of the stalker as a mentally disordered and dangerous offender does not appear to have a parallel in the American construction of stalking, which instead focused strongly on the relational aspect of stalking. Hence, it can be seen that the American construction of stalking was not adopted without amendment, but was merely the introductory means by which stalking first achieved publicity in England.

3.7 CONSTRUCTION AND REALITY

From the outset, this chapter has been based upon the assumption that the social construction of a problem does not necessarily correspond to the actuality of the problem. The extent to which this is true in relation to any particular social problem is virtually incalculable. To the strict constructionist, the actuality of the problem is of little or no significance; the construction of the problem is the actuality, and the objective reality of the existence or extent of the problem is immaterial. The contextual constructionist approach may prioritise the construction of the problem over the actuality when seeking to account for the emergence of a social problem, but does not discount the relevance and importance of the objective reality of the problem.

For the purposes of evaluating the efficacy of the legal response to stalking, it is important to evaluate the extent to which the construction and reality of stalking coincide. Two predominant typifications of stalkers emerge from an analysis of newspaper accounts of stalking. First, the stalker is characterised as a mentally disordered and dangerous man whose obsession with a celebrity or 'ordinary' stranger is likely to culminate in violence. The second characterisation is based upon the conception of a 'normal relationship gone wrong' in which the stalker, still predominantly male, is unable to accept the end of, or absence of, a relationship and will resort to extreme measures in order to re-establish, or initiate, the relationship. If the law had sought to respond only to those typifications of stalking, it is likely that a higher threshold of liability would have been established as media accounts of stalking prior to the enactment of the Protection from Harassment Act 1997 tended to focus on the more serious and extreme cases.

Fortunately, in this respect, the Protection from Harassment Act 1997 adopted an extremely general approach to the conduct that was prohibited, thus creating a wide ranging offence that encompasses a far greater breadth of stalking, and other forms of harassment, than the prototypical representations created within the media. The coverage of the nature and characteristics of stalking presented in the preceding two chapters illustrates the immense variability in conduct and motivation that can arise in stalking cases. Clearly, many of the examples used in these chapters would not fall within the prototypical models constructed within the media. Does this mean that such cases cannot be considered to amount to stalking? On one level, it is irrelevant, as legislation was enacted that prohibited the wider notion of harassment and which sets a low threshold of criminality. So the experiences of the victims would come within the remit of the law, thus it is immaterial whether or not their experience is categorised as stalking. However, on another level, it is of fundamental importance that all conduct that has the characteristics of stalking should be correctly identified. Without challenges to the prevailing perception of stalking, the construction presented in the media will become reality, a situation that may be detrimental to many who are victimised by the unwanted attention of others. Misconceptions as to the nature and severity of stalking exacerbate the harm caused by victimisation as the victim is isolated not only by the behaviour of the stalker, but also by an absence of support and understanding of others. Moreover, such misconceptions extend to the authorities and may lead to a victim's case not be addressed correctly because it is not within the popular perception of stalking cases.

3.8 SOURCES OF (MIS)CONSTRUCTION

One factor that needs to be addressed in order to understand how a social construction of stalking arose that did not directly correspond to the reality of stalking, is the processes involved in presenting the information that forms the basis of social understanding.

Clearly, the news media is an incredibly influential source of information upon which public perceptions of crime are based. It has been said that crime information represents some of the most potent imagery that the media can present:

> People become informed about crime in a variety of ways. Some people commit crime and others are victimised. Some people learn about crime from friends, relatives or neighbours who have been involved in the criminal justice system as workers or clients. Most people, however, do not have direct or indirect exposure to crime as either defendants or victims. These people, the vast majority, rely on the mass news media for their information on crime and victimisation. In this way, the news media act as a surrogate for members of the public who have limited exposure to crime and violence and as a supplement to those with more direct exposure. Accordingly, the news media can be influential in shaping opinions and attitudes about crime.[158]

---

158 Chermak, S, 'Crime in the news media: a refined understanding of how crimes become news', in Barak, 1994.

However, the presentation of news stories by the media does not present a full or complete representation of the reality of criminal behaviour. Its coverage is selective, focusing on stories that are likely to capture the attention of the reader. Moreover, the decrease in court reporters has led to a more limited availability of crime stories. There is one single Press Association reporter for the whole of the London court system, excluding the Royal Courts of Justice. Thus only one reporter covers 11 Crown Courts, including the Old Bailey, which deal with approximately 113 cases every day. Clearly, it is not possible for one person to cover each of the cases. Similar situations exist outside London. John Staples, the only regular reporter covering 10 courtrooms for Southwest News, states:

> For every one story we cover at the magistrates' and the Crown Court, about 10 are missed. It's luck a lot of the time.[159]

This fall in the number of court reporters is attributed to the increasing disinclination of newspapers to cover crime, however serious, unless there is a sensational element involved:

> There was a time when pretty much every murder would be fully covered and the newspapers wanted the stories ... Now, many murders go by without even getting a mention.[160]

Stories that are most likely to be selected are those involving crimes that are novel or dramatic. Ordinary crime is not newsworthy. The news media select exceptional, unusual and violent crimes because these stories sell newspapers.[161] Moreover, stories involving celebrities, however minor, are likely to be selected in preference to stories involving ordinary people.[162] For example, despite the dearth of court reporters available to cover serious criminal trials, Fleet Street reporters flocked to Woking magistrates' court when Tara Palmer-Tomkinson was prosecuted for speeding on the M3 motorway. This story appeared in every single national newspaper. Contrast this with the conviction of a rapist in October 1998 who had stalked his two victims, attacked and raped them, and then spent over £11,000 on their credit cards. The rapist was sentenced to 14 years, but the case was not covered by any of the newspapers, thus the rapist escaped public exposure, the victims had no public acknowledgment of their suffering and the police received no recognition of their success in catching the man.[163]

As such, the construction of crime news is distorted by the news making process. The news media have their own criteria for determining what stories

---

159 'Getting away with murder' (1999) *The Guardian*, 11 January.
160 *Ibid.*
161 Chermak, S, 'Crime in the news media: a refined understanding of how crimes become news', in Barak, 1994.
162 Roshier, B, 'The selection of crime news by the press', in Cohen and Young, 1981.
163 'Getting away with murder' (1999) *The Guardian*, 11 January.

will capture the public attention. Decisions as to what stories to include, what aspects of the story to highlight and to discard, and when the story should be released, are all made with the primary objective of attracting public attention.[164] As such, the news media present a carefully selected microcosm of the cases available which emphasise the sensational aspects of the stories.[165] Stalking cases that are bizarre, extreme, dramatic or involve celebrities are presented to the public with little or no indication that these are anything other than standard stalking cases. This forms the basis for the public perception of stalking, the benchmark against which actual experiences are measured to determine whether they amount to stalking. Few stalking cases will be as sensational or serious as those selected for inclusion in the newspapers, hence the news media are effectively acting as 'gatekeepers' who regulate access to the criminal justice system.[166] If a person does not interpret his or her experience as stalking because it does not coincide with the construction represented by the media, the matter will not be reported to the police. Consequently the victim is not afforded the opportunity to have his or her experience classified as a crime. This excludes non-prototypical cases from the legal system and creates a false construction of stalking that will continue to perpetuate itself. This results in a self-fulfilling prophesy whereby the media construction of stalking becomes the reality as a result of its influence on public perceptions.

Other agencies can also operate as 'gatekeepers' with the power to determine which cases are afforded access to the criminal justice system. Not only do these gatekeeping activities operate to filter out cases that, for whatever reason, do not accord with the gatekeepers' perception of a 'real' stalking case but, in doing so, this has a direct influence on the public perception of stalking. If a person reports his or her experiences to the police, believing them to constitute stalking, and the police refuse to take action, this person will reinterpret the experience as non-stalking. Clearly, the role of the police, although important, has a more individual impact than the media, as the construction of stalking adopted by the police is communicated to the public on a far smaller scale. Nonetheless, the police play a more direct role in shaping the construction of stalking. If the victim is uncertain of his or her legal position, reliance is placed upon the police to provide a clear, accurate and unbiased indication of whether a crime has been committed against them. However, the police themselves may respond to the construction of the problem and prioritise this over the reality of the victim's experience. The susceptibility of public officials to constructions of crime has been acknowledged:

---

164 Erikson, Baranek and Chan, 1989, p 6.

165 'Their criteria usually revolve around choosing particularly horrific cases; or if there is someone important involved; or if there is some sort of unusual twist': 'Getting away with murder' (1999) *The Guardian*, 11 January.

166 White, 1950, pp 383–90.

> Legal agents, no less than other human beings, must actively construct their own perceptual world ... The distance between perception and reality is likely to be especially great in the case of the criminal-selection process, because legal agents most often respond to events that they did not actually observe ... From the very beginning of legal processing, officials must depend on interpretations, stereotypes, definitions and accounts at least one step removed from the actual events they describe. In fact, it is in these accounts, coloured in turn by typifications of the agents themselves, that are the reality of criminal processing – not the events on which those presentations are based.[167]

Thus, a police officer, faced with a complaint from a stalking victim, evaluates the content of the complaint according to his understanding of stalking, a perception that may be based upon a combination of sources, including media representations, to determine whether it constitutes an actionable case. If it does not, his explanation to the victim will influence the way in which the victim reconstructs his or her understanding of stalking. For example, one victim was told that her situation did not amount to stalking because she was an acquaintance of the stalker. The police officer explained that stalking was carried out by strangers who had some kind of harmful intent and that her situation was merely a private dispute that did not merit police intervention. The victim accepted the police officer's determination that her experience was not stalking:

> It was just like being stalked but by somebody you know. All the things he did were stalker things so I thought it was stalking, but the policeman said that it wasn't and I hadn't realised that who it was made a difference.[168]

Once the police officer had advised the victim that her situation did not amount to stalking, she no longer conceptualised it as such, but termed her experience as 'like stalking but not by a stalker'. The conduct in question was carried out by a neighbour of the victim and included persistent silent and abusive telephone calls, standing in the bushes watching her house, following her when she went out and waiting outside her place of work. It is difficult to interpret these actions as anything other than stalking, but the victim abandoned her attempts at obtaining police intervention without questioning the accuracy of the advice of the first police officer she encountered. Her conception of stalking was adjusted to coincide with the police officer's construction thanks to her acceptance of his authority on the issue. In this way, an individual's contact with the police and others who are considered to be authoritative provides a means by which their construction of stalking is refined and amended. Unfortunately, this process does not necessarily result in a more accurate construction of stalking and may operate to reinforce and perpetuate misconceptions of stalking.

---

167 LaFree, 1989, p 236.
168 Case history 26.

Another potential source of information that has a strong influence on public perceptions of crime is found within the legal profession. Like the police, solicitors are regarded by the public and the media as authoritative sources of legal advice. The media may approach solicitors for guidance when gathering information regarding a particular crime for a feature article, as this adds authoritative weight to the content. Equally, an individual may seek advice from a solicitor either in addition to approaching the police or as an alternative. Thus, there is potential for solicitors to influence the social construction of stalking either directly, by advice to an individual, or indirectly, by general comments that are disseminated by the media. As such, legal advisors, like the police and the media, may play a powerful role in the shaping of public perceptions of crime.

Thus, it is clear that the experiences of victims will not always coincide with the public perception of stalking. This divergence may have several notable consequences. It may prevent the victim from interpreting his or her experiences as stalking, which will deter the victim from recourse to the law. This perpetuates the popular perception of stalking, as it creates a situation whereby only cases that fall within this perception come to the attention of the legal authorities. Clearly, this has implications in terms of the efficacy of legal intervention. If the full range of potential offences is not brought to the attention of the appropriate authorities, any response to the situation will not encompass these situations. The reaction of those deemed to be authoritative, such as the police and solicitors, may confirm, adapt or reject an individual's construction of stalking. The social perception of stalking is not a fixed, constant or unalterable entity, but one that is malleable and a reaction to shifts in social constructions. Thus, it is essential that the police react appropriately to stalking complaints and do not preclude an individual from having recourse to the criminal justice system merely because the individual circumstances do not reveal the prototypical stalking case.

3.9 CONCLUSION

Stalking encompasses an immense range of diverse activities undertaken for a multitude of reasons. In the face of clear evidence that this type of behaviour is not new, an explanation of the emergence of stalking as a serious social problem was sought. A constructionist analysis reveals how stalking emerged as a result of claims making in the US, from whence it migrated to England, where it was adapted to reflect prevailing social concerns. The representation of stalking in the media has proved to be an influential factor that has shaped public perceptions of stalking although it is clear that such perceptions are amenable to modification in the light of the reaction of those who are regarded as authoritative. It was during this period of emergence and modification that a legal response was deemed to be appropriate to address stalking. The following chapters will address the challenges presented to the legal system by the emergence of stalking; first by examining the efficacy of the existing law, then by considering how the law sought to adapt to provide a more effective means of intervention, and finally by assessing the legislative response to stalking.

CHAPTER 4

REMEDIES PRIOR TO THE PROTECTION FROM HARASSMENT ACT 1997

The preceding chapters established the nature of stalking, the impact of this behaviour on victims and the justifications for legal intervention in this area. What has yet to be determined is whether there was a necessity for new legislative provisions to address stalking or whether, given the nature of the conduct involved, the existing criminal and civil law provided adequate legal protection for victims of stalking. The next two chapters consider the various ways in which a stalking victim could rely upon the law for assistance prior to the enactment of the Protection from Harassment Act 1997 and question whether, given the extent of this protection, there was an identifiable gap in the law which left stalking victims with no adequate means of legal redress, thus necessitating the enactment of specific legislation.

The immense variability of the conduct concerned makes any generalisation as to the nature of stalking difficult. It is, however, possible to identify several broad categories of conduct. The conduct that has been observed to characterise stalking, both in the course of empirical research and as documented in the existing literature, can be divided into broad categories which will be used to explore potential areas of legal intervention. A distinction can be drawn between stalking cases that include aspects of conduct which contravene the law and those cases where the totality of the conduct, regardless of the legality of the composite acts, attracts legal protection. In order to provide a complete examination of these areas, this chapter first considers situations where an aspect of the stalker's conduct contravenes the criminal law. This is followed by a consideration of situations whereby the totality of the harassing conduct is amenable to legal intervention with key areas here being relationship-specific situations such as harassment within employment and family relationships. Chapter 5 extends this analysis by providing an in-depth consideration of two areas where the judiciary has sought to expand the remit of the law in order to provide greater protection for stalking victims: the Offences Against the Person Act 1861 and the tort of private nuisance.

4.1 OFFENCES COMMITTED DURING THE COURSE OF STALKING

One aspect of stalking that is immediately apparent upon examination of any selection of cases is the immense diversity of manifestations of stalking. Stalkers appear to operate from a variety of different motivations and this may impact upon the type of behaviour that they engage in towards their victims. Notwithstanding this, there is a high incidence of cases that involve the commission of at least one act which constitutes an existing criminal offence. It is somewhat surprising to note, given the diversity of stalking conduct, the relatively small range of offences that are committed by stalkers engaging in criminal behaviour. Potential areas of criminal liability will be considered using the broad categories of stalking behaviour outlined in the preceding chapters.

4.1.1 Offences against property

Acts directed against property owned by the stalking victim are prevalent, whether this be theft of property or, more frequently, its damage or destruction. Establishing liability for theft of the victim's property contrary to s 1(1) of the Theft Act 1968[1] should be a relatively straightforward matter with the main impediment arising not from the nature of the offence itself, but from the difficulties of establishing that it is the stalker who is responsible. It is frequently the case that the victim knows the stalker to be responsible for the theft of the victim's property, but lacks sufficient evidence to convince the police to take action.

Similar problems occur in relation to the damage or destruction of property, which is an offence under s 1(1) of the Criminal Damage Act 1971.[2] For example, one stalking victim's car suffered 37 slashed tyres and 17 shattered windscreens in a three month period, but she was unable to persuade the police to intervene despite her conviction that the stalker was responsible.[3] A further limitation to the use of the Criminal Damage Act is that the property damaged or destroyed during the course of stalking appears generally to be at the lower end of the scale, thus attracting a relatively minor penalty even if the stalker is prosecuted.[4] For example, one case that involved the destruction of plants and garden furniture resulted in a fine and a £250 compensation order.[5] Of course, more serious acts are targeted against

---

1   Theft Act 1968, s 1(1): 'A person is guilty of theft if he dishonestly appropriates property belonging to another with the intention of permanently depriving the other of it.'

2   Criminal Damage Act 1971: s 1(1): 'A person who without lawful excuse destroys or damages any property belonging to another intending to destroy or damage any such property or being reckless as to whether any such property would be destroyed or damaged shall be guilty of an offence.'

3   Case history 4 – even when a friend of the victim witnessed the stalker bending down next to the vehicle, the police accepted his explanation that he was checking to ensure that the car had not been damaged as he was aware that it had been repeatedly targeted by vandals.

4   Lack of sufficient evidence is not limited to the Criminal Damage Act 1971, although this appears a particularly difficult area in stalking cases, as victims frequently report that their property has been damaged during the night, with cars appearing particularly vulnerable.

5   Case history 31.

property during the course of stalking and, when this occurs, the sentence imposed does reflect this. For example, a sentence of six years' imprisonment was upheld against the stalker who, frustrated that his victim resisted all his attempts to rekindle their relationship, set fire to her house whilst she was inside it.[6]

It may be the case that the stalker will gain entry to the victim's home in order to remove or damage property, thus attracting liability for burglary under s 9(1) of the Theft Act 1968.[7] This is a relatively common occurrence in more serious stalking cases and is arguably more serious than a burglary committed by someone other than a stalker. This is due to the distress and fear caused by the knowledge that the stalker has entered what the victims often regard as their one remaining place of safety. It was the knowledge that the stalker had entered their homes that was the final straw for two stalking victims interviewed in the course of this research. One victim only managed to remain in her home for one night following the burglary of her house by her stalker.[8] In another case, it was finding that the stalker had entered her home and slept in her bed when she was away that drove a 16 year old victim to start inflicting harm upon herself with a razor blade.[9] Neither of these stalkers was charged with burglary at the time, owing to an inability to establish who was responsible,[10] thus further illustrating the probative difficulties associated with even the most straightforward offences committed by a stalker.

These are the most usual forms of property offence committed during the course of stalking. It is clear that the difficulties arise not from any complexity surrounding the actual offences, but either from an inability to identify the person responsible, if the stalker is not known to the victim, or the absence of conclusive proof that the stalker is responsible.

4.1.2 Offences against the person

Existing research suggests that the majority of stalkers are not prone to violence and any violence that does occur in the course of stalking is likely to

---

6   *R v Golding* (1998) unreported, CA (case number 97/2707/Z2).
7   A person is guilty of burglary if he enters a building or part of a building as a trespasser and with intent to steal, or inflict grievous bodily harm on any person therein, or to commit rape or cause unlawful damage – s 9(1)(a) – or if, having entered as a trespasser, he steals or attempts to steal or inflicts or attempts to inflict grievous bodily harm on any person therein – s 9(1)(b).
8   Case history 6.
9   Case history 24.
10 The difficulties of establishing criminal liability were further aggravated in these cases as neither victim knew who was responsible for stalking them. The stalker in Case history 24 was arrested some months later attempting to break into the house and a search of his home revealed property stolen in the first burglary, hence his eventual prosecution and conviction.

be of a minor nature.[11] However, there are exceptional cases where the stalker resorts to serious acts of violence.[12] The majority of incidences of physical harm that occur during the course of stalking could be dealt with under the Offences against the Person Act 1861.[13] The Act provides a range of offences that may be applicable, depending upon the severity of the harm caused to the victim and the state of mind of the stalker. If the level of injury does not suffice for a prosecution under the least serious statutory offence, assault occasioning actual bodily harm,[14] charges of common assault[15] and battery[16] may be applicable.[17] At the more serious end of the scale, the stalker who kills another person can be charged with manslaughter or murder, depending upon the surrounding circumstances.

It is not usual for the stalker to cause physical harm to the victim unless the case is one where there has been a previous relationship between the parties,[18] and then only if the relationship itself was characterised by violence.[19] However, it is far more likely that a non-relationship stalker, particularly those who are obsessed or delusional, will harm another person who is perceived as impeding access to the primary object of attention.[20] This

11 Meloy, 1996, pp 147–62.

12 As discussed in Chapter 3, these more serious cases tend to attract a higher degree of media coverage than cases with little or no violence, hence this leads to a public misconception as to the propensity of stalkers to violence.

13 The substance of these offences will be discussed in detail in Chapter 5 when considering the use of the Offences Against the Person Act 1861 against stalkers who cause their victims to suffer psychological harm.

14 Offences against the Person Act 1861, s 47: 'Whosoever shall be convicted of an assault occasioning actual bodily harm shall be liable to [imprisonment for five years]'. The offence requires an assault, in the sense of a common assault or battery, which causes 'any hurt or injury calculated to interfere with the health or comfort of the victim' so long as it is not merely 'transient or trifling' – R v Donovan [1934] 2 KB 498, p 501.

15 An assault is any act by which a person intentionally or recklessly causes another to apprehend immediate and unlawful violence – R v Savage, DPP v Parmenter [1991] 4 All ER 698, p 711, per Lord Ackner.

16 A battery occurs upon physical contact with another, however minor: 'The law cannot draw the line between different degrees of violence, and therefore totally prohibits the first and lowest stage of it; every man's person being sacred, and no other having a right to meddle with it, in any the slightest manner': Blackstone, Commentaries, Vol III, p 120 as quoted in Ashworth, 1999, p 327.

17 Criminal Justice Act 1988, s 39: 'Common assault and battery shall be summary offences and a person guilty of either of them shall be liable to a fine not exceeding level 5 of the standard scale, to imprisonment for a term not exceeding six months, or both.' Both assault and battery are torts as well as criminal offences, thus can form the basis of a civil action.

18 A stalker will only occasionally use violence against his victim in the absence of a prior relationship, as in R v Cuffin (1997) unreported, CA (case number 97/1058/Y5) where the defendant stabbed a barmaid with whom he had developed an obsession.

19 Farnham, James and Cantrell, 2000.

20 R v Bridgland (1996) unreported, CA (case number 96/3216/Z3) – the defendant was unable to accept that his ex-partner had formed a new relationship, so he broke into her home during the night and struck the man several times about the head with a ratchet whilst he was sleeping.

will usually be a partner, but has also included parents of the stalking victim, their children and other family members, friends and even an employer. This has been termed triangulation,[21] and can lead to fatal consequences as in *R v Hough*,[22] where the defendant had stalked his wife ever since she sought to end their relationship and was ultimately convicted of the murder of her new partner.[23] Attacks on third parties appear either to be motivated by revenge[24] or a belief that a particular person is the only impediment to the stalker and victim embarking on a life together.[25]

Even less common than offences of physical harm are offences of a sexual nature. In stalkers suffering from delusional disorders, this has been attributed to their social and emotional immaturity, which leads them to maintain the adolescent fantasy of idealised love – a love that is too pure to be sullied by sexual contact.[26] Many such stalkers have restricted sexual experience or have suffered sexual abuse, causing them to seek a relationship in which sex does not feature. Indeed, evidence that their victim is sexually active may prove to be an aggravating feature. Patrick Keane, who suffered from paranoia and schizophrenia, developed an obsession with the woman who lived in the flat below him but did not actively harass his victim until he heard her making love with her boyfriend. His harassment of her, which lasted for nine years, began when he sent her a card that read 'Why have sex in the room below, Patrick?'[27]

When sexual offences are committed, the stalker may be charged with rape[28] or indecent assault,[29] depending upon the level of sexual contact. Sexual coercion appears more common in situations where the parties are, or have been, involved in an intimate relationship.[30] This may be due to the

21 This phrase was first used by psychologist Dr JR Meloy, who writes extensively on the psychology of stalkers. See Meloy, 1999, pp 421–24.

22 *R v Hough* (1996) unreported, CA (case number 96/3884/X4).

23 This risk of the stalker targeting a third party perceived as impeding access to the victim is particularly high if the stalker is suffering from erotomania: Meloy, 1989, pp 477–92.

24 Case history 22 – the stalker arranged for his victim's new boyfriend to be seriously beaten as revenge for not staying away from her as he had been warned to do.

25 Case history 19 – the defendant believed that he and the victim were destined to be together as they had been in a previous incarnation, but that the victim was afraid to leave her husband as she had previously been executed for adultery. The stalker set fire to the house whilst the victim's husband and small son were inside, but fortunately neither was seriously injured.

26 Orion, 1997, p 69.

27 'Paranoid stalking is facing jail or hospital' (1997) *The Times*, 23 July; (1997) *The Guardian*, 23 July.

28 Sexual Offences Act 1956, s 1(2): 'A man commits rape if (a) he has sexual intercourse with a person (whether vaginal or anal) who at the time of the intercourse does not consent to it; and (b) at the time he knows that the person does not consent to the intercourse or is reckless as to whether that person consents to it.

29 Sexual Offences Act 1956, s 14: 'It is an offence … for a person to make an indecent assault on a woman' and s 15: 'It is an offence for a person to make an indecent assault on a man.'

30 Budd and Mattinson, 2000, Figure A5.3, p 73.

intimidating and controlling nature of stalking that creates a substantial power differential between the parties. This is likely to render the victim particularly vulnerable to threats, particularly if the relationship has been characterised by violence.[31] In such cases, there may be difficulties in establishing that intercourse was non-consensual, as there is some lack of clarity in the current law as to the nature and severity of threat required to vitiate consent in sexual offences.

For example, one victim complied with her former partner's demands for intercourse once a fortnight to prevent him from harassing her in between times. She refers to this as 'the price of peace'.[32] Another victim, prompted by a beating inflicted upon her some 18 months previously for refusing, acquiesces immediately whenever her partner initiates intercourse.[33] Certainly, these victims could not be said to be giving full and free consent to intercourse, but it is questionable whether these circumstances would suffice to vitiate the victims' consent and give rise to a potential prosecution for rape.

Such cases raise the issue of the delineation between real consent and mere submission that was addressed by the Court of Appeal in *R v Olugboja*.[34] Here, the victim, who had already been raped by the defendant's friend, complied with instructions to remove her clothing and did not resist when the defendant embarked upon intercourse. Whilst rejecting the defence contention that only violence or threats of violence would nullify consent, the Court of Appeal held that the distinction between consent and submission was a question for the jury, who should concentrate on the victim's state of mind immediately prior to intercourse, taking into account the events leading to the act and the victim's reaction to them.

The Court of Appeal rejected the defence contention that only violence or threats of violence would nullify consent. It was held that the distinction between consent and submission was a question for the jury, who should concentrate on the victim's state of mind immediately prior to intercourse, taking into account how this would be affected by events leading up to the act. The extent to which this would lead to a finding that the two stalking victims had been raped is unclear. Consent and submission are at opposite ends of a scale that encompasses a vast continuum of other reactions:

> That reasoning asserts that consent in its ordinary meaning is a state of mind, and that a person can be said to possess that state of mind notwithstanding that she feels pressured, so long as her feelings are on the right side of the point at which consent turns into submission.[35]

---

31 Walker, 1987, pp 157–66.
32 Case history 34.
33 Case history 27.
34 *R v Olugboja* [1982] QB 321.
35 Gardner, 1996, pp 275–97.

It is clear that an apparent consent may actually be a submission due to the pressure exerted upon the victim, but it is not clear where the line is to be drawn. This uncertainty was exacerbated by the finding of the Court of Appeal in *Olugboja* that a reluctant acquiescence may nonetheless amount to consent. Some useful clarification was provided in *R v McAllister*, where it was said that:

> The focus of the inquiry in all these cases is based on the sexual autonomy of the complainant. The circumstances of a possibly reluctant consent may be infinitely varied, and on each occasion the jury has to decide whether an alleged agreement to a sexual act may properly be seen as a real consent or whether it should be regarded as a submission founded on improper pressure which this particular complainant could not reasonably withstand from this particular defendant.[36]

The emphasis given to the nature of the relationship between the parties is important and may facilitate the application of rape to the stalking cases recounted above. Given that one victim has previously encountered serious violence from her partner for refusing to comply with his demands for intercourse, this is indicative of a continuing pressure exerted upon the victim that could be deemed to nullify her apparent consent.[37] Whether this would apply to the victim who agrees to intercourse on regular occasions to avoid harassment at other times is less clear. A lesser degree of threat may suffice for liability under s 2 of the Sexual Offences Act 1956, procurement of a woman by threats or intimidation, but it is still questionable whether a threat to harass the victim unless intercourse is forthcoming on a regular basis will suffice.

This discussion illustrates some of the difficulties that may arise in relation to sexual offences owing to the controlling relationship that characterises relational stalking cases. If the victim has become so intimidated by the stalker that she will agree to intercourse to minimise the continuance of harassment, can it be said that her autonomy is being upheld if this is deemed to be valid consent? The issues incumbent in these cases have not yet been tested before the courts but, given the emphasis in *McAllister* on the context in which intercourse occurs, it may be that some such cases would meet with success. Until such time, the current law on sexual offences would appear to provide little protection to victims who feel constrained by circumstances to engage in intercourse with their stalker.

---

36 *R v McAllister* [1997] Crim LR 233, *per* Brooke LJ. This was not a case of rape, but of indecent assault. However, the meaning of consent is the same for the two offences.

37 Even if this were to be accepted, this is only one element of rape. It must also be established that the defendant intended to have non-consensual intercourse or that he was reckless as to whether or not the victim consented. Owing to the period of time that had passed since the last act of violence between the parties and the victim's apparent consent, it may be that this element of the offence would be difficult to establish.

4.2 THREATENING BEHAVIOUR

It is clear that many stalking cases involve threatening behaviour by the stalker. A recent review of existing American research on threats in stalking indicated that threats occur in up to three-quarters of all stalking cases.[38] The extent to which this will constitute a criminal offence is dependent upon whether the threats are explicit or implicit, the substance of the threat and the means by which it is communicated. These limitations are unfortunate for stalking victims, as one of the most common responses to prolonged stalking is that the victim feels threatened, but this is frequently based upon conduct which is not explicitly threatening, but arises from the general situation. In most cases, this will not be actionable in law because of the distinction between the creation of a threatening atmosphere causing a generalised sense of fear and a threat of specific action causing fear that the threat will be carried out.

4.2.1 Threats to commit a criminal offence

Certain specific threats do constitute an established criminal offence.[39] Section 16 of the Offences Against the Person Act 1861 prohibits the making of threats to kill. This offence was originally limited to threats to kill which were communicated in writing, but this was amended by s 65(4) of the Criminal Law Act 1977, so s 16 now provides that:

> a person who, without lawful excuse, makes to another a threat, intending that the other would fear it would be carried out, to kill that other or a third person, shall be guilty of an offence.

Such threats appear frequently in the course of stalking either directed against the victim[40] or against another person perceived as interfering with the relationship between the stalker and the victim. As is the case with actual physical harm, the motivation for making threats to kill a third party appears to be primarily associated with either revenge[41] or to remove the person

---

38 Meloy, JR, 'Threats, stalking and criminal harassment', in Pinard and Pagini, 1999. Meloy defines a threat as 'a written or oral communication that implicitly or explicitly states a wish or intent to damage, injure, or kill the target', hence his statement of the prevalence of threats does not include threats implied from conduct.

39 Alldridge, 1984, pp 176–86 – of the threats to commit criminal offences which are identified in this article, only threats to kill and threats to commit criminal damage are relevant in a stalking context.

40 *R v Collacott* (1996) unreported, CA (case number 96/3001/X4) in which the defendant refused to accept that his marriage was over and developed an obsession with his former wife that involved relentless pursuit of her and culminated in him threatening to 'cut her fat throat from top to bottom ... then I win, she's dead'. He was sentenced to two and half years' imprisonment.

41 Case history 8 – the stalker threatened to kill his former wife's new partner, believing he was to blame for the breakdown of his marriage.

believed to be an impediment to a relationship between the stalker and the victim.[42]

This offence applies to any threats to kill, whether or not they are ever intended to be carried out[43] and regardless of whether they are made directly to the person threatened or to another person.[44] There is no requirement that the intended victim must take the threats seriously; indeed, the offence will be made out even if the threats never come to the notice of the intended victim. This may be particularly beneficial in stalking cases where victims are reluctant to take action leading to the arrest of the stalker as it provides the potential for another to intervene and make the complaint that leads to the stalker's arrest. Another favourable aspect of this offence, in terms of stalking, is that it encompasses implicit threats. Whilst it is true to say that stalkers will frequently make explicit threats, particularly towards a third party, experts in stalking risk assessment state that expressions of shared destiny are more useful indications of violence than explicit threats:

> Ironically, someone who says 'I'm going to kill you on Tuesday' may be less likely to act than someone who says 'You and I must be united on Tuesday'.[45]

The extent to which implicit threats will come within the remit of s 16 is difficult to predict. It has been held that the words 'I do not want to take her life but ... the law will take its course after the act, but I hope my children will be looked after' held a sufficient threat to justify conviction,[46] but the threats used in stalking cases can take diverse forms, some of which do not objectively imply a threat to kill, but have some shared meaning which implies a threat to the stalking victim.[47] Often, it is only the context in which an incident takes place that gives threatening meaning to an otherwise inoffensive message or act. For example, it is common for stalkers in California to send a message to their victim's pagers which simply reads '187'. This figure assumes a more menacing aspect once it is appreciated that this is the section of the Californian Penal Code for murder.[48] Whilst this conduct

---

42 *R v Ritchings* (1998) unreported, CA (case number 98/3176/W4) – the defendant told his probation officer that he planned to 'get' the partner of an actress with whom he was obsessed, described the trains he would need to catch to reach South Wales, and specified that when he got there he would 'use the knife'. He was sentenced to five years' imprisonment

43 The *mens rea* of the offence requires that the defendant intends to cause another person to fear that they will be killed, not that he actually intends to kill them.

44 *R v Collacott* (1996) unreported, CA (case number 96/3001/X4) – the threats were made to a work colleague of the person threatened.

45 Gavin de Becker, a leading security expert specialising in risk assessment in stalking cases, as quoted in Orion, 1997.

46 *R v Solanke* (1969) 54 Cr App R 30.

47 Meloy, JR, 'Threats, stalking and criminal harassment', in Pinard and Pagini, 1999.

48 Paper given by Wells, K, Deputy District Attorney, Stalking Task Force, San Diego, California given at the Stalking Seminar, Bramshill Police Training Headquarters, 22 March 2000.

has no direct analogy in this jurisdiction, research indicates a range of conduct which could be perceived as a threat to kill, such as drawing a picture of a coffin on the envelope of a letter sent to the victim,[49] the placing of an obituary notice in the newspaper,[50] arranging for funeral directors to call the victim,[51] nailing a wreath to the victim's front door[52] and sending the victim press cuttings of a stalker who had killed his victim.[53] The difficulty with these actions is that they may not be seen as an unambiguous threat to kill, but may be regarded as an act designed to upset the recipient or a manifestation of a wish that the victim were dead rather than an actual threat to kill.

The major limitation of this offence as a means of redress for stalking victims is that it is limited to threats to kill and does not encompass threats to cause harm to the victim which fall short of death, and it is these threats of lesser harm that arise more frequently in stalking cases than threats to kill.[54] Even extension of the liability of s 16 to encompass causing threats of serious harm would not alleviate the problems faced by many stalking victims and would raise problems regarding the specificity and extensity of the threat that would justify conviction. Threats may be phrased in extremely general terms and there could be difficulties in establishing that a stalker who threatens to 'get' the victim or to 'make them pay' intended to cause fear of serious harm. Additionally, it is frequently the case that the totality of the stalking conduct makes the victim feel fearful and threatened, but this is more a generalised feeling or state of mind which is based on the overall situation, not any specific threat made by the stalker:

> What about the stalker whose threat lies in mere omnipresence? Menacing behaviour need not include any credible threat but be menacing all the same. The 'threat' – and the fear – may be all the worse for being unstated and left to the imagination.[55]

---

49 Interview with Anthony Burstow, 29 March 1999.

50 Case history 24 – no arrest was made in connection with the incident although it was reported to the police.

51 Ibid.

52 Case history 8 – the victim did not report this to the police.

53 'Student jailed for harassing TV presenter' (2000) The Times, 11 January – television news presenter Sarah Lockett was harassed by a stalker who sent her various letters and articles referring to other celebrity stalking cases, including one which read: 'I think the whole Jill Dando thing was great. I was hoping a celebrity would get killed by a stalker. It made it even better that she read the news.' Jeremy Dyer was acquitted of making threats to kill as this letter was not considered to be unambiguously threatening. He was convicted of harassment and imprisoned for eight months.

54 Proposals by the Law Commission to extend the ambit of the offence to include threats of serious harm have not been adopted – Criminal Law Revision Committee, Fourteenth Report, Offences Against the Person, Cmnd 7844, 1980, paras 215–18; Law Commission, Legislating the Criminal Code: Offences Against the Person and General Principles, Law Com No 218, Cm 2370, 1993.

55 Goode, 1995, p 26.

If the threats are of such a nature that the victim fears that the stalker will cause them immediate and unlawful harm, then this may engender liability for assault.[56] However, despite the reformulation of the immediacy requirement in recent cases,[57] assault does not apply to contingent threats, nor threats to cause harm at some time in the future.[58] Neither will assault address the generalised threat communicated by the totality of the stalker's conduct, although Lord Steyn sought to bring this within the remit of assault when discussing the fear experienced by stalking victims by posing the question 'what, if not the possibility of imminent personal violence, was the victim terrified about?'[59] Although this discussion occurred in the context of psychiatric harm resulting from silent telephone calls, the question could be of general application in stalking cases. This could address situations such as the one in which the stalker did nothing other than stand and stare at the victim's house. Despite the fact that this continued for months and the stalker made no attempt to approach the victim or gain entry to her property, her primary response to his conduct was to feel threatened.[60]

These deficiencies of the law in relation to threats of harm falling short of death are made all the more inexplicable when it is considered that there is an offence which addresses threats to damage or destroy property. Section 2(a) of the Criminal Damage Act 1971 provides that:

> a person who without lawful excuse makes to another a threat, intending that that other would fear it would be carried out, to destroy or damage any property belonging to that other or a third person ... shall be guilty of an offence.

As with the offence of making threats to kill, there need be no intention to carry out the threat provided that the threat is made with the intention of causing the recipient to fear that it will be carried out. Threats to damage property appear with frequency in stalking cases but, as with any other threat, there may be difficulties with proof, especially in terms of verbal threats. Nevertheless, the offence may provide some redress for stalking victims.

Therefore, it is clear that only a narrow range of threatening conduct is covered by the criminal law. This limits the protection available for stalking

---

56 An assault is any act by which a person intentionally or recklessly causes another to apprehend immediate and unlawful violence – *R v Savage, DPP v Parmenter* [1991] 4 All ER 698, p 711, *per* Lord Ackner.

57 *R v Ireland* [1997] 4 All ER 225; *R v Constanza* [1997] 2 Cr App R 492.

58 It was believed for many years that words alone cannot constitute an assault, but this was disproved by the House of Lords in *R v Ireland, R v Burstow* [1997] 4 All ER 225 where it was said that 'a thing said is also a thing done', *per* Lord Steyn, p 236. This issue is discussed in greater detail in Chapter 5.

59 *R v Ireland, R v Burstow* [1997] 4 All ER 225, *per* Lord Steyn, p 236.

60 Case history 1 – 'At first I was just a bit alarmed when I saw him outside but as time went on I started to feel really threatened. He would stand there staring for hours and I got obsessed that I had to watch him watching me because if he went away where was he and what was he doing?'

victims. Feeling threatened is an extremely common response to being stalked, but this is frequently due to the situation itself rather than any explicit threat.[61] It would appear that the only way around this would be for the law to reformulate the notions of 'threat' and 'fear' to include the situations prevalent in stalking situations. Unless it is recognised that all conduct which causes fear can be constructed as threatening conduct and the law is prepared to prohibit this, there seems little scope for stalking victims to find redress in this area of law. The difficulties inherent with encapsulating this in any legal offence present a virtually insurmountable impediment to potential liability.

4.3 UNWELCOME COMMUNICATIONS

Threats and other unwelcome communications that occur during the course of stalking may give rise to criminal liability as a result of the means by which they are communicated to the victim.

4.3.1 Telephone communications

Making obscene, threatening, silent or general nuisance telephone calls is a frequently utilised means of harassment resorted to by stalkers with one recent and comprehensive study of stalking conduct suggesting that 78% of stalkers in the US use the telephone as a means of harassing their victims.[62] In 1995, British Telecom traced more than a million calls made to 65,000 callers at the request of the police, resulting in approximately 2,800 prosecutions or cautions, although there is no information to suggest how many of these involved stalkers.[63] Despite the high incidence of the use of the telephone as a means of harassment, a close examination of the calls reveals some disparity in the content of the calls and the purpose for which they were made. These factors need to be taken into account when considering the potential to hold the stalker criminally liable for the calls.

Section 43 of the Telecommunications Act 1984 provides that:

A person who –

(a) sends, by means of a public telecommunications system, a message or other matter that is grossly offensive or of an indecent, obscene or menacing character; or,

(b) sends by those means, for the purpose of causing annoyance, inconvenience or needless anxiety to another, a message that he knows to

---

61 Budd and Mattinson, 2000, Chapter 6.
62 Mullen, Pathe, Purcell and Stuart, 1999, pp 1244–49.
63 'Number is up for malicious phone callers' (1995) Daily Telegraph, 3 August.

be false or persistently makes use for the purpose of a public telecommunications system,

shall be guilty of an offence and liable on summary conviction to imprisonment for a term not exceeding six months or a fine ... or both.

Thus, it can be seen that s 43 creates two distinct offences. Section 43(a) relates to the content of the calls, prohibiting those which are of an offensive, indecent, obscene or menacing character, whereas s 43(b) concentrates on the purpose behind the calls, thus prohibiting repeated calls and those containing false information that are made for the purpose of causing annoyance, inconvenience or anxiety.

There are various impediments to the use of these offences in stalking cases. The problems arise either through the wording of the statute, such as the exclusionary phraseology and the sufficiency of the penalty in cases of a prolonged or serious nature, or through the inherent nature of nuisance calls, such as identifying the caller and establishing the content of the call. In order to illustrate these limitations, it is necessary to consider the various ways in which the telephone can be used in the course of stalking. It is relevant to consider the variability of content and motivation of the calls, as this may impact upon whether they are within the nature of call prohibited by this legislation.

A British Telecom study of nuisance calls used a system of categorisation whereby 60% of calls were silent, 15% obscene, 15% threatening or abusive and 10% were either hoaxes or pranks.[64] This research breaks the categories down into six categories, excluding prank calls, based upon the experience of those targeted by unwanted calls, in order to illustrate the range of calls which may be outside the remit of the legislation.

4.3.1.1 Threatening calls

Threatening telephone calls would clearly be within the 'menacing' category of calls which are prohibited by the statute. There is no requirement that the threats be directed at the person receiving the calls, nor that they threaten harm to a specific person, thus any call with sufficient menacing content would suffice. This could be advantageous for the stalking victim as the language of stalking often circumvents direct menace in favour of more indirect and implicit threats. Whilst it would not be doubted that phrases such as 'if I can't have you, no one else can' contain an implied threat, the language of shared destiny frequently utilised by stalkers, which is epitomised by 'you and I shall be united on Thursday', may not import sufficient menace to come within the provisions of the Telecommunications Act.[65] Additionally, the

---

64 *Ibid.*

65 Although this is recognised by experts as presenting a more serious risk of violence than a more explicit threat – Gavin de Becker, as quoted in Orion, 1997.

context between the parties may instil otherwise innocuous words with menace which would not be apparent to the objective listener, thus it may be problematic to fit calls which do, as a matter of fact, cause stalking victims to feel threatened within the parameters of s 43(a).

Overtly menacing calls containing direct threats appear to fall into two categories. First, there are threats made by a person known to the recipient who makes no attempt to hide his or her identity and is merely using the telephone as a convenient means of communication, possibly through a disinclination to make threats in person.[66] The second type of threatening call is made by a person whose voice is not recognised by the recipient and who has been randomly selected by the caller. For example, in *R v Onyon*,[67] the defendant telephoned women he did not know to inform them that he had their daughters held hostage and they would be raped unless the women complied with the defendant's demands to perform sexual acts and engage in self-mutilation. There are probative and evidential difficulties with both types of call that may render the protection extended by the statute of little value.[68]

4.3.1.2 Obscene calls

Obscene calls are explicitly covered by s 43(a). More than threatening calls, obscene callers tend to be unknown to the recipient, although the Home Office study of nuisance calls refers to the unevenness of demographic factors in victimisation as being highly suggestive that the majority of obscene callers know the identities of their victims.[69] The report emphasises that 'knowing is not necessarily mutual', and suggests that obscene callers usually select someone whom they have seen or spoken to that represents the caller's notion of a sexually attractive woman. This is particularly so where the purpose of the call is to aid masturbation.[70]

This is illustrated by *R v Taylor*,[71] where the defendant telephoned women who attracted him that he had seen working in local businesses. He would make comments that suggested he had been observing them for a period of

---

66 Case history 35 – 'Come back here and start acting like a wife or I'll make you so sorry'.
67 (1994) 15 Cr App R(S) 663 – there was an element of selection in that the defendant scoured local newspapers for stories about young women. Choosing those with distinctive surnames to make it easier to find their location and telephone number, he would telephone their mothers and use the information about the girl gleaned from the newspaper to add veracity to his call. He alleged to have an accomplice, a recently released sex offender, who would rape the girl unless her mother complied with his demands.
68 It should be noted that developments in telecommunications technology, such as caller display units and last number recall, have ameliorated some of difficulties inherent in establishing the identity of the person responsible for the call.
69 Buck, Chatterton and Pease, 1995.
70 *Ibid*, pp 35–36.
71 *R v Taylor* (1998) unreported, CA (case number 98/03091/X2).

time and ask if they would prefer death by strangulation or suffocation. He had taken photographs of the women he targeted which were kept with a collection of pornography which depicted women being strangled. It was found that the calls were made for the purposes of sexual gratification. Although he was unknown to his victims, there was an element of unilateral knowledge in that the victims were deliberately selected by the defendant, who was aware of the appearance of the person to whom he was speaking. Nevertheless, the victims' ignorance as to the identity of the caller, especially in the absence of repeat victimisation, renders identification of the caller virtually impossible.

The motivation of obscene calls is not necessarily sexual gratification. In *R v Wadland*,[72] the calls which terrorised 270 women into removing their clothes, mutilating their bodies and setting fire to their pubic hair were made for the feelings of power and control that this gave the defendant, whose control over his own life was slipping as his business fell increasingly into debt.

Regardless of the motivation for the call, if its content is obscene, the call will be prohibited by the Telecommunications Act. Further difficulties may arise with determining what exactly constitutes obscenity as, although obscene calls are not common, many stalkers resort to sexually targeted forms of abuse. An additional problem here is that the Act does not appear to accommodate obscene telephone calls that the stalker causes to be made by third parties. For example, the stalker who advertises the victim's services as a prostitute and makes her telephone number known in this context causes her to receive obscene telephone calls, but this would not suffice to render the stalker amenable to prosecution under the Telecommunications Act 1984.[73]

4.3.1.3 Silent calls

Silent calls are not explicitly prohibited by the statute, but may nevertheless come within either section, although this is dependent upon the circumstances surrounding the calls. If the call is perceived to be menacing, it will be covered by s 43(a). In *R v Ireland*,[74] which involved persistent silent telephone calls made over a protracted period of time, it was said that the silent caller 'intends by his silence to cause fear and he is so understood'[75] and that 'it

---

72 *R v Wadland* (1994) 15 Cr App R(S) 543 – the defendant telephoned randomly selected woman and threatened to harm their husbands or daughters unless his demands were complied with. He claimed to have made the first call in desperation, enjoyed the sense of power that he lacked in his everyday life, and this caused him to continue making the calls.

73 Advertising the victim's services as a prostitute occurred in Case histories 8 and 16. It was particularly distressing for the victim in Case history 16, owing to the high level of calls received and the content of the calls. She managed to ascertain that cards were being left in the King's Cross area of London and removed them from the telephone boxes. The cards contained the exhortation: 'Phone now and tell me what you want to do to me.'

74 *R v Ireland* [1997] 3 WLR 534.

75 *Ibid*, *per* Lord Steyn, p 547.

would be natural for the victim to regard the calls as menacing'.[76] Some callers deliberately use silence to convey a sense of menace. In one case, the caller remained silent to obscure the fact that she was a woman, acknowledging that this was due to her belief that the potential to instil fear in the recipients would be greater if they believed her to be a man.[77] She also reported a sense of satisfaction from hearing 'fear accumulating in their voices'.[78] However, recipients may not always perceive silent calls to be menacing, as there are other interpretations that may engender alternative responses in the recipient of the calls. The recipient of the calls may be annoyed and angered by the calls, but would not regard them as menacing.[79] If the call is not regarded as menacing, it will be outside the remit of s 43(a) and it will have to fit the requirements of s 43(b) if the calls are to engender liability under this statute.

Section 43(b) has two requirements. First, there must either be repeated calls or calls conveying false information. This will almost always be satisfied as silent callers habitually make repeated calls and, in any case, a single call would probably be dismissed by the recipient as a mistake or prank.[80] The key characteristic of silent calls which causes disturbance to the recipients is their repeated nature. The second requirement under s 43(b) is that the calls must be made in order to cause annoyance, inconvenience or needless anxiety to the recipient. It is important to note that it will not suffice that the calls cause these reactions in the recipient, it must be the purpose of the caller to cause these responses. It may appear reasonable to assume that there could not be any other reason to make repeated silent calls. However, an examination of some of the reasons put forward by stalkers for making calls included the hope that the ringing of the telephone would act as a prompt to her ex-partner to remind him to call her,[81] the belief that the telephone was a means by which a karmic link could be established[82] and the hope that the

---

76 *R v Ireland* [1997] 3 WLR 534, *per* Lord Steyn, p 537.

77 Case history 13.

78 This appeared to be a common feature in many of the cases where a stalker has used the telephone to harass the victim. It seems to give the stalker a sense of power and control and it reassures the stalker that his or her conduct is having an impact on the victim.

79 Case history 14 – the victim knew that his ex-girlfriend was responsible for the telephone calls and his annoyance at her conduct was based largely on the timing of the calls, which frequently occurred during the early hours of the morning.

80 The majority of victims receiving nuisance telephone calls attributed the first few calls to either prank callers or to people dialling a wrong number, but who lacked the courtesy to say so when the telephone was answered.

81 Case history 14 – 'When I started ringing, it was because he had said that he'd ring me. But he didn't so I would phone to see if he was out but if he wasn't I'd think: "Why didn't you phone me then?" and ring again so that the noise of the phone ringing would remind him that he had to call me.'

82 Case history 19 – the stalker believed that he and the victim had known each other in a previous life and that words were unnecessary to establish a karmic link between them that would re-establish their bond in their current lives, thus he would telephone and remain silent whilst mentally communicating with the victim.

answering machine would be turned on so that a carefully prepared message could be left.[83]

4.3.1.4 Dropped calls

Dropped calls, whereby the caller terminates the call immediately as the telephone is answered, are in many ways similar to the silent call. It is impossible for the recipient to gauge the purpose of the call or any clue as to the caller's identity. If the dropped calls are repeated and are made to cause annoyance, anxiety or inconvenience, they will be within s 43(b), but the difficulties associated with identifying the caller make these calls difficult to deal with effectively. For example, one victim received 67 dropped calls and 24 silent calls in one evening. This volume of calls was repeated over a period of several months and it was not until the stalker's conduct escalated into other acts of violence that it became possible to ascertain her identity, as there was no means of doing so on the basis of the calls alone.[84]

4.3.1.5 Unwanted conversation

Even conversational telephone calls that are unobjectionable in content can constitute a nuisance to the recipient if they are persistent and unwanted. A terminated relationship can lead to a series of calls. For example, following the end of a turbulent relationship, one victim received up to 20 telephone calls in a single evening from the stalker, who wished to apologise for his conduct and implore the woman to return to him.[85] Such calls are unlikely to come within s 43(b) as the purpose of the caller is not to cause anxiety, annoyance or inconvenience.

Even calls that are objectively pleasant can amount to a nuisance given the particular context of the parties. One stalker, whose constant sexual innuendo at work was upsetting his colleague and causing her to take time off from work, nevertheless persistently telephoned her in the evening to inquire after her health and to update her on what was happening at work until she eventually felt more intimidated by the telephone calls than by the constant

---

83 Case history 18 – believing the victim to be away for the weekend, the stalker composed a message outlining his feelings for her that he wanted to leave on the answering machine. However, the victim had not gone away, and the stalker would hang up immediately when the telephone was answered, but call again to try and leave the message. It did not occur to him that this could cause distress as he was concentrating on his plan to leave the message on the answering machine.

84 Case history 17 – after four months of silent and dropped calls, the stalker obtained the spare key to the victim's flat from a neighbour who was able to provide a description that established her identity.

85 Case history 20.

sexual overtones in his conduct when she was at work.[86] It is difficult to establish what the purpose of these calls was, but they certainly caused the recipient a great deal of distress which culminated in her leaving her job. It is doubtful that such ostensibly innocuous calls would be within the scope of the Telecommunications Act 1984.

4.3.1.6 Other telephone nuisance

The telephone can be used as an instrument of harassment even without the stalker being in direct contact with the victim. The stalker can use the relative anonymity provided by the telephone to represent himself as the victim and order goods and services in her name. For example, one victim spent a weekend explaining to takeaway delivery drivers and taxi drivers that she had not requested their services. Such calls could come within s 43(b), as they make use of false information to cause annoyance, but there is the difficulty of ascertaining the identity of the caller and the irony that the victim would be regarded as the recipient of the calls, that is, the taxi company, not the person to whom the conduct was directed.

Another means of indirect telephone harassment arises when the stalker does something that causes third parties to telephone the victim. In one case, the stalker placed a lonely hearts advertisement in the victim's name causing her to receive in excess of 50 telephone calls from potential suitors. The stalker then placed cards advertising the victim's services as a prostitute in telephone boxes in King's Cross causing the victim to receive numerous calls, some of an exceptionally obscene nature, from men believing her to be a prostitute.[87] The difficulty here would again be in establishing the identity of the person behind the telephone calls. Even though the obscene calls would be within s 43(a), a prosecution would hardly address the central wrongdoing in this type of situation, as it would be the actual caller who would attract criminal liability, rather than the person placing the advertisements.

4.3.1.7 Problems with the Telecommunications Act 1984

The preceding discussion illustrates the diverse nature of nuisance telephone calls and the extent to which the telephone can be used by the stalker to harass the victim. The examples also illustrate the difficulties of using the Telecommunications Act in stalking cases. The indirect nature of the contact means that it is difficult to identify the perpetrator of the calls, as the caller may remain silent or use a false name. The additional probative difficulty

---

86 Case history 21 – this gradually escalated into a situation whereby the stalker called at the victim's home in the evening with a pile of 'important paperwork' to discuss with her, some of which was two years out of date.

87 Case history 16.

comes in establishing the content of the call. Other than this, it is possible to cause harassment using the telephone in a way that is outside the remit of the legislation. It is important to note throughout that it is often the case with deliberate stalking that the stalker derives additional satisfaction from knowing that he is causing harassment whilst remaining within the parameters of lawful behaviour.[88]

The final difficulty with the use of this Act is the low level of penalty that it attracts. A protracted stalking campaign can cause distress and injury to the victim that would justify a far more stringent penalty than the maximum available under this statute and it is to be remembered that it was not until the Act was amended by the Criminal Justice and Public Order Act 1994 that this offence carried a possible sentence of imprisonment.

The potential impact of nuisance calls was encapsulated by Lord Steyn in *R v Ireland*[89] where he considered the effect that a persistent campaign of silent calls can have upon the recipient:

> It would be natural for the victim to regard the calls as menacing. What may heighten her fear is that she will not know what the caller may do next. The spectre of the caller arriving at her door step bent upon inflicting personal violence on her may come to dominate her thinking. After all, as a matter of common sense, what else would she be terrified about? The victim may suffer psychiatric illness such as anxiety, neurosis or acute depression.[90]

Thus it is clear that whilst the Telecommunications Act can address telephone nuisance which forms all or part of a campaign of harassment, there are serious limitations that detract from its efficacy as a means of intervention in many stalking cases.

4.3.2 Public nuisance

One of these limitations, the low level of the maximum penalty available, has been addressed by several judgments in which the making of nuisance telephone calls has been held to constitute a public nuisance, which is a common law offence, hence is subject to no restrictions as to the penalty available.

Public nuisance is a criminal offence at common law and may also form the basis of an action in civil law.[91] It is not an offence which is amenable to

---

88 See Chapter 1.

89 *R v Ireland* [1997] 3 WLR 534.

90 *Ibid, per* Lord Steyn, p 537.

91 Civil proceedings for public nuisance may be brought by the Attorney General as a relator action, by a local authority under s 222 of the Local Government Act 1972, or by a private individual who has suffered 'special damage' over and above that experienced by others affected by the nuisance – Buckley, 1996, pp 67–85.

precise definition and it encompasses acts and omissions that 'endanger the life, health, property, morals or comfort of the public'.[92] It differs from private nuisance in that, rather than affecting an individual, it affects the public generally,[93] thus will generally afford no protection to a single individual who is targeted by a stalker, although the wider consequences of the conduct may be taken into account. It is not unknown for a stalker to target multiple victims, often within a relatively small geographical area, thus there would appear to be potential for this offence to be used against stalkers provided the prerequisites for liability are satisfied.[94]

In order to establish whether this offence will afford a remedy to a victim of stalking, it is necessary to consider two issues. First, whether the type of conduct engaged in by stalkers can amount to a public nuisance and, secondly, whether a sufficient number of people are affected to satisfy the public aspect of the offence.

The difficulty when considering the nature of the conduct is that stalkers use diverse means to harass their victims. Fortunately, the category of behaviour covered by public nuisance is extremely broad, and it is likely that a great deal of stalking will be considered to be a danger to the victim's life, health, property, morals or comfort. Spencer considers that, since the majority of health and safety issues are now regulated by statute, public nuisance in recent years has been restricted to two situations:

> first, where the defendant's behaviour amounted to a statutory offence, typically punishable with a small penalty, and the prosecutor wanted a bigger or extra stick to beat him with, and secondly, where the defendant's behaviour was not obviously criminal at all and the prosecutor could think of nothing else to charge him with.[95]

The availability of public nuisance to combat conduct which appears to merit legal intervention, but which is not, of itself, unlawful gives it incredible scope to deal with an almost unlimited range of conduct.[96] An example of Spencer's second category can be seen in *R v Madden*,[97] where public nuisance was used to address the making of hoax bomb threats prior to this being made a statutory offence.[98] In this case, it was said that the making of a telephone call giving false information regarding the presence of explosives was conduct

---

92 *Archbold's Criminal Practice*, 1985, paras 27–44.
93 'The classic statement of the difference is that a public nuisance affects Her Majesty's subjects generally, whereas a private nuisance only affects particular individuals': *AG v PYA Quarries Ltd* [1957] 1 All ER 894, *per* Denning LJ, p 908.
94 Case histories 11 and 36.
95 Spencer, 1989, p 77.
96 Eg, in *R v Wheeler* (1971) *The Times*, 17 December, public nuisance was used to deal with the defendant, who kept a puma and two leopards in his garden. This would now be an offence under the Dangerous Wild Animals Act 1976.
97 [1975] 1 WLR 1379.
98 Now an offence under s 51 of the Criminal Law Act 1977.

that could amount to public nuisance, although the conviction was quashed by the Court of Appeal, as only eight security guards were affected by the defendant's actions and this was not a sufficient section of the public to justify liability for public nuisance.

In *R v Norbury*,[99] the use of the telephone as a means of committing a public nuisance was expanded beyond the limited scope of a hoax bomb warning to include the making of obscene telephone calls. This illustrates the first of Spencer's categories as, at the time, obscene telephone calls were covered by s 78 of the Post Office Act 1969. As the defendant had made obscene calls to 494 women in the Norfolk area over a two year period, his conduct was considered to be too serious to be dealt with by the maximum penalty of a £50 fine available under the statute, hence he was charged with public nuisance to increase the penalties available.

Obscene, nuisance and silent telephone calls are frequently used as a means of harassment by stalkers.[100] The inclusion of such calls within the scope of public nuisance may prove valuable to stalking victims and there would appear to be no reason why this could not be extended to a protracted campaign of anonymous letter writing as the distress and upset caused at being the target of an unknown person's spite and nastiness is surely analogous to that suffered by the recipient of obscene calls.

There is an obvious role, then, for public nuisance in situations where the stalker targets a large number of victims, but this is a relatively rare occurrence. It is not uncommon for a stalker to target several victims, but the paradigm stalking scenario involves a single victim. Of course, the stalking of a single person may indirectly affect those associated with the victim and there is no requirement that those affected by public nuisance be deliberately targeted, so there may be scope to include this within public nuisance. In *R v Millward*, a stalker who was infatuated with a female police officer made thousands of telephone calls over a period of two years to the police station where she worked. On one occasion, he made 363 calls in one day causing a substantial interruption to the functioning of the police station and impeded communications between the public and the police.[101] By considering the wider implications of his conduct, the court held him liable for public nuisance although only one person was directly affected by his conduct. Therefore, it would appear to be perfectly permissible to look beyond the direct victim and include those who are indirectly affected by a stalker's conduct in order to argue that it affects a sufficient amount of people to constitute a public nuisance.[102]

---

99   [1978] Crim LR 435.

100 Budd and Mattinson, 2000.

101 *R v Millward* (1986) 8 Cr App R(S) 209.

102 Although *R v Millward* appears a relatively atypical case owing to the potential disruption to the public from the police telephone being made unavailable to those with a genuine need.

The breadth of the conduct encompassed within public nuisance means that the main exclusionary factor will be whether a sufficient number of individuals are affected, thus raising the question of how many people must be adversely affected by conduct for it to constitute a public nuisance. In *AG v PYA Quarries Ltd*, it was said that a nuisance would be considered to be public rather than private if it:

> materially affects the reasonable comfort and convenience of a class of Her Majesty's subjects ... It is not necessary ... to prove that every member of the class has been injuriously affected; it is sufficient to show that a representative cross-section of the class has been so affected.[103]

Denning LJ agreed with this statement and added that it was unnecessary to specify a minimum number of persons who must be affected before a nuisance would acquire the relevant public element, but that:

> a public nuisance is a nuisance which is so widespread in its range or so indiscriminate in its effect that it would not be reasonable to expect one person to take proceedings on his own responsibility to put a stop to it, but that it should be taken on the responsibility of the community at large.[104]

The notions of a representative cross-section of a class of society and indiscriminate effect are not suggestive of a situation where a number of people are indirectly affected by conduct through their association with the primary victim. The judgments in *AG v PYA Quarries* suggest that there is something more to 'public' than the number of people who must be affected by the conduct. There must be an absence of the personal element that would be involved if public nuisance were to apply to the direct victim and all those indirectly affected by the conduct. The situation in *R v Millward* can be distinguished from this, as the public were not affected through their association with the victim, but because the defendant's actions potentially affected the speed with which the police could provide assistance.

This issue of selective targeting was considered in *R v Johnson* in which the defendant harassed 13 women with persistent unwanted telephone calls over a period of five years.[105] It was argued that this would not constitute public nuisance as the women were all acquaintances of the defendant and that it was not permissible to collect together several incidents of private nuisance and regard their cumulative affect as an offence of public nuisance. The Court of Appeal rejected this argument, saying that it was necessary to consider the cumulative effect of the defendant's conduct. This was a case where 'the public, meaning a considerable number of persons or a section of the public, was affected, as distinct from individual persons' and the fact that each of the victims was targeted because they were known to the defendant was regarded

---

103 *AG v PYA Quarries Ltd* [1957] 1 All ER 894, *per* Romer LJ, p 902.
104 *Ibid, per* Denning LJ, p 908.
105 *R v Johnson* [1997] 3 WLR 367.

as immaterial.[106] The Court of Appeal considered that any of the women living in the South Cumbria area were at risk of being harassed by the defendant should their telephone numbers become known to him and that the 13 women targeted were not to be regarded as a few selected individuals, but as an indiscriminate selection of members of the public with whom the defendant had come into contact.

The characterisation of 'the public' as a considerable number of persons and the decision that acquaintance with the defendant as the basis of selection did not place the conduct outside the parameters of public nuisance offers some encouragement for stalking victims who are amongst several targeted by the same stalker. There would appear to be no impediment to the use of public nuisance in situations such as that illustrated by the case where a 'prowler' terrorised several families living in the same village for eight months[107] and another case that involved a protracted campaign of anonymous letter writing.[108] If these cases could be deemed to amount to a public nuisance, the perpetrator could be liable for a criminal conviction or, alternatively, a civil action for an injunction or damages would be available.[109]

It remains to be seen if this will lead to the use of this offence in future stalking cases involving several victims but, as a general means of redress for the individual stalking victim, public nuisance has little to offer.

4.3.3 Written communications

Written communications feature in stalking cases in much the same way as telephone calls and break down into similar categories according to their content, although there is the added potential of sending, either through the postal service or otherwise, various items as well as written communications. Until the inception of the Malicious Communications Act 1988, only limited protection was available under s 11 of the Post Office Act 1953 which created an offence of:

---

106 *R v Johnson* [1997] 3 WLR 367, *per* Tucker J.

107 Case history 11.

108 Case history 36.

109 For an individual to bring an action for damages in public nuisance, it has to be shown that he suffered 'special damage' over and above that experienced by others affected by the nuisance. In the anonymous letter campaign case study, some of the letters contained truthful information, whilst others made false allegations. One letter accused a young woman of infidelity. Her husband became aware of this and, knowing that many of the letters contained true information, left her and sought a divorce. It would be interesting to see whether this would constitute 'special damage' for which she would be entitled to bring an action in damages and, if so, how this would be quantified.

sending, attempting to send or procuring to be sent any postal package which:

(a) encloses any indecent or obscene print, painting, photograph, lithograph, engraving, cinematograph, film, book, card or written communications, or any indecent or obscene article whether similar to the above or not; or,

(b) has on the packet, or on the cover thereof, any words, marks or designs which are grossly offensive or of an indecent or obscene character.

This section applies only to material sent through the post, hence excludes the hand delivered messages and notes attached to the victim's property which so frequently feature in stalking cases. The predecessor of this section was originally enacted to protect Post Office workers from exposure to undesirable material rather than to prohibit the using of the postal service to distribute obscene material.[110] As the Post Office is no longer permitted to open letters and parcels to inspect their contents, cases suitable for action under s 11 only come to light if packages burst open, if the obscenity is on the exterior or if the recipient makes a complaint. Additionally, the Post Office generally will only initiate proceedings if there is evidence that the material is commercially produced and there is evidence of wide scale trading, hence this section is little used.[111]

Despite the limitations upon the use of this section and the fact that it is only applicable to obscene or indecent material, the offence remains of value to address a narrow range of conduct which may arise during the course of stalking. This would be particularly beneficial if the stalker committed no other offence. For example, the man whom the local press dubbed the 'Phantom Photocopier' harassed at least 12 families living in a small Dales community by sending letters depicting caricatures of the recipients that were of an extremely vindictive and personal nature.[112] Although this conduct continued for a period of three years, only one letter sent during this period satisfied the requirements of the Malicious Communications Act 1988. Therefore, the existence of s 11 provided a valuable means of prosecuting this stalker, who had terrorised a whole community using almost wholly lawful means.

The other means by which the communication of threatening or otherwise unpleasant messages may be controlled is by the Malicious Communications Act 1988. Following the Law Commission Reports on Criminal Libel[113] and Poison Pen Letters,[114] it was proposed to create two new offences to improve statutory protection in these areas. The Law Commission recommended the replacement of the common law offence of criminal libel with a statutory

---

110 Manchester, 1983, pp 64–77.

111 There were only 10 prosecutions under s 11 in the Metropolitan Police area in 1981: *ibid*, p 73.

112 Case history 36; (1996) *Derbyshire Times*, 26 July.

113 Law Commission, *Report on Criminal Libel*, Law Com No 149, 1985, London: HMSO.

114 Law Commission, *Report on Poison Pen Letters*, Law Com No 147, 1985, London: HMSO.

offence of criminal defamation, which would be narrower in scope than criminal libel and would penalise anyone who communicated false information which was seriously defamatory with knowledge that the statement was both defamatory and false. This recommendation was never adopted, and criminal libel remains a common law offence.

In the course of examining the law of criminal libel, the Law Commission formed the opinion that there was a need for a specific offence to address the sending of poison pen letters and drafted a proposed Bill for this purpose. This measure was enacted as the Malicious Communications Act 1988 and was intended to cover letters which were outside the scope of criminal libel, fill the gaps left by s 11 of the Post Office Act 1953, which only applies to indecent or obscene material which is sent through the post,[115] and to compensate for the fact that there is no offence of threatening to cause injury at some unspecified time in the future.[116]

Section 1 of the Malicious Communications Act 1988 provides that:

a person who sends –

(a) a letter or other article which conveys –

    (i) a message which is indecent or grossly offensive;

    (ii) a threat; or,

    (iii) information which is false and is known or believed to be false by the sender;

(b) any other article which is, in whole or part, of an indecent or grossly offensive nature

is guilty of an offence if his purpose, or one of his purposes, in sending it is that it should ... cause distress or anxiety to the recipient or any other person to whom he intends that it or its contents or nature should be communicated.

Most conduct that would amount to criminal libel will be covered by the statutory provisions, but this will not render the offence of criminal libel otiose, as the sending of a malicious communication is a summary offence only which is punishable by a fine not exceeding level four on the standard scale.[117] Criminal libel is triable only on indictment and, as a common law offence, there is no restriction as to the maximum penalty that may be imposed, hence it is possible that it will be used in more serious cases which merit the imposition of a more serious penalty than that available under the Malicious Communications Act. The statute, however, covers a great deal of conduct that would not satisfy the requirements of criminal libel, hence will extend legal protection to a wider range of activities.

---

115 For a review of the scope of s 11 of the Post Office Act 1953, see Manchester, 1983, pp 64–77.

116 Knight, G, *HC Deb*, 12 February 1988, Vol 127, col 610.

117 The Criminal Justice and Police Bill 2001, cl 42(5) proposes to amend the Malicious Communications Act 1988, s 1(5) to read: 'imprisonment for a term not exceeding six months or to a fine not exceeding level 5 on the standard scale, or to both.'

It was said by the Law Commission, and confirmed during the passage of the Act, that 'communication' was to be construed widely to encompass any means of conveying information, thus would include the dropping of excrement through a letter box or the sending of a parcel containing broken glass. Spoken communications and email were deliberately excluded from the scope of the offence.[118] However, the Criminal Justice and Police Bill 2001 proposes to extend the scope of the Malicious Communications Act to include electronic communications.[119]

The statute requires not only that the communication is within one of the prohibited categories, but also requires proof of purpose on behalf of the sender. The communication must be made with the purpose of causing distress or anxiety, thus if the sender can argue that it was intended to be perceived as a joke, he will not incur liability. Equally, a person who passes on unwelcome information for honourable motives will not be liable, even if the information transpires to be untrue. It was said during the passage of the Act that it:

> sets a new boundary to the territory that is on the outer fringes of what is acceptable behaviour in contemporary society'[120] and that '[o]nly those who pursue the illegitimate purpose of causing distress or anxiety by illegitimate and wrongful means should be penalised.[121]

A distinction was then made between a man who wishes to revenge himself on a woman who has rejected his advances so he sends her a letter falsely claiming that her husband is being unfaithful, conduct that would clearly fall within the statute, and a letter which makes the same allegation but which happens to be true. Despite the obvious maliciousness behind this conduct, it would not fall within the Act. False information conveyed in the mistaken belief of its veracity would also not be covered by the Act, provided that the person communicating the information acted from honourable motives. This delineation of acceptable and unacceptable communication of false information based on the inherently unknowable motivations of the person passing the information on could be seen as a rather unsound basis for distinguishing culpability. This may prove to be a particularly limiting factor in the use of this statute in stalking cases given the multiplicity of motivations that may arise.

During the passage of this Act, it was recognised that the recipient of poison pen letters may suffer adverse effects that go beyond the shock and

---

118 This exclusion is unfortunate given the increasing prominence of email as a means of communication and its corresponding use as a means of harassment – 'Three months' jail for Internet stalker' (1999) *The Guardian*, 16 October; 'Country's first email stalker is convicted' (1999) *Daily Telegraph*, 24 March.

119 For 'letter or other article' there shall be substituted 'letter, electronic communication or article of any description': Criminal Justice and Police Bill 2001, cl 42(1)(a).

120 Patten, J, *HC Deb*, 12 February 1988, Vol 127 col 623.

121 *Ibid*, para 631.

distress of receiving the letter. The example was given of the man who felt compelled to arrange for the exhumation of his mother to quell rumours started by a series of anonymous letters that he was responsible for her death.[122] Thus, it is advantageous that the statute covers distress or anxiety caused to a person other than the direct recipient of the communication. It is, however, surprising, given the acknowledgment of the potential impact of such communications, that the maximum penalty for the offence was not set at a higher level. If the proposals to amend the Malicious Communications Act are enacted, this offence will carry a possible sentence of up to six months' imprisonment.[123]

Notwithstanding its shortcomings, the Act improved the protection available to those who receive unpleasant communications that were neither obscene or indecent, or were delivered by means other than postal delivery, hence not actionable under the Post Office Act nor serious enough to satisfy the requirements of criminal libel. To this extent, it provides clear protection against this particular form of harassment, although the relatively low penalty does little to reflect the potential impact of receipt of persistent unwanted communications that may frequently be of an extremely unpleasant nature.[124]

4.4 FALSE ALLEGATIONS

The passing of false information and the making of false allegations appears to be a relatively common feature of stalking cases. The information may either be communicated to the victim about a third party or to a third party about the victim, and either may be equally distressing and cause serious disruption to the lives of those affected. The false information can be broken down into three general and wide categories; allegations of criminal conduct,[125] imputations of immoral or socially unacceptable conduct[126] and derogatory comments about the character of the victim or a third party.[127] The extent to which these allegations come within the statutory provisions previously discussed is dependent upon the means used to communicate the information, the nature of the communication and the purpose for which it is made.

---

122 Lord, M, *HC Deb*, 12 February 1988, Vol 127, col 615.

123 Criminal Justice and Police Bill 2001, cl 42(5).

124 Particularly unpleasant items which have been sent to victims interviewed in the course of this research include blood-soaked letters, a dead rat, used sanitary towels and a *Bible* covered in raw liver.

125 Case history 15 – allegations made to the police that the victim was dealing in drugs. Case history 28 – both parties made allegations of stalking against the other to the police.

126 Case history 5 – a student claimed to be pregnant by one of her lecturers. Case history 31 – an 18 year old man claimed that his 30 year old victim had been pestering him for sex.

127 Case history 8 – the victim's estranged husband painted derogatory comments about her sexual proclivities outside her home and her place of work.

As has been discussed, one of the areas covered by both the Malicious Communications Act 1988 and s 43 of the Telecommunications Act 1984 concern the communication of false information. However, the use of these statutes to address the type of falsehoods that may be communicated as part of a campaign of stalking is limited, as both require proof of some specific purpose on the part of the person responsible for the communication, that is, the communication must be made for the purpose of causing anxiety or distress to come within the scope of the Malicious Communications Act 1988 or with the purpose of causing annoyance, inconvenience or needless anxiety for the purposes of s 43 of the Telecommunications Act 1984. Therefore, it is important to address alternative means of dealing with those who make harmful or distressing allegations during the course of stalking.

The little used common law offence of criminal libel concerns the publication of defamatory material that contains 'that sort of imputation which is calculated to vilify a man and bring him ... into hatred, contempt or ridicule'.[128] The criminal offence differs from civil libel in that it may be actionable if publication is solely to the person defamed, whereas the tort requires publication to others before the libel can be deemed to have lowered the victim in the eyes of society, but, whereas the truth of the statement is a complete defence at civil law, the criminal law requires not only that the statement be true, but that its publication is in the public interest. This avoids the difficulties associated with establishing the purpose for which the information was communicated, as criminal libel is not concerned with the purpose behind the publication of the defamatory material, but with the effect that this has upon the standing of the subject in the eyes of others.

Criminal proceedings for libel are rare, and are not encouraged by the courts.[129] The Law Commission has recommended the abolition of the offence and its replacement with a statutory offence of criminal defamation that would be narrower in scope and prohibit the communication of false information that is seriously defamatory.[130]

Nevertheless, this offence has been used with some success in some interesting harassment cases. In the most recent example, the defendant used solely lawful means to harass his victim, who had been his pen friend, for approximately five years.[131] However, when he began to write to friends and acquaintances of the victim, who was a widow, claiming to be the natural father of her son, he was charged with criminal libel and sentenced to nine months' imprisonment. In *R v Fell*, the defendant wished to sabotage his

---

128 *Thorley v Lord Kerry* (1812) 4 Taunt 355, *per* Sir James Mansfield, p 364, cited with approval in *Gleaves v Deakin* [1980] AC 477, *per* Viscount Dilhorne, p 487.

129 Smith, 1999, p 717.

130 Law Commission, *Report on Criminal Libel*, Law Com No 149, 1985.

131 *R v Penketh* (1982) 146 JP 56.

former lover's marriage in the hope that they would then be reunited.[132] He sprayed offensive and accusatory messages in aerosol paint around the village in which she lived, which caused her such distress that she attempted suicide and received treatment for severe depression. Very different motivation was apparent in *R v Leigh*, where the defendant sought to discredit the police officer responsible for the investigation which led to fraud charges being brought against him.[133] The defendant distributed 5,000 leaflets and displayed posters claiming that the officer was frequently drunk whilst on duty. He also wrote to 625 Members of Parliament, 82 judges and several national newspapers making these accusations.

There is an interesting twist in the story involved in the prosecution for criminal libel in *R v Gooding*.[134] The defendant was twice convicted for criminal libel following a prolonged campaign of obscene letters and cards and received a sentence of 12 months' imprisonment for the second offence. The most frequent recipient of these letters 'of the filthiest description', Edith Swan, who funded both private prosecutions leading to Gooding's convictions and appeared as the main prosecution witness, was eventually found to be the person responsible for sending the letters. Gooding's convictions were quashed and Swan was sentenced to 12 months' imprisonment for criminal libel. Whilst claims of false victimisation of stalking are thought to be relatively uncommon, it is important to ensure that there are means available to address these and other false claims of criminal victimisation due to the serious potential consequences for those falsely accused.[135]

Thus, the offence of criminal libel provides a means by which a specific type of stalking conduct may be brought before the criminal courts. False accusations against the victim are not uncommon in stalking cases. If these accusations are made in some permanent form, which would include painted messages and the display of posters, and are of such a nature as to expose the victim to hatred, contempt or ridicule, the sender may be liable.[136] This is so even if the accusation is true unless publication of the information is deemed to be in the public interest. Thus in *R v Greenhouse*, even though the defendant called witnesses in support of the truth of his accusation, he was still convicted of criminal libel, as his malicious publication of the information was not deemed to be in the public good.[137] The offence is triable on indictment

---

132 *R v Fell* (1976) *The Times*, 14 February.

133 *R v Leigh* (1971) *The Times*, 9 March.

134 *R v Gooding* (1921) Cr App R Vol XVI, 30 and discussion in Humphries, 1945, pp 124–35.

135 Pathe, Mullen and Purcell, 1999, pp 170–74.

136 It is difficult to understand why, in Case history 36, the 'Phantom Photocopier' was not charged with criminal libel in addition to offences under the Post Office Act 1953 and the Malicious Communications Act 1988 given the nature of some of the allegations made, which included claims of infidelity and incest.

137 *R v Greenhouse* (1887) *The Times*, 12 May.

only and reported cases suggest that conviction usually attracts a sentence of imprisonment, thus may provide a valuable means of countering this particular type of stalking conduct which overcomes many of the disadvantages associated with the statutory means of redress outlined previously.

Nevertheless, there appears to be little recourse to the law for the victim of false allegations unless these fall within the provisions of the Telecommunications Act 1984 or the Malicious Communications Act 1988, owing to the reluctance of the authorities to bring charges of criminal libel. The civil alternative places the onus of bringing an action upon the victim and does not attract legal aid, thus could be a costly and unproductive procedure owing to the limited redress available under the civil law.

4.5 LIABILITY FOR THE OVERALL HARASSMENT

The discussion thus far has focused upon the situation whereby constituent elements of a campaign of stalking amount to a discrete criminal offence. The major disadvantage with this approach concerns the uneven nature of protection that results from this for victims of stalking who are only able to rely on the intervention of the law if their stalker commits a criminal act during the course of the stalking. As many stalkers appear able to maintain several years of harassment without ever breaking the law,[138] indeed may deliberately seek to do so,[139] this creates an unfortunate situation whereby it is not unlawful deliberately to cause distress and anxiety, provided the means used are not unlawful. Therefore, it is important to consider areas of law whereby overall protection against harassment has developed regardless of the means used to cause the harassment.

4.5.1 Public order offences

The Public Order Act 1986 was the culmination of seven years' consideration of public order law and 'introduced a structured series of offences to deal with disorder at all levels'.[140] The general public order offences are hierarchical in nature, ranging from the most serious offence of riot (s 1) to the lowest level

---

138 Eg, Patrick Keane stalked his victim for nine years before the police were able to intervene after he threatened to kill her: 'Stalker convicted for causing grievous bodily harm' (1997) *The Guardian*, 23 July; 'Stalker told to expect life' (1997) *The Times*, 23 July.

139 Interview with Anthony Burstow, 29 March 1999: 'I was trying to prove a point, that they couldn't touch me. It was as much to get at the police and the whole legal system as it was to get at her.'

140 Home Office, *Policing Low-Level Disorder: Police Use of Section 5 of the Public Order Act 1986*, Home Office Research History 135, 1994, London: HMSO.

offence of disorderly conduct (s 5).[141] Although stalking could not be described as a public order offence,[142] certain manifestations of harassment may satisfy the provisions of the more minor public order offences.[143]

Section 4 contains the offence of causing fear of violence which is committed when the defendant uses words or behaviour towards another person which are threatening, abusive or insulting and which are either intended to cause the recipient to believe that immediate unlawful violence will be used or are likely to cause that response.[144] The defendant must either intend his conduct to be threatening, abusive or insulting or be aware that it may be perceived in this way.[145] It has been said that 'it is the very essence of a threat that it should be made for the purpose of intimidating or overcoming the will of the person to whom it is addressed'[146] and it has been suggested that this purpose would be satisfied by the stalker who intended that his conduct should coerce the victim into resuming a relationship with the stalker, or ceasing to associate with a new partner.[147] It is certainly true that many stalking cases appear to be pursued with the purpose of wearing down the victim's resistance in order to compel compliance with some requirement of the stalker.[148] However, the requirement that the stalker must either intend or be aware that his conduct is threatening, abusive or insulting may limit the application of this offence in stalking cases, as not all stalkers are aware that their conduct could be perceived in anything other than a positive or

---

141 Sherr, 1989, pp 85–87.

142 The Public Order Act 1986 has been described as a ladder of offences aimed at group disorder which causes fear to ordinary citizens: Ashworth, 1999, pp 338–40. During the passage of the Criminal Justice and Public Order Act 1994, a proposal which would have amended the Public Order Act 1986 to include an offence of stalking was rejected, as stalking was perceived as specific personal harm, thus unsuitable for inclusion in a statute aimed at disorderly public conduct: Standing Committee B, Criminal Justice and Public Order Bill, Cols 1280–84, 8 March 1994.

143 *R v Taft* (1997) 2 Cr App R(S) 182: the defendant had been harassing women drivers by following them in his car to deserted areas and pulling alongside them whilst appearing to be masturbating. He would then pull sharply in front of their vehicles and brake, intending to force them to stop their cars. He was convicted under s 4 of the Public Order Act 1986 and sentenced to three and a half years' imprisonment.

144 Public Order Act 1986, s 4(1)(a).

145 *Ibid*, s 6(3).

146 *Wood v Bowron* (1866) LR 2 QB 21, *per* Lush J, p 30.

147 Allen, 1996.

148 Case history 4 – the stalker persistently harassed the victim, damaged her car, threatened harm to her and to commit suicide if she refused to resume a relationship with him. Case history 8 – the stalker terrorised his former wife in order to compel her to give up her new relationship even though he had left her for another woman and was still involved in that relationship.

favourable light.[149] This is especially true of obsessive and delusional stalkers and those suffering from a mental disorder.[150]

In addition to the requirement that the words or behaviour are threatening, abusive or insulting, the conduct must also be intended to result in a fear of violence, or be such that it is likely that a fear of violence will result. This requirement has been described as 'a statutory form of assault which is capable of commission by words alone, although conduct will give additional force to any words that are uttered'.[151] Provided the conduct is threatening, abusive or insulting, it is irrelevant what form it takes, provided that the defendant has the requisite intention or awareness as to its impact. If it cannot be established that the defendant intended to cause fear of violence, the objective consideration of whether it was likely that the defendant's conduct would cause fear of violence becomes determinative. The focus will be on the propensity of the conduct to instil fear of violence into the victim regardless of the defendant's actual intention. This may assist in cases where a stalker asserts an alternative motivation for his conduct that nevertheless was perceived by the recipient to indicate that violence was likely to occur.

The main impediment to the universal utilisation of this offence against stalkers is the intention requirement. If a stalker is able to argue that he was unaware of the effect of his conduct, he may escape liability, although it will not suffice for him to assert that he did not consider the conduct to be threatening, abusive or insulting, as it must also be established that he did not appreciate that his conduct could be perceived in this light by the victim. The intention requirement may prevent use of this offence in all but the most clearly threatening situations, which is an unfortunate limitation in stalking cases, as a fear of violence is a common reaction to stalking; thus, without the intention requirement, this section could be widely used in the protection of stalking victims.

Section 4A, which was inserted by s 154 of the Criminal Justice and Public Order Act 1994, prohibits the use of threatening, abusive or insulting words or behaviour and disorderly behaviour which is intended to cause the recipient of the conduct harassment, alarm or distress. This offence concerns similar conduct to that previously discussed, but requires that it have the more general effect of causing harassment, alarm or distress to the victim rather than fear of violence required by s 4. However, as with the s 4 offence, the defendant must intend or be aware that this conduct is threatening, abusive or insulting or amounts to disorderly conduct. Section 4A also requires an

---

149 Case history 26 – despite having pursued the same person for three years, despite their persistent attempts to avoid him, this stalker has no conception that he is the stalker that she is afraid of and is concerned that she is being stalked and wishes she would let him help her.

150 Case history 19 – this stalker believes that he and his victim are joined by a karmic link and are destined to be together owing to events which occurred in their previous lives.

151 Smith, 1987, p 101.

intention to cause harassment, alarm or distress. This has been termed a 'limiting factor' due to the difficulty of such proof in practice and it has been suggested that the offence would be more effective if an awareness[152] of a risk of causing harassment had been included as an alternative mental element.[153]

The need for the defendant's conduct to cause harassment, alarm or distress ensures that this offence is potentially available in a greater number of stalking cases than the offence under s 4, as victims of stalking respond in a variety of ways and will not always be in fear of violence.[154] The requirement that the conduct should cause harassment, alarm or distress – more general notions than fear of violence – ensure that this offence is potentially available in a greater number of stalking cases then the s 4 offence. However, s 4A contains a similar impediment to its use, given the nature of stalking, due to the difficulty of establishing that the stalker intended to cause harassment, alarm or distress by this conduct.

Section 5 of the Public Order Act was introduced to enable the police to intervene at the early stages of disorder and to address various forms of offensive behaviour which may cause harassment, alarm or distress to members of the public, typically minor acts of rowdiness.[155] Liability is engendered under s 5 whereby the defendant uses threatening, abusive or insulting words or behaviour, or disorderly behaviour, within the hearing or sight of a person likely to be caused harassment, alarm or distress. Again, this offence requires that the defendant intends his conduct to be threatening, abusive or insulting, or is aware that it may be perceived in such a way.

The conduct need not actually be directed at another person and there is no requirement that any person actually experiences harassment, alarm or distress, merely that the words or behaviour are manifested in the presence of a person who could potentially be caused harassment, alarm or distress. The provision was worded in this way to avoid the necessity of producing an actual victim who suffered harassment, alarm or distress as it was felt that offensive conduct was frequently aimed at vulnerable persons who would find the requirement of giving evidence in court distressing and intimidating. Since *DPP v Orum*,[156] in which it was held that a police officer is 'a person who is capable of experiencing harassment, alarm or distress' for the purposes of s 5, it has been open to the police to arrest persons who are abusive towards

---

152 Awareness is a subjective concept akin to subjective recklessness: *Clarke v DPP* [1992] Crim LR 60.
153 Card and Ward, 1994, p 138.
154 Pathe and Mullen, 1997, pp 12–17.
155 Brown and Ellis, 1994.
156 *DPP v Orum* (1988) *The Times*, 25 July.

them.[157] The Home Office Research Study of this offence reveals that an exceptionally low level of misconduct appears to justify arrest and cites examples of firing a water pistol, shouting at a prostitute and meowing at a police dog.

The behaviour that has satisfied the 'likely to be caused harassment' requirement would appear to indicate that relatively minor conduct will suffice for liability under this section. In the light of this, it is all the more surprising that more use was not made of this offence to combat stalking, especially in situations where the stalker's conduct is causing actual harassment, alarm or arrest to an identifiable victim. However, it is not enough that the conduct causes harassment, alarm or distress, as the statute requires that the conduct itself must be threatening, abusive or insulting. The House of Lords have held that whether conduct qualifies as threatening, abusive or insulting is a question of fact that must be decided on the basis of the ordinary meaning of the words and the impact that the conduct would have on an ordinary member of the public.[158] Many incidences of stalking would not be perceived objectively as threatening, abusive or insulting, thus would not give rise to liability under this section although the actual recipient of the conduct might find the conduct manifestly threatening. For example, in Case history 1, the victim was extremely distressed by the persistence with which the stalker stood outside her house watching her. Nevertheless, this may well not be conduct that would be considered objectively to be threatening, abusive or insulting and the police certainly took this stance.[159] Therefore, even if, given the relationship between the parties and past events that have occurred, the victim feels threatened by conduct, this will not suffice if there is nothing overtly threatening in the conduct itself. Whether or not seemingly innocuous conduct is threatening is really context-dependent, but this offence requires conduct to be objectively threatening in order to qualify for prosecution.[160]

This can be seen by the way in which the pattern of conduct generally resulting in an arrest is characterised as an 'abuse, warning, arrest' spiral whereby any refusal to desist from behaving in a certain way when requested by the police leads to an arrest under s 5.[161] This could easily incorporate even

---

157 Home Office Research Study 135 found that this offence is frequently used to arrest those who are offensive towards police officers, with one-third of all arrests having a police officer as a sole victim of the offensive conduct.

158 *Brutus v Cozens* [1973] AC 854.

159 Case history 1 – 'They were so condescending. All "even if he is watching the house, what harm is he actually doing?". They said that it wasn't as if he tried to break in or threatened me or attacked me and said: "we're not quite sure what offence he's committing by standing on the pavement." They did go and talk to him but I watched them and they were all laughing together at one stage, the three of them, the two policemen and him. No way were they taking it seriously.'

160 See discussion of context-dependent crime in Chapter 2. Jaconelli, 1995.

161 Brown and Ellis, 1994, p 51.

the most harmless stalking conduct, whereby the police could warn the stalker that his conduct was causing harassment to the victim and then arrest him if he failed to desist. However, it is difficult to describe some stalking conduct as abuse. In one case, the victim's solicitor advised her to suggest s 5 to the police as a means of arresting her stalker, but the police still refused to intervene, responding: 'but he's just standing there.'[162] This idea of repeated abuse and objectively threatening behaviour ties in with the idea that this offence is intended to address disorderly public conduct rather than targeted personal harassment. The conduct described in the Home Office Research Study, although of a minor nature, does involve an element of public rowdiness and disturbance that is lacking in stalking cases. Members of the public are far more likely to be caused distress and alarm by an incident involving a man swearing and arguing with the police than they are by stalking incidents that are frequently not discernible to anyone other than the direct victim. For example, in the example cited above, the only objectively visible act was that of a man standing on the pavement which, in the absence of knowledge of the background to the situation, is unlikely to cause alarm to a bystander.

Despite the appeal of using the s 5 offence against stalkers, who so clearly cause harassment, alarm or distress, the requirement that the conduct be objectively threatening, abusive or insulting will impede many cases, and the requirement that the defendant intends or is aware that this is so will defeat even more. Equally, the absence of a public element to this type of conduct realistically moves it outside the type of conduct that the statute was intended to address, which might explain police reluctance to make use of it in stalking cases.

4.5.2 Sexual harassment in the workplace

Despite the popular conception of stalking as behaviour that occurs between strangers or intimate partners, a great deal of stalking involves acquaintances, especially where one party fosters an non-reciprocal desire to develop a closer relationship. It is not uncommon for stalking to arise from workplace relationships. One of the first areas in which a system of cohesive protection against harassment developed is that of employment law following the enactment of the Sex Discrimination Act 1975. Subjecting another person to sexual harassment can amount to direct discrimination under s 1(1)(a) of the Sex Discrimination Act, which prohibits treating a person less favourably on the ground of their sex, that is, that a person of the opposite sex was not, or would not be, treated in the same way.

The principle that sexual harassment can amount to direct discrimination was first recognised in *Porcelli v Strathclyde Regional Council*, where a female

---

162 Case history 1.

technician was subjected to a period of unpleasant treatment that included, but was not limited to, behaviour of a sexual nature by two male colleagues.[163] It was argued that as the conduct was motivated by the desire of the two male technicians to force the applicant to seek a transfer, it could not constitute sexual harassment as it lacked a sexual motivation and an equally disliked male colleague would have been treated equally badly.

This was rejected in the Court of Session where it was said that s 1(1)(a) was concerned with treatment to which people were subjected, not the motivation or objective of the person responsible. Lack of a sex-related motive did not mean that conduct could not be regarded as 'on the ground of sex' for the purposes of the Sex Discrimination Act as it was clear that:

> the campaign was plainly adopted against [the applicant] because she was a woman. It was a particular kind of weapon, based upon the sex of the victim, which ... would not have been used against an equally disliked man.[164]

Thus, if a material part of the unfavourable treatment to which a woman is subjected includes a significant element of sexually related behaviour which would not be directed towards a man, the treatment will be regarded as being based on the woman's sex within the meaning of s 1(1)(a). Lord Grieve refers to the use of sexually related behaviour as 'a sexual sword' which, as it is only used because the victim is a woman, must amount to direct discrimination.[165]

One limitation of the use of the Sex Discrimination Act was the requirement that the applicant must have suffered a detriment as a result of the harassing conduct.[166] In *Porcelli*, this was satisfied as the applicant had sought a transfer owing to her intolerable working conditions, but this will not always be the case. However, the need to establish a detriment arising from the harassment was eliminated by *Wileman v Minilec Engineering*, where it was held that 'sexual harassment is legal shorthand for activity which is easily recognisable as subjecting her to any other detriment'.[167] Therefore, being subjected to sexual harassment will, in itself, amount to a detriment and in *Bracebridge Engineering v Derby* it was held that a single act of sexual harassment, if sufficiently serious, can amount to a detriment despite the fact that 'harassment' is usually taken to connote repeated and continuing conduct.[168]

Sexual harassment is not a term used by the Sex Discrimination Act, hence there is no statutory definition that identifies the type of conduct that will be

---

163 *Porcelli v Strathclyde Regional Council* [1986] ICR 564.

164 *Ibid, per* Lord Emslie, p 569.

165 *Ibid, per* Lord Grieve, p 573.

166 Sex Discrimination Act 1975, s 6(2): 'It is unlawful for a person, in the case of a woman employed by him, at an establishment in Great Britain, to discriminate against her (b) by dismissing her, or subjecting her to any other detriment.'

167 *Wileman v Minilec Engineering Ltd* [1988] IRLR 144, *per* Popplewell J, p 147.

168 *Bracebridge Engineering v Derby* [1990] IRLR 3.

actionable. It has been described as a colloquial expression used to describe the type of discrimination made unlawful by s 6 of the Sex Discrimination Act.[169] The European Commission issued a Code of Practice that defined sexual harassment as:

> unwanted conduct of a sexual nature, or other conduct based on sex affecting the dignity of men and women at work. This can include unwelcome physical, verbal or non-verbal conduct.[170]

This definition has been applied by the courts and tribunals, but adds little clarification as to what specific behaviour will constitute sexual harassment. This issue was considered further in *Insitu Cleaning v Heads*, where it was argued that one sexually explicit comment could not amount to sexual harassment as the European Commission Code of Practice referred to unwanted conduct and the defendant could not know whether conduct was unwanted until it was done and rejected.[171] This argument was rejected and it was held that whether or not a single act of harassment will constitute a detriment is a matter of fact and degree.

Further consideration was given to this point in the recent decision of *Reed v Stedman*, where the President of the Employment Appeal Tribunal sought to establish guidelines for tribunals to refer to in sexual harassment cases.[172] It was held that the essential characteristic of sexual harassment is words or conduct which are unwelcome to the recipient and it is for each individual to determine what is acceptable to them and what they regard as offensive. If the tribunal would not characterise the conduct as offensive, this does not mean that the recipient's claim must fail, as each person is entitled to determine what conduct they find intolerable. There is some conduct that would always be regarded as unwelcome unless it was expressly invited, such as sexual touching. However, a woman is free to define her own levels of acceptance and can refuse to tolerate conduct that would objectively be regarded as unobjectionable behaviour provided that she makes it clear, by words or conduct, that such conduct is unwelcome. Once conduct has been rejected in a way that would be recognisable to any reasonable person, continuation of this conduct will generally be regarded as harassment. The tribunal must also bear in mind that once an act of a blatant sexual nature has occurred, other conduct may become objectionable and the tribunal must not separate the case into a series of specific incidents, but consider the conduct in its totality.

---

169 *Reed v Stedman* [1999] IRLR 299, *per* Morison J, p 302 (President of the Employment Appeal Tribunal).

170 European Commission Recommendation 92/131/EEC on the Protection of the Dignity of Women and Men at Work, European Commission Report, 'Protection of the dignity of men and women at work', OJ 97B.

171 *Insitu Cleaning Co Ltd v Heads* [1995] IRLR 4.

172 *Reed and Bull Information Systems Ltd v Stedman* [1999] IRLR 299.

This case is a welcome recognition that people are individuals with different levels of tolerance who will find a variety of conduct objectionable. It is for each individual to set the parameters of conduct that they find acceptable and, provided they clearly indicate what type of conduct is unwelcome, they should not be expected to tolerate conduct they find offensive even if it is generally perceived to be harmless or inoffensive. In this case, part of the conduct to which the recipient objected was the telling of obscene jokes in her presence, and she always left the room when this occurred. The Employment Appeal Tribunal held that this indicated her disapproval of such conduct, thus making its repetition unacceptable.

The President of the Employment Appeal Tribunal also made it clear that this was only the first element of establishing a claim for sex discrimination:

> The question in each case is whether the alleged victim has been subjected to a detriment and, second, was it on the grounds of sex.[173]

This second requirement is the crux of sex discrimination law that prohibits disparate treatment on the basis of sex rather than bad treatment *per se*. Thus, there must be a connection between the gender of the recipient and the conduct to which they are subjected. Inability to establish that a person of the opposite sex was, or would have been, treated differently means that the crucial gender differential that forms the basis of sex discrimination is absent and the claim will fail. This is illustrated by *Stewart v Cleveland Guest*, where the tribunal held that the display of pornographic material did not amount to sexual harassment of the applicant as it was gender-neutral conduct which a man may have found equally offensive.[174] Therefore, if the defendant can establish that the objectionable conduct is directed at both men and women and is not gender-specific, there will be no liability.[175] This has been termed the 'but I'm a bastard to everyone' defence.[176]

It was said in *British Telecommunications v Williams* that, because conduct which constitutes sexual harassment is itself gender-specific, there is no necessity to look for a male comparator.[177] This was criticised in *Smith v Gardner Merchant* as the elevation of a conclusion of fact into a principle of law.[178] The Court of Appeal agreed that conduct that amounts to sexual harassment is usually gender-specific, in which case there would be no need for a male comparator as it was bound, as a matter of fact, to be less favourable treatment as between the sexes. However, if the conduct is directed

---

173 *Reed and Bull Information Systems Ltd v Stedman* [1999] IRLR 299, *per* Morison J, p 302.

174 *Stewart v Cleveland Guest (Engineering) Ltd* [1994] IRLR 440.

175 *Insitu Cleaning Co Ltd v Heads* [1995] IRLR 4: the court would not accept that a comment to the woman regarding the size of her breasts was comparable with remarks about a man's baldness as one is of a sexual nature and the other is not.

176 Smith and Thomas, 1996, p 219.

177 *British Telecommunications v Williams* [1997] IRLR 668.

178 *Smith v Gardner Merchant* [1998] IRLR 520.

at a person because of his or her sex, but is not of an overtly sexual nature, there will still be a need for a comparator to establish disparate treatment. This was confirmed in *Reed v Stedman* where it was said that in sexual harassment cases 'the answer will usually be quite clear without resort to a comparator, actual or hypothetical'.[179]

The position of those experiencing sexual harassment in the workplace would appear, especially in the light of recent case law, to be relatively favourable compared to those harassed in other environments. Sexual harassment will, of itself, constitute a detriment for the purposes of s 6(2)(b) and, provided that the conduct is inherently sexual in nature, there is no need to prove that a person of the opposite sex would have been treated differently. The conduct need not be objectively offensive as, following *Reed v Stedman*, repetition of any conduct, however innocuous, can amount to harassment provided the recipient has made it clear that the conduct is unwanted, thus empowering those targeted to set strict boundaries of tolerable conduct and ensure that these are respected.

The obvious limitation of the Sex Discrimination Act in terms of victims of stalking and harassment is that the relevant provisions are only applicable to harassment in the workplace. Even where the stalker and his victim are work colleagues, it is clear that workplace unpleasantness which lacks a sexual element and is targeted at a particular person because they are disliked for personal reasons, rather than because they are a member of a particular sex, is not likely to be covered. In Porcelli, although the applicant was targeted for non-sexual reasons, some of the conduct was of a sexual nature, hence became a 'sexual sword' which was used because she was a woman, thus satisfying the requirements of s 1(1)(a). One victim was subjected to unpleasant conduct at work which lacked any sexual connotation, although there could be an argument that the conduct was based on her sex as it arose after she rejected a colleague's request for a date.[180] It could be claimed that she was, therefore, subjected to a detriment because of her sex as, presumably, he would not have been interested in her in a romantic way had she not been a woman. This may suffice to bring her situation within the Sex Discrimination Act, but the argument is somewhat tenuous and lacking in authority.

It is probably true to say that the area of sexual harassment in employment is one of the key areas in which the courts have been alert to identify and address harassment and to develop wide principles which embrace harassment in all its diverse manifestations. It is unfortunate that this approach is limited to harassment which occurs in the workplace, as this clearly excludes many stalking victims from the remit of the protection of this reflexive and forward thinking area of law.

---

179 *Reed and Bull Information Systems Ltd v Stedman* [1999] IRLR 299, *per* Morison J, p 302.
180 Case history 2.

4.5.3 Domestic violence legislation

Another area in which general harassment has been outlawed is within the context of familial violence, but this is contingent upon the relationship between the parties and it is true to say that the law has not been as accommodating here as it has in the context of harassment in the course of employment. Victims of stalking may qualify for protection under domestic violence legislation depending upon the nature of the relationship they have with the stalker. There is generally regarded to be a strong link between stalking and domestic violence:

> It is difficult to separate stalking from domestic violence. Understanding the complex relationship between domestic violence and stalking requires an understanding of the magnitude of domestic violence, the general cycle of domestic violence and the typical behaviour of batterers and victims.[181]

> Perpetrators stalking their former partners comprise 60% of all stalking cases in the Los Angeles area ... ex-lover stalking cases are more likely to end in violence than any other type of stalking. Most stalkings of former partners occur in the context of an increasingly violent relationship.[182]

The obvious difficulty with reliance upon domestic violence legislation is that protection is limited to those whose relationships would be considered 'domestic'. Recent legislative changes in this area of law have, however, substantially enlarged the category of persons to be protected under domestic violence provisions. However, as the Family Law Act 1996 did not come into force until 1 October 1997, which was after the main provisions of the Protection from Harassment Act came into force on 16 June 1997, it is relevant, when considering the level of protection available prior to the enactment of the Protection from Harassment Act, to consider the pre-Family Law Act domestic violence legislation.

Prior to the enactment of the Family Law Act 1996, domestic violence legislation was described as 'a hotchpot of enactments of limited scope' by Lord Scarman, who opined: 'the sooner the range, scope and effect of these powers are rationalised into a coherent and comprehensive body of statute law, the better.'[183]

The problems largely arose as domestic violence legislation was spread between three different statutes which had been introduced to deal with specific situations and which protected different classes of victims. The Matrimonial Homes Act 1983 repeated and extended the protection introduced by its 1967 predecessor, which had conferred upon the courts the ability to regulate occupation of the marital home. The Act was designed to

---

181 Salame, 1993, p 83.
182 Jordan, 1995, p 376.
183 *Richards v Richards* [1984] AC 174, pp 206–07.

deal with the property rights of married couples only, not their physical protection, as its object 'was not to protect a wife from violence but to ensure that she had a roof over her head by giving her an occupation right in the matrimonial home.[184] Occupation orders made under this Act could be granted by county courts or the High Court, both of which lacked the ability to attach a power of arrest to such an order although failure to comply gave the applicant the right to apply to the court for committal for default.

Following the recommendations of the Select Committee on Violence in Marriage, legislation was introduced to improve the protection available for victims of domestic violence. The Domestic Violence and Matrimonial Proceedings Act 1976 was the first recognition by Parliament that unmarried partners were also in need of protection from domestic violence, as it included married couples and persons who were 'living with each other in the same household as man and wife'.[185] The Act enabled parties to apply to the county court for a non-molestation order or an ouster order without the necessity of initiating divorce or separation proceedings, hence becoming an action in its own right.

The courts have been reluctant to define 'molestation' and it is generally given a wide meaning:[186]

> which extends to abuse beyond the more typical instances of physical assault to include any form of physical, sexual or psychological molestation or harassment which has a serious detrimental effect upon the health or well-being of the victim ... Examples of such 'non-violent' harassment or molestation cover a very wide range of behaviour. Common instances include persistent pestering and intimidation through shouting, denigration, threat or argument, nuisance telephone calls, damaging property, following the applicant about and repeatedly calling at her home or place of work. Installing a mistress into the matrimonial home with a wife and three children, filling car locks full of superglue, writing anonymous letters and pressing one's face against a window whilst brandishing paper ...[187]

have all been held to constitute molestation. It is clear from these examples given in the Law Commission *Report on Domestic Violence and Occupation of the Family Home* that a great deal of the behaviour which is considered to amount to molestation in a domestic violence context would be considered stalking if it occurred as part of a non-familial relationship. This is clearly illustrative of the overlap between domestic violence and stalking.

---

184 Law Commission, *Report on Matrimonial Proceedings in Magistrates' Courts*, Law Com No 77, 1976, para 3.2.

185 Domestic Violence and Matrimonial Proceedings Act 1976, s 1(2).

186 Fricker, 1988, pp 395–400.

187 *Op cit*, Law Commission, fn 184, para 2.3 (footnotes to the appropriate cases as given in the report are omitted).

Davis J asserted that the best synonym for molestation was 'pester'[188] and, in *Horner v Horner*, it was said that the word 'molest' applied to any behaviour which amounted to such a degree of harassment that it justified the intervention of the court.[189] However, despite these assertions that physical violence is not a condition precedent for the granting of a non-molestation order, research by the Woman's Aid Federation suggests that orders are rarely granted under this Act without evidence of physical violence.[190]

This Act, in contrast to the Matrimonial Homes Act 1983, which defines the rights of spouses in respect of the marital home, does not confer substantive rights on the parties, but was intended merely to provide short term relief 'so that the aggrieved part might continue to live at home while the two parties set about obtaining a solution in the long term of their practical difficulties arising from the attempt to share premises'.[191]

The final Act in the trilogy of domestic violence legislation was the Domestic Proceedings and Magistrates' Courts Act 1978, which provides that either party to a marriage may apply to a magistrates' court for a personal protection order or an exclusion order. A personal protection order will only be granted upon proof that violence has been used or threatened and that it is necessary for the protection of the applicant that an order be made. This applies only to physical violence, hence offers no protection against psychological harm or damage to property. An exclusion order prohibits the respondent from residing in, or visiting, the matrimonial home, but there is no power to extend this to a prohibition from entering the neighbourhood in which the home is situated or other geographical limitations, such as the applicant's place of work. An exclusion order requires proof of violence or threatened violence against the spouse or a child of the family (a threat of violence will only suffice if there is evidence that the respondent has used violence against some other person). Even then, the court cannot make an exclusion order unless satisfied that the applicant or a child of the family is in danger of physical injury.

Even when these statutes would cover behaviour that could be considered to be stalking, thus meriting imposition of an order concerning either protection of the applicant or occupancy of the family home, enforcement was frequently problematic. There was no facility to attach a power of arrest to an order under the Matrimonial Homes Act. Both the other Acts conferred upon the courts the limited ability to attach a power of arrest to any order made, but this was limited to cases where the respondent had caused actual bodily harm to the applicant and was deemed likely to do so again under the Domestic

---

188 *Vaughan v Vaughan* [1973] 1 WLR 1159, *per* Davis J, p 1162.

189 *Horner v Horner* (1983) 4 FLR 50, *per* Ormrod LJ, p 51.

190 Barron, 1990.

191 *O'Neill v Williams* (1984) 4 FLR 1, *per* Cumming-Bruce LJ, p 7.

Violence and Matrimonial Proceedings Act[192] and where the respondent had caused physical injury to the applicant or a child of the family and was likely to do so again under the Domestic Proceedings and Magistrates' Courts Act.[193] Even then, the power of arrest was seen as exceptional rather than routine and a Practice Note issued in 1981 states that there should be a three month limitation to the operation of a power of arrest. Additionally, even if a power of arrest is granted, it cannot make arrest for breach of an order mandatory, but merely confers upon the police the discretion to arrest that they were largely reluctant to exercise.[194] This problem led to the issue of a Home Office Circular to remind police of 'their responsibility to respond as law enforcement officers to requests from victims for help, and of their powers to take action in cases of violence'.[195]

These difficulties with the scope and enforcement of domestic violence legislation led to its examination by the Law Commission, who condemned it as complex, confusing and lacking in integration.[196] Their proposals for reform included a draft Bill which was introduced directly into the House of Lords under the Special Public Committee procedure designed to speed up the legislative process in respect of uncontroversial law reform measures based on the recommendations of the Law Commission.[197] However, the Bill encountered unexpected opposition towards the end of its parliamentary progress as backbench Conservative MPs feared that its provisions would undermine marriage by offering equal protection to unmarried persons. The Bill was withdrawn, only to reappear as Part IV of the Family Law Act 1996.

As the provisions of the Family Law Act 1996 came into force after the enactment of the Protection from Harassment Act 1997, it is not strictly relevant to consider the improved protection that was afforded to victims of domestic violence in a chapter concerned with remedies available prior to the Protection from Harassment Act. However, many of the weaknesses of the pre-1997 domestic violence legislation which would have limited its efficacy as a means of redress for stalking victims were addressed by the Family Law Act, thus it will be valuable to consider the extent of the protection available and the extent to which this overlaps with the Protection from Harassment Act.

The main weaknesses of pre-1997 domestic violence legislation were that the scope of the remedies offered by the various courts under the three Acts

---

192 Domestic Violence and Matrimonial Proceedings Act 1976, s 2(1).
193 Domestic Proceedings and Magistrates' Courts Act 1978, s 18(3).
194 Edwards, 1996.
195 Home Office Circular 60/1990, quoted in Home Affairs Committee Third Report, *Domestic Violence*, HC 245, para 14.
196 *Op cit*, Law Commission, fn 184, para 1.2.
197 Bird, 1997, p 7.

differed substantially and the protection was limited to a restricted range of applicants, that is, married persons and those in a current cohabitation situation. The Family Law Act creates uniformity of rules and procedures between the courts with competent jurisdiction in family matters, subject to certain restrictions.[198] Two categories of order are available: occupation orders[199] and non-molestation orders.[200] Eligibility for an order depends upon whether the parties are within the meaning of 'associated persons' as delineated by s 62(3), which provides that:

a person is associated with another person if –

(a) they are, or have been, married to each other;[201]

(b) they are cohabitants or former cohabitants;[202]

(c) they live or have lived in the same household, otherwise than merely by reason of one of them being the other's employee, tenant, lodger or boarder;

(d) they are relatives;[203]

(e) they have agreed to marry one another (whether or not that agreement has been terminated);[204]

(f) in relation to any child, they are both persons falling within sub-s (4);[205] or,

---

198 Family Law Act 1996, s 57 provides that all courts exercising family jurisdiction (High Court, county courts and magistrates' courts) can make orders under the Act subject to the Lord Chancellor's power to specify that certain types of proceedings will be heard in specific courts. The Family Law Act (Part IV) (Allocation of Proceedings) Order SI 1997/1896 provides that proceedings will generally be commenced in either family proceedings court or county court, but that all applications by children must be made to the High Court. Family Law Act, s 59(1) prevents magistrates' courts from hearing cases where there is a disputed question as to a party's entitlement to occupy any property unless it is unnecessary to determine that question in order to deal with the case.

199 Family Law Act 1996, ss 33–41.

200 Ibid, s 42.

201 Ibid, s 63(5) provides that this includes polygamous as well as monogamous marriages.

202 Ibid, s 62(1) defines cohabitants as men and woman who, although not married to each other, are living together as husband and wife.

203 Ibid, s 63(1) defines relatives as (a) the father, mother, stepfather, stepmother, son, daughter, stepson, stepdaughter, grandmother, grandfather, grandson or granddaughter of that person or that person's spouse or former spouse, or (b) the brother, sister, uncle, aunt, niece or nephew (whether of the full blood or the half blood or by affinity) of that person or of that person's spouse or former spouse and includes, in relation to a person who is living or has lived with another person as husband and wife, any person who would fall within para (a) or (b) if the parties were married to each other.

204 Ibid, s 44 provides that there must be evidence of an agreement to marry whether by writing (such as engagement notices in the newspaper or invitations to an engagement party), or by gift of a ring, or by ceremony entered into in the presence of witnesses. Section 42(4) provides that no application may be brought for a non-molestation order based on reliance on a former engagement more than three years after the agreement to marry was terminated.

205 Ibid, s 62(4) provides that a person has the appropriate relation to a child if they are (a) the parent of the child, or (b) has or had parental responsibility for the child.

(g) they are parties to the same family proceedings.[206]

This represents a substantial expansion of the range of persons to whom protection is available and goes far beyond the idea of domestic violence protection being available only to married couples and current cohabitants that prevailed in the preceding legislation. The drawing of boundaries regarding the limits of protection available under a family law statute has been said to define a domestic or family relationship according to modern thinking,[207] but it is not as all-encompassing as the categories proposed by the Law Commission, whose definition would have included 'those who have or had a sexual relationship with each other (whether or not including sexual intercourse)'.[208] This would have included both homosexual and heterosexual partnerships within the protection of the Act, as opposed to the actual provisions that will only extend protection against domestic violence to homosexual partners if they come within s 62(3)(c) for living or having lived in the same household. Equally, the terms of s 62(3) do not extend protection to persons who have been engaged in a relationship that has not involved cohabitation. These exclusions are significant and raise questions regarding the pertinence of a statute which facilitates the grant of a protective order against, for example, a former cohabitant's stepmother, but not against a violent non-cohabitational partner.[209]

Nevertheless, it can be seen that, despite certain limitations, there is a significant degree of protection available for victims of stalking who come within the domestic violence provisions. The widened protection provided by the Family Law Act 1996 extends this protection still further, although the scope of this extension seems illogical in many ways and could certainly be said not to extend far enough owing to its exclusion of non-cohabitational relationships.

4.6 BINDING OVER

The ability of magistrates' courts to impose an order requiring that a person keep the peace and/or is of good behaviour is of ancient origin.[210] Section 115 of the Magistrates' Courts Act 1980 provides:

---

206 Defined in *ibid*, s 63(1) and (2).
207 Lowe and Douglas, 1998, p 197.
208 *Op cit*, Law Commission, fn 184, para 3.18.
209 Hayes and Williams, 1996, pp 134–38.
210 Binding over originally derived from two sources: the peacekeeping responsibilities of all free men in Anglo-Saxon law, and the royal prerogative which enabled the King, and later his officials, to extend special protection to some individuals and to relieve others of the lawful consequences of their wrongdoing: Feldman, 1988, pp 101–28.

the power of a magistrates' court on the complaint of any person to adjudge any other person to enter into a recognisance, with or without sureties, to keep the peace or to be of good behaviour towards the complainant shall be exercised by order on complaint.

It was initially thought that the precursor of this section, s 25 of the Summary Jurisdiction Act 1879, codified the entire law on binding over, but it became clear that this offence is limited to procedure on complaint and that the powers both at common law (to take sureties of the peace) and under the Justices of the Peace Act 1361 (to bind over to be of good behaviour) have survived.[211] Despite the different origins of binding over to keep the peace and binding over to be of good behaviour, they are now considered as interchangeable concepts, although it is acknowledged that the requirement to be of good behaviour is the broader concept which is inclusive of the narrower requirement to keep the peace.[212] On a practical level, a bind over generally includes both a requirement to keep the peace and to be of good behaviour (either to a named individual or to the world in general).[213] The imposition of an order will be for a specific period of time (usually one year) and is generally backed by sureties that are liable for forfeiture if the order is breached. However, there is no other penalty for breaching the order and the sums involved are nominal (sums of around £100 are usual). A person who refuses to agree to be bound over will be committed to prison, thus refusal to be bound is treated more severely than breach of an order once it is imposed.[214]

One way in which binding over could be particularly advantageous in stalking cases comes from the fact that it is a form of preventative justice, hence there is no requirement that a person must have committed a criminal offence to justify the imposition of an order.[215] It has been said that binding over:

> consists in restraining a man from committing a crime he may commit but has not yet committed, or doing some act injurious to members of the community which he may do but has not yet done.[216]

---

211 The complex basis and interrelation of these powers is one of the justifications given by the Law Commission for their recommendation that binding over be abolished and not replaced: Law Commission, Binding Over, Law Com 222, 1994.

212 Williams, G, 1953, pp 417–27.

213 The Law Commission states that 79% of bind over orders contained both requirements: *op cit*, Law Commission, fn 211, para 2.19.

214 A person who refuses to agree to be bound over can be imprisoned for up to six months if the order is to be made under the Magistrates' Courts Act 1980 or for an unlimited period in relation to orders made at common law or under the Justices of the Peace Act 1361.

215 Blackstone, *Commentaries*, 1769, Vol 4, Chapter 18, p 248.

216 *R v Halliday* [1917] AC 260, *per* Lord Atkinson, p 273.

This ability to bring a person neither convicted nor accused of any crime before the courts and to require him to enter into recognisance to guarantee his future conduct has led to criticisms of the use of binding over:

> It would be contrary to all principle for a man to be punished not for what he has already done but for what he may hereafter to.[217]

However, this criticism is countered by the argument that binding over is not a punishment, but merely an agreement not to behave in an unlawful manner;[218] a means of averting misconduct before its occurrence.[219] Whether this continues to be the case remains to be seen. The European Court of Justice recently held that imprisonment for refusing to be bound over was justified as failure to comply with a court order, but the imposition of the bind over followed an arrest for breach of the peace, thus it may be that an order imposed in the absence of arrest and trial are not considered in the same light.[220]

A person may arrive before the magistrates' courts to be bound over in several ways. Under s 115 of the Magistrates' Courts Act 1980, a complaint is made with the sole aim of having a person bound over. Thus, any stalking victim, or the police on their behalf, can apply to the court to have their stalker bound over. Although this is viewed as part of the civil jurisdiction of magistrates' courts, the intervention of the authorities, especially at an early stage, may serve to deter stalkers from further action and will at least provide unequivocal notice that their conduct is not welcome. As it does not involve a criminal conviction, it may be less likely to aggravate the stalker into escalating his conduct against the victim, as arrest and criminal conviction frequently appear to do.[221] Equally, it should satisfy the victim's need for the intervention of the authorities and the labelling of the stalker's behaviour as 'wrong'.

At common law, the magistrates have the power to bind over any person before them[222] if it is believed that a breach of the peace will be committed in the future or that the defendant's conduct is *contra bones mores*.[223] This power exists regardless of the outcome of the proceedings before them, hence a stalker whose case is withdrawn or discontinued or who is acquitted may still

---

217 *Everett v Richards* [1952] 2 QB 198, *per* Lord Denning, p 206.

218 'A binding to good behaviour is not by way of punishment, but it is to shew that when one has broke the good behaviour, he is not to be any more trusted': *R v Rogers* (1702) 47 ER 1074, *per* Holt LCJ, p 1075.

219 Grunis, 1976, pp 16–41.

220 *Steel and Others v UK* (1999) 28 EHRR 603.

221 Chapter 6.

222 Magistrates are also empowered by common law to bind over for the purposes of preserving order in court, a wider power than that conferred by s 12 of the Contempt of Court Act 1981: Law Commission, 1994, *Binding Over*, Law Com No 222, para 2.11.

223 Contrary to a good way of life: *op cit*, Law Commission, fn 211, para 2.9.

be bound over if their conduct causes the magistrates to feel that this is appropriate.[224]

A person may also be bound over following arrest in association with breach of the peace. Although breach of the peace is not an offence known to English law,[225] a person may be arrested without warrant either for causing a breach of the peace or where it is reasonably apprehended that his conduct will lead to a breach of the peace.[226] The long standing uncertainty regarding the scope of breach of the peace was eliminated in *R v Howell*, where it was held that the requirements are:

> an act done or threatened to be done which either actually harms a person, or in his presence his property, or is likely to cause such harm, or which puts someone in fear of such harm being done.[227]

This definition of breach of the peace was favoured by the European Court of Human Rights, in their first consideration of the compliance of breach of the peace and binding over with the European Convention on Human Rights, over the broader formulation in *R v Chief Constable of Devon and Cornwall ex p Central Electricity Generating Board* which included otherwise lawful conduct which impeded others in the pursuit of their lawful business.[228] The European Court of Human Rights held that the definition in *Howell* and the subsequent cases of *Percy v DPP*[229] and *Nicol and Selvanayagam v DPP*[230]

---

224 This type of procedure was used extensively during the miners' strike, leading to the criticism that 'binding over was used to justify retrospectively charges that should not have been brought, and as a result innocent individuals "consented" effectively under duress to a curtailment of their liberty, social stigma and probability of close attention from the police. This outcome is not unique to the strike and reinforced the need for this highly unsatisfactory area of the law to be reformed.' McCabe and Waddington, 1988, pp 147–48.

225 Unlike the position under Scots law, where breach of the peace is one of the most frequently prosecuted crimes and has been loosely defined to encompass a wide range of conduct deemed to be disruptive or socially offensive. It has been used in stalking cases – *Mackie v Macleod* (1961) unreported – although its efficacy to do so its disputed. For opposing views of the value of breach of the peace in stalking cases, see Bonnington, 1996, p 1394, and Mays, Middlemass and Watson, 1997, pp 331–54.

226 Breach of the peace is one of the four situations in which the police may arrest without warrant: Cheney, Dickson, Fitzpatrick and Uglow, 1999. Since *R v Howell* [1981] 3 All ER 383, there is a power to arrest for breach of the peace where (1) a breach of the peace is committed in the presence of the person making the arrest, or (2) the arrestor reasonably believes that such a breach will be committed in the immediate future by the person arrested although he has not yet committed any breach, or (3) where a breach has been committed and it is reasonably believed that a renewal of it is threatened.

227 *R v Howell* [1981] 3 All ER 383, *per* Watkins LJ, p 389.

228 *R v Chief Constable of Devon and Cornwall ex p Central Electricity Generating Board* [1982] QB 458.

229 *Percy v Director of Public Prosecutions* [1995] 1 WLR 1382: the Divisional Court followed Howell in preference to *Ex p CEGB* in holding there must be a risk of violence before there can be a breach of the peace.

230 *Nicol and Selvanayagam v DPP* [1996] JP 155: there would be no breach of the peace if the conduct of the defendant provoked violence which was wholly unreasonable.

provided a sufficiently clear and precise statement of the scope of breach of the peace, thus enabling an individual to predict with a degree of certainty what conduct would bring him into conflict with the law.[231] Although broad enough to encompass otherwise lawful conduct,[232] the adoption of the narrower definition is unfortunate in terms of protection for stalking victims, as it is frequently the case that it is the interruption to their lawful activities which causes distress to stalking victims. Several cases involve victims who are not able to attend their place of work or study owing to the stalker's presence that would not come within the Howell definition of breach of the peace.

Having held that breach of the peace was sufficiently clear and precise, the European Court of Human Rights went on to consider whether a person bound over to keep the peace had sufficiently clear guidance as to the nature of the conduct that will breach the order. The Court held that as the bind over had been imposed following arrest for breach of the peace, it was clear that continuance of conduct similar to that which led to the arrest will constitute breach of the order. This, however, raises questions as to the validity of bind over orders imposed other than following arrest for breach of the peace. Consideration was given to this issue in *Hashman and Harrup v UK*[233] in which *Steel* was distinguished on this basis and the European Court of Human Rights held that in the absence of arrest for breach of the peace, the applicants would not have predicted what being bound over to keep the peace required them to refrain from doing. Additionally, the requirement that they be of good behaviour was particularly imprecise and offered little guidance as to what they were being ordered not to do. In the light of this decision, the future of binding over other than following a breach of the peace looks uncertain. The government have stated that once all the cases dealing with this issue have been heard by the European Court of Human Rights, they will be reviewing this area of law.[234]

Thus, it may be that the availability of binding over is curtailed in the future. This is unfortunate, as there is much to commend its use in stalking cases,[235] as has been discussed, particularly the procedure under the Magistrates' Courts Act 1980 whereby the victim is able to initiate proceedings. This is especially valuable as it facilitates intervention at an early

---

231 *Steel and Others v UK* (1999) 28 EHRR 603, paras 48–51.

232 Fenwick, 1999, pp 491–514.

233 *Hashman and Harrup v UK* [2000] 30 EHRR 241.

234 O'Brien, M, *Hansard*, HC, Written Answers, Vol 340 Col 214, 1 December 1999.

235 In *R v Dunn* (1840) A & E 599, a binding over order was sought against a stalker who persistently followed and pestered a woman, but it was refused as the power to bind over to keep the peace at the time depended upon evidence that the complainant was in danger of personal violence from another by reason of threats (actual or implied from conduct) or an actual assault. There is no longer such a requirement, and there is no impediment to a bind over being imposed if such circumstances arose today.

stage with no requirement that the stalker has committed a criminal offence. However, it has to be questioned whether binding over actually achieves anything. True, it may deter some stalkers, but the penalty for breach is merely forfeiture of sureties that are usually such a minimal sum as to provide little incentive to comply with the order. The imposition of a binding over order is largely symbolic and consequently ineffectual in many cases, as is any measure which lacks an enforceable sanction, and the power of the court to imprison for refusal to be bound, but not for breach of an order once it is imposed, is anomalous. Anthony Burstow was bound over to keep the peace three times and imprisoned for breach before the authorities appreciated the futility of this action to counter a determined stalker and sought an alternative means of intervention.

Therefore, despite the clear potential value of binding over in stalking cases, the absence of effective enforcement is a major limiting factor. Equally, it is questionable whether it will survive the sustained scrutiny of the European Court of Human Rights given its widely defined scope to limit the future conduct of those who have not yet committed any criminal offence.

4.7 EVALUATION OF THE PROTECTION AVAILABLE

This chapter has presented a consideration of the efficacy of the various means available to address stalking prior to the enactment of the Protection from Harassment Act 1997. Although each of the measures evaluated has merit in particular stalking cases, this piecemeal approach to the protection of stalking victims is deficient and inconsistent. The overriding weakness is that the protection available is uneven and contingent upon such variables as the relationship between the stalker and victim and the nature of the behaviour engaged in by the stalker.

Within certain protected relationships, harassment itself is unlawful and measures are available to deal with persistent stalkers. For those outside the remit of domestic violence and sexual harassment legislation, however, the position is less favourable but, even within these relationships, protection is not comprehensive. For example, a person who is harassed by a work colleague may be protected under sex discrimination legislation for conduct that occurs within the workplace, but if it extends beyond this, there is no protection available. Thus, a woman who was harassed by her employer had a potential means of redress for his conduct towards her at work, but no such protection when he extended his activities to pester her at home.[236] Nevertheless, the approach taken in sexual harassment cases is forward thinking and perceptive, as it provides scope for an individual to determine

---

236 Case history 21.

their own parameters of acceptable conduct and acknowledges that the history between the parties may colour *prima facie* innocuous actions and translate them into a disturbing and offensive form of harassment.[237] This is the only area of law that recognises that context-dependent nature of harassment. There has been substantial expansion of the breadth of protection of domestic violence legislation in recent years, although the most wide ranging changes only took effect after the enactment of the Protection from Harassment Act. Moreover, there are still inadequacies in the protection available, most notably the exclusion from protection of non-cohabitant partners despite plentiful evidence of widespread violence within these relationships. The most pressing question to be addressed, following consideration of these two areas of law, is why harassment is deemed unacceptable in certain situations and not others. Is it really more damaging to harass a work colleague than it is to direct exactly the same conduct towards a stranger? Surely, once it is accepted that harassment is intolerable, then this view should hold firm regardless of the identity of the victim or the nature of their association with the stalker.

However, outside these relationships, there is little protection available from the totality of harassment. Despite the potential value of the Public Order Act 1986, there is clearly reluctance on behalf of both the police and the legislature to extend the scope of these offences to situations of a wholly private nature. Equally, binding over, particularly following complaint, appears a valuable means of addressing the totality of the stalking at an early stage, but these benefits are offset by the absence of effective enforcement, thus rendering the protection merely symbolic and consequently ineffectual in many cases.

Other than this, protection is only available if substantive criminal offences are committed during the course of stalking. One of the key difficulties of determining liability upon the basis of offences committed during the course of the overall campaign of stalking is that not all stalkers will break the law. Thus, it must be questioned whether this distinction between lawful and unlawful behaviour is justifiable. Is stalking that includes criminal conduct more harmful than that which involves only lawful means? Certainly, the lawfulness or otherwise of the conduct does not appear to determine the intensity of the reaction to stalking or the extent of the harm suffered by the victims. This focus on criminal conduct overlooks the context-dependent nature of harassment as personal knowledge can identify a victim's weaknesses which can be manipulated to cause maximum distress whilst remaining within the boundaries of the law. A perfect illustration of this is the

---

237 The approach to sexual harassment in the workplace is all the more commendable when one considers that the word 'harassment' appears nowhere in the Sex Discrimination Act and that the protection which is available against sexual harassment is solely attributable to sympathetic, yet principled, judicial interpretation of the relevant provisions.

case in which the stalker used his knowledge of the victim to target her in perfectly lawful ways, which eventually led her to receive psychiatric care as an in-patient following a suicide attempt.[238] Frequently, victims are relieved, at least initially, when the stalker resorts to criminal conduct, as they believe, often erroneously, that the police will intervene and bring an end to the stalking.

However, police intervention following criminal conduct can lead a deliberate and determined stalker to ensure that his future harassment remains within the boundaries of lawful behaviour. Several stalkers interviewed admitted this, for example:

> You learn what not to do. I didn't know that sending all that stuff through the post was illegal. I mean, I knew it was wrong but not that I could get nicked for it. I was gutted when I got arrested so I soon stopped doing that and, get this, when I thought of taking photos of her I asked the [police] first if it were a criminal offence and when they said 'no' I knew I was on a winner.[239]

Equally, notorious stalker Anthony Burstow acknowledged that:

> [m]y battle was as much with [the legal system] as it was with her. I resented the interference in what was essentially a private matter and the more that they did to stop me the more determined I became to make her pay ... after I came out of prison ... I realised that I had to stop breaking the law because I'd end up back inside so I was more careful about what I did.[240]

Thus, by focusing only upon criminal offences committed during the course of stalking, a large number of stalkers are immediately placed outside the reach of the law, whether it is by chance that their conduct does not contravene the law or whether it is a deliberate tactic adopted by the stalker. If the intervention of the authorities is contingent upon the criminality of the conduct, this sends an unequivocal message to stalkers that it is permissible to stalk, regardless of the level of distress caused, provided the means of harassment utilised do not amount to a criminal offence. The law is permitting stalkers to harass with impunity provide they use lawful means. As it is clear that 'lawful' stalking can potentially cause harm of comparable severity to stalking, which involves the commission of criminal offences, there is an overwhelming need for protection that focuses on the impact of the stalking rather than the nature of the conduct.

A further limitation to the use of the criminal law to address the composite elements of stalking is that it appears ill-equipped to tackle some of the most

---

238 Case history 37 – the stalker knew about the victim's severe phobic reaction to scissors and sent her over 500 pairs during an eight month period. Additionally, he knew that a certain piece of music upset her dreadfully, having been played at the funeral of her younger brother some months previously, thus he repeatedly filled her answering machine with this music and had it played for her on the local radio station which she listened to at work.

239 Case history 38.

240 Interview with Anthony Burstow, 29 March 1999.

distressing and prevalent manifestations of stalking conduct; implicitly threatening conduct, the making of false allegations and instigating unwanted contact or supply or goods and services from third parties. Additionally, some of the offences which were specifically enacted to deal with particular problems, such as s 43 of the Telecommunications Act 1984 and the Malicious Communications Act 1988, are somewhat exclusionary and carry extremely low penalties, thus limiting their efficacy and the protection available.

Finally, the fragmentation of stalking into a series of separate incidents, whether lawful or unlawful, is a misconstruction of the problem, which both trivialises and underestimates the impact of the totality of the stalking upon the victim. The defining characteristic of stalking is its relentless and persistent nature – it is not so much the conduct which causes distress as the continuance of the conduct and the ensuing uncertainty and anxiety which this engenders in the victim. Victims experience stalking continually, regardless of the frequency of the stalker's acts, as the intervening periods are filled with trepidation. The following quotations from stalking victims encapsulate the constancy of the anxiety and uncertainty evoked by stalkers:

> The worst thing wasn't when he was outside the house ... it was when he wasn't there so I kept looking for him anyway so he [might] just as soon have done it all the time. But you wonder where he is and what he is doing. I used to spend hours sitting really still staring out of a tiny gap in the curtains, watching him watching my house, just to make sure he was still there. If he had gone, I used to get really panicky in case he was round the back trying to get in.[241]

> Our cat went missing for a week and I truly thought that she had killed him and kept expecting his mangled body to turn up on the doorstep. Of course, it didn't. He came back. He was always wandering off and I usually wouldn't think twice about it. But it makes you jumpy and suspicious. The thing is, you get so used to waiting for something else dreadful to happen that you interpret things wrongly. Every time the phone rang or someone came to the door, my heart would jump and I'd think 'what now?' It was almost better when something was happening because you were busy dealing with it. The waiting in between was worse. I was sat in with my parents watching the telly once and the phone rang and we all jumped, physically jumped in our seats, because of the tension of waiting for the next thing to happen.[242]

Therefore, a legal system that merely addresses some of the composite elements of the totality of the conduct is not providing an adequate reaction to this complex and challenging problem. One stalking victim was in court to see

---

241 Case history 32 – the victim was followed and watched for approximately six months by an unknown man who would stand and stare at her house for hours on end. She moved house in order to escape from him.

242 Case history 15 – the victim had an affair with the stalker's partner. The stalking was intensive for a eight month period but lasted intermittently for seven years, gradually decreasing until the victim is optimistic that it has now totally ended.

her stalker given a small fine for causing criminal damage to some of her plants and some garden furniture. These were the only criminal offences committed during his 10 month campaign of stalking which caused his victim such severe depression that she was forced to give up her job.[243] By breaking the whole of the conduct down into individual incidents, there is little that represents the enormity of the totality of the ordeal suffered by most stalking victims. This fragmentation increases the focus on the conduct when it needs to be upon the single element which is common to all stalking cases; the adverse impact that the conduct has upon the victim. There is a clear need for an approach to stalking that both addresses the totality of the conduct and focuses upon the impact this has upon the victim as the wrong which should be prohibited. These issues are, to a certain extent, acknowledged in the areas of tort and criminal law considered in detail in the next chapter. These areas of law were expanded to encompass stalking in recognition of the seriousness of stalking and the inadequacy of the existing law to address the problem. This chapter has presented a consideration of the problems of using existing laws which were frequently unsuited to deal with stalking and has identified the key inadequacies of this approach. This following chapter will analyse how the two areas of law sought to adapt to remedy these deficiencies and will evaluate both the success of this and the consequences of the expansion of legal principles to encompass a situation beyond their true remit.

---

243 Case history 31 – the stalker worked in a garden centre and initially showered the victim with gifts until she made it clear that she was not interested in him, at which time he began to watch her house and eventually damaged some of her property.

CHAPTER 5

JUDICIAL EXPANSION OF THE LAW

The review of the available means of legal redress for stalking victims prior to the enactment of the Protection from Harassment Act 1997 has so far revealed three key areas of difficulty. First, even in the face of years of persistent harassment, there was no basis for legal intervention unless the conduct involved the commission of an existing criminal offence. Secondly, even if a criminal offence were committed, the penalty might not appear to reflect the seriousness of the overall campaign of harassment. This might be because the offence carried a relatively low maximum penalty or because the offence formed only an infinitesimal part of the totality of the conduct. A third difficulty with the existing law was that even where the law did offer protection against harassment, this was only available to certain categories of persons in specific situations.

It is against this background that the judiciary developed areas of tort and criminal law in an attempt to expand existing legal principles to encompass novel situations, thus ameliorating these difficulties. These areas of judicial interpretation are indicative of the recognition of the need to develop a cohesive system of law to address stalking whilst illustrating the difficulties associated with expanding an existing area of law to address a situation that it was not designed to address.

5.1 THE DEVELOPMENT OF THE TORT OF HARASSMENT

The development of tort law to address a more generalised notion of harassment arose directly due to the limitations of the remit of domestic violence law. If the nature of the association between the stalker and the victim was outside of the familial relationships protected by domestic violence legislation, a victim seeking an injunction had to turn to the law of tort for a remedy.[1]

Section 37(1) of the Supreme Court Act 1981 placed the inherent jurisdiction of the High Court to grant injunctive relief 'in all cases where it appears to the court to be just and convenient to do so' on a statutory basis. This power was extended to the county courts by s 38(1) of the County Courts Act 1984. The width of the jurisdiction to grant an injunction is limited by the requirement of 'an action, actual or potential, claiming substantive relief

---

1   Cooke, 1994, pp 289–96.

which the High Court has jurisdiction to grant',[2] hence it is not enough that the applicant desires an injunction to restrain the stalker's conduct; the conduct must constitute a recognised tort, as '[an] injunction can only be an appropriate remedy where an actual tortious act has been or is likely to be committed.[3]

Unfortunately, behaviour which would be sufficient to justify the grant of an injunction under domestic violence legislation if a familial relationship existed between the parties will not necessarily fall into any of the established categories of tort. Conduct which would be considered 'molestation' is not necessarily tortious, hence leaving the victim of harassment without a remedy in civil law.[4]

This is illustrated in *Patel v Patel*, where the harassment of the plaintiff due to a family dispute led him to obtain an injunction prohibiting his son-in-law from approaching within 50 yards of his home.[5] The Court of Appeal refused to uphold this provision as the defendant could only be excluded from an area where a tort had been, or was likely to be, committed. Merely being within a certain distance of a person's property is not trespass or any other tort.[6] Although the defendant's actions had undoubtedly caused the plaintiff harassment, this was not a sufficient basis on which to grant an injunction, as the Court of Appeal explicitly stated that there is no tort of harassment.[7]

Such an unequivocal rejection of the possibility of a tort of harassment appeared to have seriously restricted the possibilities of using tort as a basis for relief in stalking cases. If there is no tort of harassment, then references to harassment would not be appropriate in injunctions prohibiting tortious conduct unless the conduct complained of amounts to one of the established torts such as assault, battery, trespass or nuisance.[8] However, it was later suggested that the plaintiff was unsuccessful in *Patel v Patel* as the court did not accept that his rights were being seriously infringed: it was described as 'a storm in a teacup'.[9] Nevertheless, this restriction upon the scope of injunctive relief renders injunctions granted in tort severely narrower in scope than those granted under domestic violence legislation. The courts will have to refuse relief to deserving applicants who may be suffering serious harassment unless the conduct fits within an established category of tortious liability. Even then, injunctive relief is limited to the prohibition of conduct that amounts to a recognised tort.

---

2   *Siskina v Distos Cia Naviera SA, The Siskina* [1977] 2 All ER 803, *per* Lord Denning, p 823.
3   *Patel v Patel* [1988] 2 FLR 179, *per* May LJ, p 180.
4   Cooke, 1994, pp 289–96.
5   *Patel v Patel* [1988] 2 FLR 179.
6   The action was based on the tort of trespass and it was not disputed that the defendant had trespassed on the applicant's property during the course of the harassment.
7   *Patel v Patel* [1988] 2 FLR 179, *per* Waterhouse J, p 182.
8   Fricker, 1988, pp 395–400.
9   *Burris v Azadani* [1995] 4 All ER 802, *per* Sir Thomas Bingham MR, pp 805–06.

This is clearly illustrated in *Pidduck v Molloy*[10] which concerned the scope of an injunction granted following a prolonged campaign of harassment whereby the defendant was restrained from, *inter alia*, speaking to the plaintiff, who was his former partner and the mother of his child. It was accepted by the court that speaking to the plaintiff was neither a tortious act nor a crime. However:

> it is the fact that the past conduct of the defendant has suggested that, if he does speak to her, it is usually for the purpose of intimidating, threatening or abusing her, all of which are capable of amounting to crimes or torts.[11]

Accordingly, the injunction was amended to read: 'not to speak to the plaintiff in an intimidatory, threatening or abusive manner.'

It was this need for a tort within which to situate the facts of a case in order to protect a meritorious applicant that led to the liberation of 'the tort recognised ... in *Wilkinson v Downton* from its status as little more than a footnote in legal history'.[12]

In *Wilkinson v Downton*, the defendant, as a joke, falsely told the plaintiff that her husband had suffered serious injury in an accident.[13] Believing this, the plaintiff suffered a violent shock 'producing vomiting and other more serious and permanent physical consequences at one time threatening her reason, and entailing weeks of suffering and incapacity'.[14] As the conduct of the defendant was outside the scope of the torts of battery and assault, and there was no remedy in negligence for nervous shock at this time, it appeared that the plaintiff would be without a remedy, but the court held that it was a tort to cause physical injury to a person intentionally. Wright J was of the view that: 'the defendant has ... wilfully done an act calculated to cause physical harm to the plaintiff ... and has thereby caused physical harm to her. That proposition without more appears to state a good cause of action, there being no justification for the act.'[15]

This decision was followed by the Court of Appeal in *Janvier v Sweeney* where the defendant, who was a private detective, threatened to traduce the plaintiff's fiancé, an internee, as a German spy and to have her arrested for having associated with him.[16] The threat was intended to frighten the plaintiff into revealing private letters belonging to her employer. This caused the plaintiff to suffer nervous trauma that was manifest by physical symptoms.

---

10   [1992] 2 FLR 202.
11   *Ibid, per* Lord Donaldson MR, p 205.
12   Brazier, 1992, pp 346–48.
13   *Wilkinson v Downton* [1897] 2 QB 57.
14   *Ibid, per* Wright J, p 58.
15   *Ibid, per* Wright J, pp 58–59.
16   *Janvier v Sweeney* [1919] 2 KB 316.

This case was viewed by the Court of Appeal as more serious than *Wilkinson v Downton* as there, the defendant was playing a particularly callous practical joke, whereas in this case, the defendant deliberately sought to frighten and intimidate the victim.

Despite the potential value of applying the principle enunciated in *Wilkinson v Downton* to harassment cases, the case was not used and '... English law and textbook writers quickly consigned this rather ill-fitting case to the footnotes of doctrinal exposition'.[17] Yet, the implications of the cases are immense as it recognises that:

> all intentional infliction of bodily harm is actionable regardless of the means employed to procure it, be it by direct physical aggression, injurious words or by setting in motion a force which directly or indirectly accomplishes the desired result. It thus offers both a unifying principle enveloping the whole area of liability for intentional physical injury and supplements the conventional trespass, wrongs of assault, battery and false imprisonment.[18]

The first use of the principle in *Wilkinson v Downton* to provide a remedy for a stalking victim came in *Burnett v George* where the defendant embarked on a campaign of harassment against the plaintiff following the acrimonious termination of a four year relationship.[19] His conduct towards her included assault, unwelcome visits to her home and telephone calls made at unsociable hours which sometimes involved heavy breathing and at other times involved verbal threats made to the plaintiff, all of which the court held 'unquestionably amounted to a general policy of molestation'.[20] The plaintiff had been granted an injunction prohibiting the defendant from 'assaulting, molesting or otherwise interfering with' her. The defendant appealed against these terms as they did not disclose a tort known to law.

The Court of Appeal confirmed that the statutory formula of justice and convenience under which the High Court and the county courts granted injunctive relief required justice to be in the form of an identifiable and protectable legal interest and conceded that molestation is not, in the absence of a matrimonial nexus or children to protect, an actionable tort, thus an injunction could not be granted to restrain it. However, if there is evidence that the health of the plaintiff is being impaired by molestation or there is interference calculated to cause such impairment, then an injunction can be granted to the extent that is necessary to avoid that impairment of health. Therefore, although the generalised prohibition against molestation and interference was too wide, as the plaintiff had given evidence that the telephone calls were having an adverse affect on her health, the injunction could be amended to prohibit the defendant from 'assaulting, molesting or

---

17 Conaghan, 1996, p 417.
18 Fleming, 1987, p 32.
19 *Burnett v George* [1992] 1 FLR 525.
20 *Ibid, per* Sir John Arnold, p 526.

otherwise interfering with the plaintiff by doing acts calculated to do her harm'.

This granting of a remedy on the basis of liability recognised in *Wilkinson v Downton* led to hopes of the emergence of a nominate tort of 'personal injury by molestation'.[21] This remedy was said to be narrower than a tort of harassment, 'involving the intended or likely impairment of the victim's health' and requiring 'lies or threats which the speaker knows are likely to cause physical injury including injury through shock'.[22]

This recognises that molestation or interference that causes impairment of health will be an actionable wrong even if the conduct of the defendant is not tortious. Thus, it is the result – the impairment of health – that is prohibited regardless of the nature of the conduct that leads to that result. This improves the protection available for victims of harassment, but is still subject to limitations. First, there must be an impairment of health, whether physical or mental, thus the victim will not have a remedy unless and until serious harm is suffered. Accordingly, victims of harassment who suffer adverse effects short of an impairment to health will still be without a remedy. Secondly, the conduct that causes the harm must be of a dishonest or intimidatory nature which is calculated to induce such harm. This requirement will exclude many prevalent forms of stalking, thus represents a further limitation to the protection available.

The requirement that the 'right to be protected by an injunction must be one that is known to law and equity'[23] has operated to exclude many deserving harassment cases from the protection of the courts. The need to deal with cases where the circumstances of the case clearly merit intervention, but the facts do not fit within the boundaries of an existing cause of action, has led the courts to 'engage in a complex perusal of existing common law in order to locate the act complained of within an appropriate cause of action'.[24] Nowhere can this be more clearly seen than in the Court of Appeal decision in *Khorasandjian v Bush*,[25] which was both hailed as a 'path-breaking and innovative decision'[26] and condemned as a decision which was difficult to rationalise.[27]

In *Khorasandjian v Bush*, following the termination of a social relationship, the defendant embarked upon a protracted campaign of harassment that included threats to harm the plaintiff, persistent telephone calls and damage

---

21 Fricker, 1992, pp 158–63.
22 Cooke, 1994, pp 289–96.
23 Martin, 1993, p 729.
24 Conaghan, 1996, p 222.
25 *Khorasandjian v Bush* [1993] 3 All ER 669.
26 Conaghan, 1996, p 418.
27 Ford, 1994, pp 14–16.

to her property. His conduct led to criminal proceedings which resulted in a conditional discharge for threatening and abusive behaviour, a period of imprisonment for making a threat to kill the plaintiff and a fine for offences under the Telecommunications Act 1984. Despite this, the defendant continued to harass the plaintiff, her mother and her boyfriend with persistent telephone calls, causing the plaintiff to obtain an injunction prohibiting the defendant from 'harassing, pestering or communicating with' the plaintiff. He appealed against the imposition of the injunction, arguing that it did not reflect any tort known to law.

In upholding the injunction, the Court of Appeal (Peter Gibson J dissenting) considered two possible causes of action: private nuisance and intentional interference with the person (the principle from *Wilkinson v Downton*).

The judges were agreed that there was potential to base the injunction upon *Wilkinson v Downton*, but differed as to how this would be applied. Peter Gibson J believed the injunction was too wide as it was not limited to an actionable wrong. He approved of the approach taken by the Court of Appeal in Burnett v George and favoured amending the injunction by adding the words 'by doing acts calculated to cause the respondent harm'.[28] Dillon LJ felt that this would render the protection provided by the injunction inadequate because 'the parts of his letters to her which are not directly intimidatory, threatening or abusive are concerned to press his unwanted suit on her as part of his campaign of harassment', thus not all of the conduct to which the plaintiff objected would be encompassed by the proposed limitation.[29]

In *Wilkinson v Downton*, it was imputed that the defendant's false statement to the plaintiff was calculated to cause harm because this was a natural and probable consequence of such conduct:

> It is difficult to imagine that such a statement, made suddenly and with apparent seriousness, could fail to produce grave effects under the circumstances upon any but an exceptionally indifferent person and therefore an intention to produce such an effect must be imputed.[30]

Dillon LJ adopted this approach and considered that harm to the plaintiff was a natural and probable consequence of the defendant's behaviour taken as a whole. It could therefore be inferred that this behaviour was calculated to cause harm, hence it was irrelevant that any single act could not be viewed as harmful. Consideration of the totality of the defendant's conduct led Dillon LJ to conclude that it was appropriate to grant a *quia timet* injunction[31] to prevent

---

28 *Khorasandjian v Bush* [1993] 3 All ER 669, *per* Peter Gibson J, p 684.
29 *Ibid, per* Dillon LJ, p 678.
30 *Wilkinson v Downton* [1897] 2 QB 57, *per* Wright J, p 59.
31 A *quia timet* injunction is granted to restrain an infringement of law that has not yet occurred, but is where there is a high probability that such an infringement will occur immediately or in the near future: Sharpe, 1999.

future harm to the plaintiff, who had not yet suffered physical or psychiatric illness, as there was 'an obvious risk that the cumulative effect of continued and unrestrained further harassment such as she has undergone would cause such illness'.[32]

However, this was very much a secondary argument for Dillon LJ, who preferred private nuisance as a basis for the injunction. Bringing the facts of this case within the cause of action for private nuisance raises two issues. First, whether the defendant's conduct would amount to an actionable nuisance and, secondly, whether the plaintiff had standing to bring an action for private nuisance.

Private nuisance is an unlawful interference with a person's use or enjoyment of land, or some right over or in connection with it.[33] This definition gives no guidance as to the nature of the conduct that will amount to an unlawful interference and it has been said that the forms that private nuisance may take are protean[34] and that, as with the tort of negligence, the categories of nuisance are never closed.[35]

The issue of whether telephone calls can amount to private nuisance has been considered in other jurisdictions. In Australia, it was held that telephone calls made late at night, disturbing the plaintiff's sleep, were an actionable nuisance.[36] In Canada, the Appellate Division of the Alberta Supreme Court held that persistent telephone calls and letters could amount to an unreasonable interference with the comfortable and convenient enjoyment of property even if the content was 'essentially agreeable' provided the communications were unwelcome.[37]

This approach was followed by Dillon LJ who held:

> Damage is ... a necessary ingredient of the tort of private nuisance ... So far as the harassing telephone calls are concerned, however, the inconvenience and annoyance to the occupier caused by such calls, and the interference thereby with the ordinary and reasonable use of the property are sufficient damage. The harassment is the persistent making of the unwanted telephone calls, even apart from their content; if the content itself as here is threatening and objectionable, the harassment is the greater.[38]

---

32 *Khorasandjian v Bush* [1993] 3 All ER 669, *per* Dillon LJ, p 677.

33 *Read v J Lyons and Co* [1945] KB 216, *per* Scott LJ, p 236.

34 *Sedleigh-Denfield v O'Callaghan* [1940] AC 880, *per* Lord Wright, p 903: 'It is impossible to give any precise or universal formula, but it may broadly be said that a useful test is perhaps what is reasonable according to the ordinary usages of mankind living in ... a particular society. The forms which nuisance may take are protean. Certain classifications are possible, but many reported cases are no more than illustrations of particular matters of fact which have been held to be nuisances.'

35 *Motherwell v Motherwell* (1976) 73 DLR (3d) 62, *per* Clement JA, p 72.

36 *Stoakes v Bridges* [1958] 32 ALJ 205.

37 *Motherwell v Motherwell* (1976) 73 DLR (3d) 62.

38 *Khorasandjian v Bush* [1993] 3 All ER 669, *per* Dillon LJ, p 676.

This extension of private nuisance could prove to be valuable for victims of stalking, as telephone nuisance figures prominently amongst the types of harassment that stalkers engage in and there is an obvious difficulty in using tort law to restrain such conduct, as it is not tortious *per se* to make telephone calls. Whether persistent telephone calls will amount to private nuisance will always depend upon the facts of the case and involve a balancing of the rights of the defendant to act in a certain way and the rights of the plaintiff to undisturbed enjoyment of his property. One of the factors to be taken into account when determining whether or not conduct amounts to private nuisance is the utility of the defendant's conduct.[39] Given the absence of utility to the conduct in stalking cases and the absence of any right to telephone another person, especially with the purpose of harassing them, it appears certain that persistent unwanted calls would generally qualify as nuisance conduct for the purposes of private nuisance.

The issue of whether the plaintiff had standing was more problematic, because she was resident in her mother's home and therefore lacked the necessary proprietary interest to bring an action in private nuisance. As private nuisance protects the use and enjoyment of property, a logical corollary of the nature of the cause of action is that only someone with an interest in the property affected by the nuisance can bring such an action.

The defendant sought to rely on this traditional conception of private nuisance as illustrated by *Malone v Laskey*, where the occupant of premises brought an action for damages after she was injured when vibrations from an adjoining property caused a water tank to fall upon her.[40] It was held that a person with no interest in the property who was a mere licensee lacked standing to bring an action in private nuisance. In *Khorasandjian v Bush*, Dillon LJ disagreed with this stance saying:

> It is ridiculous if in this present age the law is that the making of deliberately harassing and pestering telephone calls to a person is only actionable in the civil courts if the recipient of the calls happens to have the freehold or a leasehold proprietary interest in the premises in which he or she received the calls.[41]

He went on to consider the Canadian authority of *Motherwell v Motherwell*, in which the defendant bombarded her father, brother and sister-in-law with persistent telephone calls and letters.[42] The sister-in-law had no proprietary interest in the home in which she resided with her husband and children, yet was granted an injunction in her own right. In her appeal against the imposition of this injunction, the defendant sought to rely on *Malone v Laskey*,

---

39 Brazier and Murphy, 1999, pp 368–76.
40 *Malone v Laskey* [1907] 2 KB 141.
41 *Khorasandjian v Bush* [1993] 3 All ER 669, *per* Dillon LJ, p 675.
42 *Motherwell v Motherwell* (1976) 73 DLR (3d) 62.

but the court distinguished situations of mere occupation, which would not suffice to found an action in nuisance from occupation of a substantial nature upon which a claim in nuisance could be based:

> Here we have a wife harassed in the matrimonial home. She has a status, a right to live there with her husband and children. I find it absurd to say that her occupancy of the matrimonial home is insufficient to found an action in nuisance.[43]

Dillon LJ approved of this authority, acknowledging that this represented an extension of the law of private nuisance, but seeing this as justified as '[t]he court has at times to reconsider earlier decisions in the light of changed social conditions'.[44] He saw no difficulty with extending this further to cover a child living at home with her parents.[45] Peter Gibson LJ (dissenting) was highly critical of this approach and did not accept that the interest of an adult child resident in the parental home was analogous to that of the right of a wife to reside with her husband and children in the matrimonial home. This prompted him to conclude that the injunction could not properly be based on private nuisance.

At the time, this case was generally welcomed as filling the lacuna that existed due to the restricted scope of domestic violence legislation.[46] It was thought by some to affirm the existence of a new tort of harassment[47] even if it did this at 'the risk of detaching the tort from its foundations'.[48]

However, despite expanding the availability of private nuisance and extending the principle in *Wilkinson v Downton* to cover purely mental distress which creates a potential risk of physical or psychiatric harm in the future, this case was little used by stalking victims. The Court of Appeal's approval of 'substantial occupation' as a basis for an action in private nuisance in *Hunter v Canary Wharf*[49] was overruled when the appeal was heard by the House of Lords.[50] The decision in *Khorasandjian v Bush* was criticised as exploiting the

---

43   *Motherwell v Motherwell* (1976) 73 DLR (3d) 62, *per* Clement JA, p 78.

44   *Khorasandjian v Bush* [1993] 3 All ER 669, *per* Dillon J, p 676.

45   There is Canadian authority, which was not cited in *Khorasandjian v Bush*, to support the idea that children should be able to bring an action in private nuisance. In *Devon Lumber Co v MacNeil* (1987) 45 DLR (4th) 300, it was held that children of an occupier could bring an action in private nuisance for injury to their health caused by dust from the neighbouring cedar mill. Rice JA (dissenting) advanced the same argument as Peter Gibson LJ in *Khorasandjian v Bush* that an action in private nuisance involved interference with an interest in land, hence a proprietary or possessory interest in land was required in order to bring an action.

46   Bridgeman and Jones, 1994, pp 180–205.

47   Murphy, 1993, pp 926–28.

48   Ford, 1994, pp 14–16.

49   *Hunter v Canary Wharf* [1996] 1 All ER 481, *per* Pill LJ, p 498: 'A substantial link between the person enjoying the use and the land on which he or she is enjoying it is essential but, in my judgment, occupation of property, as a home, does confer upon the occupant a capacity to sue in private nuisance.'

50   *Hunter v Canary Wharf* [1997] 2 All ER 426.

law of private nuisance in order to create a tort of harassment by the back door.[51] It was accepted that changes in social conditions sometimes necessitate the development of legal principle, but the 'development of the common law should be rational and coherent. It should not distort its principles and create anomalies merely as an expedient to fill a gap.[52]

The majority of the House of Lords in *Hunter v Canary Wharf* (Lord Cooke dissenting) took a deliberately narrow view of nuisance, seeking to re-establish it as a 'tort to land' requiring a proprietary or possessory interest in order to pursue a claim. The scope of injunctions granted under private nuisance was also called into doubt as the House of Lords appeared to favour the view that only damages to property or to utility of property[53] would be recoverable in nuisance, with claims for personal injury being more appropriate to a claim in negligence. Lord Hoffmann stated: 'the plaintiff's interest in land becomes no more than a qualifying condition or springboard which entitles him to sue for injury to himself. If this were the case, the need for the plaintiff to have an interest in the land would indeed be hard to justify ... [but] the action is not for causing discomfort to the person but ... for causing injury to the land.'[54]

The majority in the House of Lords were of the opinion that Dillon LJ had used private nuisance as a device to enable him to extend to the plaintiff the degree of protection that he felt that she deserved. Whilst sympathising with his position, the House of Lords were nevertheless condemnatory of the distortion of the law of private nuisance caused by this decision:

> I can well understand Dillon LJ's concern to find a remedy for the wife or daughter who suffers from harassment on the telephone, whether at home or elsewhere. But to allow them a remedy in private nuisance would not just be to extend the existing law. It would not just be to get rid of an unnecessary technicality. It would be to change the whole basis of the course of action.[55]

The reformulation of private nuisance was seen as especially inappropriate when considering the nature of the wrong of which the plaintiff complained. Although some of the harassment of the plaintiff in *Khorasandjian* did occur at her home, this was merely because that was where she happened to be on some of the occasions when the defendant targeted her. It was not merely her enjoyment of property that was adversely affected by the defendant's conduct as:

---

51 *Ibid, per* Lord Goff, p 438.
52 *Ibid, per* Lord Hoffmann, p 452.
53 '... it is not that the land has not suffered 'sensible' injury, but its utility has been diminished by the existence of the nuisance. It is for an unlawful threat to the utility of his land that the possessor or occupier is entitled to an injunction and it is for the diminution in such utility that he is entitled to an injunction', *ibid, per* Lord Hoffmann, p 451.
54 *Ibid, per* Lord Hoffmann, p 451.
55 *Ibid, per* Lord Lloyd, p 444.

the gravamen of the complaint lies in the harassment which is just as much an abuse ... whether she is pestered in this way in her mother's or her husband's house, or she is staying with a friend, or is at her place of work, or even in her car with a mobile phone.[56]

It is possible that Dillon LJ recognised, but refused to acknowledge this point, as the scope of injunction granted in *Khorasandjian* showed no justification for the requirement of a nexus with land. The conduct prohibited was not subject to geographical limitations restricting the prohibition of harassment to that which occurred at the plaintiff's home, but was of a general nature having the effect of protecting the personal interests of the plaintiff regardless of any infringement of her property rights:

> It was so widely drawn that it covered the defendant's conduct wherever he happened to be when making the unwanted telephone calls and wherever the plaintiff happened to be when she received them. Its use of language demonstrates that the case was concerned with the invasion of the privacy of the plaintiff's person, not the invasion of interest which she might have had in any land.[57]

Despite their criticism of Dillon LJ's approach in *Khorasandjian*, it was clear that the House of Lords appreciated the gap that had existed in the law and the difficulty this presented to judges faced with a deserving applicant. On concluding that cases such as *Khorasandjian* should not be brought in private nuisance, Lord Hope stated that he 'would be uneasy if it were not possible by some other means to provide such a plaintiff with a remedy'.[58] Lord Goff expressed relief that '[t]he tort of harassment has now received statutory recognition ... we are therefore no longer troubled with the question whether the common law should be developed to provide a remedy'.[59]

This is a reference to the statutory tort created by ss 1 and 3 of the Protection from Harassment Act 1997 which came into force just months before *Hunter v Canary Wharf* was heard by the House of Lords. Thus, it is to be remembered that although this case removed the potential use of private nuisance from stalking victims, this only occurred after an alternative means of redress was in existence. Therefore, despite criticism of *Khorasandjian v Bush*, it provided a means of obtaining a civil injunction for stalking victims who lacked the familial nexus to engender protection under domestic violence legislation for four years. Also, the lengths to which Dillon LJ was prepared to manipulate private nuisance to find a means of redress for deserving victims is illustrative that the gap in the law was recognised within the judiciary and considered to be an unacceptable position. It is perhaps unfortunate that the courts continued to reformulate existing legal principles in order to fit stalking

---

56 *Ibid, per* Lord Goff, p 438.
57 *Ibid, per* Lord Hope, p 469.
58 *Ibid, per* Lord Hope, p 469.
59 *Ibid, per* Lord Goff, p 438.

cases within them, as this weakened the protection available for stalking victims and caused unacceptable distortion in the law.

It was from this position that the Court of Appeal took the nearest step that has occurred to acknowledging the existence of a specific tort of harassment. This again arose in the context of a stalking case where there was inadequate protection available to the victim.

In *Burris v Azadani*, the defendant began harassing the plaintiff after she resisted his attempts to establish an intimate relationship.[60] He bombarded her with telephone calls and letters, made uninvited visits to her house, made threats to commit suicide if she would not see him and threatened harm to the plaintiff and her children. His conduct was described by the Court of Appeal as 'an intolerable history of harassment' which caused the plaintiff to fear for her safety and that of her children. She obtained an injunction prohibiting the defendant from:

(a) assaulting, molesting, harassing, threatening, pestering or otherwise interfering with her or her children;

(b) communicating, whether orally or in writing, in person or by telephone, with her or her children; and,

(c) from coming within 250 yards of her home address.

On the first occasion that the defendant breached the order, he was warned by the court that further breaches would lead to his imprisonment. On the second occasion, he was sentenced to eight weeks' imprisonment with the sentence being suspended for six months. These breaches involved conduct in breach of terms (a) and (b) of the injunction.

On the third occasion that the defendant was brought before the court for breach of injunction, the conduct complained of involved the defendant cycling down the road in which the plaintiff lived on two occasions in breach of term (c) of the injunction. The plaintiff did not witness this and the defendant made no attempt to approach her home or communicate with her in any way. He was sentenced to four weeks' imprisonment and ordered to serve the eight week suspended sentence consecutively.

The defendant appealed on the basis that the district judge lacked jurisdiction to impose an exclusion order as it involved restraint of conduct which was not tortious nor otherwise unlawful. This argument was based upon *Patel v Patel* where the Court of Appeal held that, outside the Domestic Violence and Matrimonial Proceedings Act 1976, there was no jurisdiction to grant an injunction to restrain the defendant from exercising a public right of way or visiting premises to which he had been invited, however close to the applicant's home this may be.

---

60   *Burris v Azadani* [1995] 4 All ER 802.

The Court of Appeal considered that if an injunction can only be granted to restrain conduct which is in itself tortious or otherwise unlawful, that would be a conclusive objection to term (c) of the injunction as no tort or unlawful act is involved if the defendant merely traversed the road outside the plaintiff's house, making no attempt to contact or communicate with her, as this involved the exercise of his right to make peaceful use of the highway. However, the Court of Appeal did not accept that its powers were limited in this way:

> It would not seem to me to be a valid objection to the making of an exclusion zone order that the conduct to be restrained is not in itself tortious or otherwise unlawful, if such an order is reasonably regarded as necessary for the protection of a plaintiff's legitimate interest.[61]

This was seen as analogous to the grant of a Mareva injunction,[62] which restrains the defendant from doing that that is otherwise lawful in order to ensure that the court not thwarted in achieving their purpose. The grant of an exclusion zone would likewise 'protect the legitimate interests of those who have invoked its jurisdiction'.[63]

Sir Thomas Bingham considered that the Court of Appeal in *Patel v Patel* had not intended to lay down a general principle regarding a prohibition on the grant of exclusion zones, but had merely decided that:

> The plaintiff's complaints were a storm in a teacup, the Court of Appeal in *Patel v Patel* were understandably and very properly concerned to ensure that no unnecessary restraint was imposed on the ordinary freedom of the defendant. The view was plainly taken ... that the exclusion zone order was unnecessary for the reasonable protection of the plaintiff's interests.[64]

In view of this, Sir Thomas Bingham concluded that neither statute nor authority precluded the making of an exclusion zone order, but that such a severe restriction of the defendant's right to engage in lawful activity should only be made with good reason, reconciling the interest of the defendant to liberty and the interest of the plaintiff to protection. Schiemann LJ agreed with this notion of balancing competing interests:

> There are in these cases two interests to be reconciled – that of the plaintiff not to be harassed and that of the defendant to be allowed to move freely along the highway. An exclusion zone interferes with the latter in order to secure the former. On its face it forbids what are lawful actions. The defendant has rendered himself liable to such an order because of his previous harassing behaviour. None the less, a judge imposing such an order must be careful not

---

61 *Ibid, per* Sir Thomas Bingham MR, pp 807–08.
62 This is an interlocutory prohibitive injunction that restrains the defendant from removing his assets from the jurisdiction of the court or otherwise disposing of his assets within the court's jurisdiction prior to the final hearing of the case.
63 *Burris v Azadani* [1995] 4 All ER 802, *per* Sir Thomas Bingham MR, p 807.
64 *Ibid, per* Sir Thomas Bingham MR, p 809.

to interfere with the defendant's rights more than is necessary in order to protect the plaintiff's [rights].[65]

This suggests that the defendant who engages in harassing conduct which is tortious or otherwise unlawful renders himself vulnerable to curtailment of his lawful activities although his lawful activities must not be restricted beyond that which is necessary to protect the plaintiff:

> His liberty must be respected up to the point at which his conduct infringes, or threatens to infringe, the rights of the plaintiff.[66]

This case is a further illustration of the lengths to which the courts were prepared to go to find a remedy for victims of harassment and this has led to some contradictory academic opinion as to the basis of the decision and its impact on the law of tort. Lawson-Cruttenden sees the case as a development of the law set out in *Khorasandjian v Bush* and as confirmation of the existence of a common law tort of harassment.[67] Bailey-Harris sees no reason to view *Burris v Azadani* as based upon *Khorasandjian v Bush*, which should be viewed as an extension of two established torts – the principle in *Wilkinson v Downton* and private nuisance – rather than as a stage in the development of a tort of harassment. She suggests that the basis of *Burris v Azadani* is merely a continuation of the recently exhibited willingness to grant injunctive relief where the plaintiff has a legally recognised right or interest which falls short of a cause of action such as *Re S (Hospital Patient: Court's Jurisdiction)*.[68]

Conaghan[69] considers the possibility that *Burris v Azadani* is based upon 'a rather loose application of the *quia timet* principle', as applied in *Khorasandjian v Bush*, to uphold an injunction prohibiting conduct that could lead to physical or psychological injury,[70] thus preventing the commission of a tort before it occurred. The Court of Appeal in *Burris v Azadani* could be said to be restraining conduct which is not in itself tortious, that is, coming within 250 yards of the plaintiff's house, to exclude the plaintiff from an area where he might be tempted to commit tortious acts as he could 'succumb to the temptation to enter [the plaintiff's house], or to abuse or harass the plaintiff'.[71]

Conaghan criticises this as an extreme departure from the power to grant a quia timet injunction which traditionally requires a very strong probability of the future infringement of a recognised legal right and the likelihood of damage of a most serious nature.[72] She questions what recognised legal right

---

65 *Burris v Azadani* [1995] 4 All ER 802, *per* Schiemann LJ, pp 811–12.
66 *Burris v Azadani*, *per* Sir Thomas Bingham MR, p 810.
67 Lawson-Cruttenden, 1995, pp 625–26.
68 Bailey-Harris, 1996, pp 145–46.
69 Conaghan, 1996, pp 221–28.
70 This would constitute liability under the rule in *Wilkinson v Downton*.
71 *Burris v Azadani* [1995] 4 All ER 802, *per* Sir Thomas Bingham MR, p 811.
72 Martin, 1993, p 722.

of the plaintiff would be infringed by the defendant's presence in the neighbourhood and what degree of likelihood would be required to justify the imposition of an exclusion zone. The absence of clarity on this point is exacerbated by Sir Thomas Bingham's reliance on 'the rather elusive notion of "a plaintiff's legitimate interest", although no effort to define "interest" for these purposes is made'.[73] Conaghan concludes that 'legitimate interest' must be something other than the generally accepted legal right not to be the subject of tortious or otherwise unlawful conduct that usually suffices for the imposition of an injunction. This conclusion is based upon Sir Thomas Bingham's comment that an exclusion zone should not be restricted to situations where the conduct to be restrained is tortious or otherwise unlawful if such an order is necessary to protect the plaintiff's legitimate interests. Lawson-Cruttenden distinguishes 'legitimate interest' from 'interests which are capable of being protected as a tort' and claims that once the plaintiff has been subject to harassment, this will suffice to allow them to 'invoke the doctrine of legitimate interests' and thus be availed of the court's protection.[74]

This uncertainty regarding the basis of the decision and the absence of clarity regarding the meaning and extent of the 'legitimate interests' that the case seeks to protect rather limits the value of the case as a precedent for those seeking relief from harassment. This is especially so as the case purports to be based upon *Khorasandjian v Bush,* which was so fulsomely criticised by the House of Lords in *Hunter v Canary Wharf,* and is contrary to existing authority such as *Patel v Patel,* which held that there can be no injunction to restrain conduct which is neither tortious nor otherwise unlawful. Lack of clarity permeates the judgment and is encapsulated by Sir Thomas Bingham's statement that 'it cannot be said that there is no tort of harassment',[75] which is indicative of the reluctance of the judiciary to state specifically that there is a law of harassment.

Nevertheless, the case clearly illustrates the need for a clear and effective remedy for victims of stalking and harassment and is to be commended for trying to establish a common law tort of harassment at a time when there appeared to be no prospect of statutory intervention despite the obvious need for a clear legal basis upon which to base complaints of harassment.

5.2 THE OFFENCES AGAINST THE PERSON ACT 1861

A parallel development in criminal law which reflects a common acknowledgment amongst the judiciary of the inadequacies of the legal

---

73 Conaghan, 1996, p 227.
74 Lawson-Cruttenden, 1996, pp 418–20.
75 *Burris v Azadani* [1995] 4 All ER 802, *per* Sir Thomas Bingham MR, p 809.

protection available for stalking victims can be seen in the expansion of the Offences Against the Person Act 1861 to encompass psychiatric harm suffered by stalking victims.

Early attempts to use the Offences Against the Person Act 1861 in this way were unsuccessful. The first conviction of a stalker under the Offences Against the Person Act 1861 was quashed by the Court of Appeal owing to a misdirection by the trial judge regarding the *mens rea* required for the offence.[76] This was followed shortly afterwards by another attempt to use the Act to deal with psychological harm arising from telephone communications, although in a significantly different context. Adrian Brooks was charged under s 20 following his hoax telephone calls to the police regarding the abduction of four hour old Abbie Humphries.[77] This charge was discontinued, possibly due to the difficulties of establishing that the hoax telephone call caused psychological harm to the parents of an abducted child who must have already been suffering extreme mental anguish,[78] and replaced with one of wasting police time,[79] to which Brooks pleaded guilty and was sentenced to four months' imprisonment.[80]

It is somewhat surprising that these cases received so little media and academic attention, but they passed almost unnoticed, as did the first successful conviction under s 47 of the Offences Against the Person Act 1861 in which Robert Banks was sentenced to two years' imprisonment for persistently stealing underwear from his neighbour's washing line, causing her 'extreme psychiatric harm'.[81] Nevertheless, there is some evidence to suggest an awareness of the potential of the Offences Against the Person Act 1861 to combat stalkers. A stipendiary magistrate called for the Crown Prosecution Service to make use of this statute against a persistent stalker whom she bound over to keep the peace following a private prosecution initiated by his victim.[82] It was at this time that Robert Ireland was convicted for assault occasioning actual bodily harm as a result of the persistent silent telephone calls made to his victims.[83] It was this case, together with that of Anthony Burstow,[84] which brought the use of the Offences Against the

---

76 'Judge's error frees clerk jailed for anonymous calls' (1994) *The Times*, 16 December.

77 'Abbie calls: man on GBH charge' (1994) *The Times*, 12 July.

78 Cooper, 1995, p 405, where the implications of the calls being made to the police rather than directly to the parents are also considered.

79 Criminal Law Act 1967, s 5(2): a person is liable if he 'causes any wasteful employment of the police by knowingly making to any person a false report tending to show that an offence has been committed, or to give rise to apprehension for the safety of any persons or property, or tending to show that he has information material to any police inquiry'.

80 'Man jailed for hoax calls over Abbie abduction' (1994) *The Times*, 7 October.

81 'Underwear thief is jailed for psychological assault' (1995) *Daily Telegraph*, 31 March.

82 'Woman in fear as stalker defies court warnings' (1995) *Daily Telegraph*, 23 May.

83 *R v Ireland* (1995) unreported, Newport Crown Court, 10 March.

84 *R v Burstow* [1996] Crim LR 331, Reading Crown Court, 4 March 1996.

Person Act 1861 against stalkers who cause their victims to suffer psychological harm, and, indeed, the issue of stalking itself, firmly into the media and academic spotlight.

The common issue in these cases relates to the appropriateness of the use of the Offences Against the Person Act 1861, thus both consider whether the element of 'bodily harm', common to s 47 and s 20, encompasses psychiatric injury. Following from this, the courts went on to address the means by which this harm is to be brought about in as much as s 47 requires an assault, in the sense of a common assault or a battery, occasioning actual bodily harm, whereas s 20 requires that the grievous bodily harm be 'inflicted' upon the victim. The scope of these causative elements formed the basis of the second ground of appeal in each case.

5.2.1 Psychiatric injury as bodily harm

It was said in *R v Donovan* that 'bodily harm' has its ordinary meaning and includes any hurt or injury calculated to interfere with the victim's health or comfort.[85] Thus, the delineation between the offences is dependent upon the specified level of harm as denoted by the descriptors 'actual' and 'grievous'. Any lesser level of harm will only engender liability for common assault or battery.[86] The dividing line between actual and grievous bodily harm is not amenable to precise formulation. 'Actual bodily harm' has been said to refer to harm which, although not permanent, is more than merely transient or trifling.[87] In relation to grievous bodily harm, it has be said that there is:

> no warrant for giving the words ... a meaning other than that which the words convey in their ordinary and natural meaning. 'Bodily harm' needs no explanation and 'grievous' means no more and no less than 'really serious'.[88]

In the particular circumstances of that case, 'bodily harm' did not require further elaboration, involving, as it did, serious physical harm leading to the death of the victim. However, further consideration of the scope of the phrase is required to determine whether it encompasses injury to the victim which is not of a purely physical nature. In *R v Miller*, the defendant's actions left the victim in a hysterical and nervous condition which amounted 'an injury to her state of mind for the time being', which was held to come within the definition of actual bodily harm.[89] This has positive implications in terms of addressing

---

85 *R v Donovan* [1934] 2 KB 498, *per* Swift J, p 502.

86 Criminal Justice Act 1988, s 39.

87 *R v Donovan* [1934] 2 KB 498, *per* Swift J, p 502. Glanville Williams comments that this is a 'silly expression – as if there were some kind of contrasting harm which is not actual!': Williams, G, 1983, p 187.

88 *DPP v Smith* [1961] AC 290, *per* Viscount Kilmuir LC, p 335.

89 *R v Miller* [1954] 2 QB 282, *per* Lynskey J, p 292.

stalking, as it would appear that many victims would come within this formulation of actual bodily harm. There would, therefore, be available a means by which the criminal law could intervene even if the stalker acted in ways which were otherwise lawful, provided his conduct caused an injury to his victim's state of mind for the time being. However, there is no evidence to suggest that this course was ever considered.

The decision in *Miller* was criticised by Glanville Williams for creating a risk of over-extending the offence. He asserted that 'actual bodily harm' should connote more than trivial injury, thus should require appreciable mental harm which, as a matter of expert evidence, amounts to a recognised mental disorder.[90]

The validity of Glanville Williams' view was recognised by the Court of Appeal in *R v Chan-Fook*,[91] in which the extent of psychiatric harm that will suffice to support a charge of assault occasioning actual bodily harm was considered. In this case, the defendant suspected the victim of theft and interrogated him forcefully prior to locking him in an upstairs bedroom. Fearing that the defendant would return and cause him harm, the victim sought to escape through the window but fell, suffering various physical injuries. The prosecution, however, preferred to concentrate upon the effect of these events on the victim's mental state, asserting that this amounted to actual bodily harm. The Court of Appeal agreed with the finding in *Miller* that the word 'bodily' does not limit the harm to the skin, flesh and bones of the victim, but that it includes all parts of the body including the organs, nervous system and brain. This being so, 'bodily harm' included psychiatric injury. It was in relation to the level of psychiatric injury that would amount to actual bodily harm that the Court of Appeal departed from *Miller*, saying that it:

> does not include mere emotions such as fear, distress or panic, nor does it include, as such, states of mind that are not themselves evidence of some identifiable clinical condition. The phrase 'state of mind' is not a scientific one and should be avoided in considering whether or not a psychiatric injury has been caused; its use is likely to create in the minds of the jury the impression that something which is no more than a strong emotion, such as extreme fear or panic, can amount to actual bodily harm. It cannot.[92]

This move away from the low level of mental disturbance, characterised by transient emotional states, required to amount to actual bodily harm is in accordance with other areas of law. In considering the boundaries of the law regarding negligently caused mental harm, the Court of Appeal in *Attia v British Gas*[93] recognised that there was a boundary to be drawn between

90 Williams, G, 1983, p 187.
91 *R v Chan-Fook* (1994) 99 Cr App R 147.
92 *Ibid, per* Hobhouse LJ, p 152.
93 *Attia v British Gas* [1988] QB 304.

actual psychiatric illness, such as anxiety neurosis or a reactive depression, and lesser states, which could be described as 'merely grief, sorrow or emotional distress'.[94] Equally, when considering whether a power of arrest could be attached to an injunction under s 2(1) of the Domestic Violence and Matrimonial Proceedings Act 1976, which requires that actual bodily harm has been caused to the applicant and a recurrence of this is likely, the Court of Appeal in *Kendrick v Kendrick*[95] held that the applicant's fear of her husband would not suffice. In order to justify a finding of actual bodily harm, 'some clear evidence of a real change in the psychological condition of the person assaulted' was required.[96]

The departure from *Miller* in this respect creates parity with these other areas of law and establishes a standard of mental injury that is to be satisfied before it will amount to actual bodily harm. Having identified that a boundary exists between mere emotions and actual psychiatric illness, the Court of Appeal in *Chan-Fook* held that the determination of this boundary is a matter of expert evidence, thus concurring with the previously stated view of Glanville Williams.

Although this narrows the scope of use of s 47 in stalking cases, it does not close the door and it may, in fact, have had the opposite effect, as the recognition by the Court of Appeal in *Chan-Fook* as to the potential of using the Offences Against the Person Act 1861 against those who cause psychiatric injury may well have been the impetus for the prosecution in *Gelder* which occurred shortly after.[97] Certainly, it was only two years later that the appellate courts were considering cases under the Offences Against the Person Act 1861 against stalkers which were explicitly based upon *Chan-Fook*. This potential had probably not occurred to Hobhouse LJ, who noted at the conclusion of his judgment in *Chan-Fook* that cases involving psychiatric injury caused by assault 'will be very few and far between'.[98]

As previously mentioned, it was the cases of *R v Ireland* and *R v Burstow* which brought the use of the Offences Against the Person Act 1861 in stalking cases into the legal spotlight and the wider public arena. These cases were based upon the premises that psychiatric injury can amount to bodily harm for the purposes of the Offences Against the Person Act 1861. It was conceded by the defence in both cases that they were bound by the Court of Appeal decision in *Chan-Fook* both at first instance and in the Court of Appeal. However, Lord Bingham CJ, giving the decision of the Court of Appeal in *Burstow*, cast some doubt upon this, stating:

---

94   *Attia v British Gas* [1988] QB 304, *per* Bingham LJ, p 320.

95   [1990] 2 FLR 107.

96   *Ibid*, *per* Glidewell LJ, p 110.

97   This is speculative, as it has not been possible to obtain a transcript of this case, neither has it been reported.

98   *R v Chan-Fook* (1994) 99 Cr App R 147, *per* Hobhouse LJ, p 153.

[w]ere the question free from authority, we should entertain some doubt whether the Victorian draftsman of the 1861 Act intended to embrace psychiatric injury within the expressions 'grievous bodily harm' and 'actual bodily harm'. If he did, it is not obvious why he used the expression 'bodily' in a statute concerned with offences against the person.[99]

Not surprisingly, defence counsel for both *Burstow* and *Ireland* put great emphasis upon this statement in the joined appeal before the House of Lords. However, Lord Steyn considered that although the intention of the draftsman is an oft-referred to factor when interpreting the meaning of statutory provisions, the correct approach here was to regard the Offences Against the Person Act 1861 as an 'always speaking' statute that must be interpreted in the light of contemporary knowledge regarding the link between the body and psychiatric injury. Lord Steyn rejected the challenge to the correctness of Chan-Fook and, moreover, referred to the case as 'based on principled and cogent reasoning' that represented a 'sound and essential clarification of the law'.[100]

This finding that psychiatric injury can constitute bodily harm provides the basis for the use of the Offences Against the Person Act 1861 in stalking cases provided that the harm caused amounts to a recognisable psychiatric illness. However, there are further hurdles to an imposition of liability under the Act as it must be established that the relevant causative element of the offence is satisfied, that is, has there been an assault[101] and was the harm inflicted[102] or caused[103] to the victim.

5.2.2 Assault occasioning actual bodily harm

Section 47 of the Offences Against the Person Act 1861 contains the offence of assault occasioning actual bodily harm. The *actus reus* of the offence is satisfied by either a common assault or a battery which causes the victim to suffer actual bodily harm. It is for this reason that the offence is frequently referred to as a species of 'aggravated assault' as the only differentiation between this and common assault and battery is the severity of the resultant harm. A common assault has been defined as an act which causes another to apprehend immediate and unlawful violence[104] whilst a battery is said to be 'the actual infliction of unlawful force on another person'.[105]

---

99 *R v Burstow* [1997] 1 Cr App R 144, *per* Lord Bingham of Cornhill CJ, pp 148–49.
100 *R v Ireland, R v Burstow* [1997] 4 All ER 225, *per* Lord Steyn, p 233.
101 Offences Against the Person Act 1861, s 47: 'assault occasioning actual bodily harm'.
102 *Ibid*, s 20: 'inflict any grievous bodily harm'.
103 *Ibid*, s 18: 'cause any grievous bodily harm'.
104 *R v Savage, DPP v Parmenter* [1991] 4 All ER 698, *per* Lord Ackner, p 711.
105 *Collins v Wilcox* [1984] 3 All ER 374, *per* Robert Goff LJ, p 377.

Similarly, the *mens rea* of s 47 is limited to that required for common assault or battery, namely, intention to cause the victim to apprehend (common assault) or sustain (battery) immediate and unlawful violence or recklessness (in the *Cunningham*[106] sense) thereto. No additional mental element is required in relation to the actual bodily harm as the House of Lords held in *R v Savage, DPP v Parmenter* that 'occasioning' raises only questions of causation,[107] which is an objective issue requiring no inquiry as to the defendant's state of mind.[108] This has led to the offence being termed as one of 'half *mens rea*' as the *mens rea* does not correspond to all of the *actus reus*, being unconcerned with the 'actual bodily harm' element.[109]

Thus, if either a common assault or battery is committed and actual bodily harm ensues, the defendant will be liable under s 47, rendering the degree of culpability contingent on the degree of harm resulting from the same actions. This has been criticised by Ashworth, who sees no justification for making the penalty equivalent to the higher offence in the hierarchy of offences against the person (s 20) and the fault requirement equivalent to the lower offence in the hierarchy (common assault and battery).[110] Conversely, Gardner asserts that once a person has crossed the moral threshold of committing a common assault or battery, it is only reasonable that they are to be held liable if more serious consequences result.[111]

The absence of any requirement of intention to cause actual bodily harm or even foresight of a risk of such harm lessens the burden of proving this offence against a stalker. It is one thing to prove that an assault has taken place, but quite another, given the multiplicity of motivations that may arise in stalking cases, to establish that the stalker intended that this should cause the victim to suffer actual bodily harm in the form of psychiatric or physical injury or that he was reckless as to the possibility of this outcome. Notwithstanding this, it is not necessarily a straightforward task to establish that a stalker's actions have satisfied the requirements of a common assault. The different approaches to the elements of a common assault are illustrated in the case law preceding attempts to use the Offences Against the Person Act 1861 against stalkers and in the stalking cases that have been brought under s 47.

---

106 *R v Cunningham* [1957] 2 QB 396.

107 It has been argued that 'occasion' is a broader term than 'cause' and includes liability for outcomes that would not be attributed on the basis of causal analysis: Gardner, 1994, pp 502–23.

108 *R v Savage, DPP v Parmenter* [1991] 4 All ER 698, *per* Lord Ackner, p 712.

109 Williams, G, 1983, p 192.

110 Ashworth, 1999, pp 325–26.

111 Gardner, 1994, pp 502–23.

The cases that have sought to apply s 47 against stalkers whose actions lead their victims to suffer psychological harm illustrate the difficulties of expanding a well established area of law into new areas. Arguably, the case law concerning the composite elements of this offence had developed in such a way to preclude its application in stalking cases where psychological harm ensues regardless of whether or not such harm is capable of being encompassed within 'bodily harm'. Nevertheless, the Court of Appeal in *R v Ireland*[112] sought to interpret these existing legal principles in such a way as to facilitate the use of s 47 in stalking cases. However, the way in which the Court of Appeal went about this caused trenchant criticism[113] and attracted little support from the academic community[114] or indeed from the House of Lords when the case was further appealed.[115]

Admittedly, the factual situation in Ireland did not lend itself to an easy application of established legal principles. Unlike the majority of stalkers, Ireland limited himself to a single means of harassment, namely, repeated silent telephone calls made over a period of months. Psychiatric evidence was presented at the trial to the effect that the female victims suffered significant psychological symptoms as a result of the repeated telephone calls. In order to found a conviction under s 47 of the Offences Against the Person Act 1861, it had to be established that these calls amounted to an act which caused the victims to apprehend immediate and unlawful violence.

5.2.2.1 The conduct element of assault

The initial difficulty with which the Court of Appeal were confronted concerned the nature of the act which will suffice for an assault. There was conflicting authority as to whether words alone could amount to an assault, which casts obvious doubt over the potential for silence to constitute an assault. The difficulty stems from the oft-repeated statement in *R v Meade and Belt*[116] that 'no words or singing are equivalent to an assault',[117] although this is generally countered by the equally well quoted assertion that: 'he called out

---

112 [1997] 1 All ER 112.

113 'An aberrant decision': Griew, 1996, pp 1–2; 'the court seems to have gone beyond all reasonable bounds': Smith, 1996, p 413.

114 A notable exception being that of Ormerod and Gunn, 1997.

115 *R v Ireland, R v Burstow* [1997] 4 All ER 225: Lord Steyn notes the criticism that the Court of Appeal judgment in Ireland has received and, unlike his repeated approving references to the approach taken by the Court of Appeal in *Burstow*, he places no reliance on the reasoning or principles developed by the Court of Appeal in *Ireland*. By mentioning the criticism that the judgment received and then not supporting it, and in reaching the same final decision to dismiss the appeal on substantially different reasoning with reference to different authorities, it is easy to infer that Lord Steyn is rejecting the approach taken by the Court of Appeal.

116 (1823) 1 Lew CC 184.

117 *Ibid, per* Holroyd J, p 185.

"get the knives" which itself would be an assault, in addition to kicking the gamekeeper.'[118] Glanville Williams is critical of the reliance placed upon Meade and Belt, stating: 'the judicial authority for this supposed rule is of the slightest ... its main support derives from uncritical repetition by legal writers.'[119] He goes on to argue that the difficulty with words as a form of assault relates to the requirement of immediacy which will frequently be absent, dependent upon the words used, but that 'a verbal threat of immediate force has all the essential elements of an assault'.[120]

The potential difficulties with establishing that words alone can amount to an assault make it clear that even more difficulties arise in relation to silence, which faces the added impediment of its potential characterisation as an omission to act, which will not suffice as the basis for an assault.[121] However, the Court of Appeal in Ireland sought to avoid these problems by identifying the relevant act as the making of the telephone call:

> The making of a telephone call followed by silence, or a series of telephone calls, is capable of amounting to a relevant act for the purposes of section 47 ... the act consists in the making of the telephone call, and it does not matter whether words or silence ensue.[122]

The House of Lords did not adopt this approach to the act forming the basis of the assault in Ireland, preferring instead to examine the potential of words and silence as means of causing apprehension of immediate unlawful violence. Lord Steyn dealt swiftly with the issue of words as an assault, dismissing Meade and Belt as 'the slenderest authority' and stating: 'the proposition that a gesture may amount to an assault but that words can never suffice is unrealistic and indefensible. A thing said is also a thing done.'[123] This approach correctly acknowledges that there are circumstances in which words will certainly cause a person to fear that violence is to be immediately forthcoming. As Lord Steyn notes, it is perfectly acceptable to consider that threatening words uttered by an unseen person, speaking in the dark or from behind the victim, will cause the victim to apprehend immediate unlawful violence. As Lord Hope points out, the words and any accompanying gestures must be interpreted in the context in which they occur in order to ascertain whether the requirements for an assault are satisfied.[124] Certainly, there may be circumstances in stalking cases where a victim, owing to the persistent and

---

118 *R v Wilson* [1955] 1 All ER 744, *per* Lord Goddard, p 745.

119 Williams, G, 1957, pp 219–25.

120 *Ibid*, p 224.

121 *Fagan v MPC* [1969] 1 QB 439: the Divisional Court reiterated the traditional view that assault requires a positive act and that a mere omission will not suffice as a basis for liability.

122 *R v Ireland* [1997] 1 All ER 112, *per* Swinton Thomas LJ, p 118.

123 *R v Ireland, R v Burstow* [1997] 4 All ER 225, *per* Lord Steyn, p 236.

124 *Ibid, per* Lord Hope, p 240.

escalating nature of the conduct, fears immediate violence from the stalker although, objectively, one act in isolation would not support such a reaction. To understand the nature of the wrong in stalking, it is essential to view each act in the context of the totality of the stalking.

The House of Lords were more reticent in relation to silence as an assault. Lord Steyn was only prepared to say that he rejected the submission that silence can never amount to an assault, as the recipient of the call may 'fear that the caller's arrival at her door may be imminent', thus she may 'fear the *possibility* of immediate personal violence' in which case the caller will be liable for assault.[125] Lord Hope characterises a silent call as a positive form of communication and distinguishes this from remaining silent whilst in another's presence.[126] This is due to the opportunity, if the person is present, to observe their demeanour and assess with a reasonable degree of precision the extent of the threat which they pose. Such an opportunity is clearly absent with silent telephone calls which, coupled with an absence of a innocuous reason for remaining silent, imports a threat into the silence. Both Lord Hope[127] and Lord Slynn[128] emphasise that whether or not the silent calls in Ireland did amount to an assault was not a matter of contention, thanks to his plea of guilty. The House of Lords were merely seeking to determine whether, as a matter of law, a silent call could potentially amount to an assault.

5.2.2.2 The characterisation of violence

The approach taken by the Court of Appeal in characterising the relevant act as the making of the telephone call regardless of whether words or silence ensued has been said to be acceptable in the particular context of the case given the repeated nature of the calls and the formulation by the Court of Appeal of 'unlawful violence' as including psychiatric injury.[129] However, whilst it is reasonable that the victim must have been caused fear by the ringing of the telephone, it is not tenable to state that this was fear of unlawful violence, whether psychiatric or physical.[130] Otherwise, every telephone call made to the victim would have satisfied the *actus reus* of assault, regardless of the identity of the caller and their behaviour once the telephone was answered. The making of a telephone call is a neutral act. It is a means of establishing contact with another person analogous to walking to their front door and ringing the doorbell, hence what follows is of paramount

---

125 *Ibid, per* Lord Steyn, p 236 (original emphasis).

126 *Ibid, per* Lord Hope, p 240.

127 *Ibid.*

128 *Ibid,* p 227.

129 Stone, 1997, pp 407–10.

130 This notion of the victim being in immediate fear of violence rather than fear of immediate violence is troublesome throughout the decision.

importance in determining whether or not the requirements of assault are satisfied.[131]

The Court of Appeal in *Ireland* did not adopt this approach, but instead focused on the telephone call itself as the relevant act for the purposes of assault, stating that:

> If the Crown can prove that the victims have sustained actual bodily harm, in this case psychological harm, and that the accused must have intended the victims to sustain such harm, or have been reckless as to whether they did sustain such harm, and that harm resulted from an act or acts of the appellant, namely telephone calls followed by silence, it is open to the jury to find that he has committed an assault.[132]

Quite apart from the misstatement of *mens rea* required for the s 47 offence[133] and the fact that Swinton Thomas LJ appears to be referring to battery rather than the common assault that he professes to be addressing,[134] this statement raises difficulties in terms of the established principles of assault. Swinton Thomas LJ employs reverse reasoning, starting from the fact of harm and working backwards, to conclude that that acts in question amounted to an assault. This has been criticised as an extraordinary misapplication of *Chan-Fook*,[135] involving, as it does, confusion between causing harm (which Ireland does) with causing apprehension of immediate unlawful violence (which he arguably does not).[136] This approach of deducing violence from the fact of harm is a 'radical reconstruction' of the notion of violence in offences against the person and a clear example of result-based reasoning 'which ensures that an undeserving appellant who has engaged in anti-social conduct of a serious kind is convicted but at what cost to the principle of legality'.[137]

---

131 Stone, 1997, pp 407–10.

132 *R v Ireland* [1997] 1 All ER 112, *per* Swinton Thomas LJ, p 114.

133 *R v Savage, DPP v Parmenter* [1992] AC 699, p 742, *per* Lord Ackner: 'The verdict of assault occasioning actual bodily harm may be returned upon proof of an assault together with proof of the fact that actual bodily harm was occasioned by the assault. The prosecution are not obliged to prove that the defendant intended to cause some actual bodily harm or was reckless as to whether such harm would be caused.' It is unlikely that the Court of Appeal would be confused regarding the *mens rea* required for an offence under s 47 after such a recent judgment on this issue from the House of Lords. This lends credence to the view that Swinton Thomas LJ may not have been referring to foresight of actual bodily harm, but to foresight of psychological harm, thus 'expanding the notion of assault to embrace psychological assault'. Boland, 1997, pp 231–39.

134 Smith, 1997, pp 434–36. It has also been argued that the Court of Appeal approach in Ireland was conducive to a finding that the harm was caused by a battery rather than a common assault: Ormerod and Gunn, 1997.

135 Griew, 1996, pp 1–2.

136 Smith, 1997, pp 434–36.

137 Allen, 1996. Allen points out that this interpretation of 'violence' would not suffice under the definition of a 'violent offence' for the purposes of the Criminal Justice Act 1991, s 31(1).

To accept that unlawful violence now includes psychiatric injury would create the situation whereby it is the victim's fear of psychiatric injury that causes them to suffer psychiatric injury. This was encapsulated by JC Smith, who asks:

> Are we to imagine that P, on picking up the telephone, thinks: 'I am about to suffer a psychological injury'? Surely the idea is as ludicrous as that the appellant had *mens rea*, ie, that he was thinking: 'This'll cause him to think he's in for a nervous shock!'[138]

Nevertheless, this is what Swinton Thomas LJ appears to be suggesting when he says:

> When a telephone call is made by the appellant and the victim lifts the telephone and knows that the man is telephoning them yet again, they will be apprehensive of suffering the very psychological damage which they did suffer.[139]

This approach of equating the apprehension of immediate unlawful violence with the actual psychiatric injury suffered by the victims was unequivocally rejected by the House of Lords and was termed 'an incorrect basis from which to proceed' by Lord Hope, although, as Celia Wells notes, this is dependent upon the meaning given to 'unlawful violence'.[140] Nevertheless, the position regarding this would appear to be that of the 'hybrid' situation identified by the Court of Appeal in *Constanza* (at the leave stage) where Evans LJ stated:

> If it is the case that actual bodily harm can consist of mental illness, then that mental illness might be caused by the apprehension of physical violence. There would then be a hybrid situation in which an assault was proved, resulting in harm, but harm of a different nature from that which was feared to be imminent.[141]

This appears an entirely correct statement of the position concerning assaults resulting in psychiatric illness and is consistent with the result achieved by the House of Lords' decision in *R v Ireland, R v Burstow*.

5.2.2.3 The immediacy requirement

It is an axiomatic feature of assault that the fear engendered must be of immediate unlawful violence. The difficulties arising from the characterisation of the relevant act as the making of the telephone call and the reformulation of

---

138 Smith, 1997, pp 434–36.

139 *R v Ireland* [1997] 1 All ER 112, *per* Swinton Thomas LJ, p 118.

140 Wells, 1997, pp 463–70. Wells asserts that the correctness of the Court of Appeal decision in Ireland is dependent upon whether it is accepted that 'unlawful violence' is merely an alternative term for a battery or whether it is wider in scope and can thus include psychiatric injury.

141 *R v Constanza* (1996) unreported, CA (case number 9602137/Y3).

violence to include the psychiatric harm suffered by the victims were compounded by the judgment of Swinton Thomas LJ in *Ireland* when he states:

> As to the immediacy, by using the telephone the appellant put himself in immediate contact with the victims, and when the victims lifted the telephone they were placed in immediate fear and suffered the consequences to which we have referred.[142]

This statement arguably confuses 'fear of immediate violence' with 'immediate fear of violence', which is not the correct basis for the offence of assault.[143] Assault is not an offence which addresses the creation of an innominate sense of fear, but the narrowly defined and specific fear of being immediately subjected to unlawful violence; apprehension of an immediate battery. Swinton Thomas LJ relied on the Divisional Court decision in *Smith v Chief Superintendent of Woking Police Station*[144] in which a vagrant who peered through the victim's ground floor bedroom window was held to have satisfied the requirements of assault as:[145]

> it was clearly a situation where the basis of the fear which was instilled in her was that she did not know what the defendant was going to do next, but that, whatever he might be going to do next, and sufficiently immediately for the purposes of the offence, was something of a violent nature.[146]

Swinton Thomas LJ felt that this case was similar to that before him and asserted that '[f]ear can be instilled as readily over the telephone as it can through the window'.[147] This statement ignores both the fact that this generalised sense of fear will not suffice for an assault[148] and that it is far easier to conceive of a victim fearing immediate unlawful violence if they see a

---

142 *R v Ireland* [1997] 1 All ER 112, *per* Swinton Thomas LJ, p 114.

143 One of the common mistakes which arguably exacerbates the general difficulties with this offence is the general tendency to replace 'apprehension' of immediate violence with 'fear' of immediate violence. Although 'apprehension' and 'fear' are close in meaning, they are not synonyms. 'Apprehension' is a more specific term which is anticipatory in nature and correctly should not be used in the general way that fear is used. Ormerod and Gunn, 1997, consider this point and submit that this semantic confusion devalues the decisions in both Ireland and *R v Constanza* [1997] 2 Cr App R 492. Equally, Glanville Williams supports the use of apprehension as the requirement of the offence is to cause the victim to believe that force will be used against him rather than to fear that it will – there may be circumstances where one appreciates that another is about to resort to physical violence, but this does not cause the potential victim to be afraid: Williams, G, 1983, p 173.

144 *Smith v Chief Superintendent of Woking Police Station* (1983) 76 Cr App R 234.

145 The defendant was charged under the Vagrancy Act 1824, s 4: '... every person being found ... in any enclosed ... garden ... for any unlawful purpose ... shall be deemed a rogue and a vagabound ...' It was found that the defendant had deliberately frightened the victim, which amounted to an assault and hence an unlawful purpose.

146 *Smith v Chief Superintendent of Woking Police Station* (1983) 76 Cr App R 234, *per* Kerr LJ, p 238.

147 *R v Ireland* [1997] 1 All ER 112, *per* Swinton Thomas LJ, p 118.

148 Allen, 1996: 'a fear of anything other than an immediate battery is not sufficient.' The continuing validity of this definition has been questioned: Wells, 1997, pp 463–70.

man peering through their bedroom window late at night than it is to accept that the recipient of a silent telephone call fears the imminent arrival of the caller intent on causing harm. It is not impossible to imagine a situation whereby a stalker who makes verbal threats and who may be in the immediate locality will satisfy the requirements of assault, but it is far harder to see how silence will achieve this effect.

The Court of Appeal went on to consider the persuasive authority of *Barton v Armstrong*,[149] a decision of the Supreme Court of New South Wales, in which it was held that verbal threats communicated by telephone were capable of amounting to an assault 'if they result in apprehension of physical violence', as this would place them within 'the protection afforded by the civil and criminal law as to assault'.[150]

The reliance placed upon this case by the Court of Appeal has been criticised. Allen expresses surprise that 'a first instance decision in an Australian tort case, which is not even cited in *Halsbury's Laws, The Digest* or *Clerk and Lindsall on Tort*, could provide the support for such a radical development in English criminal law'.[151] JC Smith, comments that the findings in *Barton v Armstrong* are perfectly acceptable, but far removed from the facts of *Ireland*.[152] It is certainly true to say that, notwithstanding the use of the telephone, there is a great difference between unambiguously threatening verbal communications and silence, which may be amenable to various interpretations.[153] This aspect of the case led Allen to comment that 'even this tenuous antipodean authority provides little support for the Court of Appeal's decision'.[154]

Scope for further criticism against this reliance on *Barton v Armstrong* becomes apparent once an earlier part of the judgment, not referred to by the Court of Appeal, is considered, in which Taylor J stated:

> The gist of the offence of assault is putting a person into apprehension of impending physical contact. The effect on the victim's mind is the material factor, and not whether the defendant actually had the intention or the means to follow it up. The essence of assault is the expectation raised in the mind of the victim of physical contact from the threat of the defendant.[155]

---

149 *Barton v Armstrong* [1969] 2 NSWR 451.

150 *Ibid, per* Taylor J, p 455.

151 Allen, 1996.

152 Smith, 1997, pp 434–36.

153 This is particularly so given the nature of the situation in *Barton v Armstrong* [1969] 2 NSWR 451, in which the defendant had previously made threats to kill the plaintiff and had arranged for others to follow the plaintiff. Therefore, it was not unreasonable for the plaintiff to fear immediate violence during the duration of the telephone call owing to the knowledge that the defendant had previously hired third parties to do him harm.

154 Allen, 1996.

155 *Barton v Armstrong* [1969] 2 NSWR 451, *per* Taylor J, p 454.

Equally, the Court of Appeal in *Ireland* did not consider the later decision of the New South Wales Court of Criminal Appeal in *R v Knight*[156] in which the defendant's convictions for assault were overturned, as his threats were generalised threats of violence which could occur at any time or may not manifest at all. Lee J accepted that a telephone call could amount to an assault provided it involved threats of immediate violence. He was critical of the suggestion in *Barton v Armstrong* that the concept of immediacy could be stretched to encompass events occurring in the future and did not accept that 'fear of immediate violence has other than its ordinary literal import'.[157]

Once *Barton v Armstrong* is read in the light of *Knight* and the earlier comments of Taylor J are taken into account, it becomes clear that the Court of Appeal in *Ireland* sought to extend well established legal principles on the basis of scant supporting authority.

It is interesting to compare the approach taken to the element of immediacy by the Court of Appeal in *R v Constanza*.[158] This was also a stalking case, although the defendant used a range of diverse actions to harass his victim. Nevertheless, his prosecution for assault occasioning actual bodily harm was based upon a single incident, namely, a hand delivered letter. This letter was the culmination of 18 months' harassment, during the course of which Constanza had sent the victim over 800 letters. This particular letter was phrased in such a way that the victim felt that the defendant had finally 'flipped' and would cause her harm at any time.

The reasoning in this decision has been questioned on the basis that although the letter undoubtedly caused the victim apprehension, it was inconceivable that it caused her apprehension of immediate violence.[159] Smith, JC makes the point that, once the idea of immediate violence is departed from, the essential character of common assault is lost and replaced with what is, in substance, an offence of threats to cause violence.[160] The Court of Appeal had dealt with the issue of immediacy by holding that the requirements for an assault would be made out if the prosecution had established 'a fear of violence at some time not excluding the immediate future'.[161]

This formulation of the immediacy requirement has also caused critical comment as it is not threats of harm in the immediate future which give rise to difficulties, but the very opposite question of whether assault is restricted to

---

156 *R v Knight* (1988) 35 A Crim R 314.

157 *Ibid, per* Lee J, p 318.

158 *R v Constanza* [1997] 2 Cr App R 492.

159 Smith, 1999, p 403.

160 This is in accord with the views of Glanville Williams, who rejected the idea that a threat by letter or telephone could ever amount to an assault, preferring instead the creation of an offence of making threats: Williams, G, 1983, p 176.

161 *R v Constanza* [1997] 2 Cr App R 492, *per* Schiemann LJ, p 494.

threats relating to the immediate future. JC Smith seeks to clarify what the Court of Appeal meant by saying that although 'it reads as if a fear of violence next year ('some time') will do – as well as a fear of violence next second; but that cannot be what the Court means ... what the Court means (it seems) is that there may be an assault where the apprehension of violence extends over a long period provided that it includes violence in the immediate future'.[162]

Clearly, this interpretation would bring the formulation of immediacy in *Constanza* closer to the traditional conception of the meaning of immediacy in assault, but there is no evidence in the judgment to support his view. When granting leave to appeal, Evans LJ, having outlined the facts of the case, stated that once it was accepted that mental illness can constitute actual bodily harm, then the way in which that harm is brought about may necessitate an expansion of the conception of assault notwithstanding the earlier common law definition.[163] This statement supports the view that the cases of *Ireland* and *Constanza* involved a deliberate restatement of the immediacy requirement in cases of psychiatric harm,[164] a situation which led to the accusation that the courts were distorting the law of assault in an attempt to counter the problem of stalking.[165]

Given the degree of confusion arising from these decisions and the consequent state of uncertainty in the law of assault, clarification as to the meaning of immediacy was clearly required. The House of Lords in *Ireland, Burstow* did not, however, dwell at length on the issue of immediacy and both Lord Slynn and Lord Hutton made it clear that the issue before them did not require a decision as to how the concept of immediacy should be applied or whether it was satisfied in the case before them. Nevertheless, it is clear throughout the judgment that the traditional conception of immediacy was being reasserted and that it was not sufficient that the victim was immediately in fear: there had to be fear of immediate violence. This is reiterated by Lord Steyn throughout his judgment, although he also states that the fear of the possibility of the caller's arrival 'in a minute or two' may satisfy the requirements of assault. Jeremy Horder doubts whether this *dictum* accords with the traditional conception of the imminence requirement of force being 'there and then' applied and suggests that the emphasis on the importance of the physical proximity engendered by the imminence requirement illustrates that the law of assault is ill-equipped to deal with stalking cases.[166] Nevertheless, the House of Lords took a more traditional view of assault than

---

162 Smith, 1997, p 577.

163 *R v Constanza* (1996) unreported, CA (transcript 9602137/Y3).

164 Boland, 1997, pp 231–39. Boland puts forward the view that the Court of Appeal in both Ireland and Constanza were covertly seeking to create a new species of assault, the development of which was halted by the House of Lords.

165 Cowley, 1998, pp 155–56.

166 Horder, 1998, pp 392–403.

the Court of Appeal, reiterating the requirement of apprehension of immediate unlawful violence, despite the degree of elasticity given to the concept of immediacy by Lord Steyn, which has been said to have halted the development of psychiatric assault and done little to advance the interests of stalking victims.[167]

5.2.3 Inflicting grievous bodily harm

Once it has been accepted that psychiatric injury will suffice for actual bodily harm, there is no obstacle to construing grievous bodily harm so as to include serious psychiatric injury. However, the first conviction of a stalker under s 20 was problematic and raised issues regarding both the requisite mental state of the accused and the causative element of the offence.

Bank clerk Christopher Gelder had developed an obsession with a female customer and used the bank computer to access personal information about her. He made repeated anonymous telephone calls to her in which he made reference to this personal information, as well as comments about her appearance which suggested to her that the calls were made by someone who knew her and who was watching her movements. Following this conviction under s 20 of the Offences Against the Person Act 1861 for inflicting grievous bodily harm on the basis of the psychological injury caused to his victim, Gelder was sentenced to 18 months' imprisonment. This conviction was quashed by the Court of Appeal owing to a misdirection by the trial judge as to the requisite *mens rea* of the offence.[168]

The offence under s 20 is committed if the defendant unlawfully and maliciously wounds or inflicts any grievous bodily harm. It is accepted that the word 'malicious' encompasses both intention and recklessness. The relevant standard of recklessness is subjective '*Cunningham*' recklessness, which means that 'the accused has foreseen that the particular kind of harm might be done and yet has gone on to take the risk of it'.[169] However, the harm which is intended or foreseen need only be of a minor character; there is no requirement that the gravity of harm which ensues is intended or foreseen.[170] Therefore, it is the defendant's foresight of the consequences of his actions that is crucial in determining liability. Accordingly, the trial judge should have directed the jury to consider 'whether [the defendant] foresaw that there was a risk of harm to this woman by making the calls'.[171] It is

---

167 Boland, 1997, pp 231–39.
168 'Pest jailed for GBH by phone' (1994) *The Times*, 9 July; 'Judge's error frees clerk jailed for anonymous calls' (1994) *The Times*, 16 December.
169 *R v Cunningham* [1957] 2 QB 396.
170 The '*Mowatt* gloss' adopted by Lord Diplock in *R v Mowatt* [1957] 2 All ER 412, p 414 approved by the House of Lords in *R v Savage, DPP v Parmenter* [1991] 4 All ER 698.
171 *R v Gelder* (1994) unreported, CA, *per* Taylor LCJ.

important to note that the defendant does not have to foresee that harm of the gravity that ensues would have occurred provided he foresaw that some harm would result.[172] The subjective nature of this test poses problems in stalking cases as, whilst it is reasonable to conclude objectively that there is a risk of psychological harm arising from a series of nuisance calls, establishing what was in the mind of the maker of those calls may well prove problematic. This was highlighted by the comments of Taylor LCJ when he quashed Gelder's conviction, as he stated that the jury should have been directed to consider whether the defendant, given his infatuation and obsession with the victim, would foresee that his actions would cause her harm. As the appeal was successful on this basis, the Court of Appeal declined to address the second ground of appeal that questioned whether it was possible to inflict grievous bodily harm of a psychological nature by means of obscene telephone calls.[173]

It was this issue concerning the scope of this causative element of the s 20 offence that formed the main basis for the appeal in *R v Burstow*[174] as the courts sought to reconcile conflicting authorities as to the meaning of 'inflict' in order to determine whether a stalker who used a wide range of means to harass his victim could be liable under s 20 of the Offences Against the Person Act 1861.

Anthony Burstow developed an obsession with a former work colleague after misunderstandings as to the nature of their relationship led to acrimony. He watched and followed her, made persistent abusive and unwanted telephone calls and visited her house at times when he knew she would be alone. Once she made it clear that there would be no resumption of their friendship, Burstow began to use these means deliberately to cause his victim distress. He distributed abusive cards around her neighbourhood, scattered condoms over her garden, stole underwear from her washing line, damaged her car and sent her a parcel containing a used sanitary towel. He also burgled her home on two occasions, once stealing her wedding album and video and interfering with the plumbing so as to cause flooding when he knew she was away on holiday. This conduct had led to numerous court appearances, both civil and criminal, and he had been sentenced to imprisonment on four previous occasions. Burstow's obsession had caused him to be dismissed from the Royal Navy where he served as a Petty Officer, contributed to the break-up of his marriage and the loss of his home.[175]

---

172 *R v Mowatt* [1968] 1 QB 421, confirmed by the House of Lords in *R v Savage, DPP v Parmenter* [1991] 4 All ER 698.

173 Cooper, 1995, pp 401–09.

174 *R v Burstow* [1996] Crim LR 331, Crown Court; [1997] 1 Cr App R 144, CA; [1997] 4 All ER 225, HL.

175 Much of the information concerning this case derives from an interview with Anthony Burstow conducted on 29 March 1999.

As the intensity of Burstow's obsession increased, his conduct escalated correspondingly, leading him to commit more serious offences and consequently receive more serious penalties. It was during his third period of imprisonment, on remand whilst awaiting trial for charges of burglary, that he claimed to have made a conscious decision to ensure that he committed no further crimes in his pursuit of his victim.[176] Therefore, in the six months after his release, he sought to ensure that the stalking of his victim involved only lawful means. This, however, led to his imprisonment for contempt of court following his persistent breaches of a county court injunction. His conduct during this time ultimately gave rise to the charge of inflicting grievous bodily harm on the basis of the psychiatric injury caused to his victim by his actions.

There was evidence at the trial at Reading Crown Court that the accumulation of incidents had caused the victim to suffer severe endogenous depression with marked features of anxiety that the psychiatrist regarded as grievous harm of a psychiatric nature. The psychiatrist further believed that every contact that Burstow made with his victim, whether direct or indirect and by whatever means, caused her to suffer further psychiatric injury.

The difficulties inherent in establishing the parameters of the word 'inflict' are not particular to this issue of psychiatric harm. Even in the orthodox context of physical harm, the authorities are somewhat unclear and contradictory as to the scope of the word.[177] The clearest principle that could be distilled from the existing authorities was that 'inflict' requires a direct or indirect application of force to the body of the victim. This stems from the decision of the Supreme Court of Victoria in *R v Salisbury*,[178] which was approved by the House of Lords in *R v Wilson* where Lord Roskill described it as 'a most valuable judgment' from which he derived great assistance when deliberating the meaning of 'inflict'. He went on to say that he was 'content to accept ... that there can be an infliction of grievous bodily harm contrary to s 20 without an assault being committed'.[179] It was this accepted position that was asserted by the defence in *Burstow*.

On this basis, it is suggested that a stalker would only be liable for inflicting psychological grievous bodily harm if this resulted from some form of physical attack. This approach was consistently rejected by the courts in Burstow. At first instance, Judge Lait reviewed the authorities on the meaning of 'inflict' and concluded that *Wilson* went no further than accepting that there can be an infliction without an assault and did not indicate that Lord Roskill had accepted the *Salisbury* judgment in full, as he was restricting his findings to those that were necessary to dispose of the appeal before him.[180] This being

---

176 *Ibid.*

177 Simester and Sullivan, 2000, pp 387–89; Reed, 1994, pp 187–97.

178 *R v Salisbury* [1976] VR 452.

179 *R v Wilson* [1984] AC 242.

180 *R v Burstow* [1996] Crim LR 331, Crown Court.

so, there was no reason to give 'inflict' a narrow restrictive meaning, especially as this would place psychiatric harm outside the scope of s 20, unless it arose from a physical attack. The prosecution contention that 'inflict' was synonymous with 'impose upon' was accepted, at which time Burstow changed his plea to guilty. This approach has been criticised for 'playing fast and loose with authority'.[181]

The Court of Appeal engaged in no such manipulation of the authorities.[182] After considering the orthodox position asserted by the defence, Lord Bingham CJ noted that the cases, dealing as they did with physical harm, could be distinguished from the current situation that concerned only psychiatric injury. He concluded by stating that it was not straining language to speak of one person inflicting psychiatric injury on another. The pragmatic basis for this decision is acknowledged by Lord Bingham, who stated that it would:

> introduce extreme and undesirable artificiality into what should be a very practical area of the law if we were to hold that, although grievous bodily harm includes psychiatric injury, no offence against section 20 is committed unless such psychiatric injury is the result of physical violence applied directly or indirectly to the body of the victim.[183]

In many ways, this could be said to be a sensible response to the decision in *Chan-Fook*. Once it is accepted that the Offences Against the Person Act 1861 encompasses psychiatric injury, it becomes futile to define the causative terms in such a way that certain offences can never be made out. Notwithstanding the weight of authority which suggests that direct or indirect physical contact is required, these authorities do indeed consider only the means by which physical harm can be inflicted. In terms of practical reality, the most straightforward way of inflicting an injury upon a person's mental well being is to subject them to extreme and relentless mental torment of the type that was undoubtedly present in this case.

The House of Lords disposed of the assertion that there was a difference in meaning between 'cause' and 'inflict' by reference to the explanatory language provided by the draftsman of the Offences Against the Person Act 1861:

> Enactments taken from different Acts passed at different times and with different views, and frequently varying from each other in phraseology ... It follows, therefore, from hence, that any argument as to a difference in the intention of the legislature, which may be drawn from a difference in the terms of one clause from those in another, will be entitled to no weight in the construction of such clauses, for that argument can only apply with force

---

181 Allen, 1996.

182 *R v Burstow* [1997] 1 Cr App R 144, CA.

183 *Ibid, per* Lord Bingham CJ, p 149.

where an Act is framed from beginning to end with one and the same view, and with the intention of making it thoroughly consistent throughout.[184]

Having concluded that the difference in language between s 20 and s 18 was not to be considered a significant factor, Lord Steyn went on to consider the authorities which address the definition of 'inflict', concluding that the effect of the decisions in *Wilson* and *Salisbury* were neutral in respect of the meaning of the word. Agreeing with the House of Lords in *R v Mandair*,[185] in which it was said that the word 'cause' was wider 'or at least not narrower' than the word 'inflict', Lord Steyn concludes there is not radical divergence in the meaning of the words and that whilst they are not exactly synonymous, the current contextual usage does not preclude the idea of one person inflicting psychiatric harm on another. This overlooks, however, the context in which Lord Mackay, giving the majority verdict in the House of Lords, was considering the meaning of the words. He was, at this point in his judgment, addressing whether the s 18 offence of 'causing' grievous bodily harm was wide enough to encompass the s 20 offence of 'inflicting' grievous bodily harm for the purposes of an alternative verdict under s 6(3) of the Criminal Law Act 1967. It was the dissenting judge, Lord Mustill, who gave in-depth consideration to the meaning of the two words in a broader context and who concluded that he was:

> unable to accept that the two words mean the same, although there will of course be many states of fact to which they can both be accurately applied ... Assuming the difference in meaning to exist, 'cause' is the wider word; so a verdict of 'causing' can embrace a set of facts which do not amount to 'inflicting'.[186]

Thus 'inflict' is necessarily subsumed within 'cause', but the reverse is not true, so not every act which causes harm will amount to an infliction of harm. This is supported by the fact that s 20 refers to 'wound or inflict grievous bodily harm' as a basis for liability, both of which are included within 'causing grievous bodily harm', thus illustrating the causative scope of the s 18 offence. Accordingly, it appears eminently reasonable to assert, as the defence did, that although Burstow may well have caused his victim to suffer grievous harm of a psychiatric nature, he certainly did not inflict it upon her. Whilst Lord Steyn in Burstow seeks to circumvent these difficulties by reference to the words of the draftsman, he appears to disregard the need to consider not just what the words meant at the time of the enactment of the statute, but what the words have come to mean after over 100 years of judicial interpretation. Equally, as Celia Wells asserts, the authorities before the House of Lords were concerned with the application of s 6(3) of the Criminal Law Act 1967 and indicate a

---

184 Greaves, 1862, pp 3–4 as cited in *R v Burstow* [1997] 4 All ER 225, *per* Lord Steyn, p 234.
185 (1994) 99 Cr App R 250.
186 *R v Mandair* [1994] 2 All ER 715, *per* Lord Mustill, pp 733–34.

'sufficiently blurred interpretation of the scope of "inflicting" harm' that they are 'unhelpful on the core meaning of what "inflict" does mean', thus it may have been preferable had the House of Lords established a clear and targeted definition of the meaning of 'inflict' for the purposes of the s 20 offence.[187]

The final tactic used by both the Court of Appeal and the House of Lords in *Burstow* was to distinguish the cases before them, as they did not address the possibility of psychiatric injury. Indeed, Lord Steyn sees this as the only way around the 'troublesome authority' of *R v Clarence*,[188] regarded as a leading case for over 100 years, in which the defendant was held not to have inflicted grievous bodily harm on his wife by infecting her with a sexually transmitted disease during consensual intercourse. JC Smith questions the departure from this authority by the House of Lords notwithstanding the psychiatric/physical harm distinction, stating that such a distinction is 'difficult to follow' and questioning its rationale on the following basis:

> It surely cannot mean that if Mrs C, on discovering the infection, had sustained a neurotic injury, the judges would have said that the neurotic injury was 'inflicted' though the earlier physical injury was not.[189]

This emphasis on the distinction between the infliction of physical and psychiatric harm has led Simester and Sullivan to suggest that there are now two meanings of the word 'inflict' for the purposes of s 20 of the Offences Against the Person Act 1861 with the approach of Lord Steyn in *Burstow* being limited to psychiatric harm. The narrower approach endorsed in *Wilson* and *Mandair* should prevail in cases involving physical harm, thus retaining the requirement that the injury should result from direct or indirect impact upon the victim's body.[190] Such a further dichotomy in an already tortuous area of law is hardly to be welcomed, even in the interests of upholding such a meritorious conviction. The alternative interpretation is favoured by Virgo, who posits 'surely now "inflicts" will always be equated with "causes"' and asserts that to hold otherwise would create additional artificiality into the statute.[191] Which approach is taken remains to be seen, but it is hoped that this area of uncertainty will imminently receive the legislative attention that is necessary to establish a clear statement of the law in this area.

5.2.4 Grievous bodily harm with intent

Somewhat ironically, this most serious offence in the offences against the person hierarchy has raised few difficulties in relation to the conviction of

---

187 Wells, 1997, pp 463–70.
188 *R v Clarence* (1888) 22 QBD 23.
189 *R v Ireland, R v Burstow*: Case and Comment [1997] Crim LR 810–12.
190 Simester and Sullivan, 2000, pp 388–89.
191 Virgo, 1997, pp 251–53.

stalkers. The s 18 offence has the widest causative element of the three offences, requiring only that the defendant has caused the harm that ensues. This is combined with the narrowest mental element that will only be satisfied if the defendant intended to cause grievous bodily harm. It is this *mens rea* requirement which will generally lead to difficulties in stalking cases, as the jury may be reluctant to find that the stalker intended by his actions to cause his victim grievous psychiatric injury.

Certainly, the judge in *R v Chambers* directed the jury to acquit the defendant of the charge under s 18 of the Offences Against the Person Act 1861 owing to the difficulties of proving that he had intended to cause psychological damage.[192] The jury then found the defendant not guilty of the s 20 offence, following the judge's direction that: 'you might think she suffered annoyance, panic and emotional distress. That alone would not be sufficient for you to find these charges proven.' The case was heavily criticised, leading the judge to take the unusual step of publicly defending his approach to the case in a statement issued by the Lord Chancellor's Office.[193] However, despite the outcome of this case, it was the factual situation that caused difficulties, not the application of the law. There were no difficulties in *R v Keane*, where a stalker who had terrorised a woman for nine years, causing her to suffer post-traumatic stress disorder, was convicted of intentionally causing her this harm and was sentenced to be detained indefinitely in a mental hospital. Despite the fact that the defendant was suffering from paranoia and schizophrenia, the court found no difficulty in accepting that he had intended, by his persistent actions over a nine year period in which she moved house four times to avoid him, to cause her serious harm.[194]

In many ways, it is difficult to ascertain why Anthony Burstow was not charged with this more serious offence, as there was a great deal of evidence that appeared to suggest that he was intentionally seeking to cause his victim to suffer mental torment. One note in particular was deemed by the trial judge to show that Burstow was fully aware of the impact that he was having on his victim's life, as it read:

Do you covet the stable life of your peers? Is there a desire for normality to return at the tender age of 27.5 years, to re-discover your self-esteem and finally put to rest those recent traumas in life? Do you long for a new era when you can:

(a) wake up in the morning and smile at the day it brings, be it work or rest, weekday or weekend, and not be concerned about the motives or plans of another?

---

192 'Stalker cleared of causing harm' (1996) *The Times*, 18 September; 'Victim is left alone with her fear as jury clears stalker' (1996) *Daily Telegraph*, 18 September.

193 'Judge defends comments to jury in stalker case' (1996) *The Times*, 21 September.

194 'Stalker convicted for causing grievous bodily harm' (1997) *The Guardian*, 23 July; 'Stalker told to expect life' (1997) *The Times*, 23 July.

(b) sit at the breakfast table and discuss what lies ahead without fretting over the contents of the postbox or agonising over possible untoward news from your father's short walk for the daily paper?

(c) leave the house and, along with your family, not have to check the immediate vicinity, the road and the passing traffic?

(d) drive the car without suspicion of other vehicles ahead or behind you and be able to park and leave your car without fear of what may be there on your return?

(e) be at home, either alone or be it with Bertie and Co or in the company of others and not be fearful of your safety and, without apprehension, answer the telephone, to take one or both dogs for a walk unconcerned at whom you meet?

(f) spend lunch and other hours shopping, browsing through the town centre or village high street untroubled at who is around or without the feeling of dread that someone may be watching or waiting?

(g) return home to discuss how ordinary and normal life has been, not to just feel that you have survived another trip of another day yet unsure of what or whom may await you on the next journey outside the safe haven of the family home?

If this is a true picture of your preference for the future you must exercise complete control and totally ignore the influence of another in and on your life. But if as it appears, you leave home on each and every occasion with a frown, scowl, almost semi-permanently etched into the face, your right eyelid screwed tight, wearily watching humanity around you, unable to return home without one final glance from the porch to check for someone, then that someone still holds a significant degree of influence (control) over you and your life.

Tracey, one final point. Please remember this is totally personal and nothing will change how much I hate you – a comforting thought, is it not?

Given that there was sufficient psychiatric evidence to support a finding of grievous bodily harm, it is difficult to see, in the light of this letter and Burstow's continued pursuit of his victim, why he was not charged with intentionally causing grievous bodily harm. The letter certainly indicates that he was aware of the effect that his actions were having upon her and that he was glorying in this. After being released from prison, Burstow was outside his victim's house within one hour, making an unequivocal statement of his intention to continue to harass her. His continued activities, following his release from prison, led him to be charged under s 18 on the basis that he was now fully aware that his conduct was causing his victim to suffer psychiatric injury, thus to continue to behave as he did demonstrated that it was his intention to cause her such harm. Apparently, the prosecution were still not confident that the jury would accept this as evidence of intention to cause grievous bodily harm as opposed to an intention to cause upset or annoyance, and it was felt that there may be difficulties in establishing that she had suffered additional psychiatric harm, thus the charge was discontinued when Burstow agreed to be bound over to keep the peace.[195]

Therefore, although the interpretation of s 18 is not likely to cause difficulties, it can clearly be seen that it is the complexities of the stalking situation itself that render the use of this section unsuitable in stalking cases. This difficulty of proving additional psychiatric harm may prove an insurmountable obstacle to a second prosecution under the Act owing to the difficulties not just of establishing psychiatric harm, but also in quantifying its severity. This is particularly unfortunate, as stalking is characterised by its repeated nature that frequently remains impervious to criminal conviction and even imprisonment, as the *Burstow* case clearly illustrates. Thus, it could be that even if the Offences Against the Person Act 1861 can be interpreted in such a way that it provides a means of convicting a stalker on one occasion, subsequent convictions appear increasingly unlikely.

5.2.5 Limitations of *Ireland* and *Burstow*

Notwithstanding the criticisms of the uncertainty that these cases have caused in the law of offences against the person, these decisions represent a high water mark of judicial inclination to accommodate the interests of victims of stalking. However, the cases are nevertheless limited in the solution that is provided to those who are being stalked.

First, there will be no possibility of charges under the Offences Against the Person Act 1861 unless and until the victim suffers recognisable psychiatric harm as attested by expert evidence. This requirement is stated unequivocally by the House of Lords and was later clarified in *R v Morris*, another stalking case, where it was stated that the evidence of a general practitioner would not suffice; the expert evidence must be given by a specialist in psychiatric illness.[196] Therefore, due to the focus of the Offences Against the Person Act 1861 on the consequences rather than the nature of the conduct, the law requires that the victim must tolerate the activities of the stalker until such time as her mental health is harmed. This is a significant limitation to the potential utility of the Act in stalking cases, as not all victims will suffer psychiatric harm as a result of the stalker's conduct. There is an immense range of potential responses to stalking victimisation and how any individual reacts is contingent upon a variety of factors, including their own psychological pathology at the time of the incident and their inherent ability to withstand stress.[197] For example, Pathe and Mullen's[198] research into the

---

195 'Stalker victim left in fear as man is freed' (1998) *The Times*, 14 August. Interview with Anthony Burstow, 29 March 1999.

196 *R v Morris* [1998] 1 Cr App R 386.

197 Pathe and Mullen, 1997, pp 12–17.

198 *Ibid*.

impact of stalking on victims found that although the majority of victims suffer from post-traumatic stress symptoms, only 37% would fulfil the criteria for diagnosis of post-traumatic stress disorder according to DSM-IV.[199] This is largely due to the absence of the stressor A criterion, which requires that the trauma experienced by the victim includes actual or threatened physical harm.[200] This requirement is unfortunate, as the whole purpose of seeking to establish liability for psychiatric harm was to find a means of addressing stalking when the conduct does not involve the commission of a criminal act. To find that actual or threatened harm is a prerequisite for one of the most appropriate psychiatric diagnoses in stalking cases establishes yet another barrier to successful criminal prosecution. It seems illogical that a victim who satisfies the remaining criteria for a diagnosis of post-traumatic stress disorder should be disqualified from the assignation of the diagnosis merely because of the means by which the symptoms were caused. Although it is acknowledged that post-traumatic stress disorder is not the only psychiatric illness that a victim of stalking could suffer, it is to be remembered that there are similar diagnostic criteria for all clinically recognised psychiatric disorders, thus the requirement of psychiatric harm may operate to exclude stalking victims from the protection of the criminal law. There is evidence to suggest that a substantial number of stalking victims experience a change of personality or temperament as a result of being stalked, thus a system which allows such harm to develop prior to legal intervention, or makes such harm a prerequisite of intervention, is not taking sufficient steps to protect the well being of individuals in society.[201]

The requirement of recognisable psychiatric illness creates further difficulties when comparing the severity of this with the comparatively low threshold of physical harm that will suffice for a prosecution under the Offences Against the Person Act 1861. There is clear disparity here, as physical harm of an extremely low level will constitute 'actual bodily harm' for the purposes of s 47: 'any hurt or injury calculated to interfere with the health and comfort' of the victim will suffice provided it is more than merely 'transient or trifling'.[202] The Crown Prosecution Service guidelines suggest that prosecution under s 47 is appropriate when there are injuries such as, *inter alia*, minor cuts requiring stitches, minor fractures or extensive or multiple bruising. Injuries such as grazes, cuts, abrasions and the like will give rise to

---

199 American Psychiatric Association, 1994.

200 The current diagnostic formulation for post-traumatic stress disorder is derived primarily from early observations of survivors of relatively circumscribed traumatic events. It has been noted that this formulation 'fails to capture the protean sequelae of prolonged, repeated trauma' which makes it particularly difficult to satisfy given the nature of the conduct involved in stalking: Herman, 1992, pp 377–91.

201 Hall, DM, 'The victims of stalking', in Meloy, 1999; Pathe and Mullen, 1997, pp 12–17.

202 *R v Donovan* [1934] 2 KB 498, *per* Swift J, p 502.

the lesser charges of common assault or battery.[203] However, there is an immense degree of prosecutorial discretion involved concerning the decision whether to prosecute and under what section which, it has been suggested, is influenced by a multitude of factors other than the seriousness of harm suffered by the victim.[204] Although the dangers in attempting to establish equivalence between physical and psychiatric injuries are acknowledged, it would appear that a far lesser degree of harm will suffice to found a prosecution under s 47 of the Offences Against the Person Act 1861 if the injury is physical than if it is of a psychiatric nature. No account is to be taken of lesser mental discomfort and distraught emotional states despite the growing body of research that identifies the severe ramifications that such states can have on a person's life.[205]

It is the ongoing nature of stalking that leads to another area of concern in relation to charges under the Offences Against the Person Act 1861. The question arises as to whether it was possible to establish with any degree of precision at what stage criminal liability was incurred. With physical injuries, it is a straightforward matter to ascertain precisely when the injury occurred and what act led to this injury. The position with psychiatric harm is substantially different. One of the key features of stalking is the repeated nature of the conduct. It is reasonable to suggest that it would be an exceptional case if the victim suffered psychiatric injury when the first incident occurred; indeed, many victims acknowledge that they dismiss early incidents that occur as coincidence or paranoia and that it is only as the conduct progresses that they begin to appreciate that they are being targeted by a stalker. Additionally, many victims report that once they realised that they were being stalked, they remained optimistic that the stalker would stop and leave them alone. Obviously, the point at which any particular victim will suffer psychiatric injury is dependent upon a variety of factors. So, in this continuum of stalking behaviour, how is it to be determined when the stalker has incurred criminal liability? If the answer is to be dependent upon the impact upon the victim's state of mental health, there is clearly no stage at which the stalker could make a conscious decision to desist so as not to be in breach of the criminal law. The argument that the stalker should not be behaving in such a way has little merit if the conduct in which he is engaged is otherwise lawful. Equally, it is to be remembered that many stalkers are

---

203 Crown Prosecution Service, *Offences Against the Person Charging Standards*, 1996.

204 Clarkeson, Cretney, Davis and Shepherd, 1994, pp 4–20. This article identifies six factors other than the seriousness of the injury which influence the police response to assault: (a) initial police construction of the incident; (b) police discretion in the face of perceived demands of the prosecution process; (c) police construction of the incident as non-criminal or private; (d) the impact of public order considerations; (e) the attitude/record of the assailant; (f) the character/attitude of the complainant.

205 *Op cit*, Hall, fn 201; Pathe and Mullen, 1997, pp 12–17; Maguire and Corbett, 1987.

unaware of the potential adverse effects of their conduct on the victim. Thus, the situation created by the interpretation given to the Offences Against the Person Act 1861 by the House of Lords could be said to base criminal liability on an inherently unknowable factor.

Additional difficulties concerning the extent and application of the Offences Against the Person Act 1861 in stalking cases arise from the narrow basis of the judgments in Ireland and Burstow. As was acknowledged by Lord Slynn,[206] Lord Steyn[207] and Lord Hope,[208] there was no necessity for the House of Lords to concern themselves with issues of *mens rea* and causation as these were deemed to be established by the guilty pleas entered by both defendants at trial. Therefore, the authority is limited to a finding that the actions of these men could amount to an assault occasioning actual bodily harm and an infliction of grievous bodily harm.

The *mens rea* element of the s 47 offence is unlikely to be problematic. The House of Lords restated the traditional definition of assault, hence the *mens rea* will remain limited to intention or foresight of causing apprehension of immediate unlawful violence. The position is more complex in relation to the *mens rea* of the s 20 offence which requires that the defendant intended or foresaw some bodily harm, not necessarily of the severity which ensues. JC Smith describes the burden of establishing that a person foresaw that his act would or might cause a neurotic illness, something identifiable only by expert evidence, as distinct from mere fear or anxiety, as formidable. This leads him to question whether we can expect that only sensitive stalkers, those with greater awareness of the feelings and vulnerabilities of others, are likely to be convicted.[209] It is not certain, at present, as to how the mental element will be applied to a charge of grievous psychiatric harm and it may be, given the enactment of the Protection from Harassment Act 1997, that this issue will never be raised before the courts. Nevertheless, any future stalking cases which do arise under s 20 will need to deal carefully with the *mens rea* requirement, which may prove to be an impediment to conviction. In fact, consideration of the elements of the s 20 offence can only lead to the conclusion that the section as a whole is shrouded with uncertainty. As Virgo states:

> the increasingly inappropriate language of s 20 (where grievous bodily harm simply means serious harm, where inflicts means causes and where malice does not mean malice) can only be a source of confusion for the jury.[210]

---

206 *R v Ireland, R v Burstow* [1997] 4 All ER 225, p 227.
207 *Ibid*, pp 231 and 237.
208 *Ibid*, p 239.
209 Smith, 1997, pp 452–55.
210 Virgo, 1997, pp 251–53.

Therefore, whilst providing one means by which a stalker can be prosecuted, which overcomes the limitations discussed in the previous chapter, it would appear that recourse to the Offences Against the Person Act 1861 may cause as many problems as it solves. There are clear disadvantages to the use of this statute in stalking cases, both in terms of the protection afforded to victims and the sacrifice of legal certainty and the manipulation of established legal principles.

5.3 CONCLUSION

Chapter 4 outlined some of the potential means by which a stalker could be brought before the civil or criminal courts and the disadvantages of these, which were basically limited availability and low penalties. This chapter examined how the civil and criminal courts sought to overcome these difficulties and provide greater and more accessible redress for victims. This illustrates the recognition by the judiciary that stalking is a serious social problem that justifies legal intervention. In order to provide wide and accessible means of redress, the courts have interpreted various areas of law to ensure that the facts of particular stalking cases are within their remit. The disadvantages of this, both to victims and in terms of legal principles, have been outlined. Other than this, the preceding discussion clearly illustrates that, notwithstanding these difficulties, there was still an identifiable gap in the law which needed to be filled owing to the sheer amount of stalking cases which, notwithstanding judicial innovation, were still not within the reach of the law.

CHAPTER 6

THE PROTECTION FROM HARASSMENT ACT 1997

The Protection from Harassment Act 1997 was introduced as a direct response to the perceived need to legislate against stalking. Although the statute makes no reference to stalking, the content of the parliamentary debates prior to its enactment leave no room for doubt that the primary purpose of the legislation was to fill the gap in the law that rendered victims of stalking vulnerable to continued harassment. This chapter examines the content of the relevant sections of the Protection from Harassment Act 1997 to ascertain the scope and remit of the legislation.

6.1 SCOPE OF THE PROTECTION FROM HARASSMENT ACT 1997

The Protection from Harassment Act is generally characterised as creating two new criminal offences and a statutory tort,[1] but could equally be characterised as creating the basis for criminal liability in four ways. First, there are the two substantive criminal offences that are created – criminal harassment (s 2) and causing fear of violence (s 4) – which are the primary basis of criminal liability under the Act. Additionally, ss 3 and 5 facilitate the imposition of restrictive orders by both the civil and criminal courts, breach of which constitutes a criminal offence, hence providing a secondary basis for criminal liability under the Act.

This chapter will address the interrelation of these sections and the way in which they seek to achieve the purpose of the statute, which was to provide a fast and effective means of redress for victims of harassment. The provisions of s 1, which prohibits harassment, will be discussed in detail as this section provides the basis for the offence of criminal harassment and the statutory tort of harassment. Many of its features are replicated in s 4, which contains the offence of causing fear of violence. Having discussed these offences, the chapter will move on to consider the secondary basis for criminal liability created by the Act, which takes the form of criminal penalties for breach of court orders.

---

1   Howard, M, *HC Deb*, Vol 287, Cols 783–86, 17 December 1996.

6.2 THE PROHIBITION OF HARASSMENT

Section 1 of the Protection from Harassment Act 1997 contains the prohibition of harassment, which forms the basis of the criminal offence of harassment and the statutory tort of harassment. From the outset, questions are raised regarding the potential difficulties of founding both civil and criminal liability upon the same basis. No guidance is provided by the statute as to the circumstances in which either course of action is most appropriate – it is apparently to be a matter of personal choice for the victims. Presumably, there is nothing to prevent a victim alerting the police to the problem whilst simultaneously pursuing a civil action – a 'belt and braces' approach that may reassure the beleaguered victim that at least one course of action is likely to ameliorate the situation. Nonetheless, this clearly places the stalker in peril of double jeopardy, a particularly problematic issue in the context of this legislation, given that the breach of a civil order is a criminal offence.

Section 1 provides:

(1) A person must not pursue a course of conduct –

(a) which amounts to harassment of another, and

(b) which he knows or ought to know amounts to harassment of the other.

(2) For the purposes of this section, the person whose course of conduct is in question ought to know that it amounts to harassment of another if a reasonable person in possession of the same information would think that the course of conduct amount to harassment of the other.

(3) Sub-section (1) does not apply to a course of conduct if the person who pursued it shows –

(a) that it was pursued for the purpose of preventing or detecting crime,

(b) that it was pursued under any enactment or rule of law or to comply with any condition or requirement imposed by any person under any enactment, or

(c) that in the particular circumstances the pursuit of the course of conduct was reasonable.

The process of establishing harassment can be seen as a distinct three stage process, each stage of which must be satisfied. There must be a course of conduct by the defendant, this must cause a victim to suffer harassment, and the defendant must know or should have known that this would be so. Each of these stages raises discrete issues which may have implications for the imposition of liability for harassment, hence it is proposed to examine each stage in turn.

6.2.1 Course of conduct

There is little guidance in the Protection from Harassment Act 1997 as to what is meant by a 'course of conduct'. Section 7 specifies that a course of conduct requires conduct on at least two occasions[2] and states that conduct can include speech[3] but, other than this, there are no statutory limitations as to what form of conduct is prohibited and what circumstances constitute a course of conduct. Therefore, the wording of the statute suggests that any two incidents of behaviour may amount to a course of conduct – the first stage of liability for harassment. There are, however, various issues associated with this that require consideration.

6.2.1.1 The nature of the acts

The statute does not require that the incidents which form the basis of a course of conduct be of the same nature. Therefore, an abusive telephone call could count as one incident and throwing a brick through the victim's window could count as the second. This acknowledges the multifarious means used to cause harassment and the tendency of the majority of stalkers to engage in more than one type of harassing behaviour.[4] There is no requirement that the incidents be inherently criminal in nature. Indeed, the rationale for drawing the terms of the offence in such general terms was to ensure that conduct which is not in itself criminal will be caught within its provisions. It has been suggested that if the conduct is not harassing in itself, such as sending flowers, more than two incidents will be required to establish a course of conduct, but if the conduct is inherently harassing, such as physical or verbal abuse, two incidents will suffice to engender liability.[5] Whilst the logic of this argument may appear compelling, it may be that a more accurate conceptualisation would be to view two incidents of innocuous conduct as less likely to satisfy the other requirements of the offences of harassment – that they cause harassment and that the defendant knows or ought to know that this would be so. In many respects, the course of conduct can be seen as a neutral requirement that whilst standing alone has no criminal connotation. Thus, even if sending flowers on two occasions, for example, were to be regarded as a course of conduct, this is of little practical significance, as it would still have to satisfy the other requirements of the section before it can be said to amount to harassment. This issue is implicit in the finding of the Divisional Court in *Baron v Crown Prosecution Service*, where the emphasis was not upon whether the two letters in question could amount

---

2   Protection from Harassment Act 1997, s 7(3).

3   *Ibid*, s 7(4).

4   Budd and Mattinson, 2000.

5   Addison and Lawson-Cruttenden, 1998, pp 30–31.

to a course of conduct, but whether they could amount to a course of conduct which causes alarm or distress.[6] Equally, in *DPP v Ramsdale*, it was accepted that a substantial number of incidents had occurred, hence the course of conduct requirement was easily satisfied.[7] However, the court found, as a matter of fact, that only one of these incidents caused the victim alarm or distress, hence the offence of harassment was not made out despite evidence of incidents spanning almost two years. It is important to emphasise that the finding that two incidents amount to a course of conduct is only the first stage to be satisfied and will not suffice as the basis of criminal liability unless the other elements of the offence are present.

6.2.1.2 Omissions

It was said in *Morris v Knight* that silence cannot constitute a course of conduct, as this requires a positive act rather than a mere omission.[8] This case involved a dispute between neighbours who lived in the same block of flats and who, following a disagreement, refused to communicate even when this was necessary for the smooth running of the communal areas of the premises. The plaintiff brought an action claiming that wilful refusal to communicate when such communication was not merely courteous, but necessary, would amount to harassment. This was not accepted by the court, where it was held that harassment by omission to speak was not within the scope of the statute. However, if it cannot be said that silence can amount to a course of conduct, one can never progress to the next stage of liability and consider whether the behaviour caused the victim to suffer harassment. This is unfortunate, as there may well be circumstances in which silence could cause a person manifest distress or alarm. The very fact that silence was deliberately used as a weapon in this case is indicative of its acceptance as a means by which to cause an adverse reaction in the victim. Equally, even if a silent telephone call is characterised as a positive act, there are still situations in which one could experience harassment as a result of another's silence and certainly as a result of another's omissions. An obstructive attitude by a work colleague whereby they refuse to co-operate in any way or to pass on messages would certainly cause the recipient of the behaviour to experience distress and would be such an impediment to the effective functioning of the recipient in the workplace that harassment is sure to result.[9] However, unless there is a means to characterise this behaviour in terms of a positive act, or there is a case that says that there can be a course of conduct by omission to act, this behaviour would not engender liability under the statute. It may be that it is preferable to

---

6   *Baron v CPS*, (2000) unreported, Divisional Court, 13 June.
7   *DPP v Ramsdale* (2001) *The Independent*, 19 March.
8   *Morris v Knight* (1998) unreported, 22 October.
9   Case history 3.

adopt an approach that is in line with the imposition of liability for omissions elsewhere in criminal law by accepting that silence, or any other relevant omission, may provide a basis for liability if there is a duty to act. This would at least enable cases involving omissions to be raised before the courts.

6.2.1.3 Time between the incidents

The period of time separating the incidents may also be relevant to whether or not the conduct in question amounts to a course of conduct. Again, there is no guidance in the statute on this issue. If the telephone call is made from outside the victim's house using a mobile telephone and the brick is thrown through the window whilst the call is in progress, the proximity of the incidents could support an argument that they were part of a single incident. Alternatively, it could be argued that the situation involves two incidents of a totally different nature, hence amounting to a course of conduct. If the two incidents were two abusive telephone calls made within five minutes of each other, does this count as two separate incidents or merely one continuous act of harassment?

In *Wass v DPP*, the defendant followed, in his car, the bus upon which the victim, his former girlfriend, was travelling.[10] When the bus stopped, the defendant sought to block her passage from the bus and engage her in conversation. The victim went briefly into a nearby shop in an effort to escape from the defendant, who waited outside. Upon leaving the shop, the victim was again accosted by the defendant, who sought to persuade her to get into his car. This was the basis for his harassment conviction, which was upheld on appeal. The Divisional Court described the appeal as 'utterly hopeless' and held that the magistrates were perfectly entitled to interpret these events as conduct on two separate occasions – one before the victim went into the shop and the second when she emerged.

A different approach is evident in *DPP v Ramsdale*, which involved a protracted series of events including telephone calls, the sending of letters and cards, and photographing the victim without her consent.[11] This culminated with the defendant entering the victim's house through the bathroom window. The victim persuaded the defendant to leave, but he returned 15 minutes later and banged upon the front door. The court only addressed this final incident as giving rise to potential liability as it was found that the preceding incidents were either condoned or encouraged by the victim, or at least not rebuffed by her. The court accepted that the defendant's entry into the victim's house through the bathroom window had caused her distress, but would not interpret it as conduct on two occasions, as the conduct concerned was separated by only 15 minutes.

---

10 *Wass v DPP* (2000) unreported, Divisional Court, 11 May.
11 *DPP v Ramsdale* (2001) *The Independent*, 19 March.

These cases reach opposite conclusions on the basis of similar factual situations. Indeed, of the two cases, it would appear more logical to conclude that Wass involved a continuing incident as the defendant did not leave the area and engaged in the same type of conduct before and after the victim entered the shop. This disparity of approach highlights the uncertainty surrounding the distinction between a continuing incident of harassment and two separate incidents when only a short period of time is involved.

If both or either incident is an independent criminal offence, it could be argued that it is irrelevant, as the defendant can be charged with these offences in any case. However, it is only following conviction for an offence under the Protection from Harassment Act that a restraining order can be imposed upon the defendant, thus the victim may have good reason to prefer that charges are brought under the Act. More than this, to consider the elements of harassment individually is to disregard the nature of the wrong that the Act seeks to address. Persistent harassment, by whatever means, is harmful in a way that is not encapsulated by fragmentation of the situation into its composite elements, thus it is important to address the totality of the conduct. This was recognised by the Court of Appeal in *R v Miah* in which the defendant was sentenced to two and half years' imprisonment for harassment involving two relatively minor assaults.[12] The defendant appealed against his sentence on the basis that the assaults, viewed individually, would not have given rise to a custodial sentence. The Court of Appeal rejected this argument, pointing out that the defendant was not being sentenced for the assaults:

> In our judgment, so far as it is said that the individual content of the harassment count would not merit a sentence of two and a half years, it misses the purpose of the Act which is to provide protection and to permit punishment in circumstances where it is not the individual acts or conduct themselves, but their persistence and their impact upon the victim to which regard should be paid.[13]

As the approach of the Court of Appeal in *Miah* indicates, it is important that, wherever possible, conduct that is indicative of ongoing harassment is charged under the Protection from Harassment Act regardless of the timing of the incidents.

The second issue that arises in relation to the timing of the harassing behaviour is the extent to which two incidents separated by a long period of time will be regarded as a course of conduct. Would two abusive telephone calls one week apart constitute a course of conduct – two weeks apart, one month, three months? At what stage can it be said that the incidents are so far apart that they must considered to be unassociated and thus considered as two separate incidents? The Act offers no guidance on this issue but it has

12 *R v Miah* [2000] 2 Cr App R(S) 439.
13 *Ibid, per* Newman J.

been suggested that an appropriate context would justify incidents even one year apart being regarded as a course of conduct.[14] For example, a photograph of a new-born baby sent every year on the date that a woman had an abortion would undoubtedly cause manifest distress to the recipient and the regularity of the conduct combined with the consistent purpose would be indicative of a course of conduct.[15] This view was supported by the Court of Appeal in *DPP v Lau* by Schiemann LJ, who rejected the mathematical approach of 'incident plus incident equals a course of conduct' in favour of the need to establish a nexus between the incidents:

> The incidents which need to be proven in relation to harassment need not exceed two incidents but ... the fewer the occasions and the wider they are spread the less likely it would be that a finding of harassment can reasonably be made. One can conceive of circumstances where incidents, as far apart as a year, could constitute a course of conduct and harassment ... [For example] racial harassment taking place outside a synagogue on a religious holiday, such as the day of atonement, and being repeated each year as the day of atonement came round. Another example might be a threat to do something once a year on a person's birthday. Nonetheless the broad position must be that if one is left with only two incidents you have to see whether what happened on those two occasions can be described as a course of conduct.[16]

This case involved allegations of five incidents between the defendant and his former girlfriend. Two of the incidents were accepted by the court: a slap across the face in November 1998 and a threatening conversation in March 1999. In the absence of any nexus between these incidents, the Divisional Court was not minded to accept that these two incidents, which were of a different nature and occurred four months apart, could constitute a course of conduct. This rejection of the 'mathematical' approach provides a welcome restriction to the scope of the offence of harassment. Despite the definition of 'course of conduct' as 'conduct on at least two occasions', that should not be taken as implying that this is all that is required. As Ormerod notes, the words 'course of conduct' necessarily imply some nexus between the composite incidents – the words suggest a 'series of events with some connection'. Although the main connecting factor may well be the identity of the parties, it is not altogether clear that this alone will suffice. The analogy drawn by Ormerod regarding the meaning of a 'course of treatment' illustrates this clearly:

> Two visits to the hospital by the same patient would not necessarily be described as a course of treatment. There must be something connecting them – in the case of the treatment, one would expect it to be for the same ailment.

---

14 Addison and Lawson-Cruttenden, 1998, p 31.
15 Case Study 12.
16 *Lau v DPP* [2000] 1 FLR 799, p 803.

Unfortunately, it is not such a straightforward matter to pinpoint what the connection between incidents must be for them to be regarded as a course of conduct. Certainly, proximity in time and nature may assist but, as the foregoing discussion has established, these factors are not determinative. Neither is it necessarily the case that the conduct must be experienced by the same victim. Common sense dictates that there must be some nexus between incidents, but the nature of that nexus is elusive.

The requirement of an association that links the composite incidents is largely in accord with the way in which a course of conduct is defined in stalking legislation in the US. For example, to constitute a course of conduct under Californian law, there must be a 'pattern of conduct composed of a series of acts over a period of time, however short, evidencing a continuity of purpose'.[17] Although the Californian provisions have been the subject of a constitutional challenge regarding the meaning of 'repeatedly',[18] 'harasses' and 'credible threat',[19] no case has challenged the meaning of 'course of conduct'. However, 'course of conduct' is accepted to require a 'definite plan or relationship between the acts, not just unconnected coincidental encounters'.[20] The idea that incidents be linked by continuity of purpose could be seen to have some support in English case law. For example, *Baron v DPP* concerned two letters sent by the defendant to an employee of the Department of Social Security regarding his claim for benefit. Although ostensibly directed at complaining about the way in which the defendant's claim was being handled and an assertion of his legal rights regarding another legal action, the court felt that the background to the case coloured the nature of the letters. The defendant's previous harassment of the victim's predecessor and references to this made within the letters imbued them with a quality that evidenced an ulterior purpose common to both communications. This led the court to conclude that the letters, although four months apart and referring to that which the defendant was entitled to raise with the victim, would amount to a course of conduct although:

> Normally speaking a court might be slow to find that two letters, even if couched in intemperate language, which are separated by an interval or four and a half months, can amount to a course of conduct causing alarm and distress.

Here the two incidents were linked owing to the defendant's ulterior purpose in sending the letters, thus linking that which the court would otherwise have regarded as separate incidents.

---

17 California Penal Code, § 646.9(e).

18 *People v Heilman* (1994) 25 Cal App 4th 391 – the use of the word 'repeatedly' withstood constitutional challenge that it was void for vagueness.

19 *People v McClelland* (1996) 42 Cal App 4th 141 – 'harasses' and 'credible threat' were both held to be sufficiently clear and definite.

20 Woods, 1993, pp 449–73.

Nonetheless, there may be problems with 'annual harassment' even if the nature of the acts evidenced sufficient continuity of purpose. The offence of harassment created by s 2 is a summary offence only, hence it is covered by s 127(1) of the Magistrates' Courts Act 1980, which provides that:

> a magistrates' court shall not try an information or hear a complaint unless the offence was committed, or the complaint made, within six months from the time when the offence was committed, or the matter of complaint arose.

It could be that this section precludes the bringing of a charge of harassment when one of the incidents relied upon to establish a course of conduct occurred more than six months before the complaint was made. However, it has been argued that the offence is only complete when the second incident occurs, hence this is the time from which the six month period should commence.[21] If this is so, there is no reason why two incidents separated by one year should not form the basis of a charge of harassment provided they can be viewed as a course of conduct. Whether or not two such incidents are to be viewed as a course of conduct depends upon the context in which the incidents occur. It is submitted that the American notion of continuity of purpose would provide a good test of whether or not two such incidents are to be so regarded and would provide a useful means of narrowing the scope of the Protection from Harassment Act 1997 to those cases that it was enacted to address.

6.2.1.4 Previous convictions

Even if there is a sufficient nexus between the incidents concerned, problems may still arise if there is a significant time lapse between the first and subsequent incidents. If the first incident amounts to a criminal offence and appears to have occurred in isolation, it is likely that the defendant will be prosecuted and convicted for this prior to the commission of a second incident that is required to form a course of conduct. In such a situation, a charge of harassment based upon an incident for which the defendant has already been convicted and received punishment would place the defendant in double jeopardy. This was the stance taken in *McGlennon v McKinnon* as the court refused to consider the four previous convictions of the defendant as part of the course of conduct.[22] This being so, only one incident remained, hence the charge of harassment was bound to fail despite evidence of a clear pattern of serious harassment directed at the victim. The court held that to take these incidents into account would be to punish the defendant twice for their commission.

---

21 Addison and Lawson-Cruttenden, 1998, p 31.
22 *McGlennon v McKinnon* 1998 SLT 494.

However, failure to consider the earlier incident is arguably contrary to the intention of the statute, which was to provide the means to deal with behaviour of a continuing nature. It is the repeated nature of the conduct that is at the heart of the 'wrong' in stalking cases, thus to disregard previous incidents that were sufficiently serious as to justify criminal conviction appears to overlook the defining characteristic of harassing conduct. If the first incident is charged individually, no course of conduct is established when a second incident occurs. Provided this second incident is also a criminal offence, it may also be charged individually, but this would then preclude reliance upon it as the first incident in a course of conduct. The alternative is to take no action, lest another incident occurs which might then amount to a course of conduct, but this could leave the victim feeling unprotected.

Nevertheless, it is easy to see why the prosecutor may prefer to pursue a charge involving one identifiable incident rather than charging the defendant with harassment on the basis of a few incidents, some of which may be disproved, leaving an insufficient basis for conviction. For example, in *King v DPP*, the harassment conviction was based upon five separate incidents.[23] On appeal, each of these were attacked individually and the Divisional Court accepted that three were not incidents that could form part of a course of conduct and expressed doubt as to whether the remaining two incidents caused the victim alarm or distress. Accordingly, the defendant's conviction was quashed. If all but one incident are disproved, there can be no course of conduct, hence no conviction for harassment. In *DPP v Ramsdale*, the court felt that the victim had condoned or encouraged all but one of the incidents, thus no basis remained upon which the defendant could be convicted.[24] In light of such cases, it is clear that some cases may tempt a prosecutor to favour prosecution for an offence that requires only a single incident wherever possible; a situation which could have serious ramifications for the use and efficacy of the offence of harassment. As was recognised in *R v Miah*, the effect of the totality of the conduct may be more serious than the composite elements.

Although the statute provides that a course of conduct involves conduct on at least two occasions and can include speech, various factors may affect whether or not any two incidents will constitute a course of conduct. It would appear that any two incidents, which need not be inherently criminal in nature and which can differ from each other in nature, may be regarded as a course of conduct provided they are not so proximate in time as to be regarded as one continuing incident or so distant in time as to be regarded as two unconnected incidents. Whilst this potentially covers any possible manifestation of stalking, thus clearly enhancing the level of legal protection

---

23 *King v DPP* (2000) *The Independent*, 31 July.
24 *DPP v Ramsdale* (2001) *The Independent*, 19 March.

for stalking victims, this, of itself, creates an exceptionally low threshold for criminal liability. Ordinary people will frequently be unwittingly pursuing a course of conduct with little thought that they are fulfilling the first stage of liability for criminal harassment. Fortunately, establishing a course of conduct is not the sole criterion for liability. Once it has been established that there has been a course of conduct, the next stage is to consider whether or not that course of conduct amounted to harassment of another.

6.2.2 Which amounts to harassment of another

The Protection from Harassment Act 1997 partially defines harassment as including (thus not being limited to) 'causing alarm or distress to another person'.[25] No further definition was deemed necessary as 'harassment as a concept has been interpreted regularly by the courts since 1986'.[26] This is a reference to the Public Order Act 1986, which includes offences that make reference to behaviour which causes harassment, alarm or distress. The Public Order Act 1986, however, specifies the type of behaviour which is to cause harassment, alarm or distress, hence only threatening, abusive or insulting behaviour incurs liability, whereas there are no restrictions upon the nature of the behaviour which can engender liability if it results in harassment, alarm or distress under the Protection from Harassment Act 1997.

By making harassment unlawful regardless of the means by which it was caused, the Protection from Harassment Act focuses on the harm that results rather than the way in which it was inflicted. The focus on the harm caused to the recipient of the conduct, rather on the type of behaviour which led to the harm, is illustrative that this is to be regarded as a statute which protects individuals against harm, however caused,[27] rather than one which prohibits specified types of behaviour.[28]

This focus on the impact of the conduct upon the recipient rather than on the nature of the conduct enables the law to deal with those who use otherwise innocuous behaviour as a means of harassment. This acknowledges that many acts which are not of themselves harassing can cause harassment to the recipient because of the context in which the conduct occurs and the nature of the relationship between the parties. For example, sending a woman a picture of a baby is not an act which would be objectively perceived to be harassing, but given the relationship between the parties (they are ex-partners

---

25 Protection from Harassment Act 1997, s 7(2).

26 Howard, M (Home Secretary), HC *Deb* Vol 287 Col 784, 17 December 1996.

27 As the Offences Against the Person Act 1861, which ranks offences according to the level of harm caused to the victim regardless of the way in which this harm was brought about.

28 As the Public Order Act 1986, which focuses on the conduct of the accused and where the offences are ranked hierarchically according to the extremity of the behaviour.

and the woman aborted the man's baby against his wishes) and the context of the conduct (the pictures are sent every year on the date that the woman had the abortion) it is clear that this would be conduct which is highly likely to cause harassment, alarm or distress to the recipient.[29] Addison and Lawson-Cruttenden neatly encapsulate this, saying: 'often it is not the overt act itself which is harassing but the known, but unprovable, motives of the person concerned.'[30] This provision obviates the need to establish the motives behind the conduct or to establish if the conduct is objectively harassing; the fact that it amounts to harassment of a particular individual will suffice to satisfy this stage of liability.

By outlawing conduct that causes harassment regardless of the nature of the acts, this enables the police to intervene where they could not previously. For example, one woman was disturbed by the frequent surveillance of her home by a stranger who had approached her at her place of work. The police advised her that they were powerless to intervene until the law was broken and that the man in question was legally entitled to stand where he chose. This was repeated conduct that caused the victim a great deal of alarm and distress, hence would now provide the basis for a charge of harassment to be brought, provided it could be established that the man knew or ought to have known that his behaviour could have this effect. Thus, it is certainly true to say that 'harassment catches a wide range of conduct and potentially allows such behaviour to be considered as breaking the law'.[31]

It can be seen that the approach of criminality as contingent on the reaction of the recipient of conduct is advantageous in terms of widening the scope of behaviour amenable to legal intervention and affords protection against harassing behaviour which was not previously available. However, rendering conduct criminal merely because it is perceived to be so by the recipient has its own dangers, which may well counteract its advantages. As Addison and Lawson-Cruttenden comment, 'almost any form of activity which annoys another person could technically be described as harassment', and they give the example of the person who cries 'here comes useless' whenever a work colleague enters the room.[32] If repeated on two occasions, this would amount to a course of conduct, it may well cause the recipient to feel harassed and it may be that the court would feel that the perpetrator ought to know that this might be the consequence of his conduct. If so, criminal liability under s 2 would be established. Whilst it is clear that persistent derogatory comments may not be pleasant, it has to be questioned as to whether this type of conduct should attract criminal liability. There is a risk that too great a legal protection in such situations may render people

---

29 Case history 12.
30 Addison and Lawson-Cruttenden, 1998, p 35.
31 Mclean, D, *HC Deb* Vol 287 Col 826, 17 December 1996.
32 Addison and Lawson-Cruttenden, 1998, p 34.

increasingly incapable of ordering their own lives. Excessive paternalism will lead to increased dependency upon the law to adjudicate the most minor of life's disruptions.

Notwithstanding this, there would be some illogicality in attempting to introduce a *de minimis* standard into a statute that was explicitly intended to give primacy to an individual's reaction to conduct. The introduction of a minimal level of resistance to harassment would detract from the subjective emphasis of the Act by establishing an objective borderline between harassing and non-harassing conduct. Nonetheless, there is some indication that the courts are in favour of establishing such a borderline based upon the argument that a certain amount of unpleasantness is inevitable in social interaction.

This is clear from a consideration of the judgment of the Divisional Court in *Baron v CPS* in which a disgruntled claimant sent two unpleasant letters to an employee of the Benefits Agency.[33] The Divisional Court accepted that there were genuine grounds for complaint and that it was not surprising that intemperate language was used. It was held that the courts should be slow to find that two such letters sent four and a half months apart could amount to harassment, particularly of a public official whose exposure to abuse would tend to inure them against emotional reaction:

A line must be drawn between legitimate expression of disgust at the way a public agency has behaved and conduct amounting to harassment. The right to free speech requires a broad degree of tolerance in relation to communications. It is a legitimate exercise of that right to say things which are unpleasant or possibly hurtful to the recipient. Persons in the public service, in my view, are used to rudeness, aggression and unpleasantness of every form and the courts are likely in my judgment to expect of them a degree of robustness and fortitude beyond that which other members of the public may be expected to show.[34]

Here the court is acknowledging that a certain degree of harassment is inevitable in everyday life, but that the degree of harassment that an individual will be expected to tolerate may be dependent upon the context in which the conduct occurs. Public officials must possess a level of robustness and fortitude over and above that of an ordinary member of the public, but it is implicit in this that some degree of robustness and fortitude, albeit of a lesser degree, is expected of the public.

The level at which the line separating unpleasant conduct from actionable harassment will determine the parameters of acceptable conduct within society. Where this line is to be is a question that is likely to occupy the courts

---

33 *Baron v CPS* (2000) unreported, Divisional Court, 13 June.
34 *Ibid, per* Morison J.

in the future, as more harassment cases are heard. The finding in *Woolford v DPP* that the conduct concerned was 'at the very bottom end of the scale, close to the borderline between conduct which is not harassment and conduct which is' gives some indication of the toleration level that may be established.[35] Here, the defendant sent a card to his children wishing them happiness in their new home on the day that his wife moved with them to a new and supposedly secret address. The following day, he left two telephone messages for his wife, one telling her that he had inadvertently left the electricity off in their former home and one to welcome her to her new neighbourhood. Although this could be considered to set the level at which conduct becomes harassment at a rather low level, it should be noted that the court found that the conduct in question was 'gloating and deliberate' as it was motivated by a desire to oppress his wife rather than concern for her well being or that of the children. Whether, in the absence of this motivation, the conduct would have been deemed to have crossed the borderline between harassment and non-harassment is open to question. Although both of these cases favour the introduction of a threshold level of tolerable conduct, no guidance is given as to how and where this is to be established.

Individuals may react differently to the events, hence conduct that causes manifest alarm or distress to one person may leave another totally unperturbed. There is no provision in the Act that establishes a minimum standard of tolerance to the disagreeable actions of others, hence the level of criminality can be exceptionally low as the subjective standard of harassment encompasses the hypersensitive. This element of contingent criminality means that the law lacks certainty, as a person will not be able to predict with certainty whether a particular type of behaviour will bring him into conflict with the law as this is totally dependent upon the reaction of the recipient of the conduct. A defendant could target two different women with exactly the same behaviour, which would leave one woman unmoved and the other totally distraught. He would then be potentially liable for his actions towards the latter woman and not the former, despite the fact that his behaviour towards both was identical in every respect. The question has to be asked as to whether it is justifiable to have a criminal offence whereby criminality depends on the personality of the recipient of the conduct.

This contingent criminality may also create an anomalous situation whereby a well meaning but socially inept man who insensitively attempts to flirt with a particularly sensitive women in a way that causes her alarm could be held liable for criminal harassment, whereas the deliberate stalker who sets out to harass someone who is impervious to his activities will avoid liability. This is because harassment is a summary offence only, thus there can be no liability for attempted harassment. Section 1(4) of the Criminal Attempts Act

---

35 *Woolford v DPP* (2000) Divisional Court, 9 May, *per* Lord Bingham.

1981 provides that a charge of attempt can only relate to indictable offences or to those which are triable either way, thus there can be no offence of attempted harassment.

6.2.2.1 Indirect harassment

Even if an offence of attempted harassment were a possibility, the police would be unlikely to pursue a complaint made by a third party if the primary victim were not harassed by the conduct. However, there may be scope within the Act for a third party to experience harassment owing to the conduct of the stalker towards the primary victim, as there is no requirement that the person experiencing harassment must be the person against whom the conduct is directed.[36]

Section 1 refers to a course of conduct which causes harassment, but does not specify that the person who experiences the harassment must be the person to whom the conduct is directed. In *Lodge v DPP*,[37] it was held that harassment could include causing others to feel alarm for the safety of the defendant themselves or a third party. Addison and Lawson-Cruttenden give the example of a headmaster who is alarmed by the conduct of a man who persistently loiters near the school and offers sweets to the children and they suggest that this could amount to harassment of the headmaster, although he is not the direct recipient of the conduct.[38] They go on to suggest that the courts would only accept this notion of indirect harassment if the primary recipient were vulnerable in some way, for example, a child, elderly, or mentally incapacitated. The wording of the Act does not support this restriction, thus there is no reason why a charge could not be brought on the basis that, for example, a wife is alarmed by the attentions paid to her husband by a female work colleague.[39]

The wording of s 1 does not preclude indirect harassment and, by comparing it with the phraseology employed in s 4, this could be seen as support for the idea that s 1 does not require the complainant to be the direct victim of the course of conduct. Section 4 specifies that only the person who fears violence will be used against him has a complaint, not anyone who fears that the defendant will use violence against others.[40] The focus in s 1 is on the

---

36 Home Office Consultation Paper, *Stalking: The Solutions*, 1996, para 5.7.

37 *Lodge v DPP* (1988) *The Times*, 26 October, which dealt with causing harassment, alarm or distress under the Public Order Act 1986, s 5.

38 This also illustrates the advantage of the fact that the conduct need not be hostile or unlawful in itself to be within the terms of the Act.

39 Although there may be an argument that this would fail on the third element – that the colleague did not know nor ought she to have known that this would result in harassment of the wife. However, this would depend on the nature of the conduct and the reaction of the husband in response to the conduct – this point will be dealt with more fully in the next section.

40 Liability under s 4 is discussed further below below, p 241.

defendant's conduct, whereas the focus in s 4 is on the individual against whom the defendant's conduct is directed. This difference supports the idea that s 1 encompasses a wide notion of a victim of harassment and includes those who are harassed, alarmed or distressed by the defendant's course of conduct regardless of whom it is directed against.

This notion of indirect harassment was discussed in *DPP v Williams*, where the two incidents relied upon to establish a course of conduct were experienced by two different women who shared a house.[41] The first incident involved the defendant putting his hand through the bathroom window when one of the female occupants of the house was in the shower. She screamed, causing the other occupant to come running to see what had happened. Both women were upset and worried by this incident. The second incident took place two days later and involved the defendant staring through the second woman's bedroom window late at night. The Divisional Court upheld the harassment conviction and considered two ways in which indirect harassment may occur under the Act. The first of these was based upon the finding of fact that the first incident had alarmed the complainant even though she was not present at its occurrence. As such, it could count as the first incident in a course of conduct that was completed when she became the direct recipient of the second incident.

This approach appears to widen the scope of the Act by providing that the victim need not experience the conduct directly, but will be deemed to be the recipient of conduct via an intermediary. However, in this particular case, it is arguable that the victim, who was in the house at the time, was alarmed when she heard her friend screaming and found that this was due to the defendant's actions. Although not in the immediate vicinity of the incident, there was a degree of contemporaneity about the event that justifies the finding that it did, as a matter of fact, cause her alarm or distress. However, this notion of indirect harassment is taken further in *Kellett v DPP* where it was held that it was permissible to find that the offence had been made out even though the victim was not the direct recipient of either incident and the defendant had explicitly requested that his conduct was not made known to the victim. The facts of this case took place against the background of an acrimonious boundary dispute between the defendant and the victim, who were neighbours. The defendant observed the victim to be working on her property on occasions when he believed that she should have been at work, so he reported this to her employer. The Court of Appeal held that this could amount to harassment even though the offence was not complete until the information had been passed to the victim by the intermediary. It was irrelevant that the defendant requested that the victim should not be told that

---

41   *DPP v Williams* (1998) unreported, Divisional Court, 27 July; Finch, 2000, pp 299–301.

he had reported her as 'repetition was a natural consequence' in the circumstances. Giving the judgment of the court, Penry-Davey J stated:

> The offence was only complete when the complainant was told of the telephone calls made by the appellant in that it was the knowledge of his conduct that caused her distress. But the fact that she had been informed of the course of conduct by a third party rather than by the appellant himself did not mean that no offence was committed once she had been so informed, even in circumstances where the appellant had asked that she should not be so informed, so long as there was evidence on the basis of which the court could properly conclude, as it clearly did, that the appellant was pursuing a course of conduct which he knew or ought to have known amounted to harassment of the complainant.

This decision can be criticised for widening the scope of the Act to include 'harassment by hearsay', whereby the defendant can become liable for harassment at some time in the future if news of his conduct reaches the victim. The defendant was not in control of the dissemination of information that rendered him liable for harassment, thus his liability was wholly dependent upon the actions of another. Had the information not been passed on, the defendant's conduct and state of mind would have been exactly the same, but he would not have been liable for any offence. It has been argued that rendering criminality contingent upon the reaction of the victim creates an unacceptable degree of uncertainty in the law. A possible justification for this can be found in the nature of the harassment offence itself, as it is this subjectivity that imbues the offence with the necessary degree of flexibility to adapt to the diversity of manifestations of harassment. However, there is no such justification for making the conduct of an intermediary the determinative factor in the imposition of criminal liability. The decision of the Court of Appeal in *Kellett* has expanded the offence of harassment well beyond its reasonable parameters and has created an extremely uncertain position.

The second potential basis of liability for indirect harassment considered by the Divisional Court in *Williams* was based upon the idea of a composite group of victims. Here, the argument was that the words 'another' and 'the other' in the Protection from Harassment Act 1997 are inclusive of the plural by virtue of s 6(c) of the Interpretation Act 1978 when the victims are part of a close-knit definable group. The court did not find it necessary to consider this point, as they based their decision and the defendant's liability on indirect discrimination. However, Rose LJ found the argument based on the idea of group harassment a 'compelling submission and one which, on some future occasion, it will be necessary to adjudicate upon', otherwise there would be an extraordinary state of affairs whereby a person could watch women through the windows of a nurses' home occupied by 50 nurses on 50 occasions and not incur liability under the Protection from Harassment Act 1997 until the 51st occasion, when he visited one of the windows for a second time.

This idea of a composite group of victims was addressed in *Mills v DPP*, which concerned a neighbourhood dispute.[42] Mills was convicted of pursuing a course of conduct against two of her neighbours, both of whom were named in one single charge leading to an appeal against conviction on the basis that the charge had been bad for duplicity as the two victims had made separate allegations. The Divisional Court held that the charge was bad for duplicity as there was potential for the magistrates' court to have found a course of conduct had been pursued against one of the complainants but not the other. Otton LJ held that the Interpretation Act 1978 does make it appropriate to construe 'another' and 'the other' as including the plural, thus the wording of the section does not of itself[43] preclude the naming of more than one person as complainant in appropriate circumstances, but that neighbours lack sufficient nexus to be considered a closely knit definable group, hence this case was not one in which it was appropriate to name more than one complainant.

This issue was discussed in *DPP v Dunn* in which the conduct complained of was directed at two victims, a husband and wife, who were named in a single charge of harassment.[44] The defence argued that this was bad for duplicity as the majority of the conduct was experienced by one or the other of the victims, rather than both of them together. Reliance was placed upon the words of Otton LJ in *Mills* that group harassment would be made out in circumstances such as:

> Sisters living in the same house where they are allegedly harassed and the conduct complained of was clearly aimed at both of them on each occasion.

This, contended the defence, meant that a finding of group harassment would only be permissible if each group member were present on each occasion. This was rejected by Bell J, who stated:

> I do not believe that Otton LJ meant to say … that a charge which named two complainants could only be free from duplicity where the conduct complained of was clearly directed at both of them together on at least two occasions. Firstly, it seems to me that the conduct complained of might be aimed at two people, although only one was present. Secondly, it seems to me that the example of two sisters given by Otton LJ was only an example of a case where, in his judgment, two complainants might be named in a charge without duplicity. I did not take it to be an exclusive definition of what is required to avoid duplicity if two victims are to be named in a charge.

Bell J concluded that the acts in question were aimed at the couple as occupants of the same house involved in a boundary dispute with the defendant. As such, his conduct towards each of the individuals could be regarded as part of his course of conduct against the couple. From this it can

---

42 *Mills v DPP* (1998) unreported, Divisional Court, 17 December.
43 Judge's emphasis.
44 *DPP v Dunn* [2001] Crim LR 130.

be concluded that a married couple living in the same house will constitute a closely knit definable group. Moreover that, provided a group of individuals is deemed to amount to a closely knit definable group, acts of harassment against any of the composite members will be regarded as conduct aimed at the entire group. However, no further guidance is given as to the definition of 'closely knit definable group', thus raising questions of the relationship required between its members, the numerical parameters of such a group and whether the members must regard themselves as a closely knit definable group. Problems could also be raised as, if the group is to be viewed holistically, surely if the defendant has a defence of reasonableness against any group member, this could be viewed as a defence against the group in its totality.[45] Clearly, this is an aspect of the Act that requires judicial clarification as to its scope and remit.

These cases provide some interpretation of the notion of the 'other' who may complain of harassment under s 1 and could be argued to represent a substantial widening of the scope of the Protection from Harassment Act. It is true that there is some difference in the wording of ss 1 and 4, whereby s 4 limits the fear of violence to the person at whom it is directed and there is no such requirement in s 1 when it would have been a straightforward matter to make s 1(1)(a) read: 'which amounts to harassment of the recipient of the course of conduct.' Such a wide notion of indirect harassment whereby the complainant need not be present or witness the conduct complained of, provided they are alarmed when they hear of it from another, raises the possibility of 'harassment by hearsay'. This provides a basis for liability for harassment even in situations where there is no direct contact between the parties and where all of the incidents comprising the course of conduct come to the victim's attention via an intermediary.

Equally, *DPP v Williams* also raised the possibility of group harassment, which was supported in *Mills v DPP* and *DPP v Dunn*, thus two incidents can be directed at two different people and the defendant will still be liable provided that they can be regarded as a closely knit definable group.

It is arguable that these cases open the door even wider for liability under the Act and lower the already low level of criminal liability still further, creating unacceptable uncertainty in this area of law. On the other hand, these developments could be regarded as welcome, as they offer additional protection for those who are harassed by the actions of others. This might be particularly useful to stalking cases owing to the prevalence of triangulation,[46] whereby the target of the stalker's behaviour is not the person with whom they are obsessed, but a third party perceived as impeding access to the object of their affections.[47]

---

45 Ormerod, 2001, pp 130–33.
46 See Meloy, 1999, pp 421–24.
47 'Stalker tried to kill ex-wife's new boyfriend' (1997) *Daily Telegraph*, 16 April.

These developments could be regarded as welcome as they offer additional protection for those who are harassed by the actions of others. However, it could also be argued that these cases open the door even wider for liability under the Protection from Harassment Act 1997 and lower an already low level of criminal liability to an unacceptable level. The balance between the rights of the victim to be protected from objectionable behaviour and the need for certainty in the law, and to ensure that the law is not concerned with trivialities, is a difficult one to achieve. One thing that is clear is that further clarification as to the scope of the Act is needed.

6.2.3 The defences

Even if a course of conduct is established, this will not amount to harassment if the conduct comes within one of the three exceptions contained in s 1(3).

Section 1(3)(a) excludes conduct pursued 'for the purpose of preventing or detecting crime', which clearly covers the police and those officially employed in an investigative capacity such as persons employed by the Benefits Agency to detect benefit fraud. However, this provision is not limited in availability to those acting in an official capacity, thus is available to any person charged with harassment.

This section was raised in *DPP v Moseley* by two of the animal rights protestors, but this was rejected by the Divisional Court where it was said that it was 'difficult to see how a protest of this sort, carried over a lengthy period of time, could be said to be for the purpose of preventing or detecting crime'.[48] This does not preclude animal rights protestors advancing this defence in different circumstances, but makes it clear that the conduct in question must have the prevention or detection of crime as its primary, not ancillary, motivation. Concern was expressed during the enactment of the statute regarding the position of private detectives[49] and whether their activities would be covered by this section.[50] The situation appears to be that even these first two exceptions are only applicable if the conduct engaged is also reasonable (thus raising the question of why there are three exceptions rather than just the one exception of reasonableness).[51]

---

48 *DPP v Moseley* (1999) *The Times*, 23 June, *per* Collins J. However, it should be noted that the decision in this case centred upon the defendants' reliance upon the reasonableness defence, hence any comments regarding s 1(3)(a) are strictly *obiter*.

49 *HC Deb*, Vol 287, Cols 830–33, 17 December 1996.

50 There appeared to be dual grounds for this concern. First, that the activities of those engaged in a legitimate business should not be unnecessarily curtailed, but also that the private detective could be used to commit 'stalking by proxy', see, eg, 'Stalkers pay private eyes to do their dirty work' (1997) *Daily Telegraph*, 26 January.

51 'Clause 1(3)(c) is adequate for all those involved in legitimate crime prevention activity': Mclean, D, *HC Deb*, Vol 287, Col 833, 17 December 1996.

Section 1(3)(b) excludes conduct which was 'pursued under any enactment or rule of law', which is applicable to legally authorised activities not otherwise encompassed by s 1(3)(a), such as the statutory powers of the police to enter private premises. Again, it appears that this will not afford a defence to a party accused of harassment if the conduct is unreasonable.[52]

Section 1(3)(c) applies when 'in the particular circumstances' the pursuit of the course of conduct was reasonable. This will involve a balancing of the opposing rights of the parties in the case and will frequently be contingent upon the context in which the conduct occurs. Whilst it might be reasonable to play a loud stereo all night in a remote country house, the same conduct would surely be deemed unreasonable in a central location. It has been held not to be reasonable to repeatedly telephone and accost a person, especially once they have made it clear that this is unwelcome, even if the motivation is to attempt to save a marriage. In *DPP v Moseley*, it was held that any conduct in breach of a court order is inherently incapable of being reasonable and Roch LJ went further, stating that he felt any activity involving trespass on another's land should not be considered reasonable.

The general exclusion of 'reasonableness' in s 1(3)(c) provides scope for the law to be applied flexibly, taking into account the individual circumstances of a particular case to ensure that the rights of the one are not infringed in the interests of another. This will be particularly important where the conduct complained of is otherwise unlawful, as it is essential that this statute does not protect the interests of stalking victims by jeopardising the liberty of those innocently engaged in innocuous conduct.

6.2.4 Knows or ought to have known

The final stage in establishing liability for harassment requires that the defendant knows or ought to know that his conduct would amount to harassment of another. This creates a dual mental element for the offence, as knowledge that a course of conduct will amount to harassment is tantamount to intentional harassment,[53] whereas pursuing a course of conduct which the defendant ought to know amounts to harassment implies a moral imperative set by reference to what a reasonable person would have known.[54] Thus, this can be described as constructive knowledge, which is a species of negligence

---

52 Addison and Lawson-Cruttenden, 1998, p 18.

53 'The requirement of knowledge is regarded as having the same intensity as that of intention': Ashworth, 1999, p 191.

54 Protection from Harassment Act, s 1(2) provides that a defendant ought to have known his conduct would amount to harassment of another if 'a reasonable person in possession of the same information would think the course of conduct amounted to harassment of the other'.

that has been described as an inadequate basis for criminal liability,[55] and accused of making objective that which should remain subjective,[56] as well as possessing 'a hortatory quality that is more appropriate to the pulpit than the law'.[57] This dual mental element arguably encapsulates differing levels of culpability, as knowingly harassing is suggestive of deliberate wrongdoing, whereas failing to appreciate that conduct would be viewed as harassing is indicative of failure to live up to a certain standard of social behaviour.

The Protection from Harassment Act 1997 was deliberately phrased to include not only deliberate harassment, but also behaviour which is objectively harassing despite absence of intention to harass on the part of the perpetrator.[58] This obviates the necessity to establish an intention to harass or awareness that the conduct is capable of causing harassment which had proved so problematic when prosecuting stalkers under previously existing legislation.[59] This objective standard is seen as justified, as it is often impossible to establish the *mens rea* of stalkers who are suffering from mental or personality disorders[60] or are so preoccupied with their obsession with the victims that they are unable to comprehend that their attentions may be unwelcome.[61]

For the victim, harassment is harassment regardless of the state of mind of the perpetrator, thus it is essential to provide protection against both deliberate and inadvertent harassment. However, no distinction is made between those who did not realise that their conduct would cause harassment, but were capable of doing so had they addressed their minds to the issue, and those who are inherently incapable of perceiving the effect of their actions. Hart suggests that it is not acceptable to establish a standard of negligence which considers only an objective standard (what the reasonable person would have known) without taking into account an element of subjectivity (whether the particular person could have known this).[62] Had the counselling provisions which were included during the passage of the Act by an Opposition amendment[63] not been defeated in the House of Lords,[64] some provision would be available in the Act to deal with those whose incapacity

---

55   'Constructive knowledge is encompassed by the words "ought to have known", a conception which has no place in the criminal law', per Devlin J in *Roper v Taylor's Central Garage (Exeter) Ltd* [1951] TLR 284.

56   Dine and Gobert, 1998, p 144.

57   Earl Russell, *HL Deb*, Vol 578, Col 525, 17 February 1997.

58   Howard, M, *HC Deb* Vol 287 Col 783, 17 December 1996.

59   'Judge's error frees clerk jailed for anonymous calls' (1994) *The Times*, 16 December.

60   Allen, 1996, p 93.

61   *R v Gelder* (1994) unreported.

62   Hart, 1968, pp 152–57.

63   *HC Deb* Vol 287 Cols 837–42, 17 December 1996.

64   *HL Deb* Vol 578, Cols 523–37, 17 February 1997.

renders them incapable of appreciating the impact of their conduct on the recipient as:

> The most effective way of dealing with stalking is to remove the root cause. A stalker who has been forced to address his own offending behaviour and no longer wishes to harass the victim is far less a threat than one whose only motive not to commit further offences is the fear of legal retribution.[65]

However, such a provision is not available, and the Act will punish those who persistently harass owing to deluded beliefs as to the acceptability of their conduct in the same way that they do those who deliberately cause harassment.[66] The unavailability of a provision facilitating mental health treatment or counselling in a statute that addresses conduct that is frequently prompted by mental illness and personality disorder is particularly unfortunate given the narrow scope of the Mental Health Act 1983. Section 37 of the Mental Health Act empowers the court to make a hospital order provided that the defendant has at least one of the four types of mental disorder specified by s 1 of the Mental Health Act and hospital treatment is appropriate and available. Therefore, if hospital treatment will not either alleviate or prevent a deterioration of the defendant's condition, hospital treatment will not be deemed appropriate. In *R v Stark*, there was some disagreement between the psychiatrists as to whether the defendant's psychopathic disorder rendered him mentally ill within the meaning of the Mental Health Act.[67] However, even if it were accepted that it did, a s 37 order would not be appropriate, as treatment would not improve his condition. Hence the very fact that the defendant's disorder was deemed to be untreatable precluded the imposition of a hospital order, thus leaving the court with imprisonment as the only option despite clear evidence that his psychiatric disorder rendered him powerless to stop himself from harassing the victim. Thus, no attempt will be made to address the root cause of this defendant's behaviour or to reduce the likelihood of further harassment.

Whether the defendant ought to have known that his conduct would amount to harassment is to be established by reference to whether a reasonable person in possession of the same information as the defendant would have realised that the conduct would cause harassment.[68] If the conduct is composed of unlawful activities, there is little doubt that the reasonable person would consider this to constitute harassment even if the defendant was incapable of perceiving this. However, if the conduct is not

---

65 Howarth, G, *HC Deb* Vol 287 Col 839, 17 December 1996.

66 Lord Mottistone proposed an amendment providing a specific defence for those who were unable to appreciate the impact of their conduct owing to severe mental illness, but this too was rejected – *HL Deb* Vol 578 Cols 530–32, 17 February 1997.

67 *R v Stark* (1998) unreported, 27 March, CA. One of the few cases in which a stalker has been within the remit of the Mental Health Act 1983 was *R v Cunningham* (2000) unreported, 25 January, CA.

68 Protection from Harassment Act 1997, s 1(2).

unambiguously harassing, such as sending a person chocolates and flowers, the defendant may only be deemed to have the necessary knowledge if the recipient makes it clear that such attentions are unwelcome. To continue with the conduct would then constitute harassment, as the defendant would then be in possession of the relevant knowledge.[69]

If the defendant possesses information relating to a particular vulnerability of the victim which gives him knowledge that his *prima facie* innocuous conduct will harass the victim, this knowledge will be transferred to the reasonable man and the defendant will be liable for harassment despite the outwardly innocent appearance of the conduct.[70] Behaviour that appears innocuous may be harassing in the extreme in a particular context, such as the sending of pictures of a baby to a woman who has had an abortion. It is clear that the defendant who uses *prima facie* innocuous conduct to target a particular vulnerability of a victim will be liable provided it can be established that he was aware of the relevance of the behaviour. Addison and Lawson-Cruttenden suggest that failure to establish that the defendant appreciated the impact of his seemingly innocent conduct would entitle the defendant to an acquittal, as there is no information that can be attributed to the reasonable person that would lead to the conclusion that the defendant ought to have known that he would cause harassment.[71]

The relevance of information known to the defendant was considered in *AG's Reference (No 22 of 1999)*, where it was suggested that exploitation of a particular vulnerability of the victim will be an aggravating factor that justifies the imposition of a more severe penalty.[72] The defendant knew that the victim had previously been involved in a violent relationship and had suffered from anxiety and depression for which she had received psychiatric care. The defendant played upon this vulnerability in the course of harassing his victim and his conduct towards her included threats to inform her ex-partner of her whereabouts, which continued despite her admission to a psychiatric unit. The defendant's knowledge of his victim's vulnerable mental state and fear of her ex-partner were factors that increased the seriousness with which the court regarded his conduct. Additionally, the defendant knew that his victim was aware that he had previously been convicted of rape and this was held to be a factor relevant to determining whether he ought to have realised that his conduct would cause his victim harassment. These factors justified an increase in sentence from four and a half to six years' imprisonment.[73]

---

69 Provided it occurred on two further occasions to comply with the 'course of conduct' requirement.

70 Lord Chancellor, *HL Deb*, Vol 578 Col 528, 17 February 1997.

71 Addison and Lawson-Cruttenden, 1998, p 37.

72 *AG's Reference (No 22 of 1999)* [2000] Cr App R(S) 253.

73 Although the element of double jeopardy inherent in an Attorney General's reference caused the Court of Appeal to increase the sentence to four and a half years rather than the six years that they believed was justified.

6.3 CAUSING FEAR OF VIOLENCE

Section 4 of the Protection from Harassment Act 1997 contains the more serious offence of causing fear of violence, which carried a maximum penalty of five years' imprisonment:[74]

> A person whose course of conduct causes another to fear, on at least two occasions, that violence will be used against him is guilty of an offence if he knows or ought to know that his course of conduct will cause the other so to fear on each of those occasions.

This is, in many respects, similar to the offence of harassment, as it requires a course of conduct and applies the same 'reasonable person in possession of the same information' objective standard.[75] It is the second stage of liability that is somewhat different, as it requires that the course of conduct causes a person to fear that violence will be used against him. So, unlike the offence of harassment, this requires that the victim be the direct recipient of the conduct, thus creating an offence of far narrower scope than that of s 2. A further limitation to the scope of this offence was suggested by Lord Steyn, who points out that s 4 requires the victim to fear that violence will be used and that often victims of stalking will only be in fear that violence may be used, which will not suffice to establish liability.[76] This limitation is considered by Addison and Lawson-Cruttenden, who go further and suggest that if violence is not forthcoming on the first occasion that its use is feared, then there is no reason for the victim to be in fear that violence will be used on subsequent occasions, as past experience has shown that fear to be groundless.[77]

Attempts to widen the scope of this offence were rejected by the Court of Appeal in *R v Henley* where it was held that causing a victim to be seriously frightened of what might happen could not be equated with causing her to fear violence.[78] Equally, the Court of Appeal were not prepared to accept that fear that violence will be directed towards the victim's family would suffice. Whilst Pill LJ acknowledged that there might be a situation in which the defendant's conduct towards the victim's family members might lead the victim to fear that violence will be used against her, there was no justification for extending the offence to include fear that violence will be used against others, such as members of the victim's family. The Court of Appeal reiterated that the offence contained in s 4 is based upon the causing of fear that violence will be used against that particular victim and a generalised sense of fear, or a fear for the safety of others, would not suffice.

---

74 This is criticised by Ashworth, p 338, who states: 'the combination of a negligence standard with a maximum penalty of five years is unfortunate.'

75 Protection from Harassment Act 1997, s 4(2).

76 *R v Ireland* [1997] 3 WLR 534, p 538.

77 Addison and Lawson-Cruttenden, 1998, p 41.

78 *R v Henley* [2000] Crim LR 582.

As the offence under s 4 is both narrower in scope and harder to establish than the offence of harassment, it is advantageous for victims that s 4(5) of the Protection from Harassment Act 1997 facilitates a finding of guilty to an offence of causing harassment as an alternative verdict on a s 4 charge. This occurred in *R v McCollin* where the jury did not accept that the defendant's words had caused the victim to fear that he would use violence against her, but accepted that the words were nevertheless capable of causing harassment, alarm or distress.[79]

It would appear that the offence of causing fear of violence is both narrower in scope and harder to satisfy than the offence of harassment, which would suggest that it will result in fewer prosecutions and fewer convictions than the lower level offence. This is substantiated by Home Office figures relating to these offences:[80]

Protection From Harassment Act Data for 1998

	Prosecutions	Convictions
Section 2	4,304	2,221
Section 4	1,505	522

These figures show that there were almost three times as many prosecutions under s 2 than there were under s 4, with prosecutions under s 2 having a 52% success rate compared to a 35% success rate for prosecutions under s 4.

Certainly, there was a need for a dual level of criminal liability under the Protection from Harassment Act 1997 to ensure that adequate provisions were available to address more serious examples of harassment. However, the narrow scope of s 4 creates a situation whereby a case may be considered to merit greater punishment than that which is available under s 2, but will not fit into the more specific requirements of s 4. The wide gap between the two offences may lead to further reliance upon offences outside the Protection from Harassment Act 1997 in situations where the conduct is too serious to be dealt with by s 2, but does not fit within s 4. An example of this can be seen in *R v McBride* in which the defendant harassed three woman. Although the conduct towards all three women was similar in nature, one victim suffered a greater degree of harm than the others, becoming afraid to leave her home and suffering what the trial judge described as 'considerable mental trauma'. The harm caused to his victim was considered to be of too great an extent to be addressed by the maximum penalty available under s 2 of the Protection from Harassment Act 1997, but the circumstances of the case did not disclose the basis for a prosecution under s 4. Owing to the nature of the harm suffered by the victim, the defendant was charged with assault occasioning actual

---

79 *R v McCollin* (1998) unreported, 27 November, CA.
80 Data from the Home Office Court Proceedings Database as shown in HC Written Answers for 26 July 1999, Col 66.

bodily harm contrary to s 47 of the Offences Against the Person Act 1861 in relation to this victim, and received a sentence of two years and seven months' imprisonment. He was also charged under s 2 in relation to his other victims and received two sentences of three months' imprisonment. This illustrates the need for a 'bridging offence' to fill the gap between the two offences created by the Protection from Harassment Act 1997. Alternatively, the maximum penalty available under s 2 could be increased to address more serious cases, but this may not be desirable, given the low threshold of criminal liability.

6.4 CRIMINAL LIABILITY FOR BREACH OF A COURT ORDER

Although the Protection from Harassment Act 1997 appears to have created two new criminal offences and a new statutory tort of harassment, there are two additional means by which criminal liability can be imposed under the Act. Both of these could more correctly be considered as indirect criminal offences, as they are not available in their own right, but are dependent upon the imposition of liability under the other sections of the Act.

Section 3 of the Protection from Harassment Act 1997 imposes criminal liability for breach of civil injunction as an alternative to the more usual contempt of court proceedings.[81] Section 5 introduces the concept of restraining orders into the criminal law whereby a restrictive order can be attached to any other sentence imposed following conviction under either s 2 or s 4.[82] Breach of this order is regarded as a serious offence and carries a maximum penalty of five years' imprisonment.[83]

These provisions are indicative of the key aim of the Act, which is not solely to punish harassment that has already occurred, but to prevent any further incidents from taking place.

6.4.1 Criminal liability for breach of civil injunction

Section 3(1) provides that an actual or apprehended breach of s 1 may be the subject of civil proceedings. Although the statute makes provision for the award of damages, the main purpose of this section is to make injunctive relief readily available to victims of harassment as it is presumed that the main aim of the victim is the cessation of harassment. This section seeks to circumvent the difficulties associated with enforcement of civil injunctions[84] as s 3(6)

---

81 Protection from Harassment Act 1997, s 3(6)–3(8).

82 *Ibid*, s 5(1).

83 *Ibid*, s 5(6).

84 Addison and Lawson-Cruttenden, 1997, p 51.

provides that breach of the civil injunction without reasonable excuse will give rise to criminal liability. This removes the onus from the victim of bringing the matter to the attention of the court and of establishing the breach as it 'enables the police to act promptly and decisively on behalf of the victim, to arrest a defendant who breaches an injunction and investigate the circumstances of that breach and collect the necessary evidence'.[85]

Although the obvious benefit of this is that it relieves the burden of establishing breach from the victim, it also raises questions owing to the differing standards of proof required in the criminal and civil courts. It has been argued that this unprecedented mixture of civil and criminal provisions justifies the raising of the standard of proof required in civil proceedings to that required by the criminal courts. During the enactment of the statute, it was argued that: 'if we are to make a breach of an action in a civil court a criminal offence, we must make it clear that the same tests should be applied to the civil proceedings as would be applied in the criminal court. The standard of proof in the civil court should not be weaker than that applied in the criminal court.'[86] This would require a plaintiff seeking an injunction to establish actual or apprehended harassment 'beyond reasonable doubt' rather than the usual civil 'balance of probabilities' standard. There is scope for the civil courts to utilise a higher standard of care as Addison and Lawson-Cruttenden point out, referring to *R v Secretary of State for the Home Department ex p Khawaja*,[87] where Lord Scarman states that 'the flexibility of the common standard of proof is sufficient to ensure that the court will require the higher degree of probability which is appropriate to what is at stake'.[88]

Notwithstanding this, it is clear that the courts are applying the usual civil 'balance of probabilities' standard when dealing with the imposition of a civil injunction under s 3 and, despite some initial criticism by commentators, this aspect of the Act has caused little difficulty. The benefits of the ability to obtain an order using civil procedure whilst relying on the criminal law for enforcement were recognised and replicated with the introduction of anti-social behaviour orders under the Crime and Disorder Act 1998.[89] These orders differ from those available under the Protection from Harassment Act 1997 in that they are obtained by application of the police or local authority by way of complaint to the magistrates' court exercising its civil jurisdiction. Accordingly, as with an application for an injunction under the Protection from Harassment Act, the conduct complained of need only be established on the balance of probabilities and hearsay evidence is admissible. This is viewed as an important aspect of the anti-social behaviour order as it facilitates the

---

85 Streeter, G, *HC Deb* Vol 287 Col 968, 18 December 1996.

86 Bennett, A, *HC Deb* Vol 287 Col 847, 17 December 1996.

87 *R v Secretary of State for the Home Department ex p Khawaja* [1984] AC 74.

88 As quoted in Addison and Lawson-Cruttenden, 1997, p 21.

89 Leng, Taylor and Wasik, 1998.

giving of evidence by professional witnesses such as the police or housing officers, thus avoiding the necessity for the individuals affected, who may be intimidated by the defendant, to appear at court. An anti-social behaviour order may prohibit any future activity – including that which is otherwise lawful – provided that this is 'necessary for the purpose of protecting [local people] from further anti-social acts by the defendant'.[90] As such, it has been said to create 'individualised criminal offences for each defendant';[91] a situation that is comparable to the situation under the Protection from Harassment Act 1997, where the terms of the civil injunction or restraining order will be tailored to the circumstances of the harassment in each individual case.

The mix of civil and criminal measures highlights one of the major issues within harassment law: the need to balance the competing rights and interests of the victim, who requires protection and an accessible means of legal redress, and the person accused of harassment, who must be treated justly by the legal system. On the one hand, to require the victim to establish their claim 'beyond reasonable doubt' would be a major encumbrance, especially if legal aid is not available and the victim cannot afford legal representation. The purpose of the Protection from Harassment Act 1997 was to provide quick and effective redress for stalking victims, and this would not be achieved by requiring a criminal standard of proof before an injunction is granted. However, the converse of this argument relates to fairness to a person who is accused of harassment. If an injunction can be granted once harassment (or apprehended harassment) is established 'on the balance of probabilities', but breach of the injunction is punishable as a criminal offence, this can be seen as an indirect imposition of criminal liability for harassment which has never been established by the 'beyond reasonable doubt' standard required to engender conviction for the offence of criminal harassment.

This would appear particularly harsh if the injunction were based on apprehended harassment, where criminal liability would follow one act in breach of the injunction, as this would not suffice to establish liability for criminal harassment that requires conduct on at least two occasions. There would appear to be no scope for the criminal court to consider the circumstances that led to the imposition of the injunction to consider whether criminal liability is appropriate. In *DPP v Moseley*, Collins J held that the court was not entitled to look behind the injunction and that, once granted, an injunction was binding unless and until it was set aside.[92] Thus, it would

---

90 Crime and Disorder Act 1998, s 1(6).

91 Cracknell, S, 'Anti-social behaviour orders' (2000) 22 Journal of Social Welfare and Family Law 108, pp 108–15.

92 *DPP v Moseley* (1999) *The Times*, 23 June. This case did not involve breach of a s 3 injunction, but concerned a s 2 charge of harassment which took place whilst an injunction in which harassment was given the same meaning as in the Protection from Harassment Act was in force.

appear that this section could facilitate the 'backdoor criminalisation' of conduct which may not qualify for direct liability under s 2 for criminal harassment because, once the injunction is imposed, any breach, without reasonable excuse, will engender criminal liability which makes this tantamount to a crime of strict liability.[93]

The comment that has been caused by this mixing of civil and criminal standards could be argued to be irrelevant, as what the section actually criminalises is breach of a civil injunction, not the conduct for which it was imposed. Seen in these terms, the outcome is little different from contempt of court proceedings for breach of injunction other than that with the criminal approach, the only action required by the victim is to inform the police of the breach. The Parliamentary Secretary for the Lord Chancellor's Department defended this section against criticism during the passage of the Act, saying: 'A defendant who does not breach the court's order has nothing to fear from these provisions, but deleting them substantially diminishes the protection we want to give victims.'[94] Seen from this perspective, the injunction provides fair warning that the conduct is unacceptable to the recipient, which gives the subject of the injunction an opportunity to avoid criminal liability by conforming to the terms of the injunction.

One difficulty which has arisen due to the combination of criminal and civil provisions is illustrated in the case of *R v Cunningham*, in which the defendant had engaged in a persistent campaign of harassment against his former partner which had led to both criminal and civil proceedings against him.[95] He appealed against the sentence of 28 months' imprisonment imposed upon him following conviction under s 4 of the Protection from Harassment Act 1997:

> The issue arising from that chronology of the civil proceedings is the extent to which the judge has properly taken account of periods actually served under the two civil contempt matters and the extent to which he is at risk of being re-sentenced for matters already covered by custodial sentences.[96]

Although the Court of Appeal felt that his conduct justified the imposition of the full five years, they actually reduced the sentence to two years' imprisonment because of the confusion caused from the combination of civil and criminal proceedings arising from the same series of events and the consequent risk of double jeopardy.

There is a substantial scope for overlap between the civil and criminal provisions of the statute. This creates a risk that a defendant may be placed in double jeopardy and thus be punished for the same conduct in both the civil

---

93 Addison and Lawson-Cruttenden, 1997, p 21.
94 Streeter, G, *HC Deb* Vol 287 Col 968, 18 December 1996.
95 *R v Cunningham* (1999) unreported, 23 November, CA.
96 *Ibid, per* Ebsworth J.

and criminal courts. An examination of the interrelationship of the civil and criminal provisions and some guidance as to the stance to be taken with regards to a defendant who has already been the subject of civil proceedings would be welcomed.

6.4.2 Breach of restraining order

Section 5(1) of the Protection from Harassment Act 1997 gives the criminal court new powers to attach a restraining order to any other sentence imposed upon the defendant following conviction under either s 2 or s 4. A restraining order places restrictions upon the future conduct of the defendant in a manner analogous to bail conditions, thus removing an anomaly from the criminal law whereby the victim was protected from future conduct by the 'presumed innocent' defendant who was, however, free to resume contact once his guilt was established (albeit at the risk of further convictions). There are no limitations as to the nature of the restrictions that can be included in the restraining order other than that the order must be aimed at protecting the victim from suffering further harassment or fear of violence.[97]

Two major objections were voiced regarding restraining orders during the passage of the Protection from Harassment Act 1997. First, the fact that the restraining order could restrict the conduct towards the victim of harassment and 'any other person named in the order',[98] as the defendant had not been convicted of harassment of anyone other than the direct victim. However, it is not unusual for a stalker to target family members and friends of the victim, especially once their access to their primary target is limited. Additionally, the notion of triangulation suggests that once the stalker feels thwarted in his attempts to contact the object of his attentions, he will seek an object of blame who will then be in danger of violence.[99] This is usually the person that the stalker perceives to be standing between him and the object of his attentions, hence is commonly a partner or parent.[100] This was said to justify the widening of the remit of the protection of the restraining order. It could be argued that it is not reasonable to limit the otherwise lawful activities of a defendant towards a person who has never previously had cause to complain about his behaviour, for example, a restraining order that prohibits contact with a person who has never been the subject of harassment by the defendant.

---

97 Protection from Harassment Act 1997, s 5(2).

98 *Ibid*, s 5(2).

99 'Stalker tried to kill ex-wife's new boyfriend' (1997) *Daily Telegraph*, 16 April.

100 *R v Hough* (1997) unreported, 28 February, CA. The defendant, unable to accept that his marriage was over, stalked his estranged wife. She obtained an injunction which the defendant believed was done at the behest of her new boyfriend, so he broke into their home and stabbed the boyfriend, who died from his injuries.

In this respect, the orders are preventative in that they prevent the stalker from targeting others before he has even attempted to do so.

The second objection to the operation of restraining orders was that they may run 'until further order'[101] which, in reality, means that the defendant will be subject to the order for an indefinite period of time. It could be argued that the defendant is, or should be, entitled to know the boundaries of his sentence. The counter-argument to this is that it is frequently not possible to determine at the outset how long the victim will be at risk of further harassment by the defendant. Some stalking cases have continued for over a decade, and if the order had to be for determinate duration, this would place the onus on the victim to return to court and apply for it to be renewed. Provision is made within this section for the court, the victim or the defendant to apply to vary or discharge the order, so there is scope for the defendant to return to the court and demonstrate that there is no need for the order to continue as he poses no further threat to the victim and that all incidents of harassment have ceased.

The imposition of a restraining order may have unforeseen consequences or may impact upon the defendant in a particularly harsh manner. For example, in *R v Southwark Crown Court ex p Howard*, the defendant had been prosecuted under s 2 following his harassment of a young woman.[102] A restraining order was imposed in conjunction with his sentence, and one of the terms prohibited the defendant from going within 50 yards of the victim's home. As the defendant and the victim resided in the same block of flats, this prohibition effectively excluded the defendant from his own home, where he had lived for 25 years. The accommodation in question belonged to the local authority, who sought to evict the defendant for failing to reside within the property in contravention of their requirements, although he had paid his rent throughout his absence. His application for a variation of the order was rejected despite Bingham CJ's acknowledgment that the terms of the order had turned out to be harsher than originally contemplated or intended.

The availability of restraining orders justifies the low level of criminality in s 2. One of the main reasons thought to justify the creation of a specific statute to deal with stalking was the need to wait until the victim suffered harm, whether physical or psychological, in order to obtain a conviction under the Offences Against the Person Act 1861.[103] The low level of liability required for the offence of harassment will often mean that those convicted have only committed very few minor acts of harassment, hence justifying only a minor penalty such as a conditional discharge. This can have a restraining order

---

101 Protection from Harassment Act 1997, s 5(3).

102 *R v Southwark Crown Court ex p Howard* (2000) unreported, 12 April, Divisional Court.

103 Other means of prosecuting stalkers were possible, but their availability depended upon the nature of the conduct engaged in by the stalker and often only provided the potential of low maximum penalties.

attached which makes it clear to the defendant what future conduct is prohibited and avoids the need for the victim to suffer harm and deals with the defendant's behaviour quickly before it becomes too established in their psyche. Thus, a low level sentence imposed in conjunction with a restraining order makes it clear to the stalker that his conduct is unwelcome, which provides a 'warning shot across the bows', alerting the stalker that any future conduct will be dealt with more severely. Equally important is the ability to attach restraining orders to more serious sentences, as this ensures that persistent stalkers are brought back before the courts quickly if they do not desist from their campaign of harassment. This is especially important, as even a sentence of imprisonment does not appear to deter the more determined stalkers.[104]

6.4.2.1 The extension of restraining orders

Proposals were recently made to expand the idea of restraining orders into other areas of criminal law. The Restraining and Protection Orders Bill 1999 would have made it possible to attach restraining orders to any offence for which a sentence of five years' imprisonment could be imposed[105] or to any of a list of specified offences.[106] When introducing the Bill, Bridget Prentice referred to the success of restraining orders under the Protection from Harassment Act 1997 and proposed its extension to a range of offences.[107] She found it anomalous that those who cause their victims to fear violence may have their future conduct restricted, whilst those who actually commit violence are subject to no such restrictions. She refers to the trauma caused to rape victims when their rapist is released from prison and moves back to the neighbourhood, where the victim is forced to see him on a daily basis.

This suggests that the role of the restraining order in this Bill would be very different from its role in the Protection from Harassment Act 1997. Whilst it is clear that the continued presence of a rapist must be very stressful and frightening, this does not necessarily mean that legal limitations on his conduct after sentence are appropriate. This Bill would restrain the defendant from conduct which 'the court considers reasonably necessary to protect the victim'.[108] The restraining orders in the Protection from Harassment Act are limited to prohibitions of conduct as far as is necessary to protect the victim from further harassment or fear of violence, that is, further incidents of the same offence that he has been convicted of. The Restraining and Protection Orders Bill could impose limitations on the defendant's conduct that bear no

---

104 'Jailed stalkers still harass their victims' (1997) *Daily Telegraph*, 6 April.
105 Restraining and Protection Orders Bill 1999, cl 1(5)(a).
106 *Ibid*, cl 1(5)(b).
107 Prentice, B, *HC Deb*, Cols 346–49, 28 April 1999.
108 Restraining and Protection Orders Bill 1999, cl 1(2).

relation to the offence which has been committed, thus would arguably represent an unjustified limitation on their liberty.

It is the unique nature of the offence of harassment which justifies the imposition of a restraining order, as it is frequently not the conduct *per se*, but its repetition and the persistence of the stalker that causes the harassment. Also relevant is the fact that the Protection from Harassment Act is the only statute which requires more than one incident as the basis of liability for a single offence. Therefore, in the absence of provisions for imposition of restraining orders, the victim would have to wait for not just one, but at least two further incidents before action could be taken against the stalker. The ability to impose restraining orders in harassment cases is an acknowledgment of the particular characteristics of the offence, which do not apply in other criminal offences. However unpleasant it is for the man who raped you to move back in next door, that does not mean that the offence will be repeated, therefore there can be no similar justification for limiting his right to do so. Of course, if he then goes out of his way to use his presence as a means of harassment, action can be brought under the Protection from Harassment Act. Although the justification given for the availability of restraining orders is to prevent a repetition of the offence, this argument cannot be extended, as it is unlikely in the extreme that the Restraining and Protection Orders Bill would create a restraining order that contained a term 'you are prohibited from raping the victim'. Preventing a continuation of offending is a different matter from preventing the victim from being distressed by the presence of a person who has been convicted of harming her. Bearing in mind the examples with which Bridget Prentice supported this Bill, this would appear to include a restriction that he not be allowed to live within a certain geographical area of the victim's home, as this would be distressing. To impose restrictions on where a person lives because it might upset someone else is not a matter with which the law should be concerned.

6.5 PROBLEMS WITH RESTRICTIVE ORDERS

The current conception appears to be that restraining orders are a valuable tool in the battle against the stalker. There is some evidence emerging in the US, which suggests that such orders, whether civil or criminal, can actually exacerbate the situation. Gerbeth explains that American police term them 'orders of illusion', as they give the victim a false feeling of protection but are, in reality, just pieces of paper.[109] He illustrates this with a dramatic example of the man who 'graphically illustrated his contempt for both the order of protection and the criminal justice system. He stabbed his wife to death and

109 Gerbeth, 1992, pp 138–43.

knifed the court order to her chest.'[110] Gavin de Becker, a leading private security expert who specialises in stalking cases, believes that interventions such as restraining orders are inevitably cited by stalkers as the factor which prompted them to use violence. He terms this dynamic 'engage and enrage'.[111] Meloy describes the imposition of a restraining order as a 'dramatic moment', a phrase used to exemplify a situation which triggers the stalker's humiliation and rage and which can lead to violence, but also states that, in the majority of cases, restraining orders effectively suppress the unwanted behaviour.[112] However, another study found that 48% of stalkers violated a protective order[113] and a National Institute of Justice Report stated that restraining orders are ineffective unless zealously enforced by the police and the courts.[114]

The impact of restraining orders is yet to be determined in this jurisdiction, but research from the US suggests that they may not be the miracle solution to stalking that they appear at first glance.

6.6 CONCLUSION

Certainly, the Protection from Harassment Act 1997 represents a significant improvement in the legal protection offered to victims of stalking. A means of early intervention is provided that may prevent the conduct becoming too firmly established and should put an end to the stalking before the victim suffers serious harm. Moreover, the Act has created restraining orders that can be used to ensure that no further harassing conduct occurs, and that continuance of the conduct will be treated seriously. However, areas of the Protection from Harassment Act 1997 have been identified that merit consideration and which are possible areas for improvement. The following chapter considers the extent to which the Protection from Harassment Act 1997 has proved to be an effective means of preventing stalking.

---

110 Gerbeth, 1992, p 138.
111 Cited in Orion, 1997, pp 214–38.
112 Meloy, 1999b, pp 85–99.
113 Harmon, Rosner and Owens, 1995, p 194.
114 Cited in Orion, 1997, p 213.

CHAPTER 7

AN EVALUATION OF THE LEGAL
RESPONSE TO STALKING

This chapter evaluates the efficacy of the legal response to stalking in order to determine whether the criminalisation of stalking has proved to be a successful means of resolving the problem. The efficacy of the legal response is examined with reference to the following issues:

- Did stalking amount to a sufficiently serious social problem to merit legal intervention?
- Was the existing law inadequate to address stalking?
- How has the Protection from Harassment Act 1997 addressed the deficiencies of the existing law?
- What are the shortcomings of the Protection from Harassment Act?
- Has the Protection from Harassment Act 1997 been effective in terms of:

   (a) preventing further harassment; and,

   (b) providing protection for the victim?

Each of these issues is addressed in turn to provide a comprehensive evaluation of the legal response to stalking.

7.1 SHOULD THE LAW INTERVENE?

As the first two chapters of this book have established, stalking involves an immense range of conduct engaged in with a variety of different motivations. There is little commonality between stalking cases in terms of the specific conduct involved, the relationship between the parties and the intention behind the behaviour. The common characteristics of stalking cases are the repeated and unwanted nature of the conduct and the negative response that this conduct provokes in the victim. When stalking initially emerged as a public issue in the early part of the 1990s, it was not immediately apparent that a legal response would be forthcoming. The selective focus of the media upon celebrity victims and on cases in which stalking had been a precursor to the commission of a serious criminal offence did not convey the impression that stalking was sufficiently widespread to constitute a serious social problem that lacked a means of legal intervention. As the coverage of stalking increased in volume, it emerged that many 'ordinary' people were victims and that stalking did not necessarily involve the commission of a discrete criminal offence. It was at this stage that the issue of the efficacy of the law to address stalking was first raised.

There is no identifiable stage at which it was questioned whether legal intervention was the most appropriate means of addressing stalking. Many of the early news features included the views of psychiatrists and psychologists, which suggested that it was considered to be a medical problem rather than a legal problem, but the characterisation of stalking as a challenge for the legal system soon took predominance. However, at this stage, the question was whether the law did cover stalking as opposed to whether it should. Furthermore, there was little suggestion that stalking should fall within the remit of the civil law; the idea that it was a personal wrong against an individual that should be remedied in the civil courts is not one that emerged from the pro-intervention rhetoric. As stalking emerged as a serious and prevalent social problem, the presumption that the criminal justice system was the most appropriate means of addressing the problem appeared to emerge simultaneously.

Prior to a consideration of the efficacy of the criminal law response to stalking, it is important to question the assumption that the criminal law was the most appropriate means of intervention. Certainly, some stalking cases, owing to the nature of the conduct engaged in, fell firmly within the remit of the criminal law. However, this was due to the commission of a substantive criminal offence as a means of harassment. Thus the stalker who made repeated abusive telephone calls would come within the remit of s 43 of the Telecommunications Act 1984 and the stalker who removed items from the victim's washing line could be prosecuted for theft. The intervention of the criminal law was based upon the means used to cause harassment, not upon the harassment itself. Therefore, the stalker who engaged in solely lawful means to harass his victim was outside of the reach of the criminal law, even if his behaviour was intended to cause harassment. The question that has to be addressed here is whether the nature of otherwise lawful conduct is altered when it is engaged in with the specific purpose of causing annoyance and distress. Should a nefarious intention render unlawful that which is inherently lawful?

One of the difficulties here comes in establishing the intention behind the actions. Repeatedly targeting a victim with unlawful conduct raises a presumption that it intended to cause an adverse reaction, but can the same assumption be made regarding ostensibly innocuous conduct? How is it to be established that the repeated giving of gifts and flowers or the offering of invitations to social engagements were undertaken for less than honourable reasons? Moreover, what of the stalker whose intentions are worthy but who fails to appreciate that his conduct is unwelcome and causes distress to the recipient, or who appreciates that it is initially unwelcome, but perseveres because 'faint heart never won fair lady'? The approach of the Australian courts to establishing an intention to harass is that it will be inferred in the absence of an alternative explanation for the conduct. Even if this approach were to be adopted within the English legal system, it would be of little assistance in dealing with innocuous conduct. There are numerous reasons why such conduct could be undertaken that do not involve an intention to harass.

This is one of the difficulties of considering legislation against stalkers. Not all stalkers are deliberately seeking to cause an adverse reaction. Many labour under the misapprehension that their conduct is welcome or their feelings reciprocated, or foster a fervent wish that this will be so in the fullness of time. Such persons have no desire to cause an adverse reaction by their activities and may not appreciate that they are doing so. This diversity of motivations suggests that to view an intention to harass as the justification for legal intervention would create a situation whereby only a relatively small number of stalking cases would be addressed. There would be insuperable difficulties in establishing this intention and, in any case, it may be that the victim experiences the same degree of harm regardless of whether the conduct is engaged in to distress to the victim or in the mistaken belief that the victim will welcome the conduct.

Although the nefarious motivations of the stalker may justify legal intervention to prohibit otherwise lawful conduct, as a basis of a stalking law, the requirement of an intention to harass would provide evidential difficulties and create an unacceptable delineation between stalking and non-stalking. There is no evidence to suggest that the attentions of a deluded stalker are any less distressing for the victim than deliberate harassment of a stalker driven by malice.

Once the remit of the law is to be extended beyond innocuous conduct that is being used as a deliberate weapon of harassment, the remaining issue is whether it is justifiable to criminalise such conduct when the reason for its commission is other than to cause an adverse reaction. Can there be any justification for outlawing the giving of gifts when this is done in the hope that the recipient will view the giver more favourably as a potential partner? The justification for legal intervention to prohibit such conduct can only rest upon the harm caused to the victim and the detrimental intrusion into an individual's personal autonomy that occurs when they are prevented from going about their lawful business without interruption. If otherwise innocuous conduct prevents an individual from sleeping at night, from travelling to their place of work, or from merely spending peaceful time in their own home, surely this is conduct that should be prohibited?

The severity of the harm that can be caused by stalking should not be underestimated. Certainly, the individual incidents may not, in themselves, appear harmful, but the cumulative impact of the continuing nature of stalking behaviour should not be underestimated. Research findings indicate that the majority of stalking victims undergo a substantial lifestyle change as a result of victimisation.[1] A national survey of stalking victims in the US found that 26% of victims were absent from work because of the stalking and 7% left their employment completely.[2] Many victims relocate in order to end the stalking, with some even adopting new identities to decrease the likelihood of being found by the stalker. Such disruptions to an individual's lifestyle are indicative of the extent to which stalking can impact upon the victim's life. Moreover, there is a high incidence of psychological harm. Many victims experience sleeplessness, anxiety, depression and general fearfulness. A significant number engage in self-harm or attempt suicide. Experts suggest that approximately 37% of stalking victims satisfy the diagnostic requirements for post-traumatic stress disorder and explain that this figure would be higher but for the requirement that the harm result from actual or threatened violence, a factor that is often absent in stalking cases.[3]

Viewed from the perspective of the level of disruption caused to the victim and the severity of the harm that may ensue, there is clear justification for legal intervention to combat stalking. The question as to whether a civil or criminal remedy was appropriate is, in many respects, also answered by reference to the severity of the harm that stalking can cause. The well being and autonomy of the individual is something that the law must protect assiduously and the imposition of criminal liability for such harmful conduct not only offers a greater degree of protection to the victim, it also signifies society's disapproval for the conduct in question. As such, the use of the criminal law to combat stalking appears entirely justified.

7.2 WAS THE EXISTING LAW ADEQUATE TO DEAL WITH STALKING?

Prior to the enactment of the Protection from Harassment Act, stalking would only be actionable under the criminal law if the conduct, or an aspect of it, constituted an existing criminal offence. Many offences are committed during the course of stalking, thus it was frequently the case that an element of the stalking behaviour would give rise to criminal liability. For example, Anthony Burstow was twice convicted of the burglary of his victim's home. Although this represented only an infinitesimal proportion of the totality of his conduct against her, it nevertheless led to his arrest, conviction and imprisonment on two occasions, thus at least providing his victim with some respite from his constant harassment.[4]

---

1   Pathe and Mullen, 1997, pp 12–17.
2   Tjaden and Thoennes, 1998.
3   Pathe and Mullen, 1997, pp 12–17.
4   Interview with Anthony Burstow, 29 March 1999.

The extent to which the existing law could intervene in stalking cases was dependent on the nature of the stalker's conduct or, under civil law, the nature of the relationship between the parties.[5] This led to a situation whereby some stalking victims were protected by the law, whilst others were not. As has been discussed, the fact that a stalker engages in exclusively lawful conduct does not necessarily render victimisation less traumatic; in fact, the absence of recourse to the law may exacerbate the powerlessness and sense of isolation experienced by the victim.[6] Furthermore, for the law to intervene only when the stalking involves unlawful conduct sends a clear message to the stalker that it is perfectly permissible to harass and pester another person provided that only lawful means are used during the course of the harassment. This message was clearly received by some stalkers who went to great lengths to ensure that they remained within the law, thus attaining immunity from legal intervention. In some cases, this appears to increase the satisfaction that the stalker derives from stalking.[7]

The fragmentation of stalking into a series of criminal acts that are viewed separately from the lawful conduct can detract from the seriousness of the totality of the conduct and make any penalty imposed for an individual criminal act appear insufficient. The seriousness of the totality of a stalking campaign may be more than the sum of its composite criminal parts. For example, s 43 of the Telecommunications Act 1984 prohibits the making of threatening, abusive and obscene telephone calls; conduct that arises regularly in stalking cases. The maximum penalty for this offence is six months' imprisonment. Whilst this may suffice to address the telephoning element, if this is only a single aspect of the totality of the harassment, the penalty may seem inadequate to reflect the seriousness of the stalker's conduct. For the stalker, this may reinforce the message that it was the conduct that was unlawful, not its consequences. It was to surmount the inadequacy of the penalty under s 43 of the Telecommunications Act 1984 that Robert Ireland was prosecuted under s 47 of the Offences Against the Person Act 1861 for causing actual bodily harm following a campaign of silent telephone calls that caused the victims to suffer psychological injury.[8]

It was in recognition of the need to approach the overall course of conduct that the civil and criminal courts sought to develop the law to take a more holistic approach to stalking cases. In *Khorasandjian v Bush*, the Court of Appeal dispensed with the long standing requirement for the plaintiff to have a proprietary interest in land in order to bring an action in private nuisance.[9] This finding was necessary in order to uphold the grant of an injunction to a

---

5   See Chapter 4.
6   See Chapter 2.
7   See Chapters 1 and 2.
8   *R v Ireland* [1997] 4 All ER 225.
9   *Khorasandjian v Bush* [1993] 3 All ER 669.

young girl resident in her parents' home who was being harassed by a former partner. This remained good law until the requirement of a proprietary interest in land was restored by the House of Lords in *Hunter v Canary Wharf*.[10] Their Lordships were critical of the expansion of private nuisance that had occurred in *Khorasandjian v Bush*, whilst acknowledging that it had been necessary to afford the plaintiff the degree of protection she deserved. In restricting the scope of private nuisance to a tort against land, the House of Lords made explicit reference to the fact that injunctive relief against harassment was now available under the Protection from Harassment Act, thus obviating the need for protection under the tort of private nuisance.[11]

Equally, the expansion of the Offences Against the Person Act 1861 to encompass psychological harm illustrated judicial concern at the inadequacy of the existing criminal law to deal with stalking cases. Recognition that 'harm' for the purposes of the Offences Against the Person Act 1861 included psychological injury, and some amendment to the definition of the causative elements of the relevant offences, facilitated the use of this statute to address the totality of stalking by focusing on the consequences of the conduct.

It was the expansion of the Offences Against the Person Act 1861 to encompass the harm caused to victims of stalking, and the concomitant expansion of the tort of private nuisance, that emphasises the inadequacy of the existing law to deal with stalking. Despite these expansions, there were still gaps in the legal protection available for stalking victims, particularly in terms of the criminal law. Stalking would not give rise to liability under the Offences Against the Person Act 1861 unless and until the victim suffered the requisite degree of psychological harm, which may necessitate the victim enduring years of harassment. Clearly, despite the efforts of the judiciary to expand the existing law, there was a need for an offence that addressed the totality of the conduct whilst providing a means of intervening to halt the conduct at an early stage before serious harm is caused to the victim. This was the aim of the Protection from Harassment Act.

7.3 THE PROTECTION FROM HARASSMENT ACT 1997

The Protection from Harassment Act appeared, in many respects, to provide the ideal solution to many of the deficiencies of the criminal law in relation to stalking. Eschewing the list approach to the definition of stalking in favour of a more general approach, the statute prohibits any course of conduct that amounted to harassment of another. This appears to coincide perfectly with the core characteristics of stalking as repeated and unwanted conduct that

---

10   *Hunter v Canary Wharf* [1997] 2 All ER 425.
11   See Chapter 5.

provokes an adverse reaction in the victim. By focusing upon the reaction of the victim, the statute has the flexibility to deal with novel manifestations of stalking, as all conduct is potentially included within the definition of harassment, provided it causes the victim to feel harassed.

The definition of a 'course of conduct' as involving conduct on at least two occasions provides for early intervention whilst acknowledging the ongoing nature of stalking behaviour. The conduct requirement is neutral, so that there is no requirement that the acts themselves be unlawful or even unpleasant in nature. Moreover, they do not need to be acts of the same type, so any combination of two different acts may suffice. In addition to requiring that there be a course of conduct that causes harassment, s 1 also specifies that the defendant must know, or ought to have known, that this would cause harassment. This obviates the need to prove that the defendant intended to cause harassment by his actions, although knowingly causing harassment is tantamount to intentional harassment. The 'ought to know' requirement ensures that the stalker cannot avoid liability by asserting that he did not appreciate the possibility of a negative reaction to his conduct. It also covers the situation whereby the defendant, who is suffering from a delusional disorder or other mental disability, is inherently incapable of understanding the consequences of his actions.

Thus harassment will be established if there is a course of conduct that causes harassment to the victim and the defendant knows, or ought to know, that this would be the result. This forms the basis for both the offence of criminal harassment and the statutory tort of harassment, thus the victim has two alternative courses of action available on the basis of the same behaviour. This element of choice is important, as stalking erodes the control that victims have over everyday life, thus the choice of alternative legal action is symbolically important. Furthermore, the choice of alternative means of entry into the legal system may lead to a greater number of cases being brought, as victims are not limited to initiating an action themselves or to approaching the police – the victim can take the option that they are most comfortable with. The value of the civil approach is enhanced by the power of arrest for breach of injunction and the fact that breach of injunction is made a criminal offence. Therefore, once the victim has obtained an injunction, they are fully protected and the responsibility is not on the victim to enforce the injunction if it is breached. This is a substantial improvement to the general position regarding enforcement of civil injunctions where the onus is on the victim to bring proceedings in cases of breach.

The Protection from Harassment Act also creates the more serious offence of causing fear of violence. Similar to the offence of harassment in that it requires a course of conduct, this offence requires that the victim must fear that violence will be used against them on two occasions. This narrowly framed offence carries a more severe penalty than the offence of harassment, with a maximum penalty of five years' imprisonment. The availability of a more serious offence acknowledges that some stalking cases may involve extremes of conduct that justify more extensive punishment than that provided by the summary offence. Symbolically, it is important to have some element of hierarchy to signify to both victim and defendant the seriousness with which certain conduct is viewed.

The final way in which the Protection from Harassment Act seeks to remedy the inadequacies of the pre-existing law regarding stalking, is that it provides the means to pre-empt future stalking conduct. This is facilitated by the availability of a restraining order that can be attached to any sentence imposed by the courts and which prohibits specified conduct towards a specified party, usually the victim. Operating in a similar manner to a civil injunction or bail conditions, the restraining order provides the courts with the means not only to deal with harassment that has occurred, but also to seek to prevent future harassment from taking place. Frequently, the primary aim of prosecution is to seek a restraining order, so offering protection to the victim and ensuring that any further harassment is dealt with more harshly, as breach of restraining order carries a maximum penalty of five years' imprisonment.[12]

In summary, the Protection from Harassment Act appears to target the precise gap in the law that left stalking victims unprotected. It provides a low-level offence that facilitates early intervention into the situation that may limit the harm caused to the victim and put a rapid end to the stalking. The alternative of a civil action may encourage victims who are reluctant to approach the police or enter into the criminal justice system to instigate civil proceedings. The improved enforcement provisions ensure that the civil law route offers as great a level of protection to the victim as criminal proceedings. The offence of criminal harassment may only carry a low penalty, but is supplemented by the availability of the more serious offence of causing fear of violence that carries a maximum penalty of up to five years' imprisonment. Furthermore, a restraining order can be attached to any other penalty that is imposed by the courts, thus seeking to prevent future victimisation and to ensure that further harassment is dealt with more severely by the courts.

7.4 CRITICISMS OF THE PROTECTION FROM HARASSMENT ACT 1997

It would certainly appear that the Protection from Harassment Act has improved the legal protection available to stalking victims and has filled a gap

---

12 Harris, J, *An Evaluation of the Use and Effectiveness of the Protection from Harassment Act 1997*, 2000, Home Office Research Study 203, London: HMSO, pp 42–43.

in this respect. Notwithstanding the benefits of this legislation, it is also necessary to consider at what cost these changes were achieved.

As has been discussed, the offence of harassment requires proof only of two incidents that cause harassment. This creates an incredibly low threshold of liability that is contingent upon that which is inherently unknowable – how another person will react in any given situation.[13] This is exacerbated by the use of the 'ought to know' requirement. Given the potentially infinite variability in individual reactions to the same conduct, how can it be said that the defendant ought to have known what was occurring in the mind of another?

Although such a standard is clearly favourable for the victim, who may be just as traumatised by inadvertently harassing conduct as he or she would be by intentional harassment, it creates an unacceptably low threshold of criminal liability. What the defendant ought to know is measured according to the standards of the reasonable person in possession of the same information as the defendant. This objective standard takes no account of the defendant's inability to appreciate the impact of his conduct on another, nor does it make sufficient allowance for the potential for misunderstanding that may arise between the parties. One case that illustrates this perfectly occurred when a young man, with limited romantic experience, became attracted to a work colleague. His attempts to ask her out in the evenings were always met with polite refusals from the young woman concerned and expressions of regret that prior engagements prevented her from being able to accept. The young man saw nothing in this to suggest that his attentions were unwelcome. The recipient of his invitations, however, had no intention of going out with the young man and wished that he would stop asking her. Unable to communicate this to him herself, she informed her employer. The employer suspended the young man pending an investigation into his alleged misconduct. With no previous warning that his conduct was unacceptable, the young man was confused about what had happened and sought an explanation from the woman concerned. She became alarmed at his insistence and called the police, who arrested him. At his trial for the offence of harassment, the magistrate found that any reasonable person would appreciate that repeated refusals indicated that the invitations were unwelcome. The defendant was bitter about his conviction saying:

> I didn't think twice about asking her out a couple of times even though she said 'no'. My brother's girlfriend told me to, in any case. She said that all women say 'no' a couple of times so that they don't look too keen and to test if a bloke is really interested. She never mentioned that I could end up getting arrested.[14]

---

13 Finch, 2000, pp 273–95.
14 Case history 6.

Some events are more open to dual interpretations than others. In this case, there was potential to perceive the situation as harassment, as the victim did, or as legitimate romantic pursuit, which was how it was characterised by the defendant. The court favoured the victim's interpretation, but can it really be said that a reasonable person would reach the same conclusion? This is one of the problems with some stalking cases – the facts may lend themselves to opposing interpretations and different people respond to the same situation in different ways.

The low threshold of liability has led to the Protection from Harassment Act being used to deal with incredibly minor incidents. One of the earliest prosecutions under the statute involved two neighbours, one of whom alleged that the other's constant singing and whistling was disturbing his enjoyment of his garden.[15] Moreover, it was alleged that the erection of a large plastic owl was deliberately undertaken with the purpose of upsetting the victim's pigeons. Even though the defendant was acquitted, the fact that he had been arrested and prosecuted could be said to undermine the serious nature of the statute and the conduct that it was aimed at. Equally, another early prosecution was against an official of the Law Society who had smiled at a woman on the Underground on two separate occasions. The triviality of such cases combined with the attention-grabbing circumstances ensured that these cases were well publicised in the media. The publicity given to such trivial cases can create a negative perception of the statute that undermines the seriousness of genuine stalking cases. The creation of a *de minimis* threshold of tolerance to harassment would filter out cases perceived to be trivial, but the introduction of such an objective standard into a statute based upon the subjective reaction of the victims could be extremely problematic.[16]

The choice of civil or criminal proceedings appears to have caused too great a degree of overlap, particularly in terms of cases more suited to the civil courts being brought as criminal prosecutions. This may be due to the greater publicity given to the criminal aspects of the statute or to the fact that most victims would seek advice from the police as their first port of call, hence may become involved in criminal proceedings before considering the option of civil action. The additional problem with a civil action is that the responsibility lies with the victim to initiate and pursue an action, whereas the police and the Crown Prosecution Service deal with all aspects of a criminal proceeding. The cost of bringing an action may operate as a further disincentive, as a victim who is not legally aided will have to fund a civil action.[17]

In a criminal context, the offence of harassment not only has low threshold of liability, but also carries a low penalty, as the maximum possible sentence is

---

15 'Harassment law gets bird in police swoop' (1997) *The Times*, 31 December.
16 See Chapter 6.
17 *Op cit*, Harris, fn 12, pp 44–46.

six months' imprisonment. This may appear inadequate to address more serious cases of harassment. The purpose of the Act was to intervene quickly so that harassment would not escalate into a serious situation and provide for a low penalty that would be combined with a restraining order to ensure that no further harassment occurs. However, there is evidence to suggest that victims do not necessarily bring their problems to the attention of the police until they have experienced a substantial degree of harassment. In such situations, the conduct involved may be serious and the harm caused to the victim substantial. Although s 4 of the Protection from Harassment Act 1997 provides for a more serious offence, this is narrowly worded and requires at least two incidents that cause the victim to fear that violence will be used against them. It will not suffice that the victim fears that violence may be used against her or that she fears that violence will be used against another, the offence is limited to an extremely narrow band of behaviour. Therefore, a victim may experience stalking that is so serious that the maximum penalty under s 2, criminal harassment, is insufficient, but which nonetheless does not fall within the narrow requirements of the s 4 offence. Thus, there is still a gap in the law that is not filled by the Protection from Harassment Act, as was demonstrated in *R v McBride*, where the victim was charged with two offences under s 2 of the Protection from Harassment Act and one offence under s 47 of the Offences Against the Person Act 1861, assault occasioning actual bodily harm, due to the psychiatric injury suffered by the victim. Thus, there is clearly a need either for the more serious offence to be widened to encompass a broader range of serious harassment, for the penalty for the s 2 offence to be increased, or for the creation of a new offence that would come in between the offence of harassment and the offence of causing fear of violence in the harassment hierarchy.

During the passage of the Protection from Harassment Act, an amendment to include compulsory counselling for those convicted under the statute was approved by the House of Commons. The rationale for this was that the statute would be more effective if it tackled the root cause of the harassment. The then Conservative Government was opposed to the inclusion of this clause and it was removed by the House of Lords. Despite the doubts about the efficacy of non-voluntary counselling, the nature of many stalking cases suggests that there may have been a role for a specialist counselling programme. Moreover, many victims have expressed a desire for a form of mediation whereby they could communicate with the stalker, particularly to gain an understanding of the reasons for their victimisation. The tendency of stalking victims to engage in self-blame and to examine their own behaviour for clues as to why they were selected by the stalker suggests that, in certain circumstances, there may be a value to some controlled communication between the parties. This view is not favoured amongst professionals in the medical profession. Dr Edward Petch, a forensic psychologist who works in the secure unit of Ealing Hospital, aims to establish the first clinic dedicated to the treatment of stalkers and victims in Britain, but this would involve the parties being treated separately. Nonetheless, Dr Petch is firmly of the view that stalkers do require treatment:

> I deal with mentally disordered offenders from the more violent end of the spectrum: murderers, rapists, and sometimes multiple killers. But, in terms of my own safety, it's the stalkers that keep me awake at night. I find myself worrying about what they are capable of, and the degree of their disturbance, trying to establish what it is that is driving them. There is often a separate quality to them, an inability to acknowledge that what they are doing is wrong, or to see the effects it is having on their victims. That is quite chilling.[18]

Moreover, Dr Petch feels that the prevalence of psychological disorder in stalkers is underestimated and that the majority of stalkers suffer from either a psychiatric disorder or severe personality disorder:

> Stalking is a behaviour, not a condition. A very high proportion of stalkers will be mentally ill, maybe 75% will have a psychological abnormality ... All psychiatric diagnoses are possible – schizophrenia, mood disorders, morbid infatuation, even substance abuse. [The remainder] may not be mentally ill but will almost certainly be suffering from a personality disorder of some description, probably a disorder of attachment.[19]

In the light of this, it would appear particularly unfortunate that the Protection from Harassment Act does not address the mental health issues that are clearly relevant. Tracey Morgan, who was targeted by stalker Anthony Burstow for nine years, is an active campaigner for improvements in the law against stalking. She would like to see the introduction of mandatory psychiatric assessment for all those accused of stalking. The difficulty with this is that the Protection from Harassment Act covers a broader range of harassment, and psychiatric assessment would not be appropriate in all such cases. Moreover, as the Home Office Research Study into the effectiveness of the Protection from Harassment Act points out, such a system of assessment would be prohibitively expensive.[20]

The final criticism that can be made of the Protection from Harassment Act relates to terminology. The statute does not refer specifically to stalking; despite the repeated references to the need for a law against stalking during parliamentary debates, the word does not appear anywhere in the text of the Protection from Harassment Act. From a purely totemic perspective, this is an unfortunate omission. The labelling of conduct as criminal has an important symbolic function, thus this failure, although explicable in terms of the difficulty of defining stalking, is a fundamental weakness in the statute.

---

18 Quoted in 'Stalkers' (2000) *The Guardian*, 29 January.
19 *Ibid*.
20 *Op cit*, Harris, fn 12, p 32.

7.5 THE EFFICACY OF THE PROTECTION FROM HARASSMENT ACT 1997

In order to evaluate the efficacy of the Protection from Harassment Act in dealing with stalking cases, the measure of effectiveness to be adopted must be clearly identified. Two measures of efficacy will be adopted for the purposes of this work: first, has the statute provided adequate protection for stalking victims, and secondly, has it been successful at preventing further harassment. These factors will be assessed in relation to the following factors:

• victim awareness of the protection available;

• attitudes and actions of the police;

• the approach of the courts to enforcement; and,

• the after-care available for victims.

7.5.1 Victim awareness of the protection available

In order to assess the efficacy of the Protection from Harassment Act, it is important to gain some insight into the extent to which victims are aware of the Act and its provisions. Victims who are unaware that a potential means of intervention exists are less likely to seek help from the legal system to deal with the stalker.

During the course of this research, approximately three-quarters of the victims interviewed were aware that there was a 'stalking law', but few were able to outline its provisions with any degree of accuracy. Frighteningly, three victims who had been in contact with the police on several occasions were unaware that there was any law that covered their situation. This fact is exacerbated by the fact that one victim had reported her victimisation to the police on over 40 occasions. The other victims who had sought the advice of the police or solicitors were generally conversant with the general principle of the law, but were hazy about the precise details. For example, one victim reported:

> I've got to write everything down, apparently, and when there is enough incidents, the police will take over and arrest him. It's a bit of a bind and the list is getting really long but if it puts a stop to it, it'll be well worth it.[21]

Thus, this victim is clearly aware that the police are able to intervene, but is labouring under a serious misapprehension regarding the number of incidents that need to be established. Another victim has been equally misled by the advice of the police:

---

21 Case history 39.

I only need two incidents but there has to be witnesses. It's no good just me saying that he's done this, I have to have witnesses. And it's better if it's not my husband or son, I suppose because they would be biased. My neighbour saw him a couple of times but not when he did anything, just when he was standing in the bushes watching the house and, anyway, she's quite old and doesn't really want to get involved with the police. Our postman saw one thing and I've got his details and he's quite excited about going to court but it could be forever before he sees anything else. There was my niece who was here when he was banging on the door but I don't suppose she'd count as a witness because we're related. Anyway, that was only one time as well.[22]

Several misapprehensions are apparent here regarding the quality of the evidence that is required in order to found a complaint of harassment. The victim believes that she needs witnesses and that these must not be related to her. Neither situation is correct, although it would obviously strengthen her case if witnesses were able to confirm her evidence and their evidence would be considered to be more impartial if they were not family members. This may have been what the police were attempting to convey to the victim, but she has interpreted this as an absolute qualification. Additionally, the victim is under the impression that both incidents must be witnessed by the same person, thus she discounts two of her witnesses as they were only present on one occasion. These misunderstandings have prevented this witness from approaching the police a second time, despite the fact that the log of incidents that the police advised her to keep contains over 40 different entries.

Thus, although these victims know that a criminal prosecution is possible, they have such a fundamental misunderstanding as to the requirements of the law that a prosecution may never be forthcoming. The extent to which this confusion is due to the quality of the advice provided by the police or to the victims' misunderstanding of this advice is not clear. Other victims, however, have really benefited from the advice provided by the police:

The first chap I saw was a bit duff, he didn't seem to have a clue what was going on. But he passed me to this policewoman who was from the domestic violence unit and she was really great. I was a bit miffed at first, with her being from domestic violence, because I have never, ever been out with this man. She explained that it was just because she knew a lot about it because it happens a lot in domestic violence cases and I calmed down a bit. Anyway, she was great. I didn't understand her the first time and I think she could tell that so she told it all a different way and it made perfect sense. Once I knew what to do and what to look out for, it was dead easy. He was arrested a week later and I haven't seen him since. It's just a shame that it took me two months to find out what I had to do.

---

22 Case history 35.

Not all of the victims approached the police for advice. The best-informed victim that was interviewed during the course of this research had approached the Citizen's Advice Bureau for information and had an extremely clear grasp of the law. She was fully conversant with the requirements of the statute including the different standards required for a s 2 and s 4 offence and she appreciated that a civil action was a possibility. Moreover, as she would not qualify for legal aid, the Citizen's Advice Bureau had offered to help her fill out the appropriate forms and prepare her case if she chose the civil law option. This victim had even been encouraged to think about the provisions that she would want in a restraining order, if one were to be granted.

Sadly, some victims, although aware of the presence of the law, felt unable to make use of it. The reasons for this varied. Some victims felt that police involvement would anger their stalker and make the situation worse. Others were afraid that the police would disbelieve them, or that they would be blamed for encouraging the stalker or creating the situation.

Although approximately three-quarters of the victims interviewed were aware that there was a criminal law that was applicable to stalking, very few were aware of the existence of the civil remedy. Those who were aware of its existence were vague about the procedure that was involved and appeared intimidated by the idea of initiating legal proceedings. However, there was a marked disinclination to retain a solicitor due to the level of cost that was perceived to be involved. The victims interviewed in the course of this research were either unaware of the existence of a civil remedy or saw no advantage to pursuing this course of action when the criminal alternative was available.

The findings of this research are largely in accord with that of the Home Office research into the effectiveness of the Protection from Harassment Act in this respect:

> It is also not clear whether victims were aware of the civil option or whether those who did not wish to proceed were aware that this possibility lay open. The implication is that there may be a need for some sort of action, perhaps in the form of a publicity campaign (as with domestic violence), to draw the attention of victims of harassment to the remedies available. The police might also be well placed to give complainants advice about the civil remedy where they decide not to press charges.[23]

A need for greater publicity about the existence of the law and the options available is evident. Victims were generally either unaware of the availability of legal intervention or misguided as to the extent of the protection and their role in attaining this. Limited success can be achieved with a statute if it is not

---

23 *Op cit*, Harris, fn 12, p 54.

used due to lack of publicity either as to its existence, its availability or the extent of the protection. Hamish Brown's research into police responses to harassment included a checklist of important points to note that could be given to a victim experiencing harassment, which should prove a valuable source of information for victims.[24] However, victims need to be aware of the existence of a law relevant to their situation to ensure that they approach the police and to publicise the alternative courses of action available. Victims also need to be aware of the various sources of advice, such as the Citizen's Advice Bureau, and the availability of legal aid and fixed fee interviews with solicitors. Knowledge is a powerful weapon and one that could be invaluable to assist stalking victims to end their ordeal.

7.5.2 Police action and attitudes

Generally, stalking victims do not hold a favourable view of police involvement in stalking cases. An almost universal feeling of dissatisfaction was evident amongst those interviewed. The Home Office research study found that police officers did not have a clear grasp of the requirements of the Protection from Harassment Act. One-tenth of the arrests made under the Act were made following a single incident, contrary to the requirements of the legislation and a number of police officers were not aware of the differences between the s 2 and s 4 offences.[25] It was concern regarding the approach to policing the Act that led the Police Research Awards Scheme to fund a research project into this issue and to produce a report offering guidance to police officers.[26] This led to a number of police training days where the nature of stalking and the role of the Protection from Harassment Act were emphasised. Comparative research into the prosecution and conviction rate in various police authority areas disclosed an immense divergence between different areas.[27] The extent of the divergence between demographically similar areas was attributed to the difference in police attitudes. This might be an institutional ethos whereby the Protection from Harassment Act is not considered to be important at a high level within the police force or due to the levels of training and awareness regarding the Act within the particular police force. Some victims reported notable differences in approach within the same police station, thus the degree of assistance and support offered varied between individual police officers.

---

24 Brown, 2000, pp 13–15.
25 *Op cit*, Harris, fn 12, pp 19–27.
26 Brown, 2000.
27 von Heussen, 2000.

A consideration of the experiences of victims reveals some consistent themes regarding dissatisfaction with police attitudes to complaints of stalking.[28] First, a dismissive attitude to the conduct involved. This was a common complaint, particularly when the conduct involved was otherwise lawful. One victim whose house was watched by a stranger for nine months reported that the police said to her 'just ignore him, I'm sure he'll get fed up with it soon'.[29] This trivialised the fears that this woman felt at being the victim of this unusual and unjustified behaviour. After several complaints to the police, the victim sensed that the police were becoming irritated by her persistence and suspected that she was imagining the whole situation. On one occasion, the police approached the man and the victim could see the three men laughing together as they spoke, hardly a confidence-inspiring occurrence. It was on this occasion, whilst the victim was making the police officers a drink, that they asked her husband if she were menopausal, adding: 'it's not unusual for middle aged women to fantasise about younger men, you know.' The victim in this particular case was more aggrieved by her treatment by the police than she was by the stalking.

Other victims have reported examples of similarly cavalier attitudes from police officers. The mother of a 16 year old stalking victim persistently approached the police for assistance, as her daughter grew increasingly disturbed as a result of her victimisation.[30] The family went away for a short break to escape the persistent harassment and returned to find that the stalker had entered their house, moved the furniture, cleaned the house and left a cupboard full of groceries. When the woman reported this to the police, they seemed to find the situation amusing, saying: 'I don't know why you're complaining. I wish someone would come round and do my shopping.' When the woman responded that it had upset her daughter so much that she had made deep cuts in her arms and caught the blood in a glass, the police officer responded: 'That doesn't sound right. You ought to get her some help.' This advice may have been well meaning, but it was certainly phrased insensitively.

These may be extreme examples of inappropriate police responses to stalking victims, but other examples abound. One victim was pestered about the nature of her relationship with the stalker by a policeman, who concluded: 'You might say you've never been out with him but I don't see why he would do this to you unless there was something going on.' He refused to record her complaint of harassment and his parting advice was that the victim and the stalker should 'sit down and talk it through' even though the victim remained

---

28 The victims' interviews were analysed using the Ethnograph qualitative data analysis program and a selection of the interviews were also coded by hand to ensure accurate and consistent results.

29 Case history 1.

30 Case history 24.

adamant throughout that she had never had a relationship with the stalker.[31] Several other victims report that the police were determined to find a relational nexus between themselves and the stalker, although there is no reason why this should make any difference to the case or the police involvement. This is the danger of categorising stalking according to the nature of the relationship between the parties: the police appear reluctant to intervene in a 'private' dispute between 'domestic' parties:

> This Act was designed to deal with ... proper stalking cases ... It's not here as a means to getting back at someone who has pissed you off and that is basically what happened in this case. They split up, she's sorry then he's sorry then they row again. This isn't criminal behaviour, its life and they have got to get on with it without expecting us to come and referee.[32]

The difficulty is that the police may have their own perceptions of what a case should involve. They are as amenable to the influence of media representations of stalking as an ordinary member of the public, hence may be responding to their understanding of what a stalking case should involve. If the police officer sympathises with the stalker's situation, then he may not apply the law in a situation in which it technically should apply. One victim told of her six-month battle to have the police intervene to control the actions of her estranged husband who had been harassing her since the termination of their relationship.

He smashed up my car, had endless supplies of junk mail sent to me, ordered pizzas and taxis in my name, sent double glazing salesman round, I could go on and on. He painted 'slut' and 'whore' in huge red letters outside my house and at the office where I work and threatened to kill my new boyfriend if I didn't keep away from him. But every time the police approached him, he told them this sob story about just wanting access to the kids and how I was this vindictive cow that was making it all up to make sure he didn't get custody. So they wouldn't do anything at all and one even said to me that I ought to let the children see their father. He didn't want to see them; he just wanted to stop me seeing anyone else. The only time he took the kids out, he dumped them on his sister for the day.[33]

The police officer involved in this case was certainly convinced of the genuine motivation for the husband's actions:

> All he has done is try and get his family back. If she had the decency to respond to his letters and messages, he wouldn't have to keep sending them. He's not harassing anyone – if anything, she's causing him distress by refusing to communicate and, to add insult to injury, she wants to have him arrested. This just isn't what the Act is all about.[34]

---

31 Case history 35.
32 Case history 20.
33 Case history 8.
34 Interview with police officer involved in Case history 8.

Clearly, there are difficulties with police attitudes towards some stalking cases. The male victims of stalking, in particular, reported a distinct lack of understanding from the police. This is unfortunate, as research indicates that the apparent disparity between male and female victimisation in stalking cases can be attributed to a greater disinclination of male victims to approach the police. If the true extent of stalking is to be revealed and all cases viewed with equal seriousness, it is essential that every victim, regardless of their sex or their relationship with the stalker, feels able to seek the protection to which they are entitled.

Another frequent complaint that emerged regarding the role of the police concerned their apparent disinclination to intervene even if the complaint itself was taken seriously. As has been discussed, this can be problematic in cases viewed as 'domestic', but it also emerged as a particular problem in cases where the identity of the stalker was unknown. The common finding in all such cases encountered during the course of this research was that the police viewed the identification of the stalker as the victim's responsibility. One victim's request that the police watch her home until the stalker revealed himself was viewed with incredulity,[35] whilst another police officer appeared affronted when the victim requested that he arrange for her house to be fingerprinted after the stalker gained entry and did her laundry.[36] Obviously, police resources are finite and certain crimes demand priority attention, but is does not seem acceptable for a stalking victim to be told: 'tell us who it is and then we'll have a word with him.'

Even when victims were able to identify the stalker, the police were frequently disinclined to accept the victim's word in the absence of corroborating proof. One victim was harassed by her former boyfriend for almost three years. During a three month period, her car windscreen was smashed 17 times and she replaced 47 slashed tyres. The police refused to intervene as the victim had no direct proof that the stalker was responsible. Even when a friend of the victim caught the stalker crouched beside the car, which was found to have a punctured tyre, the police accepted the stalker's explanation that he had noticed the flat tyre and was merely taking a closer look at the damage. In this case, the police were not unsympathetic, but were stymied by the lack of evidence against the stalker:

> I do sympathise with her and I have absolutely no doubt that she is telling the truth but there is absolutely nothing that I can do. There isn't a single piece of evidence to support her allegations that this lad is responsible for the damage and, without evidence, there is no point in me arresting him.[37]

---

35 Case history 24.

36 Interview with victim's sister – Case history 7.

37 Case history 4.

There were situations in which the police were genuinely sympathetic regarding the victim's plight and were frustrated by their inability to intervene. The police officer quoted above continued:

> He was a cocky so-and-so. I knew he was responsible and he knew that I knew but we had nothing on him. Every single thing that he was accused of, he either had an alibi or a plausible explanation lined up. To be honest, nothing would have pleased me more than to see him in court but, at the end of the day, it was her word against his and, even though I believed her, I think he would have made a better witness in court.[38]

These examples present the dilemma that is at the heart of many stalking cases – whose version of events is to be preferred? Cases where the parties dispute the facts or the person accused of stalking denies responsibility can be incredibly difficult for the police to pursue. In one case, two women each accused the other of stalking and reported identical conduct. The police involved in the case were unable to decide whether one woman was responsible or whether they were targeting each other. The person at the centre of the dispute, the husband of one party and the employer of the other, reported that he was unable to determine which woman was telling the truth:

> I suppose, on balance, I do believe [my wife] because I know that [the employee] is a liar because I didn't have an affair with her, let alone father her baby. But the evidence at court against [my wife] did look damning and I can see why they found her guilty. I have this nightmare that they both did it to each other ... But I don't really know. All I know is that this has been the worst 18 months of my life.[39]

In circumstances such as these, the difficulties faced by the police in establishing sufficient evidence upon which to base a prosecution are clear. Many such problems are due not to the content of the law or to the attitudes of the police, but to the inherent nature of stalking cases. There is an element of 'sneakiness' and 'one-upmanship' about stalkers that suggests they will delight in creating a situation whereby there are beyond the reach of the law but in which all parties involved acknowledge are aware of the identity of the person responsible. This links to the characteristics of the stalker that were discussed previously, the urge to control and the need to establish ascendancy over the victim.

The final aspect of police involvement in stalking cases that caused the victims some concern was the failure of the police to keep them involved with the progress of their complaint, particularly as regards to whether or not the stalker was still in custody. Again, this was reflected by the findings of the Home Office research into stalking. Owing to the feelings of lack of autonomy and control commonly experienced by stalking victims, it may be an essential

---

38 Case history 4.
39 Case history 28.

element of the recovery process that the victim feels involved in the prosecution process. Moreover, the continuing and unpredictable nature of stalking makes it particularly important that the victim knows when the stalker is at large so that appropriate precautions can be taken. This was neatly encapsulated by the words of one stalking victim quoted in the Home Office research:

> Your whole life revolves around 'is he going to get out today?'. I want to know, I need to know because I don't just want to go to the door and see him there.[40]

There was no real consensus about the approach of the police leading up to the prosecution of the stalker – experiences appeared to vary between individual cases. Some victims reported that they were kept informed of the progress of the case and consulted about their wishes regarding the terms of the restraining order. Others had intermittent contact with the police and wished for a greater degree of involvement whilst others felt that the police dealt well with specific enquiries but would have preferred a situation whereby the police volunteered the information. Not all victims sought this degree of involvement. Some victims were content to allow the prosecution of the stalker to proceed, satisfied that the matter was being dealt with in an appropriate manner. Of the victims who wished to be kept informed, those experiencing a greater level of involvement generally expressed more favourable opinions regarding their experiences within the criminal justice system, even if the results of court proceedings were not favourable:

> I was devastated when he was acquitted but I accepted it because I knew the police and the prosecutor had done everything they could. Obviously, I wanted him to be convicted but, to be honest, the whole prosecution process made me feel better. Just watching him in the dock and knowing that he was suffering because of me really turned the tables and made me feel more able to cope. I thought that it would probably start up again after he was acquitted but it didn't. The police were great. They kept checking up on me after the trial to make sure I was alright. They seemed to think that he knew he'd had a lucky escape and wouldn't want to risk his freedom again and they might well be right. I don't know. It's stopped and I feel better. That's all I need to know.

For this victim, at least, the trial of the stalker was all part of the healing process. She was favourably impressed with the approach of the police throughout her case, feeling that they were as anxious to see the stalker convicted as she was. She described a constant level of support and involvement that restored her confidence to deal with her stalker. This was particularly important to her after the trial when she felt vulnerable to further victimisation. Other victims have not been so fortunate and have resented their exclusion from the prosecution process:

---

40 *Op cit*, Harris, fn 12, p 26.

> I only found out that he had been convicted when I read about it in the local paper. That was my case but I didn't have any part in it all. I know that he decided to plead guilty but I still needed to know. I deserved to know. I wanted to be there to see what happened. I phoned the police but they didn't know what had happened to him so I didn't know whether he was in prison or out waiting to get to me again. I should have been told what was happening.

This victim was aggrieved not just because she was not made aware of the stalker's sentence, but because she had wanted to play a part in the trial process, even if only as a spectator. To remove the victim from the prosecution process is to emphasise that the defendant is being prosecuted for contravening the law, a crime against the State, rather than for his conduct towards the victim. Obviously, this raises wider issues of the role of the victim in the criminal justice system, but it is an issue that is of particular importance in stalking cases. Should the mechanisms of justice operate without reference to the victim's needs? With a crime such as stalking, the harm to the victim cannot be remedied by pecuniary means, nor is it enough that the stalker is prosecuted. The psychological damage to the victim caused by the stalker needs to be addressed and if there is a role that the legal system can play in remedying this injury, surely it should be willing to do so.

Thus, victims often need information regarding the progress of their case and to feel involved in proceedings. Associated with this issue is the means by which information is accessible to the victim. Many victims found that a single officer was allocated to their case, which meant that if this officer were unavailable, the victim had either to wait or to explain the whole background of the case to another officer. Victims found this to be frustrating and a deterrent from approaching the police. The other extreme involved the absence of any co-ordination regarding the victim's complaint, with each incident being recorded separately, usually by different officers. Not only did the victim have to explain the history of the case on every occasion, but also this lack of association between the incidents meant that the seriousness of the case was often not appreciated by individual officers. This has the potential to seriously damage the chances of prosecution, as it is essential to establish a course of conduct. If each incident is recorded separately, incidents may not be associated with each other and vital evidence may be overlooked.

There was some evidence of good police practice in an attempt to ameliorate these problems. One notable example is the First Contact scheme in operation in the Flintshire region of the North Wales police authority. All police officers are given a simple sheet outlining the relevant provisions of the Protection from Harassment Act 1997.[41] If the police officer called to the scene is satisfied that the incident falls within the remit of the statute, a form is filled out that contains the details of the offender, the incident and the officer's

---

41 Examples of this and other first contact documentation can be found in Appendix 2.

contact details. This form is issued to the offender and is a formal warning that the conduct outlined constitutes harassment and any repetition of such behaviour will lead to arrest and prosecution. This serves to put the offender on notice that his conduct is causing harassment to another hence, should he repeat the conduct, he will not be able to argue that he did not know his conduct amounted to harassment of another. This process addresses the three elements necessary to constitute the offence of harassment. There are two clearly established incidents that have caused the victim harassment, hence her recourse to the police. The defendant is advised that he has caused harassment and made aware that further incidents would be deemed as intentional harassment and lead to his arrest, thus dealing with the mental element of the offence.

A copy of the form is passed to the Domestic Violence Officer, who keeps a central record of all potential stalking cases. The incident log in the police control room, where the report of the original incident is recorded, is dated to show that an official warning was issued, hence any other officer dealing with future incidents can easily track the history of the case. Moreover, the central administration of all stalking cases in one department ensures that all necessary information is collated together. The victim is advised to quote the reference number of the warning notice when making any further complaints to ensure that the officers make use of the system.

The issue of the warning notice serves three purposes. First, as has been discussed, it puts the defendant on notice that his conduct is unacceptable and that repetition will amount to the offence of harassment. This gives the defendant fair warning of the consequences of his actions and ensures that it is a straightforward matter to establish the requisite knowledge if a prosecution should follow. Secondly, even on the occasion of the first incident, when arrest is not an option, the issue of the warning notice reassures the victim that the police are taking the complaint seriously. The final aspect of this approach is beneficial to both the police and the victim. By ensuring that a particular unit is responsible for co-ordinating all complaints and warning notices, a small team of people who have easy access to the history of the case are always available to deal with the victim. This ensures that the victim is always able to reach somebody who is able to provide advice regarding the case and the police are able to keep all relevant information gathered together, which should lead to more effective case management.

Schemes such as First Contact go some way to addressing the problems experienced by victims in their dealings with police. A compulsory scheme outlining the action to be taken in all harassment cases should minimise negative reactions on the part of individual officers, although there will still remain an element of discretion regarding the decision as to whether to issue a warning notice. The Home Office research study found that many of the problems experienced by victims could be ameliorated if the police were given greater training in the use of the Protection from Harassment Act, which could usefully include information about schemes such as First Contact that would improve communications with victims.[42]

7.5.3 The approach of the courts to enforcement

Any law, however well drafted and comprehensive, will be ineffective if it is not enforced rigorously. There is evidence to suggest that cases brought under the Protection from Harassment Act are not being pursued with the rigour that is necessary to render the statute an effective weapon against stalking. As mentioned previously, von Heussen's comparative study into the prosecution and conviction rates under the Act in different Crown Prosecution Service regions noted a significant divergence between the figures in the regions to an extent that cannot be attributed to demographic differentials. She concludes that this divergence was due to the attitudes within the police forces to stalking cases, noting that a significant proportion of police forces failed to send a single representative to the training days that were available when the Protection from Harassment Act was introduced. The Home Office research study into the effectiveness of the Protection from Harassment Act found that the termination rate for harassment cases was 39%, a high figure when compared to the average termination rate for all crimes, which is 14%.[43] However, it was also noted that the highest termination rates occurred when the victims were known to each other; a feature shared with crimes such as rape and domestic violence.[44]

---

42 A scheme to overcome the problems of communication with all victims of crime was piloted in 1998. The One Stop Shop initiative aimed to establish a single source from which victims could receive information regarding the progress of their case. Despite the generally positive findings of the pilot study, the initiative has not been implemented nationally – Hoyle, Cape, Morgan and Saunders, 1998.

43 Harris, 2000, p 30.

44 Harris and Grace, 1999.

Figure 7.1   Complainant/suspect relationship and CPS decision

	Terminated	Proceeded with
Strangers	–	100
Acquaintances	38	62
Neighbours	46	54
Intimates	41	59
Total	39	61

This high rate of termination in cases where the victims are known to each other is attributed to the refusal of the complainant to proceed with the complaint. The Home Office research found that this was the reason given for one-third of the terminations and that in 63% of these, the defendant was the victim's partner or ex-partner. This factor could account for the reluctance of the authorities to intervene in cases involving harassment between couples:

> I mean, sometimes you wonder 'why bother?' – 24 hours later they're back in love and don't want to make a formal complaint.[45]

This may be true in some cases of harassment between partners, but it overlooks the fact that the withdrawal of the complaint may be due to a fear on behalf of the victim that a prosecution would exacerbate the problem as the defendant will not be imprisoned for long, if at all, and will have been angered by the prosecution. This links to the victim's perceptions of the level of protection that is available to them from the legal system. Many victims reported feeling that their problems would be over as soon as the police became involved, but that they were disappointed to discover that intervention by the police was not as effective as they expected.

In 47% of the cases that were discontinued, the court imposed a bind over on the defendant. This is regarded as a termination as the prosecution agrees to offer no evidence in return for the defendant agreeing to be bound over. The defendant is made aware that if the order is breached, he will be prosecuted for this as well as for the original offence. There are some doubts regarded the efficacy of such orders in general, and in harassment cases in particular, but prosecution lawyers tend to take a more favourable stance to their use, preferring to impose a bind over than to take no action at all.[46] As

---

45 Police officer quoted in Harris, 2000, p 30.
46 *Ibid*, p 31.

has been noted in Chapter 4, a defendant can be imprisoned for failing to agree to be bound over, but not for any subsequent breach of the order.

Particular problems are posed to the criminal justice system by mentally disordered offenders. Despite the prevalence of mental disorder in those accused of stalking, the Protection from Harassment Act contains no specific provisions dealing with this issue. Six per cent of the terminations in the Home Office research sample were due to the mental state of the defendant as it was felt that prosecution would not be in the public interest. Unless the defendant fits within the narrow parameters of the Mental Health Act 1983, there is little that can be done to address the core reason behind the stalking.[47] Treatment is not available as part of the legal disposal of the case and the defendant will be treated in the same was any other offender. This has ramifications for the likelihood of further offending by the stalker, as the root cause of his behaviour is not being addressed. If the stalking is manifested because of the pathology of the defendant, rather than deliberate or wilful disobedience of the law, the imposition of a criminal penalty is likely to prove an entirely ineffective measure. This issue is one that requires further research into the range of alternatives that are available.

The primary requirement of the majority of stalking victims is that the stalking should stop. Indeed, this is such a fundamental element that the cessation of stalking is one of the criteria against which the efficacy of the Protection from Harassment Act is to be measured. One feature of the Act that particularly aimed at the prevention of future stalking is the creation of the restraining order. In many cases, the imposition of the restraining order is the main aim of both the victim and the legal authorities:

> The complainants in these cases ... they are not bothered about what the punishment is going to be, they just want it to stop and if we can achieve that, then we have achieved something.[48]

Despite the attractiveness of the imposition of a restraining order in harassment cases, the Home Office research study found that they were imposed in only 56% of cases. Harris expresses surprise that they are not invariably used in all harassment cases:

> Given the perceived value of restraining orders, however, it is perhaps surprising that they were only imposed in around half of the convictions. It is not clear why they were not used in almost all other cases. It might reflect a belief in traditional measures and/or lack of faith in the new. Some practitioners appeared ignorant of the new measures. Other may have felt that

---

47 See Chapter 6.
48 Police officer quoted in Harris, 2000, p 37.

they were too draconian in some cases of a less serious nature. Sometimes prosecutors may have failed to raise the issue of a restraining order.[49]

In terms of the issue of the efficacy of the Protection from Harassment Act to prevent further harassment, the question is not solely whether a sufficient amount of restraining orders were issued, but whether their breach was enforced rigorously:

> Failure of enforcement completely undermines the significance of the order to start with.[50]

There is insufficient data currently available regarding the extent to which breaches of restraining order are prosecuted and this would appear to be a particularly important area for future research as the efficacy of the legislation is dependent upon rigorous enforcement. The strongest weapon in the armoury against stalkers would be significantly weakened if breach of the orders were not treated with the utmost seriousness.

The maximum penalty for breach of restraining order is five years' imprisonment. In the joined appeals in *R v Liddle, R v Hayes* against the sentences imposed for breach of restraining order under s 5 of the Protection from Harassment Act, the Court of Appeal took the opportunity to lay down some guidelines for sentencing.[51] Curtis J outlined a list of factors to be taken into account when determining sentence for breach of restraining order:

- Was the original offence a s 2 or a s 4 offence?
- Does the defendant have a history of disobedience of court orders?
- How serious was the defendant's conduct?
- Was there persistent misconduct or was this a solitary incident?
- What is the effect (physical and psychological) on the victim and does the defendant pose a risk to the victim and her family?
- What is the state of the defendant's mental health and is he willing to undergo treatment?
- What was the defendant's reaction to court proceedings – was there a guilty plea, does the defendant show remorse, is there recognition of the need for help?

Reference to these factors led the Court of Appeal to conclude that both Liddle and Hayes had been sentenced too harshly. Liddle's conduct was directed at his ex-wife, whom he persistently harassed despite the imposition of numerous injunctions and restraining orders. The conduct that led to the

---

49 Harris, 2000, p 56.
50 Magistrate quoted in *ibid*, p 39.
51 *R v Liddle, R v Hayes* [1999] 3 All ER 816.

current breach concerned a letter written to his wife and one incident where he spoke to her when they met accidentally. His original sentence of 21 months was reduced to one of 15 months' imprisonment.

Hayes had developed a fixation with a woman he did not know and repeatedly asked her out, despite her rejection of his advances. He was convicted of harassing her and was made subject to a lifetime restraining order, which he breached by ringing her doorbell and running away and by sending her a letter that disclosed knowledge of her daily life, suggesting that he had been keeping her under surveillance. His sentence of two years' imprisonment was reduced to 11 months.

The actual decisions regarding the two defendants' sentences suggest that Liddle's conduct was viewed more seriously than Hayes' by the Court of Appeal. The key factor that justified this appeared to be Liddle's persistent breach of court orders, although the pre-sentence report indicated that he had addressed his offending behaviour and no longer posed a threat to his ex-wife. This charge was the first against Hayes for breach of restraining order, which justified a lower sentence than Liddle despite the fact that Hayes, although not suffering from an identified mental disorder, was obsessed with his victim, but would not acknowledge that he had a problem or agree to treatment. Although no guidance was given by the Court of Appeal as to the weight to be attached to the various factors listed, it is clear that refusal to respond to the authority of the court was given greater weight than the other factors listed.

In addition to the guidance given regarding factors to be taken into account, Curtis J suggested that a 'short sharp sentence' will generally be appropriate for a first offence and that the starting point for a second infraction, on a guilty plea, should be around 15 months' imprisonment for a minor incident, with more serious conduct being fitted into the statutory framework up to the maximum five years' prescribed.

These guidelines provide an indication of the seriousness with which the courts will treat breaches of restraining orders. The list of factors to be taken into account is comprehensive and allows the courts to consider such matters as the impact of the conduct on the victim. Despite the absence of evidence as to the extent to which a breach of restraining order is pursued, it is clear that those prosecutions that do arise are likely to be treated extremely seriously.

The value of restraining orders is seen to be such that the extension of their use into other areas of criminal law has been proposed. The advisability of such an extension would require careful consideration and no comment is made upon this in the course of the Home Office research. Harris sees some value in the mandatory imposition of a restraining order in all harassment cases:

On the face of it, there appears to be some ground for considering whether restraining orders could not, with benefit, be deployed as a matter of course.

However, this begs the question of whether they do in fact achieve what they are intended to achieve: a cessation of harassment.[52]

This is the ultimate aim of the Protection from Harassment Act: to stop harassment and prevent its reoccurrence. The extent to which it achieves this purpose is questionable.

7.6 DOES THE PROTECTION FROM HARASSMENT ACT 1997 STOP STALKING?

Unfortunately, the answer to the question 'Does the Protection from Harassment Act stop stalking?' has to be 'Not always'. Some stalkers are deterred by the merest hint of police involvement, whilst others persist despite prolonged periods of imprisonment. For example, Anthony Burstow was imprisoned for three years following his conviction for inflicting grievous bodily harm upon his victim by causing her to suffer serious psychological harm. However, he continued to contact her by telephone and letter from within prison and appeared outside her house on the day she was released from prison. It appears that the determination to continue the pursuit of the victim sometimes transcends the deterrent effect of even the harshest prison sentence:

> They tend to reoffend and sometimes enforced separation through the courts is the only answer. Or enforced incarceration.[53]

An analysis of the experiences of stalkers and victims suggests that the extent to which the stalker is likely to be amenable to legal intervention is dependent upon the motivational forces involved. The tripartite typology based upon the driving force behind the stalking – the bad, the mad and the sad – can be used to good effect to illustrate the efficacy of different means of intervention.

The 'mad' stalker is likely to be delusional and will be convinced of the appropriateness of his behaviour. This stalker is not likely to be deterred by court intervention and this will not weaken his resolve to achieve his aim. Estimates as to the prevalence of mental illness in stalkers varies according to the criteria used, but Dr Petch estimates that 75% of stalkers suffer from a treatable mental disorder. Other estimates are lower, and this is clearly an issue that merits further investigation. Mental illness that leads to stalking requires treatment to remove the root cause of the offending behaviour. Such treatment will not be available in prison, but requires recourse to specialist professional treatment. The extent of the mental disorder will determine

---

52 Harris, 2000, pp 56–57.
53 Petch, E, quoted in 'Stalkers' (2000) *The Guardian*, 29 January.

whether this can be achieved on an outpatient basis or whether the stalker needs to be detained in an appropriate hospital. Many delusional disorders can be controlled with medication, but this requires that the offender seek treatment, something that they may not be prepared to do on a voluntary basis.

Despite some initial competition for 'ownership' of stalking, it finally became constructed as a problem for the legal profession. In certain cases, this is the most appropriate means of intervention, but the mentally disordered stalker may be impervious to legal measures. The Protection from Harassment Act makes no recognition of the need to address the mental health of the offender and, as such, is ineffective in offering anything more than a temporary respite to the victims of such stalkers.

There are currently insufficient resources to deal with mentally disordered stalkers, hence the proposal by Dr Petch to establish a specialist treatment centre for stalkers would appear to be the most appropriate course of action. Moreover, the law must make provision for mentally disordered stalkers to receive the treatment that is necessary to prevent further offending.

The 'sad' stalker may be the easiest of the three to deal with. Motivated by fundamental misunderstanding of the situation, he may not intend to cause distress to his victim, indeed the idea that his conduct would be anything other than well received may not have crossed his mind. It is frequently this offender who engages in *prima facie* innocuous conduct during the course of romantic pursuit. His conduct is only objectionable because it is unwanted and not because of its nature. Alternatively, the 'sad' stalker may be perfectly aware that his conduct is not welcomed but hopes that, in time, the recipient's attitude may change. Both types of 'sad' stalking have their origins in ordinary courtship behaviour, with the difference being that the pursuer's interest is not reciprocated. If this is communicated to the pursuer, who ceases pursuit in response to this, no problem arises, but if the message is not clear or the pursuer does not, or will not, understand the message, the repeated pursuit of the other will constitute stalking.

In many cases, the stalker will desist immediately when it is made clear to him that his conduct is unwanted. Alternatively, the stalker who hopes that he will convince the victim to change her mind will soon lose his determination when warned by the police that his conduct is potentially criminal. This is why the First Contact scheme described earlier is such a useful device. Once a warning has been issued by the police, the stalker can be left in no doubt that his conduct is unwelcome. In the light of this, any decision to continue should rightly be dealt with under the Protection from Harassment Act. However, the defendant is made aware of the possible consequences of his conduct at an early stage and given the opportunity to desist. Therefore, cases based upon a genuine misunderstanding about the reception of the conduct or boundaries of acceptable courtship behaviour will not necessarily lead to criminal prosecution. This is particularly important in cases where the conduct is innocuous and the rejection is not clearly communicated to the other party. The law must not be used without warning against those whose only fault is that they are socially inept. Nonetheless, the victims of such ineptitude have the right to the same form of protection against harassing conduct as those who are deliberately targeted. A warning system seems the ideal means of achieving the correct balance between the rights and interests of the parties in such cases. Even though the majority of convictions under s 2 of the Protection from Harassment Act result in an conditional discharge combined with a restraining order, this is still a criminal conviction, which may not be entirely appropriate in many 'sad' stalking cases. Alternatively, the civil remedy may be a more appropriate starting point in such cases. The difficulty with this is that the same conduct is the basis for the criminal offence and the tort of harassment, but no indication is given as to the circumstances in which each course of action is preferable.

Finally, the 'bad' stalker, who knows that his conduct is causing distress and intends that it should do so. There may be a certain degree of overlap with the 'sad' stalker, as persistent rejection can provoke anger and resentment which leads the stalker to transform into a malicious 'bad' stalker. It is hoped that early intervention by means of a warning system would prevent the escalation of 'sad' stalkers into 'bad' stalkers. Some stalkers, however, are 'bad' from the outset. These may be relational or revenge stalkers and are recognised as being the hardest to stop.[54] It would certainly appear that the criminal law is the best means of intervention here. Provided the law intervenes at an early enough stage in the harassment, the maximum penalty of six months' imprisonment is sufficient, especially when combined with a restraining order, breach of which is a more serious offence. The difficulty is that the 'bad' stalker's determination to continue harassment frequently seems to render him immune to any form of legal intervention, even imprisonment. However, not every deliberate stalker will persist to this extent in the face of arrest and imprisonment. It is very much a matter for the individual stalker, who will persist until the detriment of arrest and potential imprisonment outweighs whatever satisfaction he derives from his pursuit of the victim. The difficulty is that, in some cases, the intervention of the police appears to aggravate the stalker and merely adds to the list of grievances against the victim. For the law to be effective against the 'bad' stalker, it must have the capacity for a penalty that acts as a disincentive to continue the harassment of the victim. Although the offence of harassment does not contain such a penalty and the more serious offence of causing fear of violence is narrowly framed, the availability of a restraining order, breach of which attracts a more severe penalty of up to five years' imprisonment, would appear to fulfil this requirement. This is particularly so in the light of the

---

54   Petch, E, quoted in 'Stalkers' (2000) *The Guardian*, 29 January.

Court of Appeal decision in *R v Liddle, R v Hayes* which sets out guidelines on sentencing for breach of a restraining order.

7.7 RECOMMENDATIONS FOR IMPROVEMENTS IN PROTECTION

7.7.1 Scope of the Protection from Harassment Act

One area in which there is a great need for improvement is in the scope of the legislation. There is a clear gap in the protection offered by the offence of harassment under s 2 and the more serious offence of causing fear of violence under s 4. Although an increase in penalty for the offence of harassment would facilitate the imposition of a heavier penalty in more serious harassment cases that fall short of the requirements of s 4, it is submitted that the creation of a third offence to bridge the gap between the existing offences would be a preferable course of action. The creation of an offence of intentional harassment as a third offence in the hierarchy of harassment offences would serve to delineate between degrees of culpability in harassing conduct and provide a more severe penalty for those who deliberately cause alarm or distress. This would also be an appropriate second offence in situations whereby a conviction under s 2 did not include a restraining order to provide for more serious treatment of subsequent harassment.

Equally, some clarification, whether by amendment to the Act or by judicial intervention, is needed of some of the key terms of the offences. This is particularly relevant to this notion of the need for a nexus between incidents that the courts have begun to address. The law regarding indirect harassment is extremely unclear. A clear ruling on the appropriateness of an offence of 'harassment by hearsay' is desirable, either to confirm its existence and set down guidelines for its application, or to restrict the law to directly experienced harassment. Problems are also evident in relation to the idea of group harassment. All that can be discerned from the current case law is that family members living in the same household will constitute a closely knit definable group, but that neighbours will not. Further guidance is needed in this area.

7.7.2 Mental health provisions

It is clear that a substantial number of stalkers may act as they do because of psychiatric illness or personality disorder. The Protection from Harassment Act provides no means for such stalkers to receive treatment and the provisions of the Mental Health Act 1983 appear excessively narrow. An amendment to the Protection from Harassment Act could facilitate the psychiatric evaluation in all stalking cases where it appears necessary. This would identify those 'mad' stalkers who are in need of treatment rather than punishment and measures could be introduced to ensure that treatment was available. Although such a procedure would be costly, it would deal with the underlying cause of the harassment and may prove cost effective in the longer term. A specialist centre such as that proposed by Dr Petch could be established and convicted stalkers could be referred for treatment on an in-patient or out-patient basis, as appropriate in each set of individual circumstances. This could benefit the stalker, who would have the opportunity to receive specialist care that could prevent re-offending. This would be of obvious benefit to the victim, who currently receives only temporary respite whilst the stalker is incarcerated.

Such a centre would be staffed by experts with knowledge of the unique aspects of stalking pathology. This would have a more general beneficial affect of improving the stock of available knowledge on stalkers and enhance the prospects of successful intervention. The centre could provide an appropriate environment for further research into stalking and could address such issues as whether stalker/victim mediation would be valuable and advisable. Dr Petch proposes to establish such a centre that would not just provide treatment for stalkers, but would employ expert staff to deal with the treatment and counselling of victims of stalking.

7.7.3 Police training

A great deal of dissatisfaction was evident amongst stalking victims with the way in which the police react to stalking cases. The two predominant concerns appear to be a lack of understanding and sympathy for the plight of stalking victims and the lack of continuity in dealing with stalking cases. Although greater training of the police in general would go some way towards ameliorating both of these problems, a preferable solution, it is submitted, could be the creation of specialist units within police forces to deal with stalking cases. This would limit the need for thorough training to a far smaller number of officers and ensure that experts were available to deal with this complex area of law. The creation of stalking units would provide an automatic point of referral for all stalking cases, thus there would be less need for all police officers to be trained to deal with stalking. The presence of a small team of specialists within each police force would obviate the need for victims constantly to reiterate the facts of their case to a new officer every time a fresh incident occurs. This would provide a greater level of continuity for stalking victims and would improve the efficiency of the administration of stalking cases.

7.7.4 Greater consideration of the needs of the victim

It frequently appears that the needs of the stalking victim are overlooked once the criminal justice system becomes involved in a case. One Crown Prosecution Service solicitor exemplified this:

> There are no victims in the criminal justice system. There are just prosecution witnesses.

Although this attitude towards victims of crime may prevail regardless of the nature of the crime, it can be particularly damaging in stalking cases, where victims tend to feel disempowered and deprived of control by the process of victimisation. The law should seek to restore that which the criminal has destroyed, thus the victim's needs should be taken into account.

The creation of specialist units within the police should go some way towards addressing this point, as the victim would be clear about whom to contact within the police force. The smaller units of specially trained officers may lead to a greater level of communication between police and victim, thus providing the police with a greater awareness of the victim's needs. The victim should be informed of the progress of his or her case so that the choice as to whether or not to attend court, if not required as a witness, can be made. As has been discussed, the ability to participate in the prosecution process is an immensely valuable part of the recovery process for some victims. Certainly, victims should be kept informed of the stalker's release from prison so that he or she can be mentally prepared to deal with the reappearance of the stalker.

There is a need for greater availability of information for stalking victims. A worrying number of victims encountered during the course of this research had little accurate knowledge of their legal position. This was particularly true as regards the civil law. Some information campaign could be used to raise awareness both of stalking as an issue and of the options available to stalking victims.

Finally, some provision for the counselling of victims would be beneficial. The psychological impact of stalking victimisation can be immense and the disruption to the lifestyle of the victim almost unparalleled. The creation of a specialist treatment centre for stalkers has been discussed, but this ought, as proposed by Dr Petch, to include facilities for the treatment and counselling of stalking victims. The wrong caused by stalking victimisation cannot be remedied by the imprisonment of the stalker and the availability of a restraining order. There are profound psychological ramifications of stalking victimisation that necessitate the availability of specialist counselling for all stalking victims who wish to partake of such a service. To deal with the stalker is only addressing half of the problem that arises from stalking – it is essential that the legal system does not ignore the needs of the victims.

These recommendations would strengthen the efficacy of the Protection from Harassment Act and vastly improve the situation for victims of stalking.

7.8 CONCLUSION

The Protection from Harassment Act was introduced to deal with an extremely complex problem. Every case of stalking appears to be unique, which is hardly surprising given the infinite combinations of conduct, motivation, relationship and impact that are possible. There is no prototypical stalking case, stalking victim or stalker. As such, any statute introduced to combat stalking faces a significant challenge. In many respects, the Protection from Harassment Act provides an effective response to stalking, as it is sufficiently flexible to encompass any manifestation of stalking, however unusual. The introduction of the restraining order is probably the most important element of the legislation as this provides a means for the Act not only to tackle harassment that has occurred, but also to seek to prevent future harassment. The low level offence under s 2 provides an effective means of early intervention that may prevent many stalking cases escalating into more serious situations. Perhaps the most telling testament in support of the Protection from Harassment Act comes from notorious stalker, Anthony Burstow:

> I think it would have made a difference in my case. One of the things that surprised me early on was that the police were powerless to stop me so because of that, I didn't stop. When it got to the stage that they did start to arrest me, it was too late for me to stop – it had all gone too far. By the time the police got involved, I had invested too much in it – I had too much resentment against her to be able to stop. I wanted to but I couldn't – it had got too personal, too much was at stake ... By the time I got sent to prison, I was too immersed in the whole thing to get out and the arrest and trial was just something else to hold against her, along with the loss of my home, my job, my marriage, and all the other things that I blamed her for. I needed to be frightened off before I turned bitter. After that, it was too late. Now I don't think I'll ever be able to stop.[55]

---

55 Interview with Anthony Burstow, 29 March 1999.

APPENDIX 1: CASE HISTORIES

Case history 1

The 42 year old female victim was stalked for nine months by a man she met during the course of her employment at the Citizen's Advice Bureau. When she declined to deal with his problems (which she suspected to be manufactured in order to gain attention), he followed her home. On every occasion that the victim was home alone in the evening, the stalker stood on the pavement outside her house and stared towards the downstairs window. The victim became anxious and experienced difficulties in sleeping. She gave up her employment and rarely ventured outside of her home unless she was in company. The victim found the police to be 'extremely unhelpful, rude and condescending'. On the one occasion that the police approached the stalker, the victim could see the three men laughing together. It was following this incident that the police officers asked the victim's husband if she were menopausal or if he thought that she was fantasising about having a young lover. The stalking stopped as suddenly as it started with no noticeable reason for the cessation. The victim finds herself to be far more cautious and apprehensive than she was previously and felt unable to take a job working with the public for fear of future victimisation. She had worked for the Citizen's Advice Bureau for 12 years.

Case history 2

The 27 year old female victim was stalked for four and a half months by a work colleague whom she had believed was a close platonic friend. Although the stalker had initially sought a romantic relationship with the victim, she did not feel that he was particularly upset by her refusal. During the initial stages of a violent campaign of harassment, including extensive damage to the victim's property and threatening messages left on her answering machine, the victim turned to the stalker for support. She described her fluctuation between suspicion of her colleague and guilt for suspecting him as one of the worst aspects of the stalking. The victim sought medical assistance for sleeplessness and anxiety and was prescribed Prozac. When she felt unable to cope with the situation any longer, she left her job and moved back to her home town to live with her parents. This ended the stalking. The victim reported that the police attended promptly when she reported individual incidents, but that she never saw the same officers twice and grew tired of retelling the background to every police officer she met. As the identity of her stalker was unknown, the police were unable to offer the victim any assistance, although every incident was recorded.

Case history 3

The 23 year old male victim was stalked for 'several months' after ending his relationship with an 18 year old woman. Initially, she restricted herself to waiting for the victim after work and begging him to return to her, but later her conduct became increasingly erratic. The stalker would shout abuse at the victim in his place of work, approach his family and friends and tell them lies about the victim (including telling his 10 year old sister that he had been seriously injured in a car accident). The situation culminated with the arrest of the victim on suspicion of attempted murder after the brakes on her car were cut and she was badly injured in an accident. The victim was able to establish that he was at work during the period of time in which the damage had been caused to the stalker's vehicle. Three days after her release from hospital following the car accident, the stalker entered the victim's place of work and cut her wrists in front of the victim and several of his colleagues. She received in-patient care in a psychiatric unit and the victim has not heard from her since. He felt that the incident created a bad atmosphere at his work place and has since found alternative employment. The victim was not happy about the way he was treated by the police, feeling that they automatically believed the stalker without waiting to hear his version of events.

Case history 4

This victim was stalked for two and a half years by her former boyfriend when she was just 16. The relationship had become extremely 'intense', so the victim suggested that they 'have a break' for a few weeks. He told her: 'you may have finished with me but I haven't finished with you – it takes two people to end a relationship.' He took to waiting for the victim outside her place of work and would sit for hours just staring up at her bedroom window. She took to staying with friends to avoid him. The victim experienced extensive damage to the car that her parents bought her for her 17th birthday – she replaced 17 new windscreens and 37 new tyres in a three month period. The victim felt that police tried to be helpful, but that they could not act without proof and nobody ever saw him damage her car. Even when a friend caught him bending down next to the car, which was found to have a flat tyre, he convinced the police he had noticed that it was flat and was checking to see if it was damaged. The stalking ended when the victim started a college course in a distant town.

Case history 5

The 45 year old male victim was stalked by a woman who was a mature student at the college at which he worked as a lecturer. He noticed that she was always staying behind to ask advice, which he noted was of an increasingly personal nature, but did not think that anything was amiss until she became virtually hysterical when he returned an essay to her that he had awarded quite a poor mark. The next day, he was suspended from working pending an investigation into alleged sexual impropriety with the stalker. During the period leading up to the hearing, the stalker would call him at home and shout obscenities at the victim and his wife. She told the college authorities and the victim's family that she was carrying his child. The stress became to much for the victim's wife, who left with the children to live with her parents. Even when the internal hearing exonerated the victim, he felt that he was distrusted by the staff and students alike and sought another post in a distant town. The victim was particularly aggrieved by the treatment he received from the police, who advised him that the woman would stop shouting in the street if he went out to speak to her. He felt that the police were far more inclined to arrest him than the victim.

Case history 6

This 23 year old female victim was stalked for nine weeks by a stranger who she smiled at whilst waiting for a bus. The man took to following her home after this and she could see him lurking in the bushes watching the house. He started to waylay her and ask why she was ignoring him. She told him to 'get lost' in no uncertain terms and it was after this that the damage to her property and obscene telephone calls began. The victim arranged to spend the weekend with her sister to get a break from her problems with the stalker, but returned to find that he had forced entry into her home and all her possessions were destroyed or damaged with threatening messages painted onto the walls. The police offered her a panic button and advised her to buy heavy duty locks for the doors, but the victim was too frightened to remain in her home. She left to live with her sister and refused to return to the premises even to collect what remained of her possessions. She now suffers from panic attacks and is not comfortable leaving the house alone. The victim found the police to be sympathetic and helpful, but knew that they were unable to provide sufficient protection to ensure that she was safe from the stalker. As she did not know his name or anything about him, the police were unable to identify who was responsible, thus were unable to take action against him.

Case history 7

This victim committed suicide when she was 30 years old, exactly one year after being raped. In this interview, her sister explained that the victim had been having problems with a stalker for a 'few months' prior to the rape and believed that one of her work colleagues was responsible, although she was not sure which one. The stalking started with gifts and flowers left on her car and at her desk at work. The victim noticed that personal items had started to go missing from her home and she feared that the stalker had found a means to gain entry to the building. The victim was in the habit of leaving 'post-it' notes around the house to remind her to do things. One day she wrote two notes as she was leaving for work – 'buy bread' and 'do the laundry'. When she returned home from work, she found a loaf of bread on the kitchen table and the washing machine half way through its wash cycle. The victim decided to give the stalker a clear message that she was not interested, so she collected together all the gifts that had been left for her and burned them in her front garden. Two days later she was raped by an intruder who was wearing a balaclava. The police refused to link the stalking and the rape. The victim resigned from her job and made no effort to find alternative employment as she became increasingly withdrawn. One year after the rape, she committed suicide.

Case history 8

This female victim was stalked by her ex-husband for approximately two years after their marriage ended. The stalker left the victim to set up home with another woman. The victim saw nothing of her ex-husband and eventually met a new partner. It was at this stage that the problems began. The ex-husband would force his way into the victim's home and smash things whilst shouting abuse at the victim in the presence of her children. Her new partner was 'warned off' and refused to have any contact with her. The road outside her home and her place of work were painted with the words 'slag' and 'whore' in large red letters. An extensive selection of unsolicited goods arrived at the victim's home and she had to change her telephone number owing to the number of telephone calls she received from men who had seen her advertised as a prostitute. The police appeared reluctant to intervene, especially as they seemed to accept the stalker's story that the victim was doing these things herself so that the court would refuse him access to the children. After two years of constant harassment, the stalker met another woman and the harassment stopped.

Case history 9

This case involved two 12 year old girls. The victim was a popular girl with plenty of friends. Feeling sorry for the stalker, who always seemed 'left out', she tried to befriend her. Almost immediately, the stalker seemed to want exclusive rights to the victim – 'if we're friends, what do you want other friends for?'. The victim's parents became concerned at the amount of time that the other child was spending in their home and encouraged their daughter to spend more time with other friends. The stalker took to standing outside the victim's home for hours at a time, making all the family uncomfortable. During the summer holidays, the situation escalated to such an extent that the victim was sent to stay with relatives for a month. During this time, the victim's parents received silent telephone calls, had dog excrement pushed through their letter box and all the tyres on their car let down on several occasions. The victim dreaded returning to school and refused to go for the first week. When she finally agreed to return, she found she had been 'sent to Coventry' by her schoolmates, including those who had previously been her friends. It transpired that the stalker had told the other children that the victim had 'made a pass' at her during the summer holiday. The stress of being ostracised by her friends led the victim to refuse to return to school and her parents were forced to arrange to send her to a different school. Almost 20 years later, the victim becomes distressed when discussing the incident. She reports that it 'knocked' her confidence so much that she had never been able to return to being the lively and outgoing person that she was. At the time, there was no question of police involvement and the victim had requested that her parents did not involve the school.

Case history 10

This 14 year old stalker developed an obsession with a woman whom he saw on his way to school every day. He claims that she was always dressed provocatively, so he assumed that she wanted his attention. He followed her to find out where she lived and spent hours sitting on the bench opposite her house, hoping to catch a glimpse of her. On one occasion, he attempted, unsuccessfully, to break into her house when she was at work 'to find out more about her'. His obsession eventually led him to take hold of the victim as she walked past him and try to feel her breasts. A passer-by intervened and the stalker was arrested. He refused to discuss the events that followed, but maintained that it was the victim's fault for encouraging him. The victim declined to be interviewed.

Case history 11

This case involved multiple victims who were all inhabitants of the same village. Approximately 20 families were targeted by an unknown stalker, who made silent telephone calls, rang doorbells in the middle of the night, was seen standing in the shadows watching different houses. Women at home alone, or with young children, were the main victims. Despite several meetings in the village, the inhabitants were unable to ascertain who was responsible and the stalker was never identified. The conduct continued for approximately eight months. The victim interviewed was a teenager at the time and recalls sitting in the cupboard under the stairs with her babysitter. She remembers that at least one family moved away from the village at this time and thinks that this was due to what happened. She says that she became very safety conscious and is never comfortable spending time at home alone after dark.

Case history 12

This stalking case has continued for 13 years and is unusual in that it involves a single incident that occurs every year. The victim receives a card depicting a new-born baby every year on or around the date at which she once had an abortion. She believes that her partner from the time is responsible, but has no proof. She has never discussed the problem with anyone other than a counsellor. She feels unable to put the abortion behind her and experiences periods of extreme depression, particularly around September, which is when the cards arrive. The victim has attempted suicide twice because of her depression. She is in a relationship, but refuses to discuss the possibility of having children with her partner, an issue which she says is causing tension between them. She believes that it would be dangerous for her to have a child in case it provoked the stalker into violence.

Case history 13

Twenty-three members of the same health club received repeated silent telephone calls over a seven month period. The caller was eventually identified as one of the receptionists from the club who had targeted these particular woman owing to their successful weight loss. She felt that they were taunting her with their improved figures and that they were contemptuous of her for failing to lose weight. This stalker revelled in the distress she had caused, saying that it 'served them right'. She expressed sorrow that she had not been able to get hold of a 'voice changer' so that she could have sounded like a man, because then she would have been able to threaten the women to 'really make them pay'.

Case history 14

This 21 year old man was stalked by his girlfriend when he sought to end their relationship. She was determined that they should not split up and made sure that she 'accidentally' bumped into him on regular occasions. She was very devious, such as wheedling information about the victim's plans from his friends and family. The victim felt that he couldn't go anywhere without bumping into the stalker – 'honestly, I saw more of her after we split up than I did when we were together'. The victim became annoyed at the stalker's persistence and took greater steps to seek to avoid her. He returned home one evening to find her lying naked in his bed, having sneaked into the house when his mother popped out to the garden. The victim eventually decided to agree to go back out with the stalker as he felt that this gave him an element of control over the extent of their contact. They meet once a week. The victim dreads these meetings and wishes he could discontinue them, but says it is easier to deal with than the stalker's constant presence.

Case history 15

This victim was targeted by another woman who was angry that the victim had become romantically involved with the stalker's former partner. This led to a protracted period of harassment that has spanned almost 10 years. The stalker has caused severe damage to the victim's car, made repeated abusive telephone calls, causes numerous pizzas to be delivered to the victim and frequently orders taxis for the early hours of the morning. Unsolicited goods arrived frequently, as did various salespersons, all of whom believed that they had an appointment with the victim. The victim's employer was telephoned by a person purporting to be a police officer who warned him that the victim had been dismissed from three jobs for stealing from her employer. The most unpleasant conduct came when the stalker convinced three young lads who had been arrested for possession of drugs to tell the police that the victim was their supplier. Her family home was searched and, although no drugs were found, the victim found the experience to be extremely disturbing. She became withdrawn and the doctor prescribed anti-depressants. This made her feel detached from reality and she left her job to spend all day sitting in her bedroom staring out of the window. Eventually, the stalking stopped and the victim regained some of her confidence. The harassment continues sporadically with as much as a year passing between incidents. Nevertheless, the victim is convinced that it will never end.

Case history 16

This victim was targeted by the former wife of her partner, who blamed her for 'interfering' in her marriage, despite the fact that the couple had split up before the victim met either of them. Despite having changed her telephone number on several occasions, the victim is persistently targeted with silent telephone calls. She thinks that the stalker is able to find her new number as she is self-employed and has to make her telephone number available to business contacts. The stalking became worse when it became apparent that cards advertising the victim's services as a prostitute were being displayed in telephone kiosks in the King's Cross area of London. The victim also received membership packs from dating agencies which made it clear that another person had used the victim's details to join. The victim had limited success in convincing the police to intervene, so she took civil action and successfully obtained an injunction against the stalker. This appears to have ended the stalking.

Case history 17

This victim is a 27 year old student who was targeted by a fellow student who resented how popular the victim was. Initially, the conduct took the form of repeated silent telephone calls, with the maximum number received in any one evening being 112. The calls became increasingly frequent and the victim was advised to unplug the telephone from the socket so that the stalker would think that it was ringing but it would not really make any noise. After several evenings of peace, the victim was horrified when a large boulder was thrown through her bedroom window during the night, showering the bed with broken glass. The next morning, a glazier arrived to mend the window before the victim had even had a chance to telephone for quotes. Apparently, the booking had been made a week in advance in the victim's name. The victim found the police to be relatively sympathetic, but were told that they could not help unless they were told who the stalker was. The victim was infuriated by this and, with the help of two friends, made lists of all the people who could be responsible. By a process of elimination, they correctly identified the stalker and confronted her. The victim reported that the stalker was so distressed that she agreed not to go to the police provided the conduct did not reoccur. There have been no further incidents.

Case history 18

This stalker was romantically attracted to a work colleague and asked her out on several occasions. She did not wish to go out with him and, to avoid hurting his feelings, she made numerous excuses not to do so. In an effort to maintain good relations with him, the victim always thanked him for asking her and said that she might like to go out on another occasion. She did not intend for this to encourage the stalker – she believed that the message was clear, but that she was merely 'softening the blow'. The stalker, however, was encouraged by her attitude and kept asking her out and also took to leaving gifts on her desk at work. The victim finally had enough and reported this to her employer, who suspended the stalker. This surprised the stalker, so he stormed around to the victim's home and hammered on the door, demanding an explanation. It was at this stage that he was arrested and charged with the offence of harassment.

Case history 19

This 23 year old female victim was stalked by a man who believed that they had been lovers in a previous existence and that a 'karmic link' bound them together in all future lives. The insistence with which the stalker pursued her frightened the victim. He would wait outside her place of work and follow her as she drove home, trying to find where she lived. He ultimately obtained her address by posing as an Interflora delivery driver with a large bouquet of flowers for the victim on her day off. One of her colleagues gave the stalker the address. Observation of the victim's home led the stalker to realise that the victim had a husband and small child. Presumably to rid himself of those who impeded his access to the victim, the stalker waited until the victim was not at home and set fire to the house. Despite the presence of several witnesses, the stalker was not caught. The stress of the situation caused the victim's husband to accuse her of leading the man on and the couple separated. The victim finally became aware of the full circumstances when she was approached by the stalker's girlfriend, who was trying to get the stalker to seek psychiatric help.

Case history 20

This victim was stalked by her former partner when she felt forced to leave the relationship to escape the rigid system of rules that he wanted to live by. This included having towels of a particular size for a bath and another size for the shower (you get wetter in the bath!) and insisting that ornaments be affixed in place with Velcro so that they did not get moved and destroy the symmetry of the room. The longer the relationship lasted, the greater the control the stalker took over the victim's life. He redecorated her flat whilst she was away and traded her car in without asking her because there was a different model that he wanted her to drive. The stalker did not accept the end of the relationship and made repeated attempts to contact the victim at work, both by telephone and in person. This caused her difficulties at work. He bought her extravagant presents in an attempt to win her back, even booking a two week holiday in Athens as a surprise. The victim eventually decided to move to get away from the stalker and arranged to transfer to another branch of her employer's company.

Case history 21

This victim was stalked by her employer, who developed an obsession with her. When she sought to avoid the work place, he made continual excuses to call at her home. This made the victim extremely uncomfortable, thus she refused to answer the door to him. The stalker would move around the outside of the building, trying all the doors and windows. The victim would hide under the bed in fear that the stalker would force his way into the house. Things came to a head when the victim found out that her work colleagues had all been told that she was having an affair with her boss. She left the job and sought employment elsewhere. The stalking did not continue.

Case history 22

This victim suffered a particularly traumatic ordeal at the hands of an obsessive and violent partner. He would not allow her to have access to any money or to have friends that he did not approve of. He monitored her telephone calls and wrote down the mileage on her car every morning so that she could not go anywhere other than to college and back. He was extremely violent if she ever disagreed with him, hence she did not protest when he told her that he had decided that they would get married. She started to save up money and waited for a chance to escape from him. Somehow he found out what was going on and beat her viciously and raped her. After that, the victim dared show no sign of defiance, but waited for her first chance to get away. The stalker waited outside in the car whilst she went to have her wedding dress fitted so the victim dashed out of the back door of the shop and ran to the train station where she boarded the first train. With no money and no possessions, she arrived in a strange town and had to spend the night walking around. She does not regret this at all despite the fact that she has not been able to get in touch with her mother for five years.

Case history 23

This victim worked as a sales assistant in a large clothes shop. She noticed that two women seemed to be acting suspiciously and checked their credit card thoroughly when they attempted to pay for their goods. The card did turn out to be stolen and the women were arrested. One of the women decided to take revenge for this and set out to destroy every aspect of the victim's life. She caused her so much trouble at work by sending in friends to complain about poor service that the victim was advised to start looking for another job. She was followed home and threatened by a large gang of youths, received abusive telephone calls and was pushed into a busy street and almost hit by a car. The conduct ended after three months when the victim presumes that the stalker either grew tired of tormenting her or was imprisoned for more offending behaviour.

Case history 24

This victim was targeted by a stalker who met her once and decided that she was the only girl for him. He sent her love poetry, flowers and gifts, but did not reveal his identity. As time passed, he sent notes that berated her for not responding to his attentions. The door handles and windows of her home were smeared with excrement and the telephone would ring constantly through the night. The family went away for a short break to get some respite from the harassment, but returned to find that the man had been inside the house and had done the cleaning and left a bag of groceries in the kitchen. The police found this amusing when the incident was reported to them. The victim started to engage in self-harm and became increasingly withdrawn, so her mother hired a private detective to find out who was tormenting her daughter. This took two days and the police did act when they were presented with photographs of the stalker urinating through the victim's letterbox and throwing paint over the porch of the house. The victim's mother resented the fact that she had to pay a private investigator to do that which she considered to police ought to do.

Case history 25

This victim was targeted by a stranger whom she cannot recall meeting, but who developed a whole fantasy life around her. Initially, the stalker sent gifts and presents, but the victim began to receive distressing messages. The first of these told her that her parents had been seriously injured in an accident which caused her to rush to the hospital only to find that no such accident had taken place. Various parcels arrived for the victim, containing occult literature and erotic underwear. The victim noticed that her possessions were not always as she left them when she returned from work, and suspected that someone was getting into her home. The police were extremely supportive and watched the flat whilst the victim was at work. The man, who was arrested using a key, was a former tenant of the flat. He denied causing the victim harassment and argued so convincingly that he and the victim were partners who had argued, that the police almost believed him. The damning finding was two diaries that the stalker had been keeping. One of these detailed the fantasy life of the stalker and victim, including lists of things to do to prepare for their wedding. The other was a bizarre catalogue of hatred that included plans to kill the victim, cut her body into pieces and send bits of it to her friends and relatives. The victim knows that the stalker was arrested, but does not know what happened to him, and she has since moved away from the area.

Case history 26

This victim has moved to 14 different towns in the past three years in an attempt to escape from her stalker. The stalker has absolutely no idea that he is causing the victim distress, but is concerned that she will not go out with him because she is being stalked and she is afraid that the stalker might use violence against him. This stalker has an absolute belief that he and the victim are in love and will be together – as soon as she gets rid of her stalker. The victim hates the stalker with a passion and claims that she is afraid that she will snap and kill him. She has few employment prospects, despite having a good degree, because she has had to move so often, thus has no real work experience. She is on anti-depressants and sees a psychologist twice a month.

Case history 27

This victim was involved in an extremely violent relationship with her stalker before she managed to escape. Despite the fact that she moves to a different town every six weeks and has changed her name on three separate occasions, her stalker still manages to track her down. She claims that he does nothing else – he gave up his job so that he could spend more time looking for her. This victim lives in constant fear of the stalker and never goes anywhere without a small bag containing a change of clothes and some toiletries in case she has to make a hasty escape. Despite being extremely frightened, she does not seem discontent with her nomadic existence. She claims that living like this is a vast improvement on how her life was when she lived with the stalker.

Case history 28

This case is difficult, as it is impossible to ascertain who is the stalker and who is the victim. Two women are making virtually identical allegations of stalking against each other. This stems from rivalry over a man, the husband of one of them. The other claims to be his mistress and to have a child by him, a fact that he hotly disputes. He acknowledges the ill-feeling between the two women, but says he does not know what started it or who is actually stalking whom. He claims that his worst nightmare is that it will turn out that they are both stalking each other.

Case history 29

The victim here is a radio personality who is being targeted by a young girl who claims that they are having an affair. The victim is a homosexual who has never had any interest in young women. The stalker appears at all of the victim's public engagements and tries to engage him in conversation. Recently, she managed to locate his home and has spent several nights sitting on his front door step. Although this victim is irritated rather than alarmed, he wants the girl to keep away from him, but cannot think of any way to achieve that.

Case history 30

Although this victim was estranged from her husband, it never occurred to her that the person responsible for stalking her for nearly two years, causing tens of thousands of pounds worth of damage to her property, was the man to whom she was married for 12 years. She claimed that the break-up was perfectly amicable and that she was astounded to discover that he had been harbouring this secret resentment against her. In this two year period, the victim has had her car resprayed twice after paint stripper was poured over it, rewired her house after the stalker broke in whilst she was only holiday, blocked all the sinks and turned the taps on, and paid almost £5,000 to have her garden cleared after a load of farmyard slurry was dumped over it. She no longer has any contact with her ex-husband, although she still allows the children to visit him once a fortnight. The stalker claims that he was incensed by the way that his wife seemed to 'flourish' after the end of their relationship and that he resented this so much that he decided to make her suffer.

Case history 31

This victim was targeted by a sales assistant at the local garden centre, who developed a crush on her. As she had an account with the garden centre, the stalker found her address and kept turning up with gifts of plants and gardening books for her. He offered to help her in the garden, but she quickly became alarmed by the frequency of his visits. Her tactful attempts to discourage the stalker were not recognised, so she told him bluntly to stay away. Two days later, a large suite of expensive garden furniture was delivered that had been charged to her account. She could not convince the garden centre that she had not ordered the goods, so decided that she would keep them. The following week, she returned home from work to find the furniture in ruins and all her plants ripped out of the soil. Fortunately, her next door neighbour had noted the car registration of the person responsible and the stalker was convicted of causing criminal damage. The victim has not seen him since.

Case history 32

This victim was followed by a stranger for seven weeks. She first noticed the stalker at the local market because he was wearing a very distinctive jacket. It was the jacket, not the stalker, that she recognised on the next occasion, on the same bus that she used to get home after work. The victim still thought that it was a coincidence when the same man appeared in her local pub that night. However, it soon became clear that this was no coincidence as the man turned up outside her workplace, at the cinema and even at her nephew's christening. The victim never spoke to the man and does not know what prompted him to start following her. At the end of the seventh week, the victim awoke in the night and looked out of her bedroom window to see the man standing right outside. Her screams sent him running and the victim called a taxi that took her to her mother's house. She returned to her flat only to collect her belongings and says that she cannot imagine ever wanting to live on her own again.

Case history 33

This is a strange case, as it involves a single man and three different women. The man has behaved in exactly the same way to all three women, but only one of them feels harassed by this. The conduct involves following, surveillance and attempts to control the victim's movements and friendships. One woman realised what was going on and made her feelings clear from the outset. The second woman finds the man 'rather oppressive', but good company, whilst the third was extremely stressed by his behaviour. She found his constant presence and demands on her time incredibly alarming and was particularly upset when he started to attend the same aerobics and yoga classes that she went to. She made extensive changes to her daily routine in an attempt to avoid her stalker and was relieved when he turned his attentions to one of the other women.

Case history 34

This case is particularly distressing as it is an ongoing situation. The victim was in a brief relationship with her stalker, who was her first boyfriend. All was well at first but, as the relationship progressed, the victim felt that she was losing control over her life as her partner was making all the decisions for her – even to the extent of what evening classes he would allow her to attend. He refused to acknowledge her attempts to end the relationship and continued to make demands of a sexual nature. The victim's refusals infuriated the stalker, who became increasingly violent and left the victim fearing that she would be raped. To avoid this and to regain some control over the situation, the victim has agreed to spend one evening a fortnight with the stalker, provided that he gives her some freedom in between times. Every time they meet, the stalker requests intercourse and the victim complies because she is afraid of his violence if she refuses, and 'because it is a small price to pay for 13 days of peace'.

Case history 35

This victim is being stalked by the man who lives opposite her and whom she describes as a casual acquaintance. He, however, describes her as his 'soul mate' and sends her letters that are, on occasion, over 40 pages long, telling her how he feels about her. Sometimes the stalker appears frustrated at his lack of progress with the victim and he will pound on her front door, shouting abuse. On numerous occasions, she has seen him lurking in the bushes in the back garden, staring up at her window. Sometimes, he recites love poetry and on other occasions, he shouts obscenities. The victim is keen for the police to intervene and is diligently keeping a list of all the incidents – there are currently over 40 separate incidents – but no action has yet been taken.

Case history 36

There are numerous victims in the case of the man who has been dubbed 'the Phantom Photocopier' by the police and the local press. This man has targeted a number of families in a small village. He draws caricatures of the victims and distributes these around the village. He also creates large posters depicting the villagers, which he displays in prominent places. Some of the posters depict real events, whereas others are fictitious. This has caused much gossip, speculation and rumour in the village and has caused serious distress to many of the victims. For example, one woman who has been targeted has been depicted wearing a strait jacket – it is common knowledge amongst the villagers that she has suffered from mental health problems. However, another poster has shown the woman's husband engaging in intercourse with her daughter – this is clearly extremely distressing. One couple have split up because of this, as the husband refused to believe that the posters depicting his wife having intercourse with various other men in the village was based upon fiction. The conduct is attributed to a row that occurred in the greengrocers, in which one of the primary victims was rude to the stalker's mother.

Case history 37

This victim is being harassed by her former partner who has taken advantage of his intimate knowledge of the victim to ensure she is caused maximum distress. The victim has an extreme phobia against scissors, so the stalker has sent her over 500 pairs over a period of six months. Additionally, he knows that a particular song distresses her, as it was played at her brother's funeral and the victim often returns home to find her answering machine is full of messages that consist only of this music. Sometimes the stalker sits outside the victim's house in his car, playing the song at maximum volume on the stereo.

Case history 38

This stalker bears a grudge against a former partner. He has no wish to rekindle their relationship, but desires to 'make her pay' for some unspecified wrong that she has done to him. Initially, his revenge took the form of offensive telephone calls and ensuring that she received large quantities of junk mail. However, following his arrest for making nuisance calls, this stalker has adapted his behaviour to ensure that it does not contravene the law. The stalker takes photographs of the victim in public places and sends copies to her when they are developed. He is confident that this is not unlawful, as he asked the police if it were so prior to embarking upon the conduct.

Case history 39

This stalker believes that the victim hit his cat and killed it with her car. The victim claims that she saw another motorist hit the cat, but that he did not stop, so she tried to see if there was anything she could do. The stalker saw the victim holding his injured cat and assumed that she was responsible for its condition. Since this event, the victim regularly finds dead animals in her garden and on her car windscreen. The animals appear to have been killed by cars and not slaughtered specifically to distress her. Nevertheless, she is still incredibly upset and disturbed by this conduct and is considering moving away from the area.

Case history 40

This case involves a prolonged period of harassment based upon a desire to initiate a relationship by the stalker and his consequent inability to deal with the victim's rejection. Following a period of harassment, the victim obtained a civil injunction against the stalker which prohibited him from two specific geographical areas – the town in which the victim lived and the town in which she worked. The stalker went to a great deal of effort to obtain the largest scale map of the area to enable him to locate a position where the victim would have to pass by him, but which was outside the prohibited area. When the police approached him, believing him to be in breach of the injunction, he was able to show them a map with the prohibited areas outlined in red and his own position, outside these areas, marked with a cross.

APPENDIX 2: FIRST CONTACT INFORMATION

Grateful acknowledgment is made to North Wales Police for their permission to use the following information.

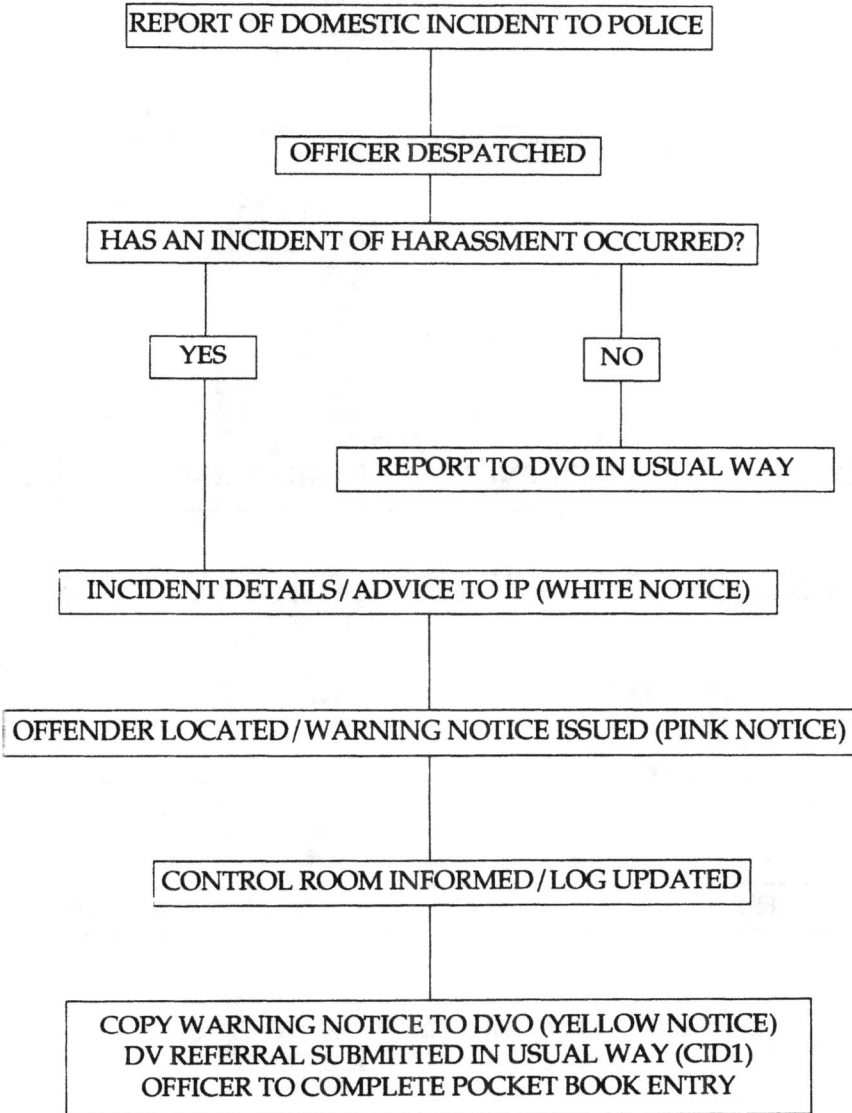

```
          ┌─────────────────────────────────────────────┐
          │   REPORT OF DOMESTIC INCIDENT TO POLICE      │
          └─────────────────────────────────────────────┘
                            │
                ┌───────────────────────────┐
                │    OFFICER DESPATCHED      │
                └───────────────────────────┘
                            │
          ┌─────────────────────────────────────────────┐
          │   HAS AN INCIDENT OF HARASSMENT OCCURRED?    │
          └─────────────────────────────────────────────┘
                   │                         │
              ┌─────────┐              ┌─────────┐
              │   YES   │              │   NO    │
              └─────────┘              └─────────┘
                   │                         │
                   │          ┌──────────────────────────────┐
                   │          │  REPORT TO DVO IN USUAL WAY   │
                   │          └──────────────────────────────┘
                   │
     ┌──────────────────────────────────────────────────┐
     │   INCIDENT DETAILS / ADVICE TO IP (WHITE NOTICE)  │
     └──────────────────────────────────────────────────┘
                   │
 ┌────────────────────────────────────────────────────────────┐
 │  OFFENDER LOCATED / WARNING NOTICE ISSUED (PINK NOTICE)     │
 └────────────────────────────────────────────────────────────┘
                   │
       ┌────────────────────────────────────────────┐
       │   CONTROL ROOM INFORMED / LOG UPDATED       │
       └────────────────────────────────────────────┘
                   │
  ┌───────────────────────────────────────────────────────────┐
  │   COPY WARNING NOTICE TO DVO (YELLOW NOTICE)              │
  │   DV REFERRAL SUBMITTED IN USUAL WAY (CID1)              │
  │   OFFICER TO COMPLETE POCKET BOOK ENTRY                  │
  └───────────────────────────────────────────────────────────┘
```

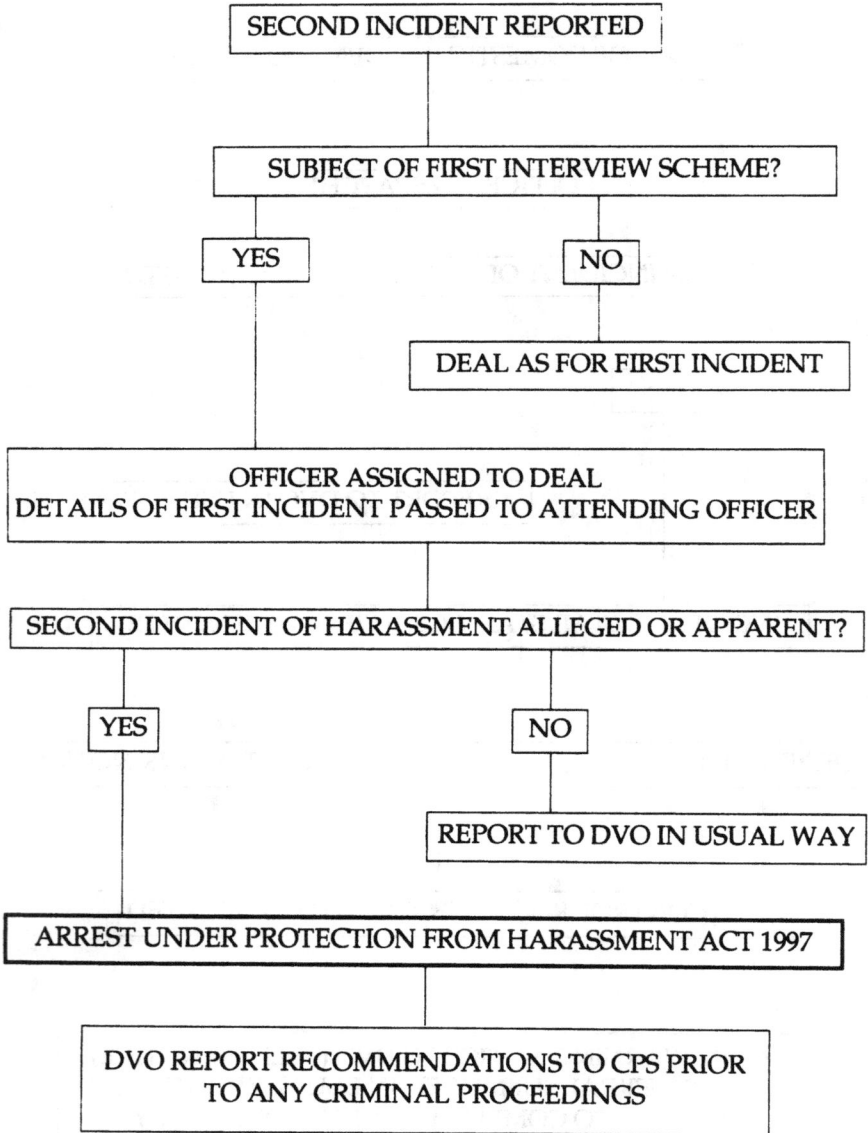

SECOND INCIDENT REPORTED

SUBJECT OF FIRST INTERVIEW SCHEME?

YES

NO

DEAL AS FOR FIRST INCIDENT

OFFICER ASSIGNED TO DEAL
DETAILS OF FIRST INCIDENT PASSED TO ATTENDING OFFICER

SECOND INCIDENT OF HARASSMENT ALLEGED OR APPARENT?

YES

NO

REPORT TO DVO IN USUAL WAY

ARREST UNDER PROTECTION FROM HARASSMENT ACT 1997

DVO REPORT RECOMMENDATIONS TO CPS PRIOR
TO ANY CRIMINAL PROCEEDINGS

NORTH WALES POLICE
Heddlu Gogledd Cymru

FAMILY PROTECTION TEAM
Flintshire Division
Halkyn Police Station
Pentre Road
Halkyn
Flintshire
CH8 8BS

Our Ref:	HJ/UJJ	Tel: 01352 707593
Your Ref:	**226-E-070200**	Fax: 01352 781436
Date:	Friday 10 March 2000	

Dear

Further to the incident whereby Police Officers dealt with a matter of Harassment against you. You were issued with a Notice with an Incident Reference Number thereon and the person concerned has been warned.

You have now entered a Protection From Harassment Scheme, which is operating in this Division. If you have further problems in relation to Harassment please call Police and quote this incident reference to us, so that we may refer to the original report. If further Harassment occurs which results in an Offence under the Protection from Harassment Act 1997, Officers will require a Statement from you so that a full investigation can be conducted and the alleged offender dealt with accordingly.

If you have any questions in relation in this matter please do not hesitate to contact me on 01352 707593.

Yours sincerely,

Helen JONES, DVO

Flintshire Family Protection Team
FAMILY PROTECTION TEAM
HALKYN POLICE STATION
PENTRE ROAD
HALKYN
FLINTSHIRE
CH8 8BS
TEL 01352 781435 EXT 3193
January 14, 1999
Dear Sir/Madam,

(The following is to be read with reference to the attached booklet containing forms CID 61)

As from the beginning of this month we have been piloting a new repeat victimisation strategy in Flintshire. The scheme involves greater use of the Harassment Act 1997. It has been introduced initially to tackle the repeat nature of many of the Domestic Violence incidents that we are called to deal with but in essence will apply to any situation whereby an individual is subject to continual Harassment.

The mechanism of the scheme is as follows:

1. A call is received at police control room and an officer is dispatched to deal.

2. If the officer is satisfied that an incident of Harassment has occurred then the victim will be issued with the white copy of Form CID 61, on which will be written the incident reference and officers details.

3. The alleged offender will be located and issued with a red copy of Form CID 61. This form formalises the warning procedure that in the past has usually only been words of advice.

4. The yellow copy of Form CID 61 is forwarded to the local Domestic Violence Officer for filing. The rear if the yellow form comprises a statement which the officer issuing will complete to confirm issue of the warning notice.

5. The original incident log is updated by police control room to effect that Forms CID 61 have been issued.

6. If the victim has cause to report a second incident to police the original incident can be referred to and an officer dispatched. If the officer is satisfied that a further incident of Harassment has occurred, then an arrest may be made under the Act.

The perceived advantages to the scheme are:

a) The victim is given reassurance that positive action has been taken.
b) The alleged offender is given a clear message that this behaviour will not be tolerated and that to persist in these actions may be tantamount to criminal proceedings.

HARASSMENT ACT 1997

Section 2 'Criminal Harassment' (Arrestable Offence)

'A person must not pursue a course of conduct which amounts to the Harassment of another and which he knows or ought to know amounts to Harassment of the other.'

Course of conduct?

Conduct on at least *two* occasions. The conduct does not have to be the same on each occasion and can include speech.

Harassment?

Almost any form of behaviour that annoys or distresses another person could technically be Harassment but it is important to apply the 'reasonable person' test. Also remember it is the effect on the victim that is important NOT the intention of the offender.

Penalties

Summary offence – up to 6 months' imprisonment and/or fine up to £5,000.

Section 4 'Fear of Violence' (Arrestable Offence)

'A person whose course of conduct causes another to fear, on at least two occasions, that violence will be used against them is guilty of an offence if they know or ought to know that their course of conduct will cause the other so to fear on each of those occasions.'

Course of conduct

As above.

Fear of violence

Can include speech. Remember to apply 'reasonable person' test.

Penalties

Either way offence – Magistrates' court, up to 6 months' imprisonment and/or £5,000 fine and restraining order.

Crown court, up to 5 years' imprisonment and unlimited fine and restraining order.

Restraining Orders

Under Section 5 of the Act, where a person is convicted of an offence contrary to Section 2 or Section 4, the court may make a restraining order to prohibit the offender from doing anything described in the order. Restraining orders will be made to:

Protect the victim or anyone mentioned in the order from

(a) further conduct causing harassment, or

(b) further conduct which will cause fear of violence.

CID 61

OIS / _____ / _____
(Rhif Log/Log No.) (Dyddiad/Date)

Dyma eich cyfeirnod digwyddiad unigryw. Dylunwch y rhif hwn os oes achos gennych i hysbysu'r Heddlu am ail ddigwyddiad o'r natur hwn. Os ydych yn colli'r rhif, cysylltwch â'ch Swyddfa Heddlu leol a gofyn am y Swyddog Trais Teuluol

This is your unique incident reference. Please quote this number if you have cause to report a second incident of this nature to the police. If you lose this number then please contact your local police station and ask for the Domestic Violence Officer

Mewn argyfwng deialwch
999

In an emergency dial
999

Cyflwynwyd gan: Enw, Rheng, Rhif / Issued by: Name, Rank, No. _____

Llofnod y swyddog / Signature of officer: _____

Rhanbarth/Heddlu / Division/Force: _____

CID 61

HYSBYSIAD O RYBUDD

WARNING NOTICE

OIS / _____ / _____
(Rhif Log/Log No.) (Dyddiad/Date)

ENW LLAWN (y person sy'n derbyn y rhybudd)
FULL NAME (person being warned)

DYDDIAD GENI/DATE OF BIRTH

Mae hwn yn Rybudd Swyddogol. Amlinellir eich bod wedi cyflawni gweithred o aflonyddu yn erbyn:

This is an Official Warning. You are suspected of having committed an act of harassment against:

_____ (Enw'r achwynydd/Name of complainant)

Os gelwir yr heddlu i ail ddigwyddiad deliai y bydd wch yn cael eich arestio, a'ch cyhuddo o dramgwyddo dan Ddeddf Amddiffyn rhag Aflonyddwch 1997.

If police are called to a second incident you may be arrested and charged with an offence under the Protection from Harassment Act 1997

Cyflwynwyd gan: Enw, Rheng, Rhif / Issued by: Name, Rank, No. _____

Llofnod y swyddog / Signature of officer: _____

Rhanbarth/Heddlu / Division/Force: _____

Derbynnwyd copi o'r flurflen hon/Received copy of this form: _____

NORTH WALES POLICE

Statement of Witness Criminal Justice Act 1967, Section 9. Magistrates' Court Act 1980, Section 102. Magistrates' Court Rules 1981, Rule 70.

Statement of _____

Age (if over 18 enter "over 18") _____

Occupation ...... POLICE OFFICER .... Number ....

"I completed a FORM CID 61 of which the second page of this statement overleaf is a true copy issued on the date referred to in it. The original FORM CID 61 was then given to the person warned.

The person warned was advised that if police were called to a second incident of Harassment against the complainant named overleaf, then he/she may be liable to arrest for an offence under the Protection From Harassment Act 1997.

This statement consisting of two pages, is true to the best of my knowledge and belief and I make it knowing that, if it is tendered in evidence, I shall be liable to prosecution if I have wilfully stated in it anything which I know to be false or do not believe to be true".

Date _____

Signature _____

Rank No. _____

BIBLIOGRAPHY

Abrams, KM and Robinson, GE, 'Stalking part I: an overview of the problem' (1998) 43 Canadian Journal of Psychiatry, pp 473–76

Abrams, KM and Robinson, GE, 'Stalking part II: victims' problems with the legal system and therapeutic considerations' (19978) 43 Canadian Journal of Psychiatry, pp 477–81

Addison, N and Lawson-Cruttenden, T, *Blackstone's Guide to the Protection from Harassment Act 1997*, 1997, London: Blackstone

Addison, N and Lawson-Cruttenden, T, *Harassment Law and Practice*, 1998, London: Blackstone

Ainsworth, PB, *Psychology and Crime: Myths and Reality*, 2000, Harlow: Pearson Education Ltd

Alldridge, P, 'Threat offences: a case for reform' [1984] Crim LR, pp 176–86

Allen, MJ, 'Look who's stalking: seeking a solution to the problem of stalking' [1996] Web Journal of Current Legal Issues

Allen, MJ, *Textbook on Criminal Law*, 3rd edn, 1999, London: Blackstone

Allison, JA and Wrightsman, LS, *Rape: the Misunderstood Crime*, 1993, London: Sage

Altheide, DL, 'The news media, the problem frame, and the production of fear' (1997) 38(4) Sociological Quarterly, pp 647–68

Anderson, I, '*Hunter and Others v Canary Wharf Ltd*: the tort of nuisance – not for women and children?' (1998) 10(2) Child and Family Law Quarterly, pp 201–10

Anderson, KJ and Accomando, C, 'Madcap misogyny and romanticized victim-blaming: discourses of stalking in *There's Something About Mary*' (1999) XXII(21) Women and Language, pp 24–28

Anderson, SC, 'Anti-stalking laws: will they curb the erotomanic's obsessive pursuit?' (1993) 17 Law and Psychology Rev, pp 171–85

Anonymous, 'My ex-husband won't leave me alone' Good Housekeeping, March 1980, pp 32–34, 39–40

Ashworth, A, *Principles of Criminal Law*, 1992, Oxford: OUP

Attinello, KL, 'Anti-stalking legislation: a comparison of traditional remedies available for victims of harassment versus Californian Penal Code Section 6469' (1993) 24(4) Pacific Law Journal, pp 1945–80

Auchincloss, EL and Weiss, RW, 'Paranoid character and the intolerance of indifference' (1992) 40(4) Journal of the American Psychoanalytical Association, pp 1013–37

Bailey-Harris, R, 'Case note on *Burris v Azadani*' (1996) 26 Family Law, pp 145–46

Barak, G (ed), *Media, Process and the Social Construction of Crime: Studies in Newsmaking Criminology*, 1994, New York: Garland

Barron, J, *Not Worth The Paper: The Effectiveness of Legal Protection for Woman and Children Experiencing Domestic Violence*, 1990, Bristol: Women's Aid Federation

Barry, MM, 'Protective Order Enforcement: Another Pirouette' (1995) 6(2) Hastings Women's Law Journal, pp 339–62

Bassis, MS, Gelles, RJ and Levine, A, *Social Problems*, 1982, New York: Harcourt Brace Jonovich

Bean, P, 'Stalking and the New Crime Bill' (1996) 160 Justice of the Peace, p 1043

Berger, PL and Luckmann, T, *The Social Construction of Reality*, 1967, London: Allen Lane

Best, J, *Images of Issues: Typifying Contemporary Social Problems*, 2nd edn, 1995, New York: Aldine de Gruyter

Best, J, *Theatened Children: Rhetoric and Concern about Child Victims*, 1990, Chicago: University of Chicago Press

Billings, PW, 'Why the English legal system fails to adequately protect victims of obsession' (1996) 1(3) Journal of Civil Liberties, pp 183–215

Bird, R, *Domestic Violence and Protection from Harassment: The New Law*, 2nd edn, 1997, Bristol: Jordans

Bjerregaard, B, 'Stalking and the First Amendment: a constitutional analysis of State stalking laws' (1996) 32(4) Criminal Law Bulletin, pp 307–41

Boland, F, 'Psychiatric injury and assault: the immediate effect of *R v Ireland, R v Burstow*' (1997) XIX(2) Liverpool Law Rev, pp 231–39

Bonnington, A, 'Stalking and the Scottish courts' (1996) 146 NLJ 1394

Box, S, *Deviance, Reality and Society*, 1971, London: Holt, Rinehart and Winston

Bradfield, JL, 'Anti-stalking laws: do they adequately protect stalking victims' (1998) 21 Harvard Women's Law Journal, pp 229–66

Brake, M and Hale, C, *Public Order and Private Lives: The Politics of Law and Order*, 1992, London: Routledge

Brazier, M, 'Personal injury by molestation – an emergent or established tort' (1992) 22 Family Law, pp 246–48

Brazier, M and Murphy, J, *The Law of Torts*, 10th edn, 1999, London: Butterworths

Bridgeman, J and Jones, MA, 'Harassing conduct and outrageous acts: a cause of action for intentionally inflicted mental distress' (1994) 14 Legal Studies, pp 180–205

Brown, D and Ellis, T, *Policing Low Level Disorder: Police Use of Section 5 of the Public Order Act 1986*, Home Office Research Study 135, 1994, London: HMSO

Brown, H, *Stalking: an Investigator's Guide*, 2000, London: HMSO

Buck, W, Chatterton, M and Pease, K, *Obscene, Threatening and Other Troublesome Telephone Calls to Women in England and Wales*, Research and Planning Unit Paper 92, 1995, London: Home Office

Buckley, RA, *The Law of Nuisance*, 2nd edn, 1996, London: Butterworths

Budd, T and Mattinson, J, *The Extent and Nature of Stalking: Findings from the 1998 British Crime Survey*, Home Office Research Study No 210, 2000, London: HMSO

Bureau of Justice Assistance, *Regional Seminar Series on Implementing Anti-Stalking Codes*, 1996, Washington: Department of Justice

Burgess, AW, Baker, T, Greening, D, Hartman, CR, Burgess, AG, Douglas, JE and Halloran, R, 'Stalking behaviours within domestic violence' (1997) 12(4) Journal of Family Violence, pp 389–403

Card, R and Ward, R, *The Criminal Justice and Public Order Act 1994*, 1994, Bristol: Jordans

Cairns-Way, R, 'The criminalisation of stalking: an exercise in media manipulation and political opportunism' (1994) 39 McGill LJ, pp 379–400

Caplan, L, *The Insanity Defence and the Trial of John Hinckley Jnr*, 1987, New York: Dell

Carmody, C, 'Deadly mistakes' [1994] ABA Journal pp 68–71

Carroll, A, *Constitutional and Administrative Law*, 1998, Harlow: Pearson

Carter, D and Dymond, A, *Quiet Enjoyment: Arden and Partington's Guide to Remedies for Harassment and Illegal Eviction*, 5th edn, 1998, London: Legal Action Group

Cheney, D, Dickson, L, Fitzpatrick, J and Uglow, S, *Criminal Justice and the Human Rights Act 1998*, 1999, Bristol: Jordans

Clark, RE and LaBeff, EE, 'Ending intimate relationships: strategies of breaking off' (1986) 6 Sociological Spectrum, pp 245–67

Clarkson, CMV, 'Law Commission Report on Offences Against the Person and General Principles: (1) violence and the Law Commission' [1994] Crim LR, pp 324–33

Clarkeson, C, Cretney, A, Davis, G and Shepherd, J, 'Assaults: the relationship between seriousness, criminalisation and punishment' [1994] Crim LR, pp 4–20

Cohen, S, *Folk Devils and Moral Panics: the Creation of Mods and Rockers*, 1980, Oxford: Martin Robertson

Cohen, S and Young, J (eds), *The Manufacture of News: Social Problems, Deviance and the Mass Media*, 1981, Beverley Hills: Sage

Coleman, C and Moynihan, J, *Understanding Crime Data: Haunted by the Dark Figure*, 1996, Buckingham: Open University

Coleman, FL, 'Stalking behaviour and the cycle of domestic violence' (1997) 12(3) Journal of Interpersonal Violence, pp 420–32

Conaghan, J, 'Harassment and the law of torts: *Khorasandjian v Bush*' (1993) 1(2) Feminist Legal Studies, pp 189–97

Conaghan, J, 'Equity rushes in where tort law fears to tread: the Court of Appeal decision in *Burris v Azadani*' (1996) 4(2) Feminist Legal Studies, pp 221–28

Conaghan, J, 'Gendered harms and the law of tort: remedying (sexual) harassment' (1996) 16(3) Oxford Journal of Legal Studies, pp 407–31

Conaghan, J, 'Enhancing civil remedies for (sexual) harassment: section 3 of the Protection From Harassment Act 1997' (1999) 7(2) Feminist Legal Studies, pp 203–14

Conaghan, J and Mansell, W, *The Wrongs of Tort*, 2nd edn, 1999, London: Pluto

Cooke, E, 'A development in the tort of private nuisance' (1994) 57 MLR, pp 289–96

Cooper, RJ, 'Grievous bodily harm by telephone' (1995) 59 Journal of Criminal Law, pp 401–09

Corwin, M, 'When the law can't protect them' (1993) *Los Angeles Times*, 8 May

Cosgrove, S, 'Erotomania', *New Statesman and Society*, July 1990, pp 31–32

Cowley, D, 'Assault By letter' (1998) 62 Journal of Criminal Law, p 155

Cracknell, S, 'Anti-social behaviour orders' 22 Journal of Social Welfare and Family Law, pp 108–15

Cretney, A and Davis, G, 'Prosecuting "domestic" assault' [1996] Crim LR, pp 162–72

Cretney, SM and Masson, JM, *Principles of Family Law*, 6th edn, 1997, London: Sweet & Maxwell

Croall, H, *Crime and Society in Britain*, 1998, London: Addison Wesley Longman

Daly, K and Maher, L (eds), *Criminology at the Crossroads: Feminist Readings in Crime and Justice*, 1998, New York: OUP

De Becker, G, *The Gift of Fear*, 1997, New York: Little Brown and Co

De Becker, G, *Protecting the Gift*, 2000, New York: Little Brown and Co

De Clérambault, G, *Psychoses Passionelles*, 1922, Paris: Universitaires de France

Diacova, N, 'California's anti-stalking statute: deterrent or false sense of security?' (1995) 24(2) Southwestern University Law Rev, pp 389–421

Diefenbach, DL, 'Portrayal of mental illness on prime-time television' (1997) 25(3) Journal of Community Psychology, pp 289–302

Dietz, PE, Matthews, DB, Martell, DA, Stewart, TM, Hrouda, DR and Warren, J, 'Threatening and otherwise inappropriate letters to Member of the United States Congress' (1991) 36(5) Journal of Forensic Sciences, pp 1445–68

Dietz, PE, Matthews, DB, Van Duyne, C, Martell, DA, Parry, CDH, Stewart, T, Warren, J and Crowder, JD, 'Threatening and otherwise inappropriate letter to Hollywood celebrities' (1991) 36(1) Journal of Forensic Sciences, pp 185–209

Dine, J and Gobert, J, *Cases and Materials on Criminal Law*, 1998, London: Blackstone

Dine, J and Watt, B, 'Sexual harassment: moving away from discrimination' (1995) 58 MLR, pp 343–63

Dine, J and Watt, B (eds), *Discrimination Law: Concepts, Limitations and Justifications*, 1996, London: Addison Wesley Longman

DiVasto, PV, Kaufman, A, Rosner, L, Jackson, R, Christy, L, Pearson, S and Burgett, T, 'The prevalence of sexually stressful events among females in the general population' (1984) 13 Archives of Sexual Behaviour, pp 59–67

Downes, D and Rock, P, *Understanding Deviance: a Guide to the Sociology of Crime and Rule Breaking*, 3rd edn, 1998, Oxford: OUP

Edwards, *Reducing Domestic Violence ... What Works? Use of the Criminal Law*, 2000, London: HMSO

Elliot, DW, 'Frightening a person into injuring himself' [1974] Crim LR, pp 15–25

Emerson, RM, Ferris, KO and Gardner, CB, 'On being stalked' (1998) 45(3) Social Problems, pp 289–314

Enoch, D and Trethowan, W, *Uncommon Psychiatric Disorders*, 3rd edn, 1991, Oxford: Butterworths Heinemann

Erikson, RV, Baranek, PM, and Chan, JB, *Negotiating Control: A Study of News Sources*, 1989, Toronto: University of Toronto Press

Esquirol, JED, *Mental Maladies: A Treatise on Insanity* (trans: R de Sanssure), 1965, New York: Hafner (originally published in 1845)

Farley, JE, *American Social Problems*, 1987, Englewood Cliffs, NJ: Prentice-Hall

Farnham, FR, James, DV and Cantrell, P, 'Association between violence, psychosis and relationship to victims in stalkers' (2000) 355 The Lancet, pp 199–205

Feldman, D, 'The Kings Peace, the Royal Prerogative and public order: the roots and early development of binding over powers' [1988] 47(1) CLJ, pp 101–28

Fenwick, H, 'The right to protest, the Human Rights Act and the margin of appreciation' (1999) 62(4) MLR, pp 491–514

Finch, E, 'Contingent criminality and the inadvertent stalker' (2000) 5 Journal of Civil Liberties, pp 273–95

Finch, E, 'Peaceful protest or campaign of harassment: protestors harassment and reasonableness' (1999) 5 Web Journal of Current Legal Issues

Finch, E, 'Two incidents and two victims: can this constitute a course of conduct?' (2000) 64 Journal of Criminal Law, pp 299–301

Fitzgerald, LF, Swan, S and Fischer, K, 'Why didn't she just report him? The psychological and legal implications of women's responses to sexual harassment' (1995) 51(1) Journal of Social Issues, pp 117–39

Fleming, JG, *The Law of Torts*, 7th edn, 1987, Sydney: Sweet & Maxwell

Ford, JD, 'Squaring analogy with principle or vice versa' [1994] 53 CLJ, pp 14–16

Foucault, M, *Discipline and Punish: the Birth of the Prison*, 1977, London: Allen Lane

Frazier, PA, Cochran, CC and Olson, AM, 'Social science research on lay definitions of sexual harassment' (1995) 51(1) Journal of Social Issues, pp 21–39

Fremouw, WJ, Westrup, D and Pennypacker, J, 'Stalking on campus: the prevalence and strategies for coping with stalking' (1997) 42(4) Journal of Forensic Science, pp 666–69

Fricker, N, 'Molestation and harassment after *Patel v Patel*' (1988) 18 Family Law, pp 395–400

Fricker, N, 'Personal molestation or harassment: injunctions in actions based on the law of torts' (1992) 22 Family Law, pp 158–63

Fritz, JP, 'A proposal for mental health provisions in State anti-stalking laws' (1995) 23(2) Journal of Psychiatry and Law, pp 295–318

Fuller, R, 'The problem of teaching social problems' (1938) 44 American Journal of Sociology, pp 415–35

Gardner, J, 'Rationality and the Rule of Law in Offences Against the Person' [1994] 53 CLJ, pp 502–23

Gardner, S, 'Appreciating *Olugboja*' (1996) 16 Legal Studies, pp 275–97

Gardner, S, 'Stalking' (1998) 114 LQR, pp 35–37

Gearty, C, 'The place of private nuisance in a modern law of torts' [1989] 48(2) CLJ, pp 214–42

Gerbeth, VJ, 'Stalkers: who they are' (1992) 40(10) Law and Order, pp 138–43

Gilligan, MJ, 'Stalking the stalker: developing new laws to thwart those who terrorise others' (1992) 27 Georgia Law Rev, pp 285–314

Goode, E and Ben-Yehuda, N, *Moral Panics: the Social Construction of Deviance*, 1994, Cambridge, Massachusetts: Blackwell

Goode, M, 'Stalking: crime of the nineties?' (1995) 19(1) Criminal Law Journal, pp 21–31

Grabe, ME, 'Tabloid and traditional television news magazine crime stories: crime lessons and reaffirmation of social class distinctions' (1996) 73(4) Journalism and Mass Communication Quarterly, pp 926–46

Griew, EJ, '*Ireland*' (1996) Archbold News, Issue 6, pp 1–2

Grunis, AD, 'Binding over to keep the peace and be of good behaviour in England and Canada' [1976] Public Law, pp 16–41

Gunter, B, *Television and the Fear of Crime*, 1987, London: John Libbey and Co

Gusfield, JR, *The Culture of Social Problems*, 1981, Chicago: Chicago UP

Guy, RA, 'The nature and constitutionality of stalking laws' (1993) 46(4) Vanderbilt Law Rev, pp 991–1027

Harmon, RB, Rosner, R and Owens, H, 'Obsessional harassment and erotomania in a criminal court population' (1995) 40(2) Journal of Forensic Sciences, pp 188–96

Harmon, RB, Rosner, R and Owens, H, 'Sex and violence in a forensic population of obsessional harassers' (1998) 4(1) Psychology, Public Policy and Law, pp 236–49

Harris, J, *An Evaluation of the Use and Effectiveness of the Protection from Harassment Act 1997*, 2000, Home Office Research Study 203, London: HMSO

Harris, J and Grace, S, *A Question of Evidence? Investigating and Prosecuting Rape in the 1990s*, 1999, Home Office Research Study 196, London: HMSO

Hart, HLA, *Punishment and Responsibility: Essays in the Philosophy of Law*, 1968, Oxford: Clarendon

Hartgen, CA, *Crime and Criminalisation*, 2nd edn, 1978, New York: Praeger

Hayes, M and Williams, C, *Family Law: Principles, Policy and Practice*, 1999, London: Butterworths

Hayes, M and Williams, C, 'Non-molestation protection – only associated persons need apply' (1996) 59 Family Law, pp 134–36

Heidensohn, F, *Crime and Society*, 1989, Basingstoke: Macmillan

Heil, A, 'Lovesick' Mademoiselle, December 1986, pp 128–30, 136–38

Herman, JL, 'Complex PTSD: a syndrome in survivors of prolonged and repeated trauma' (1992) 5 Journal of Traumatic Stress, pp 377–91

Herold, ES, Mantle, D and Zemitis, O, 'A study of sexual offences against females' (1979) 14 Adolescence, pp 65–72

Herring, J, 'Assault By telephone' [1997] CLJ, pp 11–13

Herring, J, 'The criminalisation of harassment' [1998] CLJ, pp 10–13

Hester, S and Eglin, P, *A Sociology of Crime*, 1997, London: Routledge

Hicks, RD, *In Pursuit of Satan: the Police and the Occult*, 1991, New York: Prometheus

Hilgartnner, S and Bosk, CL, 'The rise and fall of social problems' (1988) 94 American Journal of Sociology, pp 53–78

Holmes, RM, 'Stalking in America: types and methods of criminal stalkers' (1993) 9(4) Journal of Contemporary Criminal Justice, pp 317–27

Home Office, *Review of Public Order Law*, 1985, London: HMSO

Horder, J, 'Reconsidering psychic assault' [1998] Crim LR, pp 392–403

Hoyle, C, Cape, E, Morgan, R and Saunders, A, *Evaluation of the 'One Stop Shop' and Victim Statement Pilot Projects*, 1998, Home Office Research Study, London: HMSO

Humphries, T, *Criminal Days: the Recollections and Reflections of Travers Humphries*, 1945, London: Hodder and Stoughton, pp 124–35

Irfield, P and Platford, G, *The Law of Harassment and Stalking*, 2000, London: Butterworths

Ingman, T, *The English Legal Process*, 8th edn, 2000, London: Blackstone

Jaconelli, J, 'Context dependent crime' [1995] Crim LR, pp 771–82

James, A and Raine, J, *The New Politics of Criminal Justice*, 1998, London: Longman

Jamrozik, A, and Nocella, L, *The Sociology of Social Problems: Theoretical Perspectives and Methods of Intervention*, 1998, Cambridge: CUP

Jason, LA, Reichler, A, Easton, J, Neal, A and Wilson, M, 'Female harassment after ending a relationship: a preliminary study' (1984) 6 Alternative Lifestyles, pp 259–69

Jason-Lloyd, L, 'The Protection From Harassment Act 1997: a commentary' (1997) 161 Justice of the Peace, p 787

Jenkins, P, *Intimate Enemies: Moral Panics in Contemporary Great Britain*, 1992, New York: Aldine de Gruyter

Jordan, T, 'The efficacy of Californian stalking law: surveying its evolution, extracting insights from domestic violence' (1995) 6(2) Hastings Women's Law Journal, pp 363–83

Kell, D, 'Psychiatric injury and the bodily harm criterion' (1995) 111 LQR, pp 27–32

Kerrigan, K, 'Breach of the peace and the European Convention' (1999) 63(3) Journal of Criminal Law, pp 246–50

Kidder, LH, Lafleur, RA and Wells, CV, 'Recalling harassment, reconstructing experience' (1995) 51(1) Journal of Social Issues, pp 53–69

Kienlen, KK, Birmingham, DL, Solberg, KB, O'Regan, JT and Meloy, JR, 'A comparative study of psychotic and non-psychotic stalking' (1997) 25(3) Journal of the American Academy of Psychiatry and Law, pp 317–34

King, RD and Wincup, E (eds), *Doing Research on Crime and Justice*, 2000, Oxford: OUP

Kitsuse, MI and Spector, M, 'Towards a sociology of social problems: social conditions, value judgements and social problems' (1973) 20 Social Problems, pp 407–19

Kolb TV, 'North Dakota's stalking law: criminalising the crime before the crime' (1994) 70(1) North Dakota Law Rev, pp 159–86

Koffman, L, *Crime Surveys and Victims of Crime*, 1996, Cardiff: University of Wales

Kunen, JS, 'The dark side of love' People, October 1987, pp 89–98

Kurt, JL, 'Stalking as a variant of domestic violence' (1995) 23(2) Bulletin of the American Academy of Psychiatry and Law, pp 219–30

Lacey, N and Wells, C, *Reconstructing Criminal Law*, 2nd edn, 1998, London: Butterworths

LaFollette, M and Purdie, R, *A Guide to the Family Law Act 1996*, 1996, London: Butterworths

LaFree, GD, *Rape and Criminal Justice: the Social Construction of Sexual Assault*, 1989, Belmont: Wadsworth

Lane, JC, 'Threat management fills void in police services' (1992) The Police Chief, pp 23–29

Law Commission, *Binding Over*, 1994, Law Com No 222, London: HMSO

Lawson-Cruttenden, T, 'The emergence of a tort of harassment' (1995) 25 Family Law, pp 625–26

Lawson-Cruttenden, T, 'Is there a law against stalking?' (1996) 146 NLJ, pp 418–20

Leng, R, Taylor, R and Wasik, M, *Blackstone's Guide to the Crime and Disorder Act 1998*, 1998, London: Blackstone

Lilly, JR, Cullen, FT and Ball, RA, *Criminological Theory: Context and Consequences*, 1989, California: Sage

Lingg, RA, 'Stopping stalkers: a critical examination of anti-stalking statutes' (1993) 67(2) St John's Law Rev, pp 347–80

Lockton, D and Ward, R, *Domestic Violence*, 1997, London: Cavendish Publishing

Loveland, I (ed), *Frontiers of Criminality*, 1995, London: Sweet & Maxwell

Lowe, NV and Douglas, G, *Bromley's Family Law*, 9th edn, 1998, London: Butterworths

Lunney, M and Oliphant, K, *Tort Law: Text and Materials*, 2000, Oxford: OUP

Maguire, M and Corbett, C, *The Effects of Crime and the Work of Victim Support Schemes*, 1987, Aldershot: Gower

Manchester, C, 'Obscenity in the Mail' [1983] Crim LR, pp 64–77

Manis, JG, *Analysing Social Problems*, 1976, New York: Praeger

Martin, J, *Modern Equity*, 14th edn, 1993, London: Butterworths

Matthews, R and Young, J (eds) *Issues in Realist Criminology*, 1992, London: Sage

Mays, R, Middlemass, S and Watson, J, 'Every breath you take – every move you make – Scots law, the Protection From Harassment Act 1997 and the problem of stalking' (1997) 6 Statute Law Rev, pp 331–54

McAnaney, KG, Curliss, LA and Abeyta-Price, CE, 'From imprudence to crime: anti-stalking laws' (1993) 68 Notre Dame Law Rev, pp 819–909

McCabe, S and Wallington, P, *The Police, Public Order and Civil Liberties*, 1988, London: Routledge

McCann, JT, 'Subtypes of stalking (obsessional following) in adolescents' (1998) 21 Journal of Adolescence, pp 667–75

Mead, D, 'The Human Rights Act – a panacea for peaceful public protest?' (1998) 3 Journal of Civil Liberties, pp 206–23

Meier, RF, *Crime and Society*, 1989, Boston: Allyn and Bacon

Meloy, JR, 'Unrequited love and the wish to kill: diagnosis and treatment of borderline erotomania' (1989) 53(6) Bulletin of the Menniger Clinic, pp 477–92

Meloy, JR, *Violent Attachments*, 1992, Northvale, NJ: Jason Aronson

Meloy, JR, 'Stalking (obsessional following): a review of some preliminary studies' (1996) 1 Aggression and Violent Behaviour, pp 147–62

Meloy, JR, 'Predatory violence during mass murder' (1997) 42 Journal of Forensic Science, pp 326–29

Meloy, JR, 'The clinical risk management of stalking' (1997) 51(2) American Journal of Psychotherapy, pp 174–84

Meloy, JR, (ed), *The Psychology of Stalking: Forensic and Clinical Perspectives*, 1998, San Diego: Academic Press

Meloy, JR, 'Erotomania, triangulation and homicide' (1999) 44 Journal of Forensic Science, pp 421–24

Meloy, JR, 'Stalking: an old behaviour, a new crime' (1999) 22(1) The Psychiatric Clinics of North America, pp 85–99

Meloy, JR and Gothard, S, 'Demographic and clinical comparison of obsessional followers and offenders with mental disorders' (1995) 152 American Journal of Psychiatry, pp 258–63

Michael, J and Adler, M, *Crime, Law and Social Science*, 1933, New York: Harcourt Brace Jonovich

Mithers, CL, 'Can a man be too mad about you?' Mademoiselle, October 1982, p 36

Monti, G, 'The reasonable woman standard in sexual harassment litigation' (1999) 19(4) Legal Studie, pp 552–79

Morville, DA, 'Stalking laws' (1993) 71 Washington University Law Quarterly, pp 921–35

Mullen, PE and Pathe, M, 'Stalking and the pathologies of love' (1994) 28 Australian and New Zealand Journal of Psychiatry, pp 469–77

Mullen, PE, Pathe, M, Purcell, R and Stuart, GW, 'Study of stalkers' (1999) 156(8) American Journal of Psychiatry, pp 1244–49

Muncie, J and McLoughlin, E (eds), *The Problem of Crime*, 1996, London: Sage

Murphy, J, 'The emergence of a tort of harassment' (1993) 143 NLJ, pp 14–16

Nehilla, TJ, 'Applying stalking statutes to groups – a first amendment freedom of speech analysis' (1995) 99(4) Dickinson Law Rev, pp 1071–95

Newark, FH, 'The boundaries of nuisance' (1949) 65 LQR, pp 480–90

Noble, M, 'Harassment – a recognised tort?' (1993) 143 NLJ, pp 1685–86

Norrie, A, 'After *Woollin*' [1999] Crim LR, pp 532–45

O'Reilly, GW, 'Illinois' stalking statute: taking unsteady aim at preventing tactics' (1993) 26(4) John Marshall Law Rev, pp 821–64

Orion, D, *I Know You Really Love Me: a Psychiatrist's Journal of Erotomania, Stalking and Obsessive Love*, 1997, New York: Macmillan

Ormerod, DC, 'Comment on *DPP v Lau*' [2000] Crim LR, pp 581–82

Ormerod, DC, 'Comment on *Dunn*' [2001] Crim LR, pp 130–33

Ormerod, DC, 'Comment on *R (A Child) v DPP*' [2001] Crim LR, pp 396–98

Ormerod, DC, 'Comment on *R v H*' [2001] Crim LR, pp 318–32

Ormerod, DC and Gunn, MJ, 'In defence of *Ireland*' (1997) 3 Web Journal of Current Legal Issues

Packer, HL, *The Limits of the Criminal Sanction*, 1968, Stanford, California, CA: Stanford UP

Palmer, C, Moon, G and Cox, S, *Discrimination at Work: The Law on Sex, Race and Disability Discrimination*, 3rd edn, 1997, London: Legal Action Group

Pathe, M and Mullen, PE, 'The impact of stalkers on their victims' (1997) 170 British Journal of Psychiatry, pp 12–17

Pathe, M, Mullen, PE and Purcell, R, 'Stalking: false claims of victimisation' (1999) 174 British Journal of Psychiatry, pp 170–72

Pease, K, 'Obscene telephone calls to women in England and Wales' (1985) 24(4) Howard Journal, pp 275–81

Perez, C, 'Stalking: when does obsession become a crime?' (1993) 20(2) American Journal of Criminal Law, pp 263–80

Pinard, G and Pagini, L (eds), *Clinical Assessments of Dangerousness: Empirical Contributions*, 1999, New York: CUP

Proctor, M, 'Stalking: a behavioural overview with case management suggestions' (1995) 29(3) Journal of California Law Enforcement, pp 63–69

Quinney, R, *The Social Reality of Crime*, 1970, Boston: Little, Brown

Reed, A, 'Offences against the person: the need for reform' (1994) 59 Journal of Criminal Law, pp 187–97

Renzetti, CM and Lee, RM (eds), *Researching Sensitive Topics*, 1993, New York: Sage

Richardson, S and Bacon, H (eds), *Child Sexual Abuse: Whose Problem? Reflections from Cleveland*, 1991, London: Venture

Richardson, S, Best, J and Bromley, D (eds), *The Satanism Scare*, 1991, New York: Aldine de Gruyter

Roach Anleu, SL, *Law and Social Change*, 2000, London: Sage

Roberts, AR and Dziegielewski, SF, 'Assessment typology and intervention with the survivors of stalking' (1996) 1 Aggression and Violent Behaviour, pp 359–68

Roesch, R, 'Creating change in the legal system' (1995) 19(4) Law and Human Behaviour, pp 325–43

Rogers, WVH, *Winfield and Jolowicz on Tort*, 15th edn, 1998, London: Sweet & Maxwell

Romans, J, Hays, J and White, T, 'Stalking and related behaviours experienced by counselling centre staff members from current or former clients' (1996) 27(6) Professional Psychology: Research and Practice, pp 595–99

Rook, PFG, *Rook and Ward on Sexual Offences*, 2nd edn, 1997, London: Sweet & Maxwell

Rubenstein, M, *Discrimination: a Guide to the Relevant Case Law on Race and Sex Discrimination and Equal Pay*, 12th edn, 1999, London: Eclipse

Rubington, E and Weinberg, MS (eds), *The Study of Social Problems: Seven Perspectives*, 5th edn, 1995, New York: OUP

Safran, C, 'A stranger was stalking our little girl' Good Housekeeping, November 1992, pp 183, 263–66

Salame, L, 'A national survey of stalking laws: a legislative trend comes to the aid of domestic violence victims and others' (1993) 17(1) Suffolk University Law Review, pp 67–112

Samuels, A, 'Stalking defined' (1997) 18(3) Statute Law Rev, pp 244–49

Sandberg, DA, Dale, EM and Binder, RL, 'Characteristics of psychiatric inpatients who stalk, threaten or harass hospital staff after discharge' (1998) 155(8) American Journal of Psychiatry, pp 1102–05

Sarbin, TR and Kitsuse, JI (eds), *Constructing the Social*, 1994, London: Sage

Sartre, J, *Truth and Existence* (trans: A van den Hoven), 1992, Chicago: Chicago UP

Schwartz-Watts, D and Morgan, DW, 'Violent versus non-violent stalkers' (1998) 26(2) Journal of the American Academy of Psychiatry and the Law, pp 241–45

Schwartz-Watts, D, Morgan, DW and Barnes, CJ, 'Stalkers: the South Caroline experience' (1997) 25(4) Journal of the American Academy of Psychiatry and the Law, pp 541–45

Searle, JR, *The Construction of Social Reality*, 1995, New York: Free Press

Segal, J, 'Erotomania revisited' (1989) 46 American Journal of Psychiatry, pp 1261–66

Selfe, D and Burke, V, *Perspectives on Sex, Crime and Society*, 1998, London: Cavendish Publishing (see now 2nd edn, 2001)

Sharpe, RJ, *Injunctions and Specific Performance*, 1999, Toronto: Canada Law Books

Sheldon, S, 'Who is the mother to make the judgment?: the constructions of woman in English abortion law' (1993) 1(1) Feminist Legal Studies, pp 3–22

Sheridan, L, Davies, GM and Boon, JCW, 'Stalking: perceptions and prevalence' (2001) 16 Journal of Interpersonal Violence, pp 231–45

Sheridan, L, Gillett, R and Davies, G, 'Stalking – seeking the victim's perspective' (1999) 30 Issues in Legal and Criminological Psychology, pp 345–59

Sherr, A, *Freedom of Protest, Public Order and the Law*, 1989, Oxford: Blackwells

Simester, AP and Chan, W, 'Intention thus far' [1997] Crim LR, pp 704–19

Simister, AP and Sullivan, GR, *Criminal Law: Theory and Doctrine*, 2000, Oxford: Hart

Smith, ATH, *Offences Against Public Order*, 1987, London: Sweet & Maxwell

Smith, IT and Thomas, GH, *Industrial Law*, 1996, London: Butterworths

Smith, JC, 'Comment on *Burstow*' [1997] Crim LR, pp 452–55

Smith, JC, 'Comment on *Ireland*' [1997] Crim LR, pp 434–36

Smith, JC, 'Comment on *Woollin*' [1998] Crim LR, pp 891–93

Smith, JC, *Smith and Hogan Criminal Law*, 8th edn, 1996, London: Butterworths

Smith, JC, *Smith and Hogan Criminal Law*, 9th edn, 1999, London: Butterworths

Sohn, EF, 'Anti-stalking statutes: do they actually protect victims?' (1994) 30(3) Criminal Law Bulletin, pp 203–41

Spector, M and Kitsuse, JI, 'Social problems: a reformulation' (1973) 21 Social Problems, pp 145–59

Spencer, JR, 'Public nuisance – a critical examination' [1989] 48(1) CLJ, pp 55–84

Spitzberg, BH and Rhea, J, 'Obsessive relational intrusion and sexual coercion victimisation' (1999) 14(1) Journal of Interpersonal Violence, pp 3–20

Spitzberg, BH, Nicastro, AM and Cousins, AV, 'Exploring the interactive phenomenon of stalking and obsessive relational intrusion' (1998) 11(1) Communication Reports, pp 33–47

Stake, RE, *The Art of Case Study Research*, 1995, New York: Sage

Stephenson, GM, *The Psychology of Criminal Justice*, 1997, Oxford: Blackwells

Stone, R, 'It's bad to talk: assault by telephone' (1997) 133 LQR, pp 407–10

Strikis, SA, 'Stopping stalkers' (1993) 81 Georgia Law Journal, pp 2771–81

Sumner, C, (ed), *Crime Justice and the Mass Media*, 1982, Cambridge: CUP

Tappan, PW, 'Who is the criminal?' (1947) 12 American Sociological Review, pp 96–102

Tharp, M, 'In the mind of the stalker', US News and World Report, 17th February 1992, pp 28–30

Thompson, K, *Moral Panics*, 1998, London: Routledge

Thornton, P, *Public Order Law*, 1987, London: Financial Training Publications Ltd

Townshend-Smith, R, 'Harassment as a tort in English and American law: the boundaries of *Wilkenson v Downton*' (1995) 24(3) Anglo-American Law Rev, pp 299–326

Tjaden, P and Thoennes, N, *Stalking in America: Findings from the National Violence against Women Survey*, 1998, Washington: Department of Justice

Trindade, FA, 'Intentional torts: some thoughts on assault and battery' (1982) 2 Oxford Journal of Legal Studies, pp 211–37

Trindade, FA, 'The intentional infliction of purely mental distress' (1986) 6(2) Oxford Journal of Legal Studies, pp 219–31

Tuggle, CA, 'The Bias Towards Finding Bias in Television News' Communication Reports (1998) Vol 11, No 1, pp 65-72

Tuke, DH (ed), *A Dictionary of Psychological Medicine*, 1892, London: Churchill Livingstone

Van Dijk, P and van Hoof, GJH, *Theory and Practice on the European Convention on Human Rights*, 1998, The Hague: Kluwer

Vaughan, D, *Uncoupling: Turning Points in Intimate Relationships*, 1986, Oxford: OUP

Virgo, G, 'Offences against the person: do-it-yourself reform' [1997] 57 CLJ, pp 251–53

Von Heussen, E, 'The law and social problems: the case of Britain's Protection from Harassment Act 1997' (2000) 1 Web Journal of Current Legal Issues

Walker, N, *Crime and Criminology: A Critical Introduction*, 1987, Oxford: OUP

Walker, SJ, 'When 'no' becomes 'yes': why girls and women consent to unwanted sex' (1997) 6 Applied Journal of Preventative Psychology, pp 157–66

Wallis, M, 'Outlawing stalkers' (1996) 2(4) Policing Today, pp 25–29

Wasik, M and Taylor, R, *Blackstone's Guide to the Criminal Justice and Public Order Act 1994*, 1995, London: Blackstone

Weiner, D, 'Criminal responsibility and the infliction of harm' (1995) 69(1) Law Institute Journal, pp 30–33

Weiner, RL, 'Social analytical jurisprudence in sexual harassment litigation: the role of social framework and social fact' (1995) 51(1) Journal of Social Issues, pp 167–81

Welch, JM, 'Stalking and anti-stalking legislation: a guide to the literature of a new legal concept' (1995) 23(3) Reference Services Rev, pp 53–59

Wells, C, 'Stalking: the criminal law response' [1997] Crim LR, pp 463–75

White, DM, 'The gate keeper: a case study in the selection of news' (1950) 27 Journalism Quarterly, pp 383–90

White, R and Perrone, S, *Crime and Social Control: An Introduction*, 1997, Oxford: OUP

Wilcox, B, 'Psychological rape', Glamour, October 1982, pp 232–44, 291–96

Williams, DGT, 'Preventative justice and the courts' [1977] Crim LR, pp 703–09

Williams, G, 'Preventative justice and the rule of law' (1953) 16(4) MLR, pp 417–27

Williams, G, 'Assault and words' [1957] Crim LR, pp 219–25

Williams, G, *Textbook of Criminal Law*, 2nd edn, 1983, London: Stevens

Williams, WL, Lane, J and Zona, MA, 'Stalking: successful intervention strategies' (1996) 63(2) The Police Chief, pp 24–26

Wilkins, L, *Social Deviance*, 1964, London: Tavistock

Wilson, D and Ashton, J, *What Everyone in Britain Should Know About Crime and Punishment*, 1998, London: Blackstone

Wolfgang, ME, Savitz, L and Johnston, N (eds), *The Sociology of Crime and Delinquency*, 1970, New York: John Wiley and Sons

Woods, LT, 'Anti-stalker legislation: a legislative attempt to surmount the inadequacies of protective orders' (1992) 27 Indiana Law Rev, pp 449–73

Wright, JA, Burgess, AG, Burgess, AW, Laszlo, AT, McCrary, GO and Douglas, JE, 'A typology of interpersonal stalking' (1996) 11(4) Journal of Interpersonal Violence, pp 487–502

Wright, JA, Burgess, AG, Burgess, AW, McCrary, GO and Douglas, JE, 'Investigating stalking crimes' (1995) 33(9) Journal of Psychosocial Nursing, pp 38–43

Wright, M, 'Victims, mediation and criminal justice' [1994] Crim LR, pp 187–99

Young, J, *The Exclusive Society*, 1999, London: Sage

Zona, M, Sharma, K and Lane, JA, 'A comparative study of erotomania and obsessional subjects in a forensic sample' (1993) 38 Journal of Forensic Science, pp 894–903

INDEX

For Product Safety Concerns and Information please contact our EU
representative GPSR@taylorandfrancis.com
Taylor & Francis Verlag GmbH, Kaufingerstraße 24, 80331 München, Germany